PIRATES
of the
CARIBBEAN

Buccaneers, Privateers,
Freebooters and Filibusters
1493-1720

English language edition Copyright © 2002 Conway Maritime Press, London.
Volume Copyright © 2002 Lunwerg S.L., Beethoven 12, 08021 Barcelona.
Text Copyright © 2002: Cruz Apestegui

Translation by Richard Lewis Rees

This English-language edition first published by
Conway Maritime Press in 2002.
Conway Maritime Press is a division of Chrysalis Books plc
64 Brewery Road
London N7 9NT
www.conwaymaritime.com

A member of **Chrysalis** Books plc

The present edition has been translated with the help of the General
Direction of Book, Archives and Libraries of the Spanish Ministry of
Education, Culture and Sports, in the European Year of Languages.

9 8 7 6 5 4 3 2 1

A CIP catalogue record for this book is available from the British Library.

ISBN 0 85177 932 8

Created and designed by Lunwerg Editores,
Beethoven 12, 08201 Barcelona, Spain

Editorial & Typesetting (English edition) by Page Nine,
Falmouth, Cornwall, England

Printed in Spain

Pirates
of the
CARIBBEAN

Buccaneers, Privateers,
Freebooters and Filibusters
1493-1720

Cruz Apestegui

Conway Maritime Press

FOREWORD

Plundering at sea is as old as navigation itself. From the moment when some decided to travel the seas and transport goods in ships, others aspired to take the riches carried aboard for themselves. Throughout history, this war was waged against a force superior by virtue of its flexibility and disparate nature to that of the most consolidated of states.

Where gold and silver abounded – as they did in the New World – and where the inevitable need arose to transport these riches back to a homeland separated by an ocean from its colonies, piracy spread like wildfire. If to this geographical circumstance we add the imposition of a monopoly trading system, the problems for those maritime nations were exacerbated; had the profits been retained where they were made, they might have led to an open, competitive economic system.

In this book, Cruz Apestegui conveys a comprehensive overview of piracy, privateering, and buccaneering in the 16th and 17th centuries, both in the European Atlantic and in the waters of the Indies – a far from easy task. The author has expended enormous effort to sift the truth from the chaff of unfounded legend and hoax. It must be said that he has risen very successfully to the challenge. The outcome is a text that combines scientific rigour and readability to include hitherto unpublished original material and an updated bibliography.

Essentially, Cruz Apestegui's book is a solidly informed view of the Spanish Empire's struggle against corsairs, buccaneers, and pirates, of battles fought wherever the need arose in the Atlantic and Pacific oceans and the Caribbean sea. For the European powers, jealous of Spain's American possessions and wealth, engaging in piracy was the way to wage war against the Iberian colossus.

The reader will appreciate that, from today's point of view, it is extremely difficult to distinguish between what constituted acts of piracy and acts of legitimate trade. Indeed, the same problem prevailed at the time the events actually took place. In this context, the career of the Dutch West India Company is highly significant, as are the attitudes of England and France during what were, theoretically at least, times of peace.

The stance of 'Adam's dispossessed' changed radically when the Spanish monopoly began to founder irreparably after the signing of the treaties of Westphalia and Madrid. Jamaica, Curaçao, and Santa Dominica provided the gateways to the commercial banquet and sealed the fate of filibusters and pirates, although their activities did not cease entirely until well into the 18th century.

These pages present a gallery of 'Adam's dispossessed', honourable traders who became noble lords, corsairs in times of war and so-called times of peace. Furthermore, the reader will learn of the rise and fall of the trading companies and of the filibusters, for whom, at least for a while, the sun never set.

FERNANDO SERRANO MANGAS
The University of Extremadura

CONTENTS

The altarpiece of St George by Pere Nisard. Museo de la Iglesia de Mallorca.

AN OLD, VERY LUCRATIVE MÉTIER

According to Greek myths, on his voyage to the Garden of the Hesperides in Mauritania, Hercules thought he had reached the end of the world. He separated two mountains known as Calpe (Gibraltar) and Abila (on the African coast) to link the Mediterranean with the unknown ocean beyond and, on their summits, he built two pillars to show future generations just how far his glorious exploits had taken him. Over the horizon lay the sea of darkness that would remain unexplored for a long time to come.

The struggle to dominate the sea and to master navigation is as old as humanity itself, indeed, for the peoples of antiquity such as the Phoenicians, Greeks, Carthaginians and Romans, maritime exploration was of prime importance. Commercial exchange between coastal societies was made possible by a uniting sea linking an increasingly complex, well organised system of trading posts and regular shipping routes. And in later epochs, the possibility of improving a quotidian life, the thirst for adventure and the promise of vast fortunes were incentive enough to attract a great number of adventurers to engage in a highly lucrative activity: piracy.

At the beginning of our historical era successive major campaigns had all but eradicated pirates until, from beyond the then frontiers of Europe, life-threatening opportunists again became the scourge of the seas of the known world.

ANTECEDENTS

The Frozen North Wind

Throughout Europe the decline and fall of the once-mighty Western Roman Empire had given way to a succession of monarchies of Germanic origin. In the mid 8th century the Franks had managed to halt the Muslim advance from the south, and their domains stretched through today's Germany and Italy, to form the Carolingian Empire.

In the North Sea regions, day-to-day life continued as ever in small villages inhabited by peasants and fisherfolk. Until one day the fearsome Vikings in their light sailing vessels or oared boats destroyed peaceful lives of these coastal communities – the Norsemen brought with them the strategy of surprise and an incredible capacity to attack quickly, plunder and return to the sea.

Viking incursions took place every year, in the spring and summer months. The islands of the North Sea, England, Ireland and France were sacked by small flotillas manned by between thirty and 100 freemen. Once on land, these invaders became bloodthirsty warriors who razed everything in their path to the ground. Their campaigns extended to the Mediterranean and they were the scourge of the North until the

With the advent of maritime trade – wool, wine and wheat – cod fishing in the North Sea and whale hunting by the Basques and the Cantabrians, the 13th century witnessed intense traffic in the English Channel. Constant attacks on trading vessels led to the coastal towns grouping together in brotherhoods.

11th century. Their objectives were rich prizes: jewels, gold, silver and silk. They took no hostages for ransom, killed anyone foolish enough to resist and took prisoners who became their slaves in the North Lands. Churches and monasteries were their principal targets, for they were well aware of the treasures contained therein.

Late in the 9th century the Vikings modified their strategy. Now they organised major military expeditions with a view to founding new settlements, they gave up piracy and established kingdoms and duchies comparable to those of their enemies.

The Beginnings of Maritime Trade

In the 11th century trade began to spread throughout Europe.[1] England formed a major trading fleet, devoted to the exchange of cloth and spices. The cities of Flanders, with Bruges at the head, and German cities led by Lubeck, Hamburg and Cologne, as well as the kingdoms of Castile, Navarre and Portugal, with trading ports such as Santander, Bilbao, Deva, Fuenterrabía, Bayona and Lisbon, engaged in intense commercial traffic. In order to facilitate mercantile exchange, such cities began to group together. Lubeck and Hamburg, for example, created a federation, the Hansa, which fostered their commercial relations. By establishing trading posts throughout Europe, and fostering agreements between states, they obtained privileges and secured safe passage at sea.

The major wool, wheat and wine trades of Bordeaux and the Iberian Peninsula, cod fishing in the North Sea, and expeditions by Basque and Cantabrian whalers who pursued their quarry as far as the waters of Spitsbergen, created a constant traffic of ships that were invariably forced to enter the English Channel.

Associated with this prosperity, it seems that, in the 13th century, the ancient Viking custom of seaborne attack began a new lease of life. The coastal communities of Cornwall, Scotland and Ireland, traditionally devoted to fishing, discovered the old, lucrative métier of piracy. The privileged location of their ports and, in particular, their knowledge of winds and currents, gave the pirates a definite advantage. What began as attacks against Hansa, Genoese and Castilian vessels soon threatened to extend to any ship that entered these waters.

Early in the 14th century, protests reached even the Privy Council but the English Crown was powerless to solve the problem. The main cities in the south of England, Sandwich, Romney, Winchelsea, Hythe and Rye, with Dover and Hastings taking the lead, constituted the League of the Cinq Ports[2], (despite being seven their title referred to only five ports). These cities organised a squadron to combat the pirates and, at the same time, secured major fiscal privileges. However, what began as a system of defence became a band of pillagers, who imposed their own arbitrary rule on Channel traffic.

A number of cities to the west – Plymouth, Dartmouth, Poole and Fowey – set up a kind of brotherhood to combat the Cinq Ports.[3] Its area of influence embraced the coasts of Brittany and Normandy and later extended to the Iberian Peninsula. The constant conflicts between England and France and their traditional allies, Portugal and Castile, favoured the formation of attack and reprisal squadrons that continually sacked the Cantabrian ports. In Bayona the *Hermandad de Mareantes*[4] was constituted, whose objectives were identical to those of the brotherhoods and leagues of northern Europe. And the *Hermandad de las Marismas de Castilla*[5] was created, embracing the cities on the Cantabrian cornice, from Bayonne in France to Bayona in Galicia. Its ships sailed in two organised convoys departing annually for Flanders, once between April and May and once between August and September.

Although the Hermandad was neutral, during the War of Brittany its ships attacked English vessels in the Bay of Biscay. Protests soon reached the Castilian Court where, in 1328, Alphonso XI listened to complaints about the abuses committed by the ships of the Hermandad de las Marismas:

…malefactors and pirates from Fuenterrabía, San Sebastián, Guetaria, Motrico, Lequeitio, Portugalete, Castourdiales, Laredo, Santander, San Vincente de la Barquera, Avilés, Ribadeo, Vivero, Coruña, Noya, Pontevedra and Bayona del Miño….[6]

International conflict broke out in the middle of the 14th century. Edward III, King of England and Duke of Aquitaine, and Philippe de Valois, King of France, sought the support of Castile in order to secure command of the sea. Despite Luis de La Cerda's support for the French cause during the war of succession to the Duchy of Brittany, Castile remained neutral. Consequently, Edward granted Bayona the privilege of exclusive wine trade with England, much to the chagrin of the Hermandad de las Marismas.

Early in November 1349 a fleet, under the command of Carlos de La Cerda, Luis's brother, captured several wine-carrying ships and put their crews to the sword.

The gravity of the situation reached such proportions that in 1350 Edward III, not knowing to whom he could turn, wrote to the bishops of York and Canterbury asking them to pray for the protection of the country against the onslaught of pirates.

…The Spaniards, with whom I had planned to renew the recently signed treaty through the marital union of our daughter, have attacked many merchant vessels of our nation and others sailing the seas with their cargo of wine, wool and other merchandise, robbing them and putting the crews inhumanely to the sword…. Such is their arrogance that having assembled a huge fleet in Flanders, with crews of armed men, not only do they boast of having entirely destroyed our ships and come to dominate English waters, but also of having invaded our kingdom and exterminated our subjects….[7]

The activities of the Mediterranean ports, such as Palma, chief city of the island of Mallorca, were very important during the 13th and 14th centuries. Trade with the East, through the trading posts set up by the Venetians, supplied the whole of Europe with products of extraordinarily high quality.

In case God should be deaf to his prayers, however, Edward assembled a major fleet. He embarked together with his sons, the Prince of Wales, known as the Black Prince, John of Gaunt, later Duke of Lancaster, and the Count of Richmond, then still a mere boy of ten, and 400 men of distinction. The ships were equipped with artillery, crossbowmen, archers and men of arms. The *Thomas* was the flagship.

News of the English fleet reached Flanders, where the Hermandad reinforced its ships and chose Carlos de La Cerda as commander.

The English and the Castilians met at Winchelsea,[8] where the vessels of the Hermandad had anchored. Having got to windward, the Hermandad set upon the English ships. The outcome of the battle was the capture of between fourteen and twenty-six Hermandad ships – according to different chronicles – and the loss of two of the finest English vessels. On both sides the losses were enormous. Nevertheless, to celebrate the victory, Edward was proclaimed King of the Sea by his jubilant subjects.

The following year, a twenty-year treaty[9] was signed at the Tower of London recognising the right of Hermandad de las Marismas ships to trade with any English port, and both sides compensated each other for the damage and losses they had suffered. The Hermandad delegates Juan López de Salcedo, Diego Sánchez de Lupart and Martín Pérez de Golindano,

Trade with the Low Countries, particularly with Flanders and the German cities of the Hanseatic League (or Hansa),
became the mainstay of European economy.

THE 'BROTHERS OF VICTUALS'

In 1243 Lubeck and Hamburg signed an agreement to combat pirates who lurked at the mouths of the major German rivers, in the Baltic islands and the North Sea.

During previous years there had been seamen who, weary of fighting inside and outside the protectionist mercantile organisations, opted to seek their fortunes as pirates. Two of these were Godekins and Stertebeker[10] (according to author

Philip Gosse, his nickname might be translated as *The Drunkard*) who, late in the 14th century, joined forces, together with Moltke and Manteufel (the man-devil) to form the *Vitalienbrüder* (the Brothers of Victuals), more familiarly known as the Friends of God and Enemies of the World). Themselves former Hansa traders, they were perfectly familiar with the routes of its heavy merchant vessels where they spread terror for several years.

The Hansa received complaint

after complaint, until the federation decided to take punitive action. However, its bulky vessels were unable to compete with the fast, light ships of the Vitalienbrüder. Furthermore, the Brothers were quick to react and, in 1392, they stormed and sacked Wisby, the Hansa's main headquarters, taking hostages for whom they demanded substantial ransoms. They then assaulted Bergen with identical results. The Vitalienbrüder had managed to paralyse shipping in the

Baltic and the North Sea to the extent that not even fishing boats dared leave harbour. The authorities organised two punitive expeditions, both of which met with failure.

In 1402, however, good fortune turned its back on the Vitalienbrüder. A large fleet from Hamburg managed to intercept their vessels on the high seas. After a bitter struggle a fabulous booty was recovered, which more than covered the costs of the expedition, and Stertebeker was put to death.

THE HERMANDAD DE LAS MARISMAS DE CASTILLA

Serious doubts exist as to when the Hermandad de las Marismas de Castilla was formed and who its members were, although the most commonly held opinion is that it was a federation of all the major Cantabrian coastal towns. It seems that early in May 1296 delegates from Santander, Laredo, Bermeo, Guetaria, San Sebastián, Fuenterrabía and Vitoria met at Castourdiales to discuss the constitution of a brotherhood strictly governed by a set of regulations.

Three delegates set up their headquarters in Castourdiales, the first of whom received a seal with which to formalise the Brotherhood's documents. The emblem symbolising the Hermandad consisted of a castle over the waves and the legend *'Sello de la Hermandad de las villas de la marina de Castilla y Vitoria'*.

signed the treaty with King Edward. The Hermandad had lost a battle but won the war.

For their part, the Bretons also mustered their forces against English attacks, and held the latter's fleet in check during the Hundred Years' War. Worthy of special mention is the figure of Jeanne Belleville,[11] a woman famous throughout France for her beauty. Her husband, Lord Olivier Clisson, had been beheaded in Paris in the summer of 1303. His widow swore to avenge herself. Having mortgaged her lands and sold furniture and jewels to purchase and equip three ships, she set sail under the name of La Dame de Clisson and soon became the scourge of the French coast. Exceptionally ferocious, she engaged in burning towns and villages, cutting throats and sinking ships. She boarded other vessels accompanied by two of her young sons, who were as fierce and intrepid as their mother. Jeanne Belleville, whose fate is unknown, may be considered one of history's first female pirates.

Bands of pirates such as the Brave Boys of Fowey, who plundered the coast of Normandy, and individuals like St Ives and William Kyd were famous throughout the 14th century. All attempts by the English Crown to curb the activities of its own pirates proved fruitless principally because the Crown was incapable of controlling its nobles, who were entrusted with the task of imposing order in their respective regions. Far from doing this, however, they financed the formation of pirate squadrons that provided them with huge profits.

Unlawful activities also continued in Castile. In 1477 three men from Guipázcoa and two from Vizcaya embarked as passengers on an English ship bound for Castile.[12] When the crew were resting after having battled against the elements during a storm, the foreigners killed thirty-three Englishmen and threw their bodies overboard. They took the ship to Galicia where they negotiated sale of its cargo with Pedro Pérez de Sotomayor. However, the crime was discovered when some of the bodies of the murdered seamen were washed ashore. The murderers were condemned to death by the Hermandad de las Marismas.

It was not until 1495, having signed an agreement with France, that Henry VII established a set of regulations to govern the activities of corsairs, who were allowed to engage in piracy only during time of war and exclusively against enemy ships and those of their allies. This formula had already been applied on the Iberian Peninsula in the form of the Ordenanzas of Pedro IV of Aragon (1356) and the Regulación de las Presas Marítimas, issued in 1480 by the Catholic Monarchs.

Thus were opened the gates of opportunity, justified by the right of reprisal, through which piracy was to develop into the Modern Era.

The Resurgence of Muslim Piracy

The fall of Constantinople to Mohammed II and its re-christening as Istanbul in 1453 marked the end of the Byzantine Empire and the consolidation of a new Islamic power in the eastern Mediterranean. The route across Asia was once again wholly in Muslim hands and the lucrative trade activities of the Venetians and Genoese were seriously threatened.

On the Peninsula, the Catholic Monarchs had managed to unify their kingdoms and now began their onslaught against the last remaining Muslim bastion in Europe, the Kingdom of Granada. However, despite their military prestige, their control of the Mediterranean and the discovery of the Americas, their problems continued.

The taking of Granada led to a permanent diaspora of Moriscos who, given the choice of either renouncing their faith or abandoning the Peninsula, preferred the latter option. Most settled on the north coast of Africa, where penury, humiliation and hatred of the monarchs who had stripped them of everything fostered the resurgence of

ATTACKS AND REPRISALS.
ARRIPAY AND PERO NIÑO

The corsair Harry Pay, *Arripay* to the Spanish, operated under commission from the English crown.[13] A native of Poole, Dorset, he was the scourge of the north coast of the Peninsula, his most renowned feat being the theft of the Holy Crucifix from the Church of Santa María in Finisterre. Harry Pay was a hero in his home town, and his return from each campaign was an occasion for celebration.

Reprisals were not long in coming, however. Pero Niño, who would later become Admiral of Castile, one of the boldest seamen of the 15th century, vowed to devote his life to imposing order on the sea.

Born in Cantabria,[14] his father was a squire and his mother was chosen as the future Enrique III's nurse. He was educated at the court of Juan I according to the principle that 'he who must learn the art of chivalry should not waste time in the study of letters'.

Having taken part in a number of campaigns on land, in 1403 the king made him a seaman in charge of two galleys and a *nao* (a type of carrack). He was twenty-five years old. In the Mediterranean, he pursued several corsairs such as Juan Castrillo and his sidekick known as Amaynar, Diego Barrasa and Nicolás Jiménez.

After the breakdown of the Paris truce and the resurgence of hostilities between France and England, Castile was forced to come to the assistance of the former in compliance with a pact of mutual aid. Pero Niño took to the sea with three Castilian galleys, which operated jointly with two French galleys – in all some 1,500 men including the rowers. He sailed along the coast of France, attacking English settlements there as he went.

In England he attacked Chilbury, a village of some 300 inhabitants, which was sacked and razed to the ground. He then attempted to storm Plymouth, but was received by artillery fire and had no alternative but to retreat. Next he attacked Portland, where he took a number of prisoners.

Niño's flotilla reached Poole, Harry Pay's home town, which the Castilians decided to attack alone. Pero Niño launched a ferocious onslaught, ordering his men to take no prisoners and to raze everything to the ground. They burned the town, beginning with the palace and the supply stores. Revenge was sweet but reinforcements reached the English, and Niño's men, amid what the chronicles describe as a genuine hail of arrows, were forced to retreat back to the galleys to avoid death or capture.[15]

One Phillipot sought revenge with 1,000 men, managing to capture fifteen Cantabrian ships, but such recompense was insignificant compared to the havoc wreaked by Niño, which put paid to the town's commercial importance.

In the spring, three whaleboats joined the expedition and Niño took to sea once again. While patrolling the coast of Calais, the Spaniards sighted an English convoy carrying the daughter of the King of England to Holland, where she was to marry. Harry Pay was at the head of the convoy. Niño's men attacked, and the English received them with arrows, darts, stones and fire. The Castilians fired burning bolts and sent a fireship into the convoy. At the height of the battle, the wind changed

The activities of corsairs belonging to the brotherhoods began to cause serious problems in relations between the different European monarchies. In the mid 14th century, Pedro IV of Aragon drew up a set of regulations in an attempt to restrict their activities; France, England and Castile did not follow suit until the end of the century.

direction and the sea became angry. The English attacked Niño's galley, which was rescued from the fray by one of the whale-boats. According to the chronicler, one more hour of calm would have assured the Castilian's victory.

Since provisions were running short, Niño decided to return to France, where he sought help to attack the island of Jersey, defended by 4,000 or 5,000 Englishmen. Assisted by cavaliers from Brittany, the men made landfall and attacked the island. With fifty men, Niño set upon a group defending a standard with the cross of St George. The insignia having been captured, the remaining defenders fled. The magnificent spoils included 10,000 gold crowns and 'twelve lances, twelve axes, and twelve bows with their corresponding arrows...', which were given to Niño for a period of ten years.[16]

The campaign came to an end when Niño was ordered to return to Spain. Back at Court, he led an eventful life, married three times, on each occasion with a lady of noble descent, and lived to the ripe old age of seventy five.

Palma de Mallorca around 1480, as depicted on the St George altarpiece by Pere Nisard. Museo de la Iglesia de Mallorca.

Berber privateering, fomented in turn by the Berber states and protected by the Sultan of Istanbul. A number of renegades acquired fame and fortune among the Muslim hosts.

On the Christian side, the Knights of St John of Jerusalem, who had settled on the island of Rhodes, and a multitude of grand masters from Vizcaya, Aragon and France chose privateering as a lucrative alternative to legitimate trade.

The correlation of forces was reasonably balanced, until one summer day in 1504, when two papal galleys[17] loaded with valuable merchandise were making the crossing from Genoa to Civitavecchia. Foreseeing no danger on the peaceful waters of the Mediterranean, the two ships sailed out of sight of one another. When the leading galley, captained by Paolo Victor, was passing the island of Elba, the watch sighted a small galliot. The captain decided to proceed without waiting for the second galley, since he did not imagine for a moment that the galliot harboured any kind of threat. However, when it came within firing range, the galliot turned about. Standing on its decks and hanging from its yards was a

During the first half of the 16th century, the resurgence of Muslim piracy blocked maritime trade in the Mediterranean. Aruj and Kheireddin Barbarossa became the most famous and feared corsairs in the waters between the straits and the north coast of Africa.

host of Turks armed to the teeth. Having fired a first volley of arrows, the Turks boarded the galley and, to the astonishment of the crew, quickly took control. The slaves were freed and the Christians locked in the hold. The brains behind such an audacious feat was a tall, robust individual with a thick reddish beard, Aruj 'Barbarossa', one of two corsairs who would sow panic in the Mediterranean until the mid 16th century. After Aruj's

death, his brother Kheireddin 'Barbarossa' took his place and acquired such power and fame that he became *Kapitan Pasha*, (admiral), of the entire Turkish fleet.

Having been told of the existence of a second galley, Barbarossa ignored the advice of his lieutenants and ordered his men to dress in Christian clothes, put the galliot in tow and wait for the other ship to catch up. The ruse proved effective. The crew of the second galley thought that the flagship had made a capture and was now waiting for them to come abreast to continue the crossing together. Barbarossa repeated his previous manoeuvre and quickly overpowered the newcomers. With his booty he sailed to Tunis, where he was proclaimed a hero.

News of this assault by an unknown pirate spread like wildfire through Europe, and it marked the beginning of pirate and corsair activities that were to be the scourge of the Mediterranean until the early 19th century.

The Caribbean, an Exceptional Setting

Talk of corsairs and pirates brings to mind idyllic beaches and ships with billowing sails. Literature and the cinema have created the image of the honourable rogue in heroic confrontation with the commercial system in defence of the underprivileged. In contrast, Spanish documentary sources and contemporary chronicles convey the idea that piracy was the cause of all the misfortunes of Spain's colonies in America. Reality would lie somewhere between these two versions, although not necessarily equidistant from both.

From its beginnings in the 15th century, piracy in the Caribbean acquired its own specific characteristics that would persist until the early 18th century and undoubtedly formed part of the context of war at sea.

Spain defended her acquired rights in the Caribbean region, while other interested European nations fostered privateering as the means to obtain what they had failed to achieve either militarily or diplomatically: to break the Spanish trade monopoly. Religious fervour became, in itself, a cause of conflict.

However, to believe that the Spaniards themselves did not engage in privateering would be ingenuous to say the least. The collaboration and complicity of the Catholic Monarchs' subjects, burdened by taxes and left by the home country to their own devices as far as basic necessities were concerned, was crucial to the advent of smuggling, Caribbean piracy in embryonic form. Furthermore, many successful attacks against American strongholds would have failed without the collaboration of renegades.

The military campaigns organised by the English Crown during the war with Spain, in which corsairs participated for their own profit, and the specific encouragement of smuggling by the Queen and distinguished courtiers, served to blur the borderline between privateering and piracy.

In the 17th century the situation changed radically. For Spain, international peace had been temporarily secured and, in order to combat smuggling the authorities devastated vast areas of the Caribbean, leaving land free for colonisation by the French and the English.

A new war was the pretext for Holland's full-scale assault of the American coast. Trading companies, halfway between mercantile organisations and institutional organisms, sent in their corsairs to conquer new enclaves. The settlements on St Kitts, Providence and other smaller islands were the embryo of what would become the filibusters' den par excellence: La Tortuga.

England took the initiative and conquered Jamaica in 1655. Defence requirements made the island a new lair of filibusters and, with Dutch Curaçao, also became the centre of the black slave trade in the Caribbean.

The power balance between European nations and the consolidation of their colonies in America led to a change in the situation early in the 18th century. Following the Treaty of Utrecht, and with the American market partially open, piracy became a problem that affected everyone. Collaboration between the colonial authorities and the decisive campaign launched by England would eventually put paid to piracy in the Caribbean.

Sources of Information

Although attempts have been made on numerous occasions to study privateering and piracy, legends and speculation have been rife since the first exploits of Drake and Hawkins in the Spanish colonies.

The apparent lack of primary documentary sources has been an obstacle to comparison between official writings and contemporary eyewitness accounts. These documentary sources do exist, however, but it is practically impossible to analyse systematically the vast number of documents, letters, reports and accounts of the presence of pirates and corsairs in Caribbean waters. Furthermore, the supreme effort this would involve goes far beyond the scope of this book.

The Spanish sources, scattered among the different national archives and many contained in documents not directly related to the theme, provide clarity and eyewitness accounts as a supplement to chronicles of the time. These substantially enrich the view of a problem that, by virtue of its complexity and implications, must be subjected to constant reappraisal.

A WHO'S WHO OF PIRATES, CORSAIRS, BUCCANEERS AND FILIBUSTERS IN AMERICA

It is no easy task to make a fine distinction between pirates, corsairs, buccaneers and filibusters. In the first place, their activities were very similar, different versions of the old métier of sea wolves, the only differences being the circumstances in which they operated. Possibly the clearest concept is that of piracy, defined by Azcárraga[18] as 'an armed seafaring expedition, unauthorised by any State, whose aim is to seek profit', he added that pirates 'were a threat to commercial interests in general, rather than those of a specific country'.

Thus pirates were the enemy of maritime trade as a whole, and they were motivated by the lure of profit. They submitted to the authority of no sovereign and made no distinction between nations when it came to choosing their quarry.

Corsairs or privateers operated in a similar way although according to a set of rules. Azcárrega defines privateering as 'the naval enterprise of a private individual against the enemies of his State, who operates with the approval and subject to the authority of a belligerent power with the exclusive objective of causing losses to enemy trade and to that of other nations allied with the enemy'.

Privateering was given legal status by the right of reprisal, and corsairs attacked only those ships that engaged in trade under the banner of nations considered to be enemies. They were granted letters patent in exchange for part of the booty, which they would deliver to the State.

There were two kinds of privateering: that carried out in wartime and that carried out by exercising the right of reprisal, however, a very fine line marked the differences between them. Thus, during the second half of the 16th century the English invoked right of

Searching for hidden treasure – few escapades can have so captivated childhood imaginations.

reprisal to engage in privateering in Spanish waters. Francis Drake, th most famous of Queen Elizabeth's 'sea dogs', may have begun his career as a privateer under a letter of reprisal. The French, for their part, engaged in privateering as an act of war, not of business.

Spanish corsairs employed as coastguards to combat smuggling in peacetime deserve separate mention, as this was another form of exercising the right of reprisal. Similar circumstances extended to privileged companies who defended their monopolies through engagement in privateering.

The terms buccaneer and filibuster are exclusive to the Caribbean and to a specific period in history, the 17th century. The buccaneers were those adventurers

who, after the settlement of the north of Hispaniola had been evicted by the Spaniards, occupied the area and devoted themselves to drying meat. The name, probably of Karib origin, although some authors claim that it comes from the Arawak, derives from the word the Indians used to describe this process of preserving meat.

Buccaneers appeared in the second quarter of the 17th century, hunted livestock that had returned to the wild, mainly pigs and cattle, and, once the meat had been cured and salted, it was sold or exchanged for other provisions. The fact that they supplied smugglers active in the area, thus fostering illegal trade, led to actions against them by the authorities of Santo Domingo. The main characteristic of the lifestyle of

the 'brethren of the coast', as buccaneers called themselves, was the democratic discipline they exercised among themselves.

Taking advantage of the opportunity to obtain meat and hides from the buccaneers, adventurers from the smaller islands settled on La Tortuga, off the coast of Venezuela, and became filibusters. Aided by the major European powers, for almost fifty years they agreed to prey on Spanish possessions only, commissioned by the colonial authorities of La Tortuga or Jamaica. Some doubt exists as to the origin of the name, although it most probably comes from the Dutch *vrijbuiter* (freebooter) or *vrie boot* (fly boat) which the French translated as *flibustier*.

The world as presented in a 16th-century Spanish book of navigation.

CHAPTER I

ADAM'S DISPOSSESSED
(1493-1561)

The Legend of the Indies

After his return to the Iberian Peninsula, Christopher Columbus announced in a letter to the Catholic Monarchs[1] that he had reached the Indies by sailing west. He had discovered six islands rich in gold and inhabited by people similar to the Guanches, the legendary inhabitants of the Canary Isles. The *Carta de Colón*, dated 3 March 1493, was sent to numerous dignitaries at the Castilian court and was soon translated into several languages and printed in Florence, Rome, Antwerp, Paris and Basle. Thus began the story of a land of untold riches on the far side of the ocean. But the secret best kept by Columbus and his men was the route they had followed to reach the new lands – that was enshrouded in utmost secrecy.

The first treasures soon reached Europe along with news that the Spaniards had set up a trading post on *Hispaniola* (the island today divided into Haiti and the Dominican Republic) from which to begin the colonisation process.

In 1507, the Academy of Vosges published an edition of Ptolemy's *Cosmographiae*, in which the idea was first expressed that the new lands discovered by Columbus were, in fact, a new continent. The prologue, *'Cosmographiae Introductio'*, stated that the Florentine sailor, Amerigo Vespucci, had proved this, and it was proposed that the new continent should be called 'America' in his honour.

So arrived new myths of cannibals, sea monsters, gold and riches untold, and terrible rulers who did not hesitate to execute anyone who dared to cross the sea. All this served to stimulate the greed of the sea wolves lying in wait between the Canaries, the Azores and the Iberian Peninsula ready to pounce on vessels returning from the Americas.

A Highly Perilous Zone

While the route to the Americas was a closely guarded secret, everybody knew the final destination of returning ships bringing treasures from the new lands. They were bound for Seville and its *Casa de Contratación* (House of Transactions – the administrative centre for Spain's New World empire). To find a ship on the ocean was tantamount to looking for a needle in a haystack but to wait for her in those places in which she would take water and provisions was more like fishing for trout from a river bank.

Even so, early attacks were few and far between. On his first voyage, Columbus encountered French corsairs near the Canary Isles, and on his third crossing he decided to return via Madeira to avoid a flotilla stationed at Cape St Vincent.

The Berber corsairs, particularly the Barbarossa brothers, who abandoned the waters of the Mediterranean to reach the Canaries, and French attackers in the Azores area and the Straits of Gibraltar, were the principal dangers for ships homeward bound across the ocean. Arming the flotillas was initially considered the most effective measure, and to foster this practice a Royal Decree[2] was issued in 1502 ordering carracks to be built as escorts, above all to ships weighing over 1,500 tons.

Safeguarding the coasts with armed patrol vessels that hounded enemy ships proved to be an effective way to protect shipping and, in 1505, the system was put into practice by arming fustas (two-masted boats) in Seville and sending them to the Straits.

Ocean-going ships had not yet been the victims of attacks that made the adoption of exceptional measures necessary. But the alarm sounded in 1507 when assaults began to occur with greater frequency. It was proposed that additional measures be adopted to supplement the defence and coastguard patrols. To this end, in the summer of 1507 Juan de la Cosa organised the first armada whose mission was to protect ships returning from the Indies. The Casa de Contratación raised funds from traders to arm two caravels.

However, no major action was taken to protect ships on their way back from the Indies until, in 1512 and 1513, two artillery ships were sent to the Canaries to escort the returning fleets.

Privateering, outlawed by the Catholic Monarchs in the last quarter of the previous century, was now fomented as a coastguard service, and a Law[3] was passed according to which the booty would be divided into five equal parts: one for the King; two for the officers and crew; one for the owner of the ship; one for the charterer of the expedition. When the booty was captured by a king's ship, the last two portions were deposited in the royal coffers.

It was not until 1521, with the outbreak of the first war between France and Spain (1521-1526), that systematic

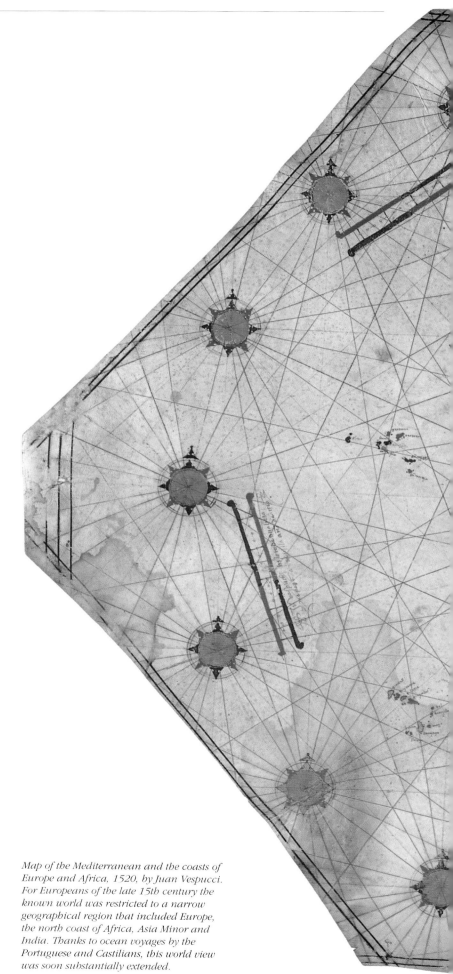

Map of the Mediterranean and the coasts of Europe and Africa, 1520, by Juan Vespucci. For Europeans of the late 15th century the known world was restricted to a narrow geographical region that included Europe, the north coast of Africa, Asia Minor and India. Thanks to ocean voyages by the Portuguese and Castilians, this world view was soon substantially extended.

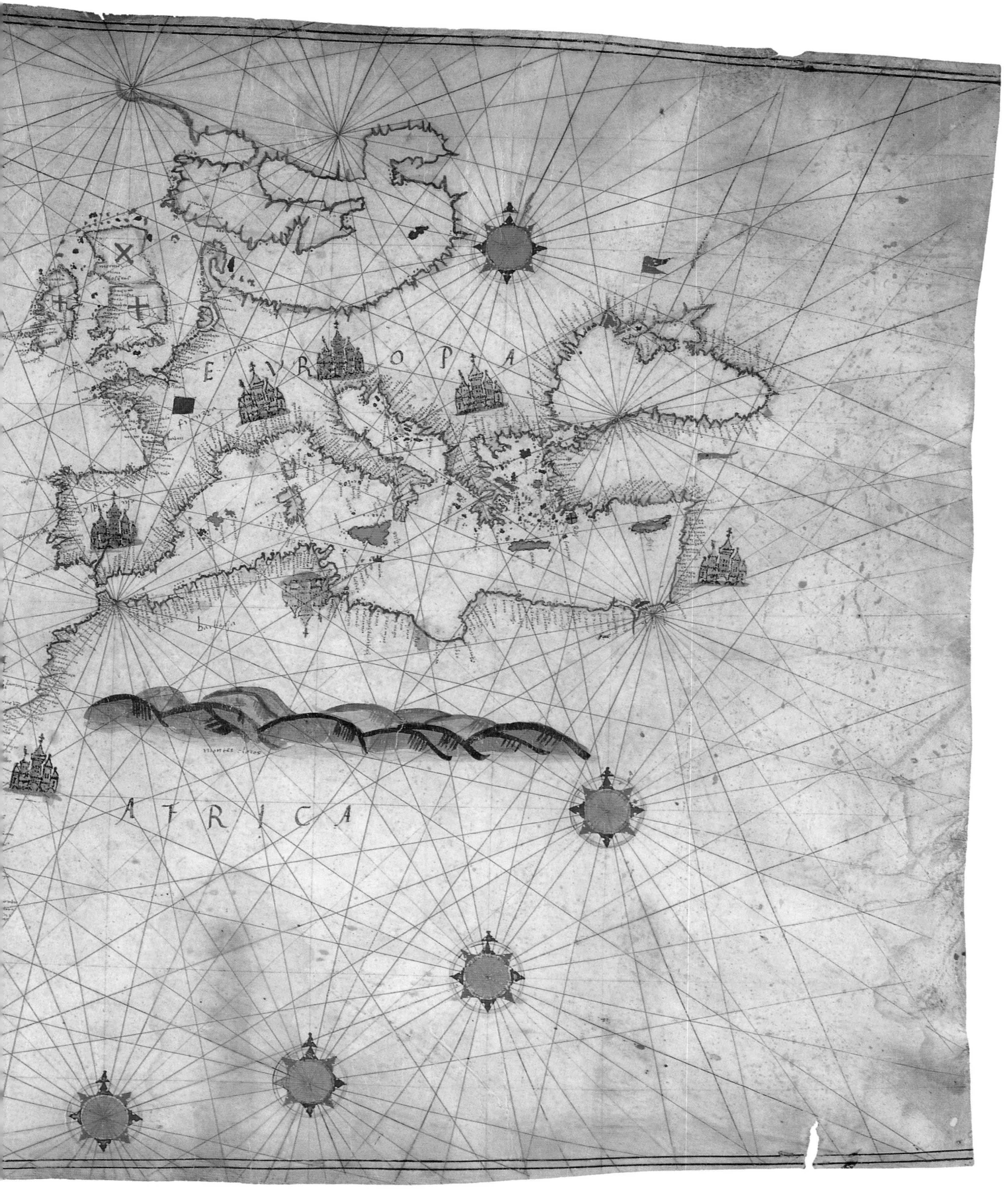
E V R O P A
A F R I C A

The Inter Caetera *bull issued by Pope Alexander VI on 4 May 1493 in favour of the Catholic Monarchs.*

TO WHOM DOES THE SEA BELONG?

With the discovery of the new lands to the west and south of Europe, disagreements arose between the crowns of Castile and Portugal over the rights conceded them by the Treaty of Alcovaça. Delegations from both countries who met in 1493 were unable to settle the dispute, so it was decided to bring the case before Pope Alexander VI.

Thanks to the astuteness of the Castilian ambassadors, the alacrity of the Catholic Monarchs and the fact that both the Pope and his notary had originally been the subjects of Ferdinand and Isabella, the Curia Romana was extra-ordinarily prompt to issue bulls (Papal edicts) in favour of Castile.

Juridical instruments were required to meet two needs on the part of the Crown of Castile. First, a bull of donation had to be issued that would ratify Castile's rights of ownership as discoverer of the new lands and, second, the dividing line between the areas of Castilian and Portuguese influence in the world had to be established. The *Inter Caetera* and *Eximiae Devotiones* bulls, dated 3 May 1494, satisfied Castile's initial claims by granting the monarchs those lands that belonged to no other Christian sovereign.

The second Inter Caetera bull established a line of demarcation from pole to pole that passed through the meridian of the Azores. Castile was granted rights to all territories west of the Atlantic archipelago.

On 26 September 1493 the *Dudum siquidem* was issued, a true victory for Castile, which recognised the Castilians' rights to eastern isles that they discovered by sailing west, and those in the Indian Ocean.

Portugal did not accept the limits established in the Inter Caetera bull, so Castilians and Portuguese sat down to negotiate. Finally, by the Treaty of Tordesillas, signed on 7 June 1494, a new line of demarcation was drawn 370 leagues (1,185 miles) west of the Cape Verde Islands. The ocean now had owners, which ratified the concept of *Mare clausum*, with the concession of reciprocal guarantees of free passage.

Meanwhile the disinherited kingdoms of Europe, France and England, sent their explorers – and their pirates and corsairs – into the Atlantic in an attempt to break the Iberian monopoly.

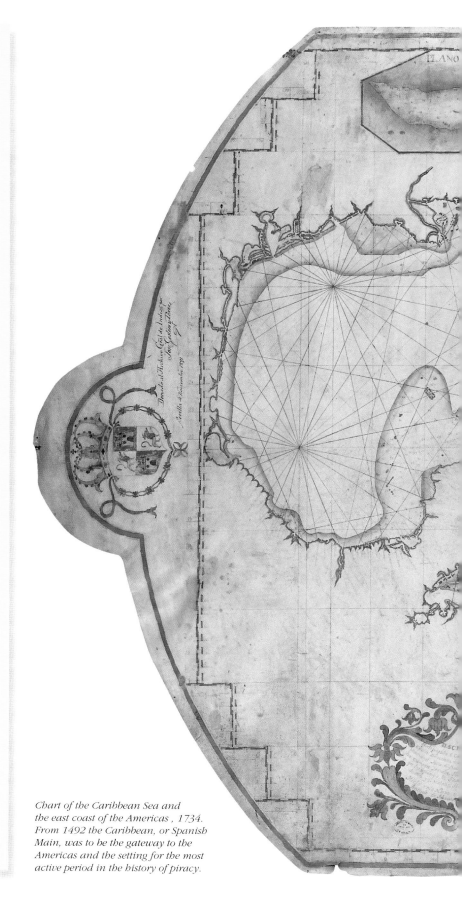

Chart of the Caribbean Sea and the east coast of the Americas , 1734. From 1492 the Caribbean, or Spanish Main, was to be the gateway to the Americas and the setting for the most active period in the history of piracy.

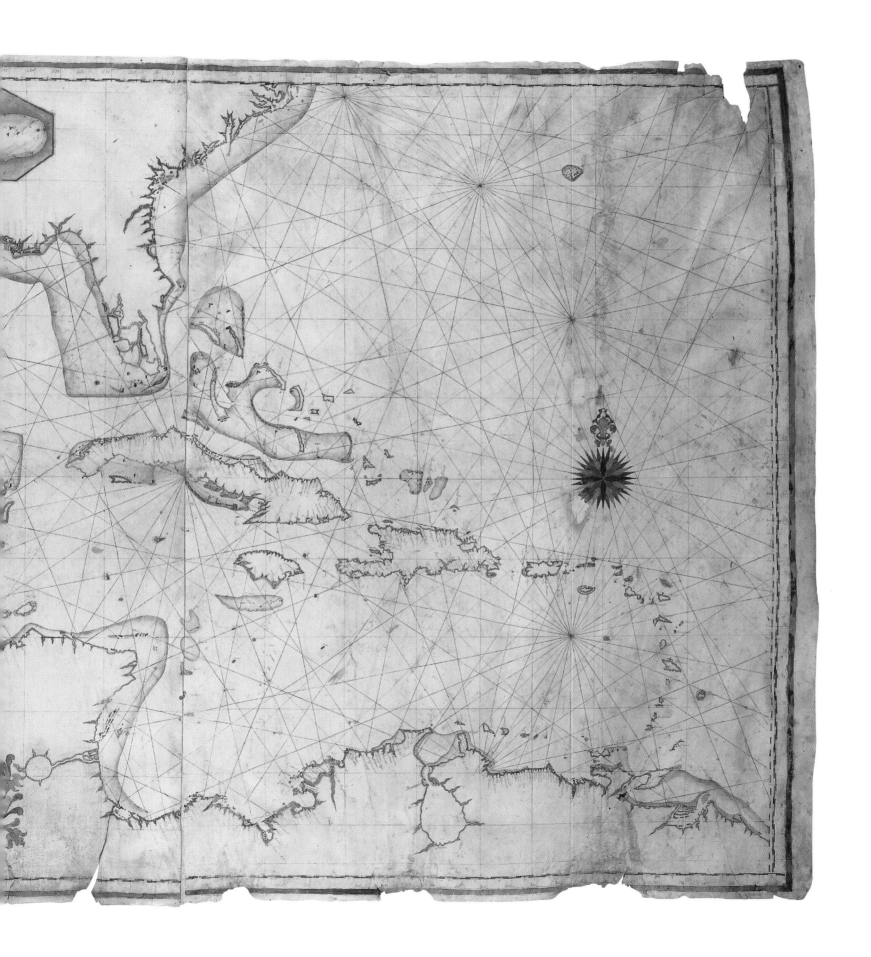

The booty captured by Florín included '…eighty-eight thousand castellanos in gold bars…many rich jewels and pearls, some as big as almonds, and many chalchiuíes, precious stones similar to emeralds…". Among other treasures was Montezuma's famous plume of feathers.

attacks by corsairs in the service of Francis I of France created the need for permanent escort armadas.

El Florentino, Success and Failure

The legend of the first pirate to capture treasures from the Americas begins with reports of his name and origins. Jean Fleury, Juan Florín or El Florentino are three of the names attributed to an individual who was born, apparently in Florence, early in the 16th century, although some French authors claim that his place of birth was Vatteville-sur-Seine.[4] Most agree, however, that his pseudonyms conceal the identity of Giovanni da Verrazzano, brother of the Florentine, Girolamo Verrazzano, a geographer in the service of Francis I.[5] And there is no disagreement over his occupation: piracy.

El Florentino served Jean d'Angó, an Italian charterer who had settled in Dieppe, for whom he captured all the ships that came within his reach. The two men had reached an exceptional agreement with the French king: they received an annual sum of 4,000 crowns in exchange for not attacking ships sailing under the French flag and for simultaneously harassing the ships of his enemies. D'Angó soon amassed a considerable fortune and acquired respectability, becoming alderman, inspector of the salt depots, captain and gaining other ranks and positions of power in his adopted city.[6]

The pirate and his men were active in the area bounded by the Azores, the Canaries and the Iberian Peninsula, where they lay in wait for unsuspecting ships. One of their first actions was the persecution, as far as Puerto de la Luz, of a flotilla of seven vessels transporting colonists to the Canaries, some of which El Florentino managed to capture. The governor of Gran Canaria, Pedro Suárez de Castilla,[7] armed five ships to pursue the pirate, and managed to free a number of both ships and captives.

Jean Fleury's greatest feat, the fruit of coincidence, took place in the spring of 1522. Three caravels had been sent by Cortés carrying the *Quinto Real* (Royal Fifth)[8] of the treasures obtained during the conquest of Mexico, as well as many other gifts for illustrious personages. Gold, silver, emeralds and other precious stones, masks, capes and the famous crest adorned with the green feathers of the quetzal shared the hold with numerous exotic animals. Furthermore, Cortés had sent a number of Indians and products of the New World: sugar, skins and maize.

Legend had it that the curse of the Indians would bring great misfortune to those who stole their treasures and, indeed, from the very beginning the voyage was plagued by bad luck.

After a hard crossing, the ships were nearing the Azores. On the horizon, a number of sails announced the presence of El Florentino's fleet, which rushed to attack and take two of the caravels. The third, carrying the treasure, managed to find refuge on the island of Santa María, without alerting the corsairs to the manoeuvre. They waited a few days and, when they decided that the coast was clear, the caravel took to sea once more, this time escorted by three others belonging to Domingo Alonso, which had arrived from Santo Domingo, Hispaniola. Florín, however, had remained in wait and intercepted the flotilla near Cape St Vincent. Despite the quality of the defence, the corsairs managed to take two

Colmenar, now Villa de Monbeltrán, in the pass from the Meseta to Andalusia through the Sierra de Gredos, was the site of Jean Florín's execution.

of the caravels: the one carrying the treasure and one of Domingo Alonso's carrying gold, pearls and a great quantity of sugar. Alonso Davila, the commander of the flotilla, was taken prisoner.

The booty was enormous[9]: '...eighty-eight thousand castellanos in gold bars; the treasure of the great Montezuma that Guatemuz had in his power, which was a fine gift for our great Caesar, for there were many rich jewels and pearls, some as big as almonds, and many chalchiuíes, which are precious stones like emeralds...'.

Florín gave the best pieces to Francis I, and news of the vast treasures of the Indies spread like wildfire through France. Festooned with honours and prestige, Florín soon set sail once more, although he never again managed to make such huge profits.

The Emperor Charles V wrote to the King of France to protest against the actions of Florín, and urging him to

return what had been stolen. The Frenchman's ironic reply has gone down in history:[10] '... How is it that you and the king of Portugal have kept the world for yourselves, leaving nothing for me? Show me the part in Adam's last will and testament that says you are the sole heirs to those lands and have the right to take all you can from the sea.'

The King of France thus justified the attacks and, encouraged by the stance adopted by their king, French corsairs occupied permanent positions in the Spanish shipping lanes. The Spanish authorities took immediate action. In June of that year, 1522, the order was given to arm a squadron against the corsairs and, in September, a covenant was signed with the Comercio de Sevilla to fund the squadron with proceeds from taxes. Different formations took to the sea in subsequent years.

In 1526, a new war (1526-1529) broke out between Francis I and Charles V. This time, both rulers mobilised their corsairs, presumably acting in legitimate self defence. The Emperor once again lifted the ban on

PRIMUS CIRCUNDIDISTI ME

Log book of the voyage of Juan Sebastián Elcano, 1519-1522.

In January 1519 there was one recurrent topic of conversation at the Castilian court. Under the auspices of the king, a major expedition was being prepared in Seville, commanded by the Portuguese seaman, Ferdinand Magellan, to sail westwards to the Moluccas (today Maluku, Indonesia), the spice archipelago and a trade monopoly controlled by the Portuguese. The plan was to sail south to the Cape of Good Hope and then eastwards.

Five ships were ready to embark on the venture: the *Trinidad*, weighing 110 tons, commanded by Magellan himself, who held the rank of captain general; the *San Antonio*, weighing 120 tons, captained by Juan de Cartagena, general overseer of the armada; the 90-ton *Concepción*, captained by Gaspar de Quesada; the 85-ton *Victoria*, with Luis de Mendoza, general treasurer; and the *Santiago*, weighing 75 tons, commanded by the pilot Juan Serrano.

Men of a wide variety of origins embarked on the mission: thirty-one Portuguese, including Magellan and most of the pilots; twenty-nine

Italians, mostly Genoese and Venetian; seventeen Frenchmen; six Greeks; six Flems; five Germans, engaged as artillerymen; four Englishmen; one Morisco; two Malayans; four black slaves and 165 Spaniards, most of them Vizcaíno. Among them, two exceptional protagonists: Juan Sebastián Elcano, a native of Guetaria, first mate of the *Concepción*, responsible for the successful outcome of the expedition, and Antonio Pigafetta, known as Antonio Lombardo, the captain's servant, who wrote the chronicles.

On 10 August 1519 the five vessels left Seville and sailed down the Guadalquivir, although they had to wait until the 27th to set off for the open sea from Sanlúcar.

In the almost three years it took them to fulfil their mission, they travelled over 17,000 leagues (about 51,000 miles), visiting the Cape Verde Islands, the coast of Brazil and Río de la Plata. Having wintered in San Julián, they discovered and passed through the Straits of Magellan. In the Pacific they reached the Marianas, the Philippines, Mindanao, Borneo, the Moluccas and Timor, finally returning

via the Indian Ocean, the Cape of Good Hope, Cape Verde and Sanlúcar.

In his manuscript, Pigafetta described fantastic places and animals, birds that killed whales, the tree that gave water, women that fertilised the wind, the giant Patagons and the pygmies of the island of Arucheto, whose inhabitants reached only elbow height and whose ears were so large that when they slept, one served as a pillow and the other as a blanket.

Of the 270 men, 160 died in the venture, while others suffered a variety of fates. Magellan himself was killed on the island of Mactan, on 27 April 1521, during a skirmish with the natives.

The ships, too, met different destinies: the *Santiago* was dismasted and wrecked on the coast of Patagonia; the *San Antonio* deserted in the Straits of Magellan and returned to Spain with its forty-five men; the *Concepción* became unserviceable and had to be abandoned and burned on the island of Bobón; an attempt was made to repair the *Trinidad* in the Moluccas and then sail her eastwards to

Panama, but she never reached her destination. Only the humble ship the *Victoria* fulfilled her mission and returned to the Peninsula by the planned route.

On 6 September 1522, two weeks short of three years after she had set sail from Spain, the *Victoria*, with her crew of eighteen commanded by Elcano, reached Sanlúcar. The sails of the *Victoria*, painted in Tadore with the cross of Santiago and the legend *Esta Es La Vera Figura de Nuestra Buenaventura*, greeted the city of Seville.

Elcano was received by the king in Valladolid, where his lineage was ennobled and he received a coat of arms featuring the globe and the legend *Primus Circundidisti Me*.

The expedition was of prime scientific importance. The passage to the Pacific and the western route to the Spice Islands had been opened. Years later, the anecdotal voyage of Francis Drake, on which all he did was follow the itinerary already marked out by Magellan and Elcano, was unjustly hailed, thanks to English propaganda, as the first circumnavigation of the world.

The constant presence of French corsairs in the waters of the Iberian Peninsula led to the formation of coastguard squadrons to protect ships returning from America on their passage from the Azores and Seville. Álvaro de Bazán, who was promoted to the office of Capitán General de la Mar Océana, began his career by devising and setting up the coastguard defence. His 1555 campaign rid European waters of corsairs for a time. As the Marquis of Santa Cruz, he was appointed commander of the Enterprise of England – the Spanish Armada – by Philip II of Spain. The death of Santa Cruz, probably of typhus, in early 1588 removed him from command.

privateering and many seamen decided to try their luck in the venture.

One was Martín Pérez de Irízar,[11] also known as Martín de Rentería or El Capitán de Rentería, a famous seaman from Guipázcoa who distinguished himself as one of the most successful corsairs in the service of the Spanish Crown. Pérez de Irízar's territory extended from Cape St Vincent to the Italian Peninsula, where he controlled the passage of ships through the Straits and pursued corsairs to their lairs in the Mediterranean.

Florín's luck was running out. When sailing the Straits of Gibraltar near Cape St Vincent, on 3 October 1527,[12] he encountered a warship, one of six forming the Vizcaya squadron, captained by Martín Pérez de Irízar, on its way to Cadiz. Pérez de Irízar recognised the French colours and launched his attack. After a bitter struggle, in which thirty-seven Spaniards were killed and fifty wounded, the two French galleons – one of which Florín had captured from Martín Aldabe – surrendered and 150 prisoners were taken. One of them identified

himself as Juan Florín and offered the fabulous sum of 300,000 ducats in exchange for his freedom.[13]

In view of such an astonishing proposal, the prisoner was taken to the Casa de Contratación in Seville, where he admitted having stolen and sunk more than '…150 ships, galleys and galleons, zabras and brigantines…'.[14] It was decided to send the prisoner to the Court, where the Emperor himself would decide his fate and that of some of his comrades. While Florín was being transported under escort, a messenger was sent ahead to inform Charles of the French pirate's arrival. The response was categorical: Florín was to be executed at the very spot the Emperor's reply was received.

Fate decreed that the execution should take place at Puerto del Pico,[15] on the Roman road that links the Meseta and Andalusia via the Sierra de Gredos. Florín was executed in Colmenar[16] (now Villa de Monbeltrán), together with his second-in-command, Michel Feré, and a third individual called Mezières.[17]

As a reward for the capture of Florín and other actions against corsairs, the Emperor granted Pérez de Irízar,[18] by a privilege signed in Barcelona on 6 June 1529, the coat of arms of three barracks that commemorated his main feats: the taking of seventeen of Barbarossa's galleys after a battle lasting a whole day; the defeat of Florín; the capture of a Greek corsair and the release of forty-seven prisoners destined to be galley slaves of the Viceroy of Sicily.

The French Corsairs, a Weapon of War

Throughout the reign of Francis I, his continual wars against the Emperor and his alliance with the Turkish Sultan favoured the institutionalisation of privateering as a permanent activity in the ports of France.

The activities of these privateers were centred mainly in two areas, one on each side of the ocean. In the waters between the Canaries and the Azores, attacks against ships returning from America were frequent, as were attempts to plunder some of the islands in the Canary archipelago. Assaults on American strongholds began in 1528.[19] An unidentified pirate captured a Spanish caravel near Lanzarote and forced the captain to show him how to cross the ocean. He reached Margarita and, sailing along the coast, came to Puerto Rico, where he sank the caravel near Cabo Rojo. On the island he

JURIDICAL FORMULAE GOVERNING PRIVATEERS

Privateering was carried out not as the initiative of private individuals but as an activity commissioned by governments with authority and jurisdiction in the waters where it took place. In general terms, privateering was understood as a way to hinder enemy trade and provisioning during wartime, although it was also a way to form squadrons against the enemy. Exceptionally, it was carried on in peacetime as a measure of reprisal.

Privateers were licensed by a contract, letter of marque or commission. The most common formulae are described below.

LET PASS One of the navigation permits issued to English ships in the West Indies. The document consisted of a letter in which the issuing authorities identified the bearer and requested that the competent authorities in the waters in which he was to sail allow him free passage to a specific destination. Abuse and distortion of the terms of the Let Pass led to the inclusion of clauses of good faith in some of the documents.

The Spanish fostered the issue of their own Let Passes in order to cross their own jurisdictional waters when the destination was beyond their frontiers. They also issued *cartas de seguro* and safe conducts, by which they asked their allies to allow free passage and not to take action of reprisal.

Corsairs such as Richard Guy, William James and Edward Mansfield used this document as legal credentials to engage in privateering.

LETTER OF MARQUE Another legal formula by which to denote a privateer, which apparently made a distinction between crews that received regular payment, 'as any merchant marine sailors', and those who wrested cargo from their original owners, like pirates of old.

It seems that letters of marque were issued in wartime only, and they were the most permissive documents of their kind. They were first issued in the 13th century and it was one of them, dated 1404, that legitimised the activities of Harry Pay.

Letters of marque were scarce in the 16th century, being issued only to figures of considerable influence, such as Cumberland, Chidley and Raleigh.

Around 1701, English trading vessels and privateers that sailed under the Union Jack did so with a letter of marque and were distinguished from ships of the Royal Navy – the only vessels authorised to carry the Union Jack – by two Bordeaux-red spots near the flagstaff.

LETTER OF REPRISAL This was a special kind of letter of marque whose origins go back to the late 13th century. When an issue had not been resolved through legal channels, such as refusal on the part of the Spanish authorities to accept complaints about pillaging carried out by their corsairs, the French or English authorities issued letters of reprisal authorising the aggrieved party to make good his losses through reprisal. He was thus allowed to capture ships and cargoes as if in wartime. The booty could not exceed a stipulated quantity, equivalent to the losses, plus expenses, plus a small premium. The profits were split three ways between the charterer, the officers and the crew. The flag was similar to that used by ships sailing with letters of marque.

The requisites needed to obtain a letter of reprisal were specified in 1585. The prospective bearer was required to file a complaint at the High Court of the Admiralty against a specific country in the form of a reasoned allegation backed by one or several witnesses.

The document had to specify the name of the ship, its tonnage, the names of the captain and crew, of the orderly, munitions and the charterer.

The bearer of the letter was required to pay a tariff, and was granted a period of six months in which to engage in privateering. Once this period had lapsed, the licence expired, although privateers often operated with expired licences, subsequently reaching an agreement with the Admiralty on the sum to be paid in compensation on their return to England.

Before sailing, the bearer of a letter of reprisal was required to deposit a bond at the Admiralty to cover possible damages to third parties and to guarantee strict compliance with the terms stipulated in the licence. The sum in question was usually £3,000 per ship.

An inventory had to be drawn up of all plundered goods and, when sold, the buyers were forbidden to exchange them.

---

stormed, sacked, and finally burned the city of San Germán,[20] the first such victim on the coasts of America.

In 1537, during the third Franco-Spanish war (1536-1538) Francis I formed a large fleet of privateers, divided into two[21] squadrons operating independently of one another. The one commanded by Maiguet, whom the Spaniards called May Get or Señor de Roubost, consisted of twelve vessels and patrolled the waters between Cape St Vincent and the Canaries. The second, commanded by Admiral Bnabo, consisted of one galleon, two naos and a caravel, and sailed along the African coast as far as the Canaries.

Maiguet began his operations by assaulting a fleet from Santo Domingo, capturing two galleons. The Spanish squadron of three warships, commanded by Miguel Perea[22], set off in pursuit, recovered the captured ships and caused two of the French vessels to surrender. Maiguet was killed in the battle.

Bnabo was more fortunate.[23] He met a merchant fleet of thirteen naos and one caravel that, in mid January, had sailed with no escort from Sanlúcar. He attacked the fleet, several of whose ships surrendered, and set his own caravel adrift with all the prisoners on board. Thanks to the skill of one of these, Nicolás de Nápoles, the boat made landfall at Chipiona.[24]

The French remained in the area and, near Lanzarote, captured Juan Gallego's nao. Next Bnabo approached the coast in order to abandon, on one of its beaches, all the women he had taken prisoner – all except for two girls whom he decided to take with him.

His adventures came to an end early in March off Santa Cruz de Tenerife. Bnabo attempted to storm the city, only to find Miguel Perea's small armada, composed of three warships, waiting for him. This 'armadilla' had joined the flotilla of the Portuguese Simao Lorenzo and was on its way to the Indies. Perea forced several of the French

Cuba, and particularly the cities of Santiago and Havana (shown above in a perspective plan of 1567) was especially vulnerable to attacks by corsairs and pirates. Men such as Roverbal, in 1543, and Sore, in 1554, perpetrated assaults that had disastrous consequences for the inhabitants.

vessels to surrender, including Bnabo's flagship. He freed some forty prisoners, whom he took to Las Palmas in the Canaries, and then continued on his journey. In the meantime, Lorenzo inflicted further reprisals by destroying a number of settlements that the French had built on the island of Lobos.

American waters were also the scene of operations by French corsairs. During the third war several ships in the areas of Chagres and Havana were attacked.[25] As a preventive measure, and for the first time, the gold and silver from the Americas were ordered to remain in Santo Domingo until a large fleet could collect them and transport them back to Spain.

In April 1538, an attempt was made to storm Santiago de Cuba, but the attackers were repelled by Diego Pérez's caravel. And another attack on San Germán also ended in failure.[26]

The first English attack in the Caribbean took place in 1540. On 17 August, Cervantes de Loaysa wrote a letter to the Emperor informing him that a 400-ton English ship had captured a Spanish nao with a cargo of hides, sugar and cassia fistula. The English ship became stranded in Cabo Tiburón and the crew were forced to take to the caravel, abandoning some of their artillery. The captain of the English was a Frenchman, who fled during the fighting and later gave himself up to the island authorities.

In 1541, peace having been signed with France, the Emperor of Spain sent Diego Fuenmayor as ambassador extraordinary to the court of Francis I with the mission of persuading the French king to withdraw all his corsairs

THE ATLANTIC ROUTES

When Spanish ships crossed the Atlantic Ocean from the Iberian Peninsulas, they did so by following routes that soon became known to all European navigators.

The American continent was reached by sailing south. Vessels normally departed from Sanlúcar de Barrameda, set a course for the Cape Verde Islands and made their first stopover in the Canaries. Merchant ships reached the Canaries twelve or fourteen days after setting sail and would come in sight of the Cape Verde Islands 4 or 5 days later.

Having reached 16° latitude, they would head westwards for Deseada (today La Désirade, off Guadeloupe (1), although they might also sail further south to latitude 14° on a course for Trinidad (2). During the crossing, the trade winds would drive the ships to the Windward Islands, and they would arrive at Trinidad thirty days after their departure, making Deseada some ten or twelve days later.

Several routes in the Caribbean led to the main destinations and it would take most vessels more or less the same time to arrive. Puerto Rico in the north would be reached some fifty days after having departed from Sanlúcar, Santo Domingo two or three days later. Sixty-five days were needed to arrive at Havana and some seventy-five days to reach San Juan de Ulúa. About the same time was needed to reach the southern destinations. Ships arrived at Cartagena after a voyage of some fifty days, while seventy-two or seventy-three days were needed to make Nombre de Dios.

The return voyage was far more difficult, since sailing the Caribbean was very slow. Havana would be reached in sixty days from San Juan de Ulúa (off Veracruz), in seventy from Nombre de Dios on the Isthmus, and in about fifty from Cartagena.

Ships crossing the Caribbean (3) set sail from Havana, passed through the Bahamas Channel (today the Straits of Florida) and then set a course for Bermuda, which they would sight some twenty days later. Sailing a course of 35°, ten days later they would reach the Azores, where ships would be informed of their eventual destination, either Lisbon (4) or Seville (5), depending on whether or not enemies were present in the vicinity of Cape St Vincent. Sometimes the route was changed and ships would sail to the Canaries from the Azores in an attempt to reach the coast of Andalucía coast from the south. At last, Sanlúcar would hail merchant vessels seventy days after they had left Havana.

A very important route was the one followed by the Flanders Fleet, which set sail from Laredo in Cantabria (6) for the Dutch ports via the coast of Brittany and the English Channel.

This same route was followed by boats that sailed to the cod and whale fisheries of Terranova (Newfoundland) (7), which they would reach after a stopover in Iceland. They would then return via the Azores (8) to the Cantabrian ports.

The English, French and Portuguese followed a line parallel to the Portuguese coast,(9) ever on the lookout for the occasional ship returning from the Azores, to reach the Canaries. In general they would then sail to the African coast to obtain black slaves, and from here they would set off on the crossing, further south (10) than the routes followed by the Spaniards. On other occasions they would sail straight for the American coast, (11) still keeping south of the Spanish routes.

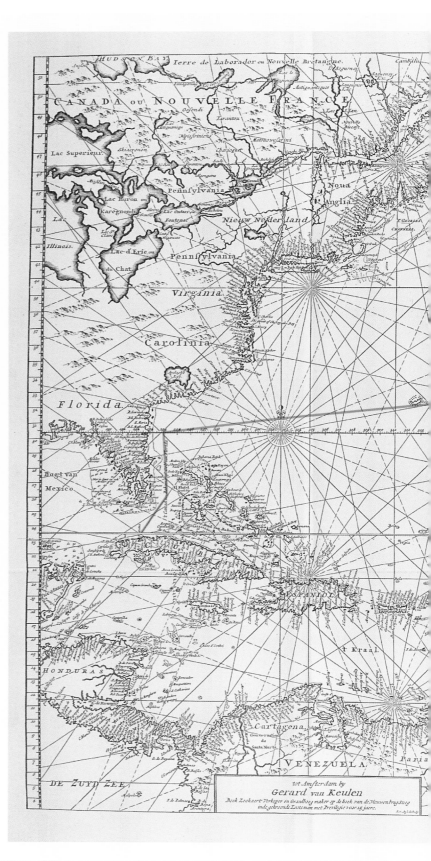

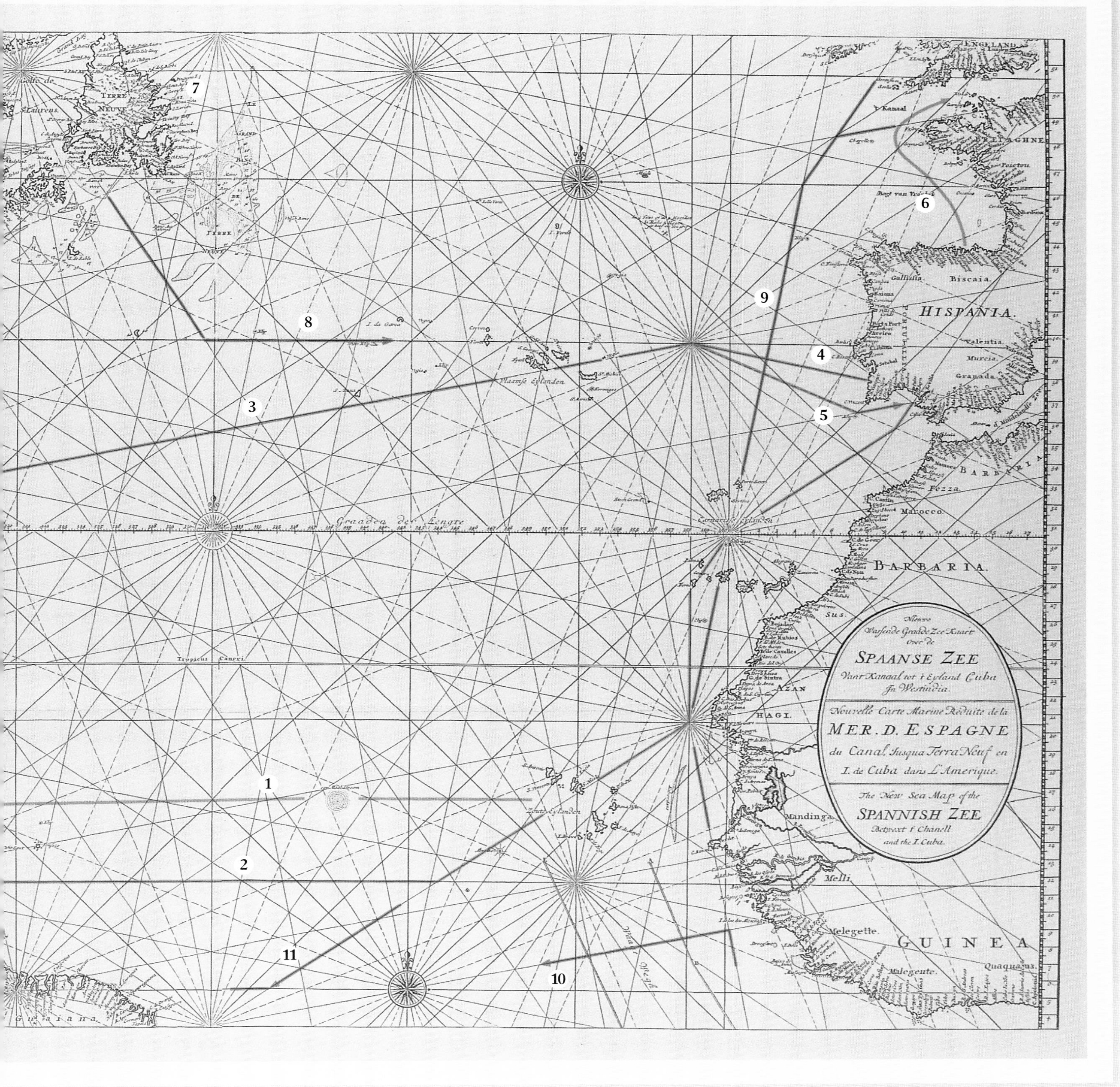
SPAANSE ZEE
Vant Kanaal tot 't Eyland Cuba
In Westindia.
Nouvelle Carte Marine Reduite de la
MER. D. ESPAGNE
du Canal Jusqua Terra Neuf en
I. de Cuba dans L'Amerique.
The New Sea Map of the
SPANNISH ZEE
and the I. Cuba.
ENGLAND
BRETAGNE
HISPANIA.
Biscaia.
Gallisia.
Valentia.
Murcia.
Granada.
BARBARIA.
Marocco.
Fezza.
Mandinga.
Melli.
Melegette.
GUINEA
Malegente.
Quaquaus.
Kanaal
Graaden der Lengte
Tropicus Cancri
Vlaamse Eylanden
Canarise Eylanden
Zoute Eylanden
TERRE NEUVE
Golfo de S. Laurens.
1
2
3
4
5
6
7
8
9
10
11

NAVIGATION INSTRUMENTS

Since it was impossible to rely on points of geographical reference during ocean crossings, seamen had to find other ways to ascertain their exact position. To this end, they needed to know two coordinates, longitude and latitude, as well as the exact route to follow in order to reach their destination.

The problem of setting the course had been solved with the introduction of the compass in the mid 13th century. In order to avoid errors of parallax, the compass was attached to the compass card, which together pivoted on the beam.

In the mid 16th century the box that housed the compass, the *mortero*, was suspended in a device invented by G. Cardano, so that it would not be affected by the rocking of the ship. Calculation of the route was complemented by observation of the currents, and corrections were made based on the relative positions of the ship's wake and its trajectory.

A further problem to be faced in sailing the ocean was the fact that the compass pointed towards the magnetic, not the geographical, north. The difference, called magnetic declination, was tabulated in the 16th century.

With the first voyages to the African coast, the need arose to establish a reference with regard to north-south position, and this was achieved through knowledge of latitude, that is, the height of the celestial pole above the horizon from a specific point of observation.

During the day, latitude was measured in terms of the height of the sun using first the quadrant, and later the astrolabe, which was radically simplified by the Portuguese. Other widely used instruments were the gimmal, the grommet, and the cross-staff, also known as Jacob's staff.

Another parameter was needed to ascertain the exact position of the ship – longitude, which could not be determined with the instruments available at the time. The only way to measure the number of leagues travelled was by estimating the speed of the ship and entering it on a chart. The later introduction of log chips made this task far easier.

1. Tiller housing
2. Cross-staff
3. Hourglass
4. Astrolabe
5. Astrolabe
6. Diagram of a log chip

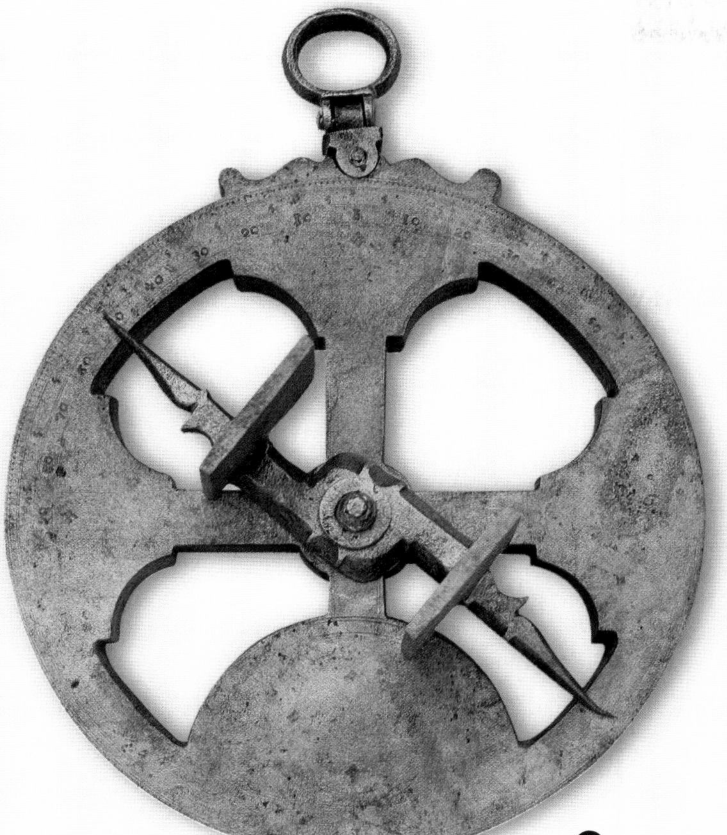

1-1853
1571

❹

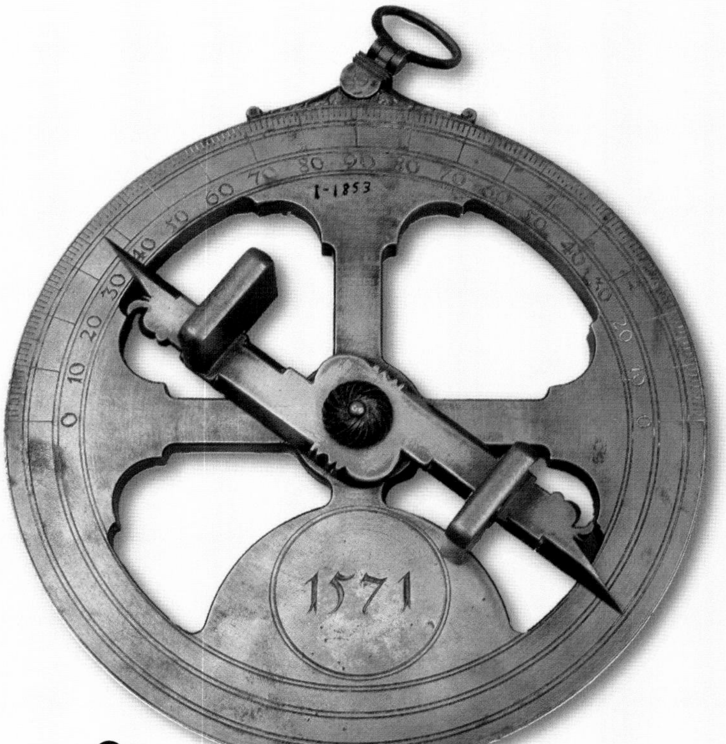
❺

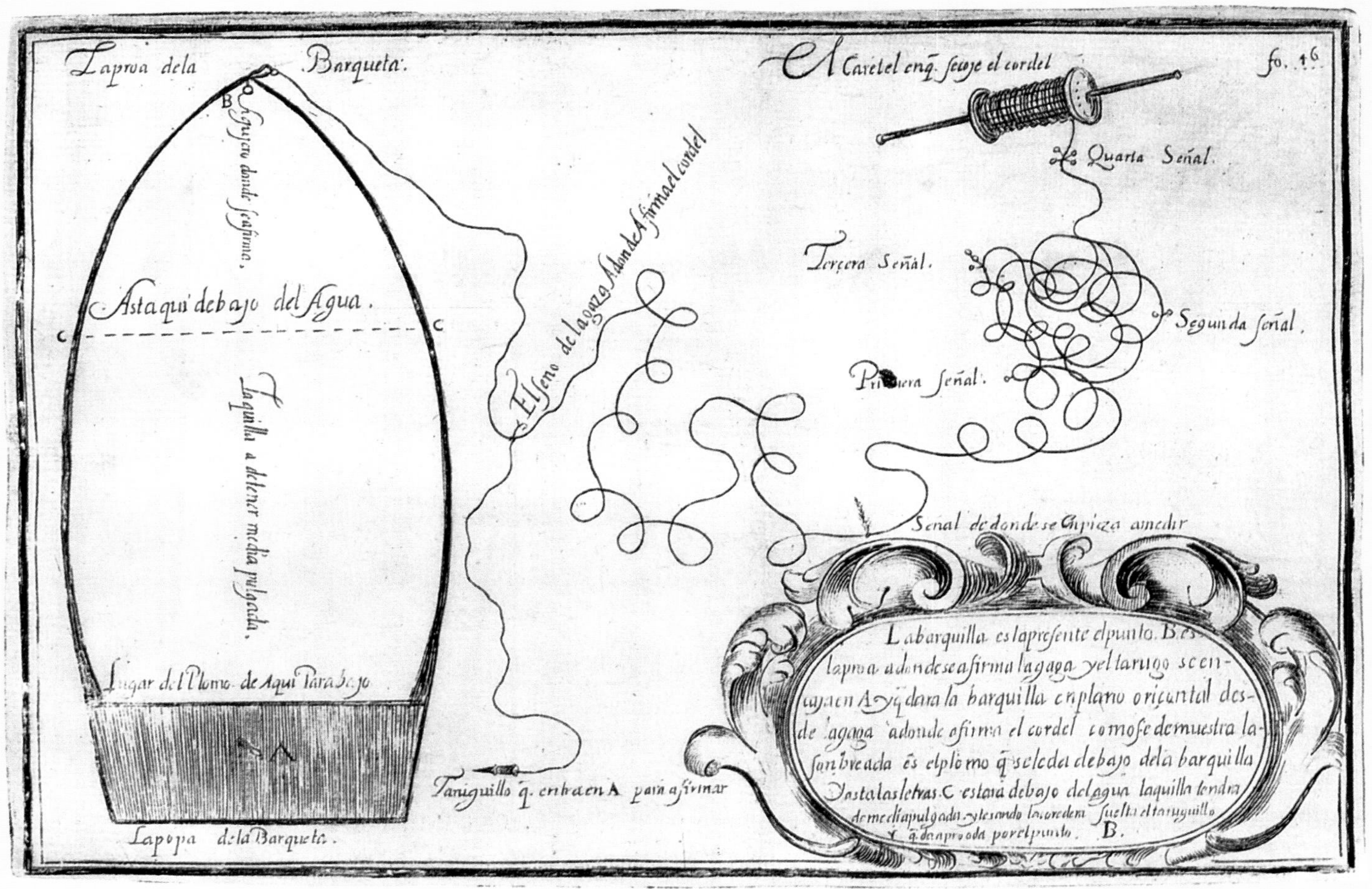

Laproa dela Barqueta.
Aguxero donde se asirma.
Astaqui debajo del Agua.
Laquilla a detener media pulgada.
Lugar del Plomo de Aqui Para bajo
Lapopa dela Barqueta.
El seno de la gaza Adonde Afirma el cordel
Taruguillo q. entra en A para afirmar
El Caretel enq. se coje el cordel
fo. 46
Quarta Señal.
Terçera Señal.
Segunda señal.
Primera señal.
Señal de donde se empieza amedir
Labarquilla es la presente el punto. B. es
laproa adondese afirma lagaga yel tarugo se en-
caja en A y q. dara la barquilla en plano oriçuntal des-
de lagaga adonde afirma el cordel como se demuestra la-
sonbreada es el plomo q. se le da debajo dela barquilla
Asta las letras. C estara debajo del agua laquilla tendra
de media pulgada y teniendo la corredera suelta el taruguillo
y q. da aproada por el punto. B.

❻

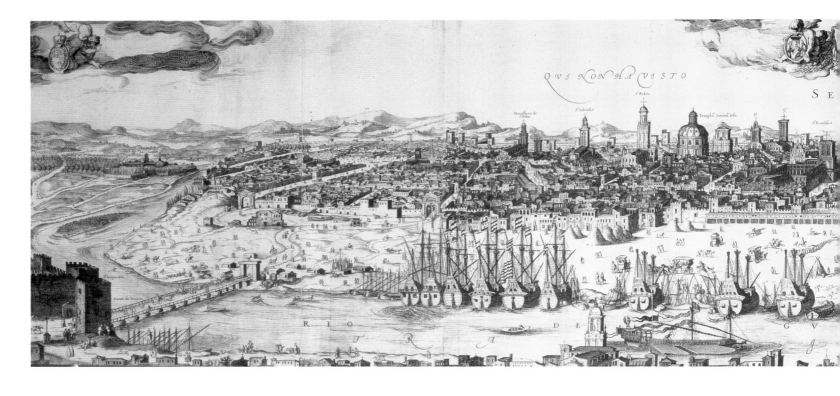

TOWARDS A NEW ADMINISTRATIVE STRUCTURE

With the discovery of new lands across the Atlantic, the Spanish monarchy required a new administrative structure to govern the Indies and to guarantee controlled expansion within the transatlantic possessions and safety for shipping.

In May 1497 the export of products to the new lands was declared tax exempt and, by a Royal Decree dated 3 September 1500, the *Acta de Navegación* was issued that favoured trade by Spanish vessels. The first official *Armada de Indias* (Indies Fleet) set sail in the year 1501.

Different commissions were set up to take charge of governing the Indies until, on 14 February 1503, Queen Joan issued a letter patent in Alcalá de Henares by which she ordered the *Casa de Contratación* (House of Transactions) to be set up in Seville, at which all merchandise from the Indies and the Canaries, 'and all other islands yet to be discovered', had to be registered.

The *Audiencia* (Colonial High Court) of Santo Domingo was set up and exploration continued in the southern continent and the Antilles.

In 1508 the post of *Piloto Mayor de la Casa de Contratación* was established, and the first man to hold the position was Amerigo Vespucci, who had gained renown by his conclusion that the newly discovered lands did in fact constitute part of a continent. The mission of the Piloto Mayor was to inspect navigation instruments, appraise the abilities of ships' pilots and to set the courses that would take the fleets to the Indies.

With the constitution of the viceroyalties of *Nueva España* (Mexico) and *Tierra Firme* (South America) in the mid 16th century, the administrative structure was finally consolidated. *Audiencias* and *Casas Reales* were set up, responsible for justice and finances respectively, and other administrative instruments were created in order for the huge bureaucratic machine to run smoothly.

On 14 February 1503, Queen Joan issued a letter patent in Alcalá de Henares by which she ordered the Casa de Contratación (House of Transactions – the centre of government for the New World) to be set up in Seville (above), at which all merchandise from the Indies and the Canaries, 'and all other islands yet to be discovered', had to be registered.

from the sea and return all the unlawfully confiscated goods to their rightful owners. All his good offices proved fruitless, however. The fourth Franco-Spanish war (1542-1544) served as a pretext for further action against American strongholds.

One of the most notorious corsairs was Jean François de la Roque, Seigneur of Roverbal, who had taken part in the French expeditions to Canada as Jean Cartier's lieutenant. Roberto Ball, Robert Wall or Roverbal, as he was known to the Spaniards, appeared in American waters in the middle of 1543 with a flotilla first sighted off the coast of Baracoa, a city he attacked and plundered. Later, en route to Havana, he was caught in a storm off Matanzas and his fleet was dispersed. As luck would have it, one of his tenders reached Havana, which was completely undefended. The French obtained a *tributo de quema* (payment levied in lieu of burning the city)[27] and provisions, thanks to which the flotilla was able to proceed on its voyage.

Having regrouped his ships, Roverbal sailed southwards, reaching *Tierra Firma* (an area of South America roughly equivalent to today's Colombia and Venezuela) at Rancherías, which he stormed. From there he sailed to Santa Marta[28] and, on 16 July, he entered the port. The city was undefended; the governor, Luis de Lugo, had gone inland with almost the entire garrison to

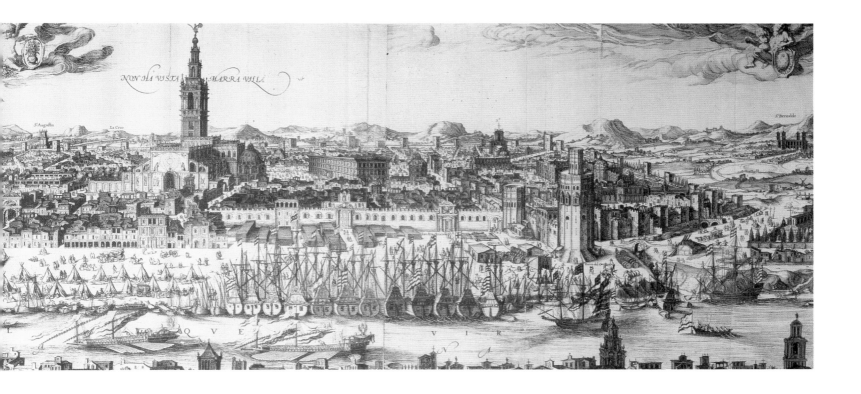

put down an Indian rebellion. Roverbal took the city easily and plundered the churches, going to the extreme of digging up the dead in search of silver. He again tried to get a tributo de quema but having failed to do so he sank the ships anchored in the harbour, set fire to the wooden houses, slaughtered the livestock, robbed the vegetable gardens and cut down the fruit trees. Then he abandoned the city, taking with him four bronze cannons that the defenders had not had time to use. Such was the dejection of the citizens[29] that to prevent Santa Marta from being abandoned, men, ammunition and 3,000 pesos were sent so that the city could be rebuilt.

In 1544 Roverbal sailed to Cartagena de Indias, a city he had planned to storm with the help of a 'renegade' called Ormaechea[30] who had lived there. On the night of 24 July he stormed the city and took it practically unopposed. His booty amounted to 35,000 pesos in plunder, 2,500 taken from the Royal Coffers and a further 2,000 gained in the form of a tributo de quema.

Despite the Peace of Crepy, which put an end to the Franco-Spanish war in 1544, French corsairs continued with their actions. Jean Alphonse de Saintonge[31] was a French pirate based at La Rochelle. He was famous for his attacks on squadrons, although his most daring exploit was the storming of Puerto de la Luz in the Canary Isles. After one of his actions he returned to base with the squadron of Pedro Menéndez de Avilés in hot pursuit.

Avilés followed Saintonge into the harbour of La Rochelle, recovered five ships that the Frenchman had

THE MARTYRS OF BRAZIL

In 1553 the Portuguese galleon *Santiago* set sail for Brazil. Among her passengers was Father Ignacio Acevedo and thirty-eight other Jesuits who had been sent to the missions in Rio Paraná.

The ship was attacked by Jacques Sore and the Jesuits taken prisoner. On discovering their identity, Sore ordered them to be martyred. One by one their arms were cut off and the victims, still living, were then thrown overboard.

It was on account of such actions that Sore became notorious for his extreme cruelty.

ROVERBAL ATTACKS CARTAGENA

In the summer of 1544 Roverbal's French squadron set sail to take Cartagena, guided by a renegade. The figure of the renegade, identified by some as Ormaechea and by others as a pilot called Corzo, is regarded as having been crucial to the success of the operation.

All sources coincide in the fact that Ormaechea, or Corzo, had been brutally whipped by Alonso de Bejines, lieutenant of the *adelantado* (governor of a frontier province), Pedro de Heredia. Ormaechea then apparently fled to France, where he convinced Roverbal of the benefits he would obtain from an assault.

The attack took place on the night of 24 July and substantial booty was taken. Thanks to the good offices of the renegade, only one Frenchman was wounded in the operation. The fatality was Alonso de Bejines, whom Ormaechea stabbed to death while shouting 'this is the reward for those who, for no reason, dishonour the good!'

AMERICAN SILVER

The true treasure of America was undoubtedly silver and thousands of tons of the precious metal were transported across the ocean to become legal tender throughout Europe.

The great Mexican and Zacatecan mines, discovered in 1547, and those of Guanajuanato in 1549, along with the immensely rich mine of Potosí, in Bolivia, constituted the basis of the American mining industry, to which smaller mines also contributed, such as those of Cuencamé, San Luis de Potosí, Sombrerete and Pachuca, which were first worked around 1552.

Bartolomé Medina's discovery in 1554 of cold amalgamation, also known as the *método de patio*, made mass production of silver possible. Thanks to this method, silver was extracted from base mineral ores that hitherto had been regarded as worthless – around 3 or 4 marcos (one marco is the equivalent of 230 grams) were extracted per quintal (46 kg). Mercury, mined in great quantities in Almadén, Spain, was used as the reactive agent.

The silver bars were transported in cartloads or on the backs of mules to Peru and Mexico, where they were weighed and marked. Some were then minted as coins and taken to Europe by the fleets of Tierra Firme and Nueva España.

THE TRADE BAN

At the end of the fifth Franco-Spanish war, on 6 June 1556 the Spanish authorities issued a Royal Decree addressed to the colonial authorities, stipulating that anyone caught trading with foreigners in the Indies, in any of their 'provinces and ports and belonging to whatever nation', in gold, silver, pearls, precious stones, fruit or any other merchandise, or supplying them with provisions, arms or ammunition, would be put to death and all their worldly goods confiscated.

The purpose of the decree was to reinforce the commercial monopoly by introducing stringent dissuasive measures to check the spread of smuggling. The French, and subsequently the English, thus saw their trading opportunities severely restricted.

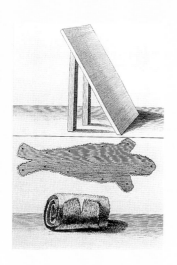

Curriers at work using sideframes (left) for scraping seal skin.

captured and attacked the flagship, *Le Marie*, eventually killing her pilot. With the wind against him, however, he was unable to leave the port, and the Governor of La Rochelle threatened to cannon Avilés's ships from the fortress, accusing him of opening fire in the waters of a nation with which a peace treaty had been signed. Avilés argued that he was pursuing a pirate, not a corsair, since the peace treaty guaranteed that hostile acts justified by engagement in privateering would cease. The governor was forced to accept Avilés's reasoning and allowed the Spaniards to take to the sea with all their booty.

Conflicts with England, which originated in Henry VIII's divorce from Catherine of Aragon on account of her failure to produce an heir to the throne, broke out once more. In 1545 the functionaries at the Casa de Contratación[32] were ordered to confiscate the goods of English subjects residing on the coasts of Spain, in reprisal for the illegal capture of two Spanish ships. The procedure for these confiscations consisted of calculating the value of what had been stolen and confiscating goods worth up to a third more in value.

Then hostilities again broke out between France and Spain, after the death of Francis I and the accession to the throne of Henry II. The fifth war (1551-1556) marked the beginning of a period of open conflict at sea.

In the Canaries the need arose to create militias, and a coastguard flotilla was armed under the command of Jerónimo Bautista[33] who thwarted several French attempts to settle on the islands. In April 1552 the flotilla forced an armada of French corsairs to surrender, and took eighty prisoners.

One of Saintonge's sons, Antoine-Alphonse,[34] attempted to repeat his father's exploits at Puerto de la Luz. He chose Santa Cruz de Tenerife as his objective, but the stronghold had been forewarned and the artillery managed to repel the corsairs. The escapade cost Saintonge his life.

Now at war on several fronts, Spaniards were again authorised[35] to take to the sea as privateers, forming squadrons with which to fight the French. Furthermore, they were exempted from paying the Quinto Real, the fifth part of the booty that was normally presented to the king, so that those charterers who risked their fortunes in defence of the king's interests could do so in the hope of greater profits.

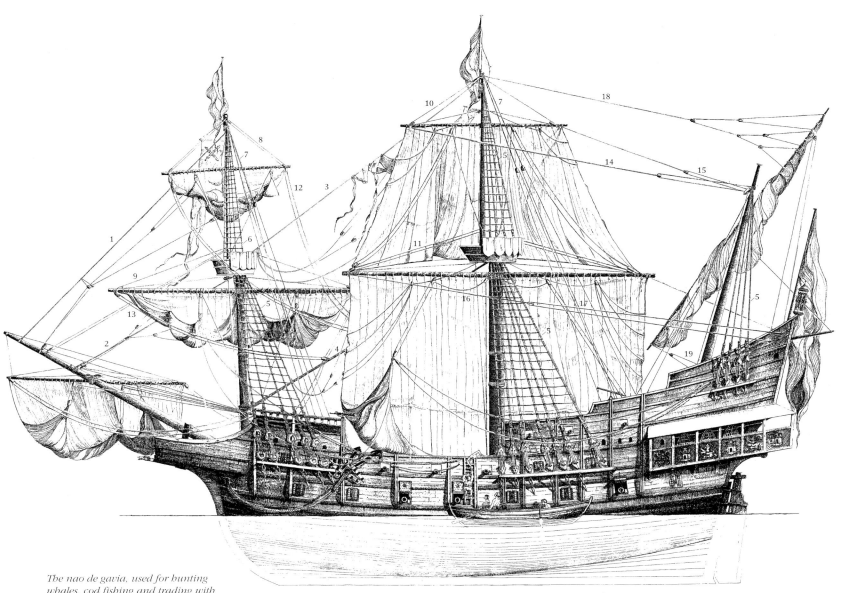

The nao de gavia, used for hunting
whales, cod fishing and trading with
Flanders, proved to be the most suitable
for Atlantic crossings. The different kinds of 17th-century and 18th-century
ocean-going ships all evolved from vessels of this type.
1. Foretopmast stay; 2. Foremast stay; 3. Mainmast stay; 4. Main stay;
5. & 6. Shrouds; 7. Backstays; 8. Fore topsail lifts; 9. Foresail lifts;
10. Main topsail lifts; 11. Main sail lifts; 12. Fore topsail braces;
13. Foresail braces; 14. & 15. Main topsail braces; 16. & 17. Mainsail braces;
18. Mizzensail lifts; 19. Bowline block and tackle.

The American Campaign by the First 'Peg Leg'

In 1553 King Henry II of France issued his first *lettre de
marque*, authorising François le Clerc[36] to engage in
privateering and provided his expedition with three
warships. Le Clerc, nicknamed *Pata de Palo* (Peg Leg)
assembled an imposing fleet consisting of six large ships
– including the three from the king – four tenders and
1,000 men. His lieutenant was Jacques Sore, whom the
Spaniards called Jacques de Soria or Jacques Suez, a
fanatical Huguenot notorious for his cruelty, whose
exploits included the assault on the Portuguese galleon
Santiago near the coast of Tenerife.

Once the fleet had crossed the ocean, Pata de Palo's
forces split up. The larger contingent, under his and
Robert Blondel's command, consisting of six large naos
and four oar-powered tenders, sailed to the Greater
Antilles. In March they attacked[37] San Germán in Puerto
Rico, then the islands of La Mona and Saona, and finally
Río Soco and Azua on Hispaniola. In April, still on the
island, they attacked the city of Yaguana, which they
sacked and burned, sharing out a booty of 100,000
pesos. On the 29th of that month they stormed
Montecristi,[38] then retraced their steps and attempted to
take Puerto Rico.

On August 2 1553, on his return voyage from the
Americas, Pata de Palo stormed[39] Santa Cruz de las
Palmas. Then he planned a new action against La
Gomera, although this was less successful. Once back in
France, Henry II rewarded François le Clerc by ennobling
his lineage.

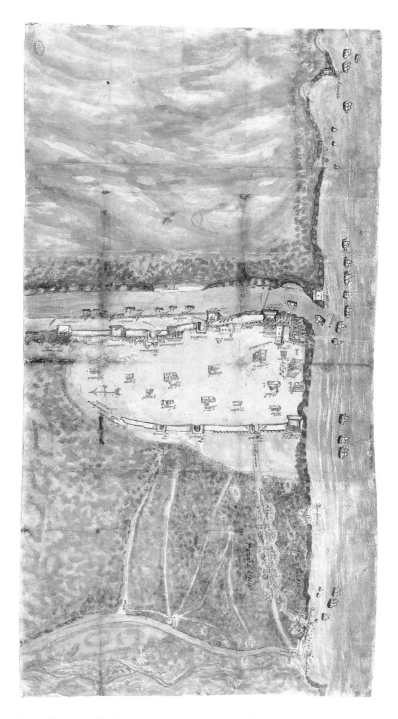

Santo Domingo, the first American city and seat of the Audiencia de Indias and the colonial government, played a prominent role during the first half of the 16th century. It became a compulsory stopover for the Spanish fleets and provided shelter for the coastguard squadrons, becoming the most important defence post in the Caribbean.

Facing page:
In the continual conflicts between France and Spain, corsairs were a highly efficient weapon of war. But they did not cease their activities during times of truce. In 1559, Martin Cote perpetrated one of the most daring and profitable operations against Spanish strongholds in America when he stormed Santa Marta and Cartagena.

Meanwhile the squadron commanded by Sore sailed to Santiago de Cuba,[40] which they stormed without difficulty and made off with a booty of 80,000 pesos.

In 1555, guided by the 'renegade' Diego Pérez,[41] Sore reached Margarita off the coast of Nueva Andalucía (today's Venezuela). When challenged by the watch, Pérez replied that they were a merchant ship from Castile. They were allowed to pass and anchored in the harbour without arousing suspicion. At dawn, Sore disembarked with his men, killed the sentries and surprised the still-sleeping islanders who were in no position to put up a resistance. He quickly took the city, which he sacked, and then demanded a tributo de quema. He did the same in Borburoata and Santa Marta.

Spurred on by his good fortune, Sore attempted the same exploit in Río Hacha. Once it had been occupied, Diego Pérez himself negotiated the tributo de quema, which amounted to 4,500 pesos. While Diego Pérez took to the mountains with part of the profits, Francisco Velázquez, who had been transported to the ship as a hostage, was waiting to be freed on payment of his ransom. But Sore, who had demanded a further ransom and the delivery of Pérez, was forced to set sail. When he was twenty leagues from the coast he set the prisoner adrift in a small boat without oars, sails or provisions, but luck was with Velázquez and he managed to make landfall. When he reached Río Hacha, he discovered the identity of the renegade, who was subsequently hanged.

Sore set off on his return journey to Europe, although he could not resist making a last attempt on Havana,[42] which he reached on 10 July together with some 500 men. With him were his lieutenant, the Navarrese Juan del Plan or del Plano, and his pilot, a Portuguese from Las Terceras called Pedro Bras, both renegades. The population of Havana amounted to about 100, with whom the Cabildo managed to form a defence force of six or seven cavalry and four foot soldiers[43] together with the governor Angulo and forty Indians. The fortress was manned by twenty-four men, whom the *alcaide* (keeper), Juan de Lobera, ordered to hold out while he withdrew to a nearby village.

The defenders of the fortress managed to withstand the onslaught for two days, 10 and 11 July, until at dawn on the 12th Sore stormed the fortress from the rear by burning the gate. He took control of the castle, took the defenders prisoner and demanded a ransom of 30,000 pesos in exchange for their lives.

On the night of the 18th, while the pirates were celebrating their victory, Angulo managed to put together a force of 35 residents, 220 blacks and 80 Indians, and together they assailed the pirates, killing fifteen or sixteen and wounding Sore. The operation was not as successful as expected and Sore, blinded by rage, murdered thirty-one Spanish prisoners with his own hands. Then, to celebrate the victory, his pirates 'donned the chasubles and ornaments of the priests, grotesquely daubed their faces and paraded thus before the main altar. One of them, disguised as a bishop, led a pig tied to a rope. The images of the Virgin and the saints were disfigured, the

canvases rent with daggers, and the priests forced to insult the holy scriptures....'[44]

However, the misfortunes suffered by Havana did not end here. In October, two months after Sore had abandoned the city and the residents had begun to rebuild it, they were attacked once again.[45]

Spain adopted exceptional measures. In 1555 the armada of Álvaro de Bazán, famed and feared for his exploits in the Straits and on the African coast, rid the seas around the Canaries of French corsairs. The armadas proved their effectiveness as escorts to merchant vessels and were a prototype to the subsequent system of fleets.

Portuguese carracks sailing off a rocky coast. Note that the artist has depicted the same ship in different views.
Joachim Patinir (1480-1524)

On the juridical side, suspicion that attacks by corsairs had their real and fictitious aspects – the latter serving as an alibi for the inhabitants of the Indies to elude the ban on trade – a law[46] was enacted prohibiting any transactions with 'foreigners or corsairs'. It seems that the law had little effect, however, for the following year it was re-enacted.

Unexpectedly, the Spaniards found a new ally in their fight against the French. In 1557, in an England ruled by Mary Tudor,[47] a proclamation was issued authorising engagement in privateering against French interests as a means to reinforce control over the English Channel.

In Spain, as a further incentive for armadas and fleets to pursue enemy corsairs, late in 1558 it was decreed that the fifth part of the booty, normally reserved for the king, would be for the captains of galleons and commanders of fleets that had seized it.[48]

The Franco-Spanish truce of 1559 did not put an end to French operations in the Indies. The pirate Martin Cote

or Cotes,[49] accompanied by his lieutenant, Jean[50] who, according to some chroniclers was Martin's brother, attacked Santa Marta and Cartagena in Tierra Firme.

Cote, commanding six ships, reached Santa Marta, which he successfully stormed, suffering very few casualties, most of whom were the victims of poisoned arrows fired by the Indians. He demanded a *tributo de quema* of 15,000 pesos, which he then increased by 600 in exchange for not sacking the city.

Having secured his booty, Cote set sail for Cartagena, arriving there on 11 April. The city had been forewarned, however, and Governor Bustos had made preparations for its defence. The beach was sown with poisoned spikes and a number of fortifications were built. At the same time, a defence force was mustered consisting of ten harquebusiers and twenty horsemen, reinforced by a contingent of local residents and 500 'Indian archers', whom the *cacique* (local chief), Maridado, had offered to the Spaniards.

Cote's forces were far superior in numbers. One thousand of his men disembarked but, though well armed, they were held at bay by the harquebusiers while the latters' ammunition lasted. When the firing stopped, Cote ordered his men to attack, but they were repelled

In the late 16th century there was a proliferation of villages around Bayajá, on the north coast of the island of Hispaniola in the late 16th century.

by the horsemen, the Indians and numerous citizens, all armed with cold steel.[51]

In the struggle many Frenchmen lost their lives, including Cote's lieutenant Juan. But faced by the superior numbers of the enemy, the Spaniards retreated to the mountains, letting the pirates occupy the city. Chroniclers have not calculated the booty, although apparently it was not substantial, despite the fact that the French were paid a ransom for the prisoners and secured a tributo de quema.

While Cote and his men were in Cartagena, a dispute between the pirate and one of his chaplains resulted in the latter having his head blown off. Cote ordered him to be buried near the main altar of the cathedral. There the corpse remained until the city was recovered and the bishop ordered it to be disinterred and thrown into a dungheap, 'as befitting a perfidious preacher of heresies'.[52]

A number of French attacks by the French took place between 1559 and 1560, particularly against the town of Campeche. Names such as Guillen Megandez and Francisco Vissin,[53] whom the Spaniards called Vitanual, became famous for their offensives against ships engaging in trade between the Peninsula and the Indies.

Coinciding with news of the end of the war, an exceptional occurrence took place in Campeche that would be repeated only very occasionally through history. A corsair, together with his men, gave himself up to the authorities saying that, having heard news of peace between Spain and France, he could no longer engage in war.[54] Some of the men were sent to Mexico to appear before the Viceroy, while others were allowed to remain and settle in the city.

During the 1560s, smuggling by the French, Portuguese and English reached epidemic proportions. Collaboration on the part of Spanish colonists and the connivance of Indies authorities contributed to exacerbate the problem, despite extraordinary measures adopted by the Crown.

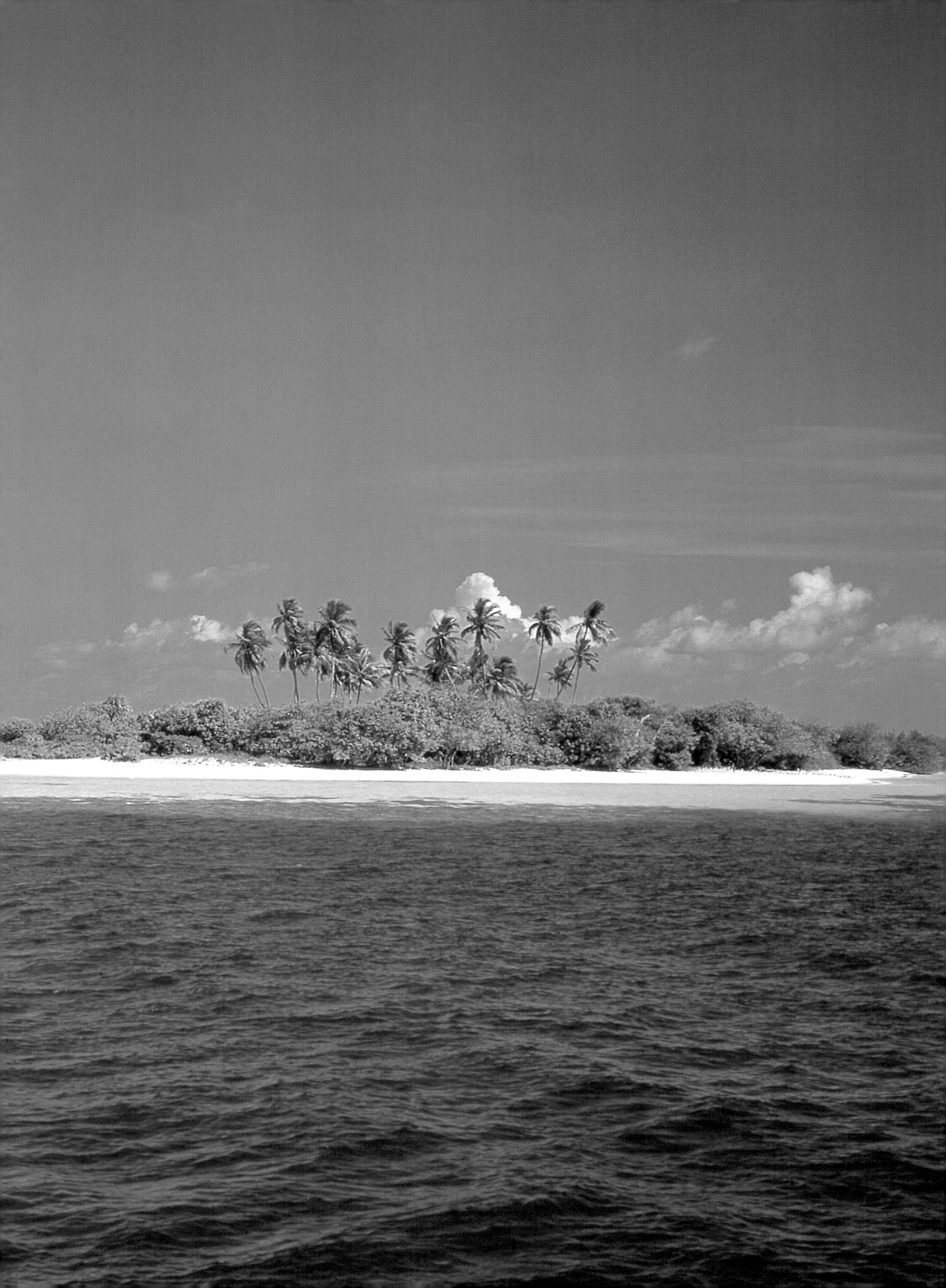

Chapter II

FROM HONOURABLE TRADESMEN TO NOBLE CAVALIERS
(1561-1588)

A PERIOD OF CHANGEABLE RELATIONS

Following the marriage, in 1509, between Catherine of Aragon, and Henry VIII, King of England, the alliance between Spain and England against France, their common enemy, marked a policy of mutual understanding and good relations. English trade with Spain and its islands had become regular after the signature of the Treaty of Medina del Campo in 1489, and now flourished.

By the time Henry VIII died in 1547, however, relations had soured; but the early death of his son Edward VI in 1553 gave rise to a new era in which the 1554 marriage between Mary, Queen of England, and Philip of Spain, Prince of Asturias, meant the re-establishment of the alliance with Spain and the reinstatement of the Catholic Church in England.

It was at this time that trade relations between England and Spain became especially intense. The English were treated as subjects of the King of Spain and trade flowed smoothly under the control of the Seville monopoly.

However, the era was to be short-lived. In 1558 Mary died and was succeeded by Elizabeth, who had adopted the Anglican faith and broke off relations with Philip II. In Spain, the stock-breeding crisis led to a decline in wool

One of the many small islands in the Antilles.

trading and the traditional markets in the British Isles suffered greatly as a result. In England, the severance of the alliance with Spain and the country's neutrality in the war against France gave rise to the basis for future events: the exclusion of the English from trade with the Indies would result in the total breakdown of relations.[1]

It was in this context that English 'merchant adventurers' would be the protagonists of an exceptional episode in the history of privateering and piracy. Claiming the right to trade freely wherever their ships might take them, the English attempted to cut through Spanish prohibitions by imposing enforced trade, a system first employed by John Hawkins.

The disaster of San Juan de Ulúa led to a breakdown in relations between Spain and England that would last until 1572. There ensued a change in English policy, in which the objective was no longer to foster trade through contraband but rather to appropriate Spanish treasures and to attempt to establish colonies from which to embark on riskier undertakings. These would be the golden years of Francis Drake.

ENFORCED TRADE AND CONTRABAND

The traditional attacks by English corsairs against Spanish fleets sailing to the ports of Flanders, or the constant harassment of vessels on their way to the whale or cod fisheries of Terranova, changed in the mid 16th century. After an initial period of lying in wait for Portuguese ships off the coast of Guinea, the waters of the Azores, frequented by Spanish merchant vessels, became far more attractive.

The first English success took place in 1560, when a seaman from Southampton, Edward Cook, captured a nao on its return journey from America. Attempts at subsequent captures continued, invariably in seas that the English knew well – between the Azores and Madeira.

At the same time England introduced a policy by which she attempted to establish her own areas of influence and, without entering into open conflict with Spain, to weaken Spanish hegemony. The English sought belligerently to re-assert their control of the Channel, through which Spanish ships were obliged to pass on their way to the traditional markets in Flanders. To this end, England issued the document, *Fighting in Territorial Waters*[2] in 1562.

The unfriendly relations between Queen Elizabeth and King Philip, the desire to extend markets and the need of American ports to obtain provisions from beyond the limits of Seville control, all encouraged English merchants to enter into the American venture. To do this, however, they needed someone with sufficient technical knowledge and the necessary contacts to open the path to American trade. That man was John Hawkins.

John Hawkins Reforms the Royal Navy

John Hawkins (Juan Acle or Aquines to the Spaniards) was destined to be a man of the sea. He was born in Plymouth in around 1530, the son of a rich family of merchants. Some authors associate part of the family fortune with a voyage that his father, William, made to Brazil in the 1530s, where he would have obtained large quantities of brazilwood.

If John's origins were privileged, his marriage was decisive, linking him with the family of Benjamin Gonson,[3] the navy treasurer. Gonson introduced his son-in-law to the most important merchants in London and provided him with the possibility to exert increasing influence in naval matters. In 1577, together with Gonson, John Hawkins was appointed to the five-member Royal Navy Directory and, by 1588, he was

Sir John Hawkins, 1581.
Anonymous, English School.

commander of one of the divisions that confronted the Spaniards during the Enterprise of England.

His work in the Royal Navy contributed to its modernisation,[4] both technically – with the adoption of faster, more manoeuvrable ships – and administratively – Hawkins persecuted the squandering and corruption of previous eras.

In 1562 Hawkins visited the Canary Isles and, through his contacts with other merchants, came to realise how profitable the black slave trade with the Indies could be. Contraband, begun by the Portuguese who sold at prices substantially lower than the official ones, was a highly attractive business proposition. His contact with Pedro Ponte, one of the Governors of Tenerife, would have been crucial to Hawkins's decision to try his luck. The only problem was that trafficking was forbidden and, while relations between the English and the Spanish might have not been as good as in the past, they had not been completely severed.

John Hawkins's second voyage was his first contact with the coast of Tierra Firme, South America. His arrival in Margarita, where he discovered the rancherías (pearl-fishing settlements) of Cumaná, Borburata, Curaçao, Río Hacha and Cartagena, brought him substantial profits through his engagement in 'enforced trade' – part coercion, part complicity.

Hawkins's First Voyage to the Indies

John Hawkins sailed from Plymouth in October[5] 1562 in command of the 120-ton *Solomon*, the 100-ton *Swallow* captained by Thomas Hampton, and the 40-ton *Jonas*. His contingent amounted to 100 men and it seems that he counted on both the moral and financial support of his father-in-law.

Having made a stopover in the Canaries, where Ponte provided him with the pilot, Martínez, Hawkins finally reached Hispaniola. He caulked and repaired his ships in Puerto Plata, and then proceeded to La Isabella, Cuba, to do some trading, alleging that he had been forced to make landfall and needed capital to pay for the repairs. When the governor got wind of this, he sent Cristóbal Bernáldez at the head of seventy cavalry to prevent Hawkins from concluding his deals.

First there was a skirmish but, thanks to the good offices of Martínez, the Spaniards eventually agreed to establish commercial transactions to mutual benefit. The authorities levied taxes in the form of a consignment of slaves and a Portuguese caravel that Hawkins had captured. Even so, the Englishman made substantial profits and obtained a certificate of good conduct from the Governors of Hispaniola, who had benefited from the

ATLANTIC
OCEAN
GULF OF MEXICO
NEW SPAIN
FLORIDA
STRAITS OF FLORIDA
GREAT ABACO
BAHAMAS
DRY TORTUGAS
FLORIDA KEYS
CAY SAL BANK
HAVANA
SAN SALVADOR
CONCEPTION I.
ACKLINS I.
GREAT BAHAMA BANK
BANCO DE CAMPECHE
C. San Antonio
C. Corrientes
LOS PINOS
CAICOS
YUCATÁN
CAMPECHE
VERACRUZ
SAN JUAN DE ULUA
CUBA
SILVER BANK
NAVIDAD BANK
GRAND CAYMAN
C. de la Cruz
MONTE CHRISTI
PUERTO PLATA
GONAVE
HISPANIOLA
SANTO DOMINGO
MONA
SAONA
PUERTO RICO
ANEGADA
VIRGIN GORDA
EL SOMBRERO
ANGUILLA
ST BARTHELEMY
SAN MARTIN
ST CROIX
BARBUDA
ANTIGUA
GUADALOUPE
LA DESIRADE
GUADALOUPE PASSAGE
DOMINICA
MARTINIQUE
ST LUCIA
ST VINCENT
BARBADOS
GRENADA
TOBAGO
TRINIDAD
ACAPULCO
JAMAICA
C. Tiburón
VACA
PEDRO BANK
TRUJILLO
HONDURAS
SERRANILLA BANK
NICARAGUA
PACIFIC OCEAN
CARIBBEAN SEA
C. de la Vela
RÍO HACHA
CURAÇAO
MARGARITA
MARACAIBO
CARTAGENA
BURBOROATA
La Guaira
CARACAS
NEW GRANADA
NEW ANDALUCIA
TIERRA FIRME
PORTOBELLO
NOMBRE DE DIOS
PANAMA
1st EXPEDITION
2nd EXPEDITION
3rd EXPEDITION
4th EXPEDITION
0 80 160 240 320 km

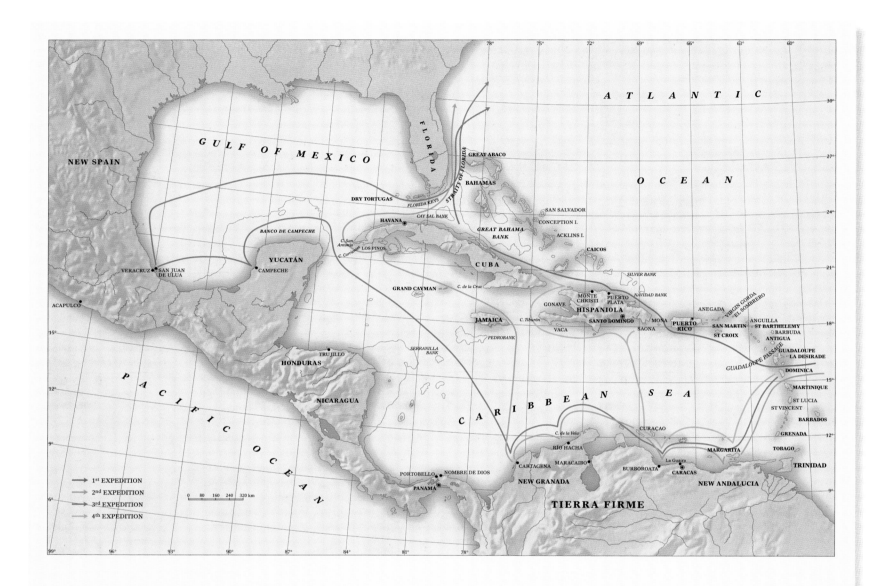

JOHN HAWKINS'S SMUGGLING VOYAGES

In the mid 1500s the Spanish colonies in America were in a highly precarious situation. A report by paymaster Ruiz de Vallejo, presented on 21 April 1568, revealed that smugglers came 'well stocked with oil, wine and other victuals and goods lacking in these lands, which the inhabitants desperately needed, and no form of punishment might prevent them from purchasing in secret everything they needed. Furthermore, to escape detection, they do so under cover of night.'[7]

Despite threats from the authorities, all manner of strategies were employed to evade controls. The smugglers claimed that they had been forced in to dock to carry out repairs and to take in provisions, while the local Spaniards used a variety of different arguments to escape punishment.

Often a simulated attack would be agreed upon, and the Spaniards would claim that they had been the victims of 'enforced trade'. On other occasions, they allowed goods to be unloaded while repairs were being carried out and, with the complicity of the local authorities, transactions took place behind a false door. The Dutch introduced 'sloop trading', in which smugglers would make a pre-arranged signal and, under cover of night, the inhabitants would flock to the sloop to trade.

Hawkins was a true master of the art of smuggling and organised four major expeditions, probably in connivance with Pedro Ponte, thanks to the latter's connections on either side of the Atlantic:

First expedition (1562-1563) to Hispaniola. *Green*

Second expedition (1564-1565) to Tierra Firme, Curaçao, Isla de los Pinos and Florida. *Red*

Third expedition (1567-1569) to Tierra Firme, Yucatan, and culminating in the disaster of San Juan de Ulúa. *Blue*

James Lowell's expedition (1566-1567), sponsored by the Hawkins family, to Tierra Firme, Curaçao and Hispaniola. *Yellow*

operation. He invested[6] his gains in the purchase of skins and returned to England. The voyage was considered a great financial success and, strategically, the route to the Indies was no longer a secret from the English.

Contraband with Institutional Support (1564-1565)

Encouraged by his success and a political climate favourable to the establishment of colonies in America,[8] and spurred on by Ribault during his exile in England,[9] Hawkins organised a second voyage that enjoyed the support of major sponsors. The main shareholder in the venture was the queen herself, who supplied the 700-ton Royal Navy galleon *Jesus of Lubeck*, purchased from the Hansa in 1545 and valued[10] at £2,000. Other sponsors were Lord Clinton (the Lord High Admiral), Benjamin Gonson, William Winter (the Royal Navy Inspector), the Earl of Pembroke, Lord Robert Dudley, Sir William Cecil (Lord Burghley, the Queen's first counsellor), Sir William Garrard, Sir William Chester, Edward Castlyn and the Hawkins family.

Learning of Hawkins's intentions, the Spanish ambassador, Diego de Silva, registered an official protest. The Queen assured the ambassador that she would prevent the fleet from sailing, but for obvious reasons she allowed Hawkins to go ahead with his plan.

On 18 October 1564 Hawkins sailed from Plymouth on the *Jesus of Lubeck*, accompanied by the 140-ton *Salomon* and a further two ships belonging to his family: the 50-ton *Tiger* and the 30-ton *Swallow*, all with well-trained crews. The voyage began badly, however,[11] since 'one of the officers was hit by a tackle block and killed instantly'.

Having reached Ferrol, in northwest Spain, the ships set sail together and headed south, sighting Tenerife on 6 November. Hawkins made for the port of Adeje, where he disembarked to greet Pedro de Ponte, with whom he stayed for five days, resting and repairing some of the damage to his ships.

In mid November the flotilla set sail for Guinea, and remained off the African coast until late January 1565. They spent their time capturing negroes to be traded in the Indies, and a number of Hawkins's men were killed in confrontations.

On 29 January the fleet departed from Sierra Leone and thence set sail for the Indies, arriving at Dominica forty days later. Since the Indians were hostile, Hawkins

During his return voyage to England, Hawkins visited the French settlements in Florida, where he witnessed the deplorable plight of Laudonnière's men. Having given them what help he could, he continued on his voyage and brought news to England of the uses of tobacco: '…a kind of dry weed placed in a clay bowl with a reed attached. The weed is set alight and the smoke is sucked through the reed, which assuages their hunger, so that they may go for four or five days without food or drink…'.

proceeded to Margarita, where his problems began. He and his men were warmly welcomed by the *alcalde* (mayor), who gave them provisions, but the governor refused to receive Hawkins, denied him permission to trade and prohibited him from engaging the services of a pilot to guide him along the coast. Furthermore, he informed the viceroy and Santo Domingo of the Englishman's presence.

Seeing that it was impossible to trade and take in provisions, Hawkins set sail again on 20 March, made port in Cumaná, Tierra Firma (Venezuela), sailed past La Tortuga and, on 3 April, reached Borburata.

Having anchored, Hawkins disembarked on the beach, declared that he was English, that his intention was to trade, and requested permission to do so legally. The locals replied that 'the king had forbidden them to trade with any foreign nation, under threat of having their worldly goods confiscated, so they would be grateful if he left them alone, returned from whence he had come and expect no help from them, for they were loyal subjects and could not infringe the law…'.

After several days of dialogue, the wealthier locals bought a number of negroes and, to avoid problems of customs duties, gave them to the poor.

On 17 April, Governor Alonso Bernáldez arrived. In writing, Hawkins alleged that he had come 'on a ship of the Queen of England bound for Guinea, but the bad weather and winds had forced him to land here. Consequently he needed to repair his ships and secure large sums of money to pay his soldiers, as he had promised to do, knowing that they would not leave without obtaining what was due to them.' Using this veiled threat, he requested a licence to trade.

The profits from his transactions were largely eaten away by high taxes, however, and, in the face of the inflexible stance of the Spaniards, Hawkins made a show of his military strength. In exchange for not using force, the Englishman asked to be allowed to trade, indicating that he was prepared to pay the usual commercial tax rate of 7.5 per cent.

The governor accepted his conditions, but Hawkins demanded hostages as a guarantee that they would be met. The hostages were provided and, over the next few days, Hawkins was able to trade unmolested.

On 4 May he set sail with the product of his transactions. He had managed to sell[12] 151 negroes, cloth, wine and other merchandise, for which he received 12,528 pesos, and he scrupulously paid his taxes at the rate of 7.5 per cent. Subsequently, Governor Bernáldez[13] was tried for his part in the affair and forced to reimburse the value of the negroes and the merchandise purchased by the local people, as well as the taxes that had not been paid.

Two days later, Hawkins and his men reached Curaçao and, having taken Alcalde Lázaro Bejarano prisoner after he had ingenuously come on board to pay a complimentary visit to the Englishmen, they traded skins and took in provisions. In fact, the transactions took place under threats,[14] which became reprisals when Hawkins suspected the Spaniards of deliberately delaying his departure.

They continued their voyage, making port in Aruba, Cabo de la Vela and Las Rancherías, where they were informed of the course for Río Hacha, which they reached on 19 May.[15]

Hawkins addressed the Royal Treasurer, asking him for permission to trade and declaring that he was an honest merchant, reinforcing his claim with a certificate issued by the Governor of Borburata.

To avoid any unpleasantness, the Spaniards allowed him to trade but offered such ridiculously low prices that the Englishman declared that '...they were treating him extremely harshly, attempting to ruin him when his prices were so reasonable that no other trader could compete with them.'

THE FRENCH ADVENTURE IN FLORIDA

In 1562 religious wars broke out in France, in which Huguenots, Catholics and Protestants would be engaged until 1598. In light of this violent unrest, some decided to try their luck on the far side of the Atlantic and set up a colony in Florida. Admiral Coligny, head of the Huguenot party, was the driving force behind the idea.

The site chosen was ideal for his purposes: there were no Spanish colonies and from here they dominated the Bahamas Channel, the passage that the Spanish fleets must use.

In February 1562, a first reconnoitring expedition led by Captain Jean Ribault sailed from Dieppe. They made landfall in Florida on a small island on the river known to the Indians as Edisto or Pom-Pom (today the River Santa Cruz), which the French renamed Mai, since they had arrived on the first day of that month.

Ribault built the fort of Charlesfort in honour of Charles IX of France, and left his second-in-command, one Albert, in charge of thirty men. He then took to sea and sailed back to France. Those who had remained suffered such terrible calamities that they rose in revolt, killed Albert and abandoned the fort. On their return voyage to France, lack of provisions forced them to practise cannibalism, until eventually they were rescued by an English ship.

In the meantime Ribault, who had had to flee to England for a time, prepared a new expedition. An advance guard captained by his new lieutenant, René Goulaine de Laudonnière, set sail in late April 1564 and reached the banks of the San Juan river, where they built a new fort, La Carolina.

Ribault had also reached the Caribbean. Near Yaguana he captured two small Spanish ships, ruthlessly tied up the prisoners and threw them overboard, an act that would later bring terrible consequences.

Word reached Cuba of the Frenchman's plans, which consisted of the fortification of Punta de los Mártires, Florida, and placing galleys there to block the passage of the fleets. He then intended to attack Havana with 800 men, free the slaves, whom he would incorporate into his own forces, and then proceed with a campaign against Santo Domingo and Puerto Rico.

When the news reached Spain, the king ordered the immediate evacuation of Florida and the establishment of a Spanish colony. In order to carry out the mission, he appointed Pedro Menéndez de Avilés – an Asturian seaman of almost fanatical religious convictions who had rid the Cantabrian waters of pirates – adelantado of Florida.

In Cadiz a fleet was prepared under his command, with Diego Flores Valdés as admiral, 995 armed men, four priests and 117 colonists. The plan was for him to join forces with the fleet of Esteban de las Alas, transporting farm implements and colonists from Santander, Avilés and Gijón.

However, news of Ribault's departure forced Avilés to set sail on July 29 1565 without waiting for reinforcements. He learned of Ribault's plans and positions from three French mutineers.

A storm dispersed his fleet. Avilés managed to reach Puerto Rico and, without waiting for the rest, sailed for Florida, where he arrived on August 28. There he established a settlement that he called San Agustín, in honour of the saint whose day it was.

In early September they located the French, and Avilés ordered them to abandon the territory, threatening war if they did not. The French replied with jokes and insults, but fearing an attack they took to sea during the night. The Spaniards returned to San Agustín, where 500 men disembarked and began to build the city.

Avilés learned the position of La Carolina from an Indian, and proceeded to the fort. Two hours before dawn he attacked, using cold steel only. Everyone at the fort – save the women and ship's boys under the age of fifteen – was put to the sword, the total number of deaths amounting to seventy.

King Athore and René Goulaine de Laudonnière, lieutenant to Jean Ribault. Engraving by América de Bry.

René Goulaine de Laudonnière managed to escape with sixty men.

Having resolved the situation on land, Avilés turned his attention to the sea, where three ships were anchored commanded by Ribault's son Jacques. The French were called upon to surrender, Avilés promising to return them, women and ship's boys included, to France on one of his ships. Receiving no reply, he ordered the artillery to open fire, sinking one of the ships.

Then Avilés went in pursuit of those who had fled into the jungle. Some twenty fell victim to harquebus fire, while a dozen more attempted to hide among the Indians, but the latter handed them over. The rest, including Laudonnière, managed to reach Jacques Ribault's ships.

Avilés ordered his men to return to San Agustín, fearing that the main body of the French forces would attack the colony. First, however, he rechristened the French fort with the name of San Mateo, whose day it was, and made the position secure. From the Indians he learned that a

detachment of 200 pirates was lurking in the jungle. He went after them and managed to capture them. As an act of reprisal against Ribault's brutal treatment of the crew of the ship he had taken near Yaguana, Avilés inflicted exemplary punishment: he decapitated the prisoners three by three, except for eight who swore they were Catholics.

The flotilla in which the French attempted to withdraw was wrecked and 350 survivors were discovered by the Indians. They were taken prisoner, including Jean Ribault, who offered to pay the sum of 100,000 ducats in exchange for his life. They were all executed, however, except for a few who swore they were Catholics and boys under the age of fifteen. Avilés hung a placard on the corpses saying 'Hanged, not as French but as Lutheran heretics'.

Twenty days after the executions, the Indians announced the presence of a new contingent of 170 Frenchmen who were mustering near Cape Canaveral. The French had fled into the forest and

Avilés promised to spare their lives if they surrendered: 150 capitulated.

Ribault's forces had been annihilated on land but they still had to be swept from the sea. The two surviving ships of the squadrons of Captains Fourneaux, Etienne and Lacroix still remained in the Caribbean.

At the end of 1565 they took the ship in which Diego de Mazariego, the former Governor of Cuba, was sailing, and they anchored near Mariel. Governor García de Osorio sent a frigate and two vessels commanded by Pedro Menéndez Márquez, Avilés's nephew against the French; the outcome of the confrontation was the capture of one of the ships, the liberation of Mazariego, six Frenchmen dead and forty surrendered. The captains managed to flee on one of the two ships, while the prisoners were taken to Seville where they were hanged.

When the few survivors of Ribault's fleets got back to France, the ensuing wave of anti-Spanish protest reached diplomatic level. The Spanish reaction was one of firm rejection.

Another Huguenot captain swore revenge and took to sea in August 1567. Dominic Gourges, a *gentilhomme* who had sold all his possessions and become a corsair, sailed with the apparent intention of capturing negroes in Guinea to sell in Brazil. He captured some in Cape Verde and sold them in the Antilles to one Ceballos, who informed him of the possibility of assaulting the forts of Florida.

Gourges sailed to the fort of San Mateo, hoisted his flag and entered the harbour without any difficulty. On making landfall he came across one of the survivors of Ribault's fleet, Pierre Bren, who had remained hidden among the Indians. Bren was on good terms with Saturiba or Saturioua, an Indian chief hostile to the Spanish, and managed to secure an agreement between Saturiba and Gourges to attack the Spanish positions.

Gourges stormed San Mateo and another Spanish fort that had been built on Charlesfort, taking thirty-eight prisoners. To avenge Ribault's men, he hanged some and handed the rest over to the Indians, who tortured them to death. In imitation of Avilés's cruelty, he placed placards on the corpses saying '…Not as Spaniards, but as murderers'. Gourges then sailed back to La Rochelle, where he was welcomed as a hero.

Gourges published his 'feats' in a book entitled *History of the Reconquest of Florida*, as a result of which he was hotly pursued by the agents of the Spanish ambassador, Francés de Alava, and he was forced to seek refuge in Rouen. He died in 1583, when he was on the point of joining the French fleet sent to the Azores to support the Prior of Crato.

To prevent further attacks, in July 1568 Avilés took ships and reinforcements to San Agustín, which finally made the colony secure. Then he was appointed Governor of Cuba, in Havana, where he kept the coasts clear of pirates until his return to Spain in 1573.

On the morning of May 21, Hawkins fired a culverin to summon the citizens. He had mustered 100 armed men, equipped the launch with two light bronze cannons, and placed four double cannons in two boats. Having been alerted, the Spaniards came to the beach with banners and armed men, but they retreated when the English began to fire from the boats. When Hawkins's men landed, the Spanish cavalry, thirty men with javelins and leather shields, drew back. After negotiations had taken place, the Spanish agreed to trade, but Hawkins demanded hostages before withdrawing his men.[16] Over the next few days they traded freely and took in fresh water. On the night of May 31 Hawkins set sail without further incident. Later, he applied the same strategy in Cartagena with identical results.

At last Hawkins set a course for Hispaniola and, on June 4, came in sight of Jamaica. Thinking they had reached their destination, they sailed to leeward and crossed the channel to the island of Cuba. But they were mistaken about their real position and sailed straight past a watering place, not realising their error until they reached the island of Los Pinos. Finally, they continued to the Cape of San Antonio and reached the coast of Florida early in July.

Lacking an expert pilot, they passed La Tortuga looking for landmarks that would lead them to Havana, but night fell and they sailed past the city without making harbour.

They were thus forced to sail up the Bahamas Channel and, after a number of incidents, on July 15 were at 26° north. They sailed on along the coast until they reached 30.5° north, in French territory, took in fresh water and anchored for the night. Leaving his ships in deeper waters, Hawkins took the pinnace to look for French settlements, question the Indians and enter all the coves and estuaries.

At last he located Laudonnière, who had built a fort in which he had remained with a few soldiers. At war with the Floridians, his provisions were running out, but, since he and his men numbered only a few, he dared not leave the fort except when absolutely necessary.

Hawkins gave him twenty barrels of flour, four casks of kidney beans and other victuals. Furthermore, he lent[17] Laudonnière one of his tenders so that he and his men could return to France. In exchange, the Englishmen received twenty pipes of wine similar to those of Orléans, which the Frenchmen had made from wild grapes.

Coastal plantations, such as this sugar plantation were subject to numerous and repeated attacks. Here we see the process of gathering cane, crushing it beneath the stone wheel, boiling it down and taking it away in large vats. Note that the workers are slaves – both European and African.

On July 28 Hawkins set off to cross the Atlantic. The wind direction and lack of provisions forced them to Terranova, where they caught large quantities of fresh cod and took in other provisions. From here, the favourable winds took them back to England and, after an uneventful voyage, they docked in Padstow on September 20 1565.

Those who had invested in the venture made substantial profits. On November 5 1565, Diego de Silva, the Spanish ambassador to England, wrote to Philip II stating that the dividends shared out among the backers of the enterprise amounted to 60 per cent. As a special reward, Hawkins was knighted. Once again the Spanish ambassador filed a formal protest, but it went unheeded.

While Hawkins's first voyage had meant the discovery of the route to the Americas, his second had provided exhaustive knowledge of itineraries that would make subsequent, far more ambitious ventures possible.

A New Contraband Expedition (1566-1567)

The third voyage organised by William and John Hawkins was commanded by James Lowell, who was accompanied by a young man of twenty-four called

Francis Drake. Lowell had been a trading agent on Tenerife and was well versed in the Spanish language and customs.[18] They left Plymouth in November 1566 and crossed the Atlantic via Guinea. In the Caribbean, they made port in Margarita and there spent the Easter of 1567 in the company of the fleet of the Frenchman, Jean Bontemps, with whom they entered into a temporary association.[19]

They attempted to sell slaves in Borburata but, although they used force, they managed to make only 1,500 pesos. They visited Río Hacha, where they attempted to trade separately, but the Spanish refused to cooperate and, in retaliation, Lowell disembarked ninety-four moribund negroes[20] and continued on his journey. (In a subsequent expedition, Hawkins had the effrontery to demand payment for the negroes.)

Having taken in water and provisions in Curaçao, they proceeded to Hispaniola, where they committed some thefts, and finally they sailed up the Bahamas Channel on their way back to England. The adventure yielded little profit, due probably to the lack of institutional support or the absence of such a daring individual as John Hawkins.

The Last Smuggling Campaign,[21] the Disaster of Veracruz (1567-1569)

Disappointed by the results of Lowell's expedition and, in the knowledge that both profits and support were much greater when he himself took the reins, John Hawkins prepared to engage in a new smuggling venture. Once again, he enjoyed ample financial and political support, the Queen herself supplying two ships, the *Jesus of Lubeck* and the 300-ton *Minion*. The rest of the flotilla consisted of the 150-ton *William and John*, the 100-ton *Swallow*, the 50-ton *Judith* and the 40-ton *Angel*, all fully equipped with weaponry and manned by experienced crews.

In the meantime, the Spanish ambassador's spies had informed him of the forthcoming expedition, and once again de Silva filed a formal protest. Receiving no satisfactory reply, and determined to obtain one, he filed a second protest. The Queen's only answer this time was that he was mistaken about the flotilla's destination and that she knew nothing more about the matter.

Preparations continued and everything seemed to be going very well for Hawkins. This time, however, the

Distorted versions of events in San Juan de Ulúa, news of repression in the Low Countries, and the death in stange circumstances of Isabel de Valois, Sebastian of Portugal and Prince Charles, fuelled anti-Spanish propaganda and led to a systematic campaign to denigrate Spaniards. Tales of the slaughter by them of innocent Native American communities served as a justification to attack the towns and cities of Spanish America. The 'Black Legend' – the propagandistic view that Spanish rule was inherently corrupt and bigoted – was taking shape.

Spanish were determined to intimidate the Englishman. A flotilla of seven warships entered Plymouth without making the customary salute and headed straight to where Hawkins was preparing his expedition. It was the custom for ships entering a foreign harbour to hoist their topsails and standards as a greeting and a sign of goodwill; this forced the vessels to reduce speed and placed them at the mercy of the port artillery. On this occasion, however, the Spaniards disregarded the custom.

When Hawkins realised what was happening, he opened fire on the Spaniards, forcing them to separate and make the greeting. After the incident, the Spanish

THE SHIPS

Several kinds of ships were used by corsairs. During the initial, fundamentally English, period of privateering of the 16th century, the vessels were classified according to four main types.

Man-of-War. Equivalent to the Spanish galleon, the man-of-war might weigh up to 700 or 800 tons, carried a large crew and up to thirty cannons, and generally belonged to the Royal Navy. Cumbersome to manoeuvre, she normally operated with the support of smaller vessels.

Merchantman. A multi-purpose merchant vessel of which there were several kinds. In general they were armed with demi culverins supplemented by sakers and other forms of small artillery. They proved to be very effective in the assault of small towns.

Barque or Tender. With one or two masts, weighing between 50 and 100 tons, armed with small artillery and with large crews, this was the corsair's ship par excellence.

Pinnace. A small vessel used as a troop carrier. It would occasionally have a sail, although generally it was powered by oarsmen.

Other commonly used types of vessel were:

The Fire Ship. Not a type of vessel as such, the fire ship was used in major operations, towed by a pinnace, set on fire with its cannons loaded and sent into a flotilla or harbour of enemy ships.

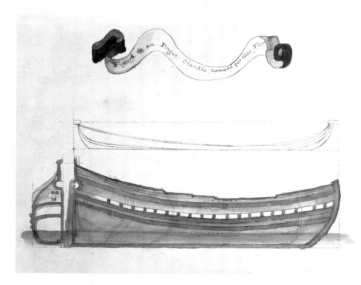

The Pingue. A typical Dutch boat. Ideally suited to the shallow waters of the Caribbean, it was often used in small-scale incursions.

The Barca Longa. The Spanish equivalent of the pinnace.

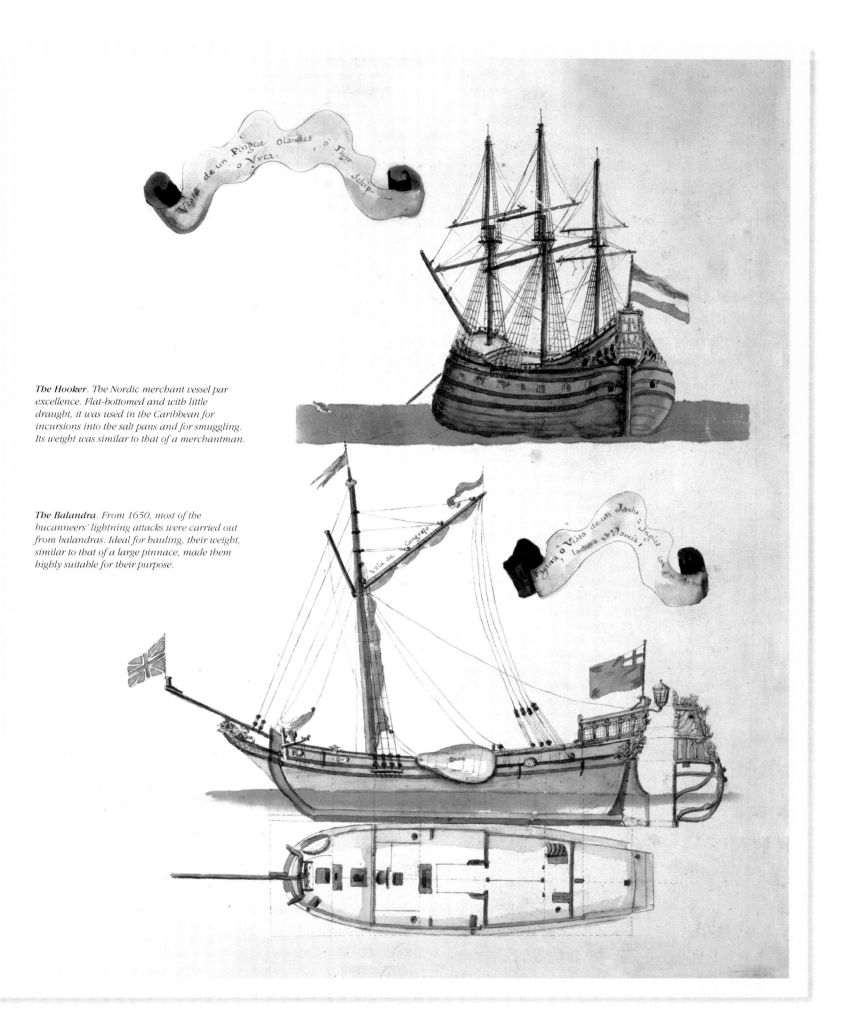

The Hooker. *The Nordic merchant vessel par excellence. Flat-bottomed and with little draught, it was used in the Caribbean for incursions into the salt pans and for smuggling. Its weight was similar to that of a merchantman.*

The Balandra. *From 1650, most of the bucanneers' lightning attacks were carried out from balandras. Ideal for hauling, their weight, similar to that of a large pinnace, made them highly suitable for their purpose.*

THE INDIES FLEETS

Constant assaults by French and English corsairs on merchant ships returning from America led the Spanish authorities to devise an effective defence system. The proposed solution was that the ships should sail together in fleets, escorted by armed vessels that would transport the treasure on the return voyage. The system was given its definitive structure between 1561 and 1566, and was subjected to a number of modifications in 1590.

Two fleets were organised each year, one to Nueva España, which sailed from Sanlúcar in April, and the other to Tierra Firme, which set sail in August. Both fleets would spend the winter in American ports and, when the winter was nearing its close, begin the return voyage to the Peninsula.

In January, the ships of Nueva España weighed anchor bound for Havana, and in February the Tierra Firme fleet sailed from Cartagena with the same destination. Both fleets met in Havana, waiting for the vessels from Honduras to join them before setting off on the Atlantic crossing. The departure took place no earlier than March 10 and no later than July 15.

The fleets traditionally entered the Caribbean by way of the Guadeloupe Passage and continued along the *ruta interior* (inner route) as far as Santo Domingo. Before 1560 the fleets would separate in this port.

The Tierra Firme fleet often used the Granada Channel and then continued along the coast of Nueva Granada (Venezuela) as far as Cartagena. It then proceeded to Nombre de Dios to collect the silver from Peru and then returned to Cartagena to avoid the sandbanks that prevented them from sailing north to Havana.

As from 1700, the Nueva España fleet began to use the *ruta de fuera* (outer route) to Havana via the Canal Vieja on the north coast of Cuba.

1. *Ruta interior* of the Nueva España fleet.
2. Diversion followed by the galleons of Honduras.
3. Crossing the bank of Yucatan on the *ruta interior*.
4. Crossing the bank of Yucatan on the *ruta de fuera*.
5. The Veracruz-Havana return route. Depending on the winds and the weather conditions, it was possible to sail more or less to the north.
6. *Ruta de fuera* of the Nueva España fleet.
7. Route through the channel between Caicos and Mayaguana (the Caicos Passage). This route was used by the fleets, especially that of Tierra Firme, in emergencies. From 1655 it was the usual route for the return voyage of English ships from Jamaica.
8. Deviation from the Caicos Passage.

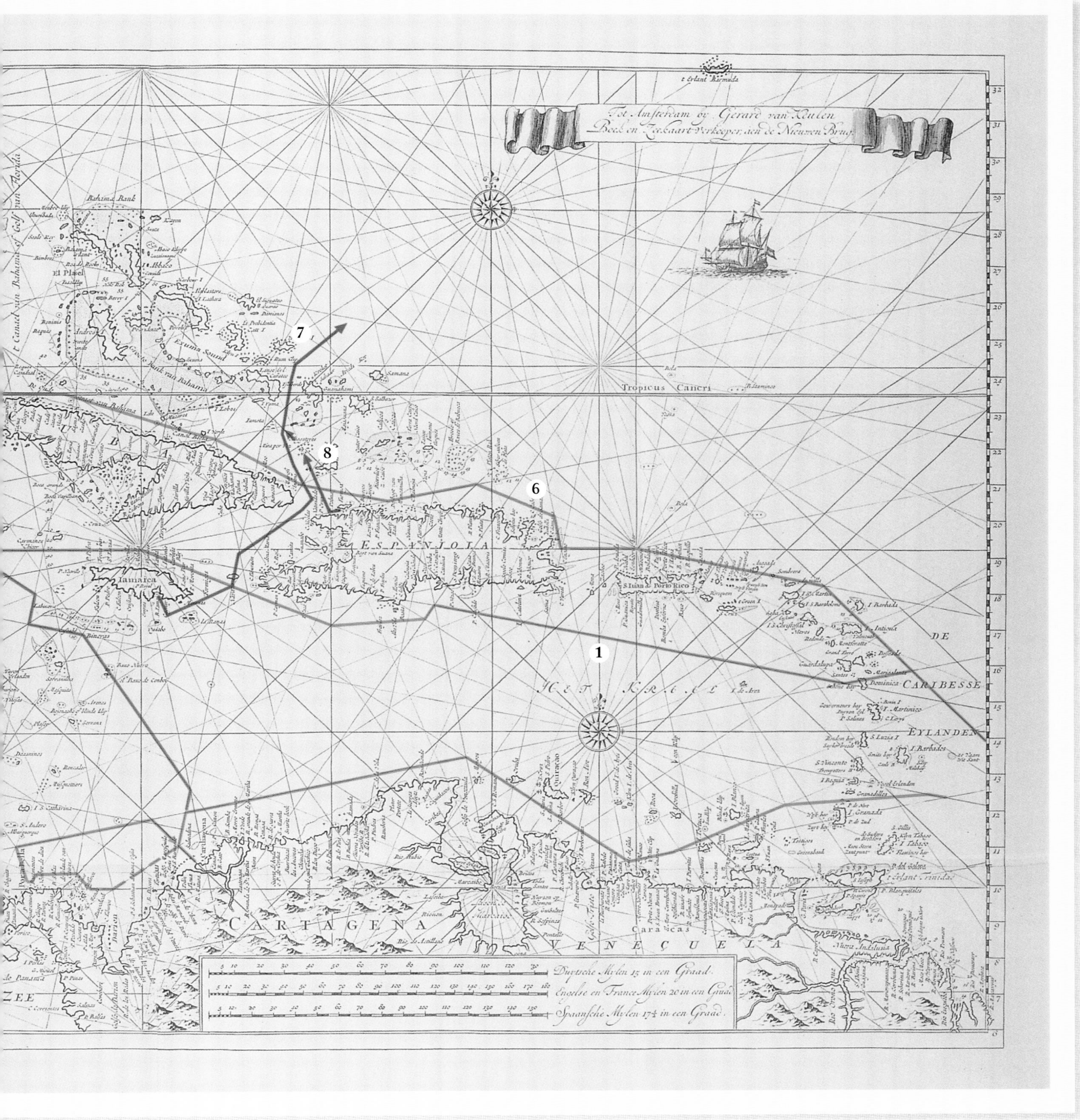
t Eylant Barmuda
Tot Amsterdam by Gerard van Keulen
Boek en Zeekaart Verkooper, aen de Nieuwen Brug
Bahama Bank
El Placel
Exuma Sound
Tropicus Cancri
7
8
6
1
ESPANIOLA
Jamaica
S. Iuan de Porto Rico
DE
CARIBESSE
EYLANDEN
I. Barbados
I. Granada
Curaçao
CARTAGENA
VENEÇUELA
Nueva Andalusia
Duytsche Mylen 15 in een Graad.
Engelse en France Mylen 20 in een Graad
Spaansche Mylen 17½ in een Graad.

commanders complained to the port authorities and the Spanish ambassador to the Queen, who this time felt forced to demand an explanation from Hawkins. The latter's excuses did nothing to resolve the issue, but it certainly was clear that this time the Spaniards had determined to use force against the Englishman and that Hawkins would boldly retaliate.

The English flotilla finally sailed from Plymouth on 2 October 1567 with William Clarke and Francis Drake among the sailors. On the way to Tenerife they captured a number of ships, one of which, the *Espíritu Santo*, was re-christened *Grace of God* and given to Jean Planes to command.

They reached Gambia and Senegal but resistance on the part of the natives forced the English to withdraw. Later they attacked a number of French ships and wrested their slaves from them. On October 28 they reached Sierra Leone, where they made 470 negroes captive and set sail for the Caribbean. Their first landfall was in Dominica, where Hawkins, not wishing to pit his strength, limited himself to taking in fruit, water and meat.

HAWKINS SEEKS CONVERSION

By 1571 it seems that John Hawkins's prestige had fallen considerably. His large private fleet could not trade at Spanish ports where an embargo had been decreed on English ships, and he attempted to solve his problems unassisted by English diplomacy. Through an intermediary, George Fitzwilliams,[22] he signed a capitulation on 11 August in which he committed himself to serving the King of Spain with the aim of 'restoring the Catholic faith in England, destroying the tyranny of Elizabeth and defending the freedom and rights of the Queen of Scotland'.

Hawkins was required to supply sixteen ships with 420 cannons and 1,585 men. In return, he would receive 16,987 ducats per month, a pardon and 'amnesty for all the harm he has caused in the Indies'.

The agreement was conceived at the Escorial, thanks to the intervention of the Duke of Feria and of secretary Zayas, a close friend of Arias Montano. It seems that it was linked to the new strategy that was planned to begin with the substitution of the Duke of Alba by the Duke of Feria as Governor of Flanders, but the death of the latter, the king's favourite and probably Hawkins's partner, on 8 September, led to a change of plans.

In December the Spanish ambassador in London, Guerau de Spes,[23] informed the Spanish court of Hawkins's concern that he might be discovered, since the Earl of Leicester was insistently asking him why, since his fleet was ready, he did not take to sea. Philip II himself noted in the margin 'We must make sure that our plans are not thwarted here too, as in all the rest'. Due to a lack of determination on the part of the Spaniards, the plan fell through.

They proceeded to Margarita, where they also took in provisions. In Borburata they did some business and later, in Río Hacha, they managed to sell part of their merchandise after exercising force and burning a number of houses.[24] In Santa Marta a simulated combat took place and, after the governor had capitulated, they managed to sell 114 negroes and a substantial amount of merchandise.

On 1 August 1568 they reached Cartagena. Although the construction of fortifications had begun, the stronghold was not yet adequately defended, having only two pieces of artillery and very few soldiers. Hawkins was unaware of this, however, and all he saw from the sea were the walls of the small forts of El Boquerón and La Caleta.

Hawkins challenged the stronghold, as was his custom, and Martín de Alas, the city governor, replied that[25] 'the only language in which they could communicate was that of the sword and the harquebus'. Taking the Spaniard's word as good, the English opened fire.

The defenders had devised a strategy to deceive the enemy – they would fire the cannons and then change their position repeatedly to create the impression that their forces were greater. The ruse worked and, after a blockade of eight days, Hawkins set sail once more.

As winter was approaching, Hawkins decided to reach the Bahamas as quickly as possible; he was unable to fulfil his objective. West of Cuba, a storm caused considerable damage to his ships, particularly the *Jesus of Lubeck*, and he was forced to enter the Gulf of Mexico.

Off the coast of Campeche they captured the merchant ship of Francisco Maldonado, who assured them that the best place to repair ships of such tonnage was San Juan de Ulúa.[26] Hawkins also learned of the imminent departure of the fleet of Nueva España and believed that at last his great opportunity had come. On 14 September 1568 ten English vessels,[27] mistaken for the fleet of Nueva España bringing the new viceroy, Martín Enríquez de Almansa, arrived in Ulúa.

The following day, the treasurer and other city authorities came to greet the newcomers, in the belief that they would welcome the viceroy. Invited to come on board, they were taken prisoner. Hawkins alleged that he had been forced to anchor here, and threatened to kill his prisoners if he was not allowed access to the island of Gallega,[28] which had a fort.

Then, the imminent arrival of the true fleet of Nueva España made him change his tactics: he hid his ships behind the islet and took up positions in the city. His plan was to steal the treasure that was being sent from Veracruz for collection by the Spanish fleet. He believed that all he need do was wait.

In a moment all his plans were thwarted. Antonio Delgadillo, the port purveyor, had informed Veracruz of the presence of the English and the droves of mules carrying the treasure had made an about-turn. On the 17th, the sails of the fleet of Nueva España appeared on the horizon – the English had no chance of escape without a fight.

The forces were equal. Although the Spanish fleet consisted of thirteen galleons, only one was a warship. The fleet was also carrying many passengers and combat was out of the question until they had disembarked; this operation took place on the 20th, as far from the English flotilla as possible.

Hawkins had enough time to prepare his defence. He re-allocated his ships and took up positions on the walls. Enríquez's fleet anchored, blocking the escape route, and remained on the look out. Both sides waited for the other to attack, and they were both prepared to fight, although their motives were very different. Hawkins's objective was to break through the blockade and return home with what he had managed to obtain; for the viceroy, it would be dishonourable to make a pact with the Englishman, and his intention was to take Hawkins prisoner. Negotiations began and hostages were exchanged, but it soon became clear that this would lead nowhere. Reinforcements of 120 men arrived from Veracruz and, undetected, took up their positions on the Spanish ships.

As night fell on 22 September, Viceroy Enríquez deployed his men. One hundred and thirty Spanish harquebusiers embarked on launches and took up their positions on the hooker *San Salvador*, which was placed between the armadas, close to the English ships.

According to Spanish sources, the attack began at around nine in the morning when Ubilla, waving a white handkerchief, signalled to the viceroy, who ordered the attack by sounding a trumpet. In response, the English opened their artillery fire and a fierce battle ensued.

The Spanish vice-admiral's ship caught fire and lost its cargo when a well-aimed cannon ball exploded a barrel of gunpowder. The *Jesus of Lubeck* was so severely damaged after an intense exchange of cannon fire with

A bay in Hispaniola, today the Dominican Republic. The landscape has remained largely unchanged over the past four centuries except for the proliferation of coconut palms introduced from the Pacific by the Spaniards.

the Spanish flagship that she had to be abandoned. Aboard her the Spaniards found the hostages and took 'General Aquines's Silver Vessel, clothing and other articles of little value, and forty-five or fifty slaves'.

Delgadillo and his troops stormed Gallega and, by midday, the Spaniards had taken control of the islet and the castle. The English flotilla now became the target of cannon fire from both land and sea. Only three English defenders survived the attack on the island. In the afternoon, the *Angel* and the *Swallow* foundered, and the entire English contingent was forced to escape on board the *Minion*, the only ship left – the *Judith*, commanded by Drake, had fled.

With the *Minion* and a tender, Hawkins attempted to return to England. He lost the tender and, at Panuco (in the north of today's Veracruz), he had to disembark 104 men, whom he promised to come back and collect one year later, for on the ship there was nothing to eat except for 'skins, cats, dogs, rats and mice, parakeets and monkeys…'. After a string of calamities, they reached Plymouth on 3 February 1569. Spanish spies informed Madrid that only fifteen men had returned on the *Minion*.

Those whom Hawkins had left in Panuco suffered all kinds of misfortunes.[29] They were attacked by the Chichimeca Indians who stole everything down to their clothes. Naked and with many suffering from malaria, they had great difficulty in making their way through the jungle but at last they arrived in Tampico, where they were taken prisoner by Luis de Carbajal.

Sent to Mexico City, they suffered a variety of fates. Some ended their days in hospital, some were forced to work in the wool mills of Texcoco, others in the mines, and the young boys were sent to monasteries. Only a few ended up in the service of illustrious personages. Finally, after the arrival of Pedro Moya de Contreras, come to establish the Inquisition in Nueva España, proceedings were opened against them that ended in an *auto da fe,* and a variety of sentences were passed.

Back in England, Drake's and Hawkins's distorted accounts of events – in which they accused Ubilla and the viceroy of treachery, and which were further enflamed by official policy – raised anti-Spanish feelings among the populace, although the loss of a Queen's galleon was hard to justify. Hawkins accused Drake not only of leaving him to his fate but also of having unlawfully appropriated the cargo of the *Judith*; it led to tense relations between the two men.

Despite the disasters, the Hawkins family business was flourishing. By 1570 they had become the owners of one of England's most important private fleets, thirteen of whose ships were larger than 60 tons and whose total tonnage was 2,090. Their privateering activities continued unabated. In November 1571 John signed a document[30] by which he committed himself to paying the sum of £1,000 as a guarantee of good conduct in the execution of a commission to persecute corsairs and pirates in English waters. Other illustrious English seamen such as Martin Frobisher, William Winter and Thomas Prydeaux signed similar documents. Nothing, it would seem, had changed but the venue.

Crisis and New English Policies (1568-1572)

During the 1560s, Europe was caught up in a spiral of events that would give rise to a new order. The French Huguenots, from the ports of the Bay of Biscay, hounded ships trading between Spain and Flanders, and in The Netherlands the resurgence of nationalist sentiments around the Protestant Reformation would culminate in the rebellion of 1567.

A great number of Dutch vessels imitated their co-religionaries from La Rochelle and, by 1568, all resources were invested in coordinating the maritime offensive against Spain – the English ports provided shelter in this endeavour. The *Watergeuzen* (sea beggars) launched a campaign to harass Spanish interests in the Channel and it produced a number of successful results.

England's support for the Dutch rebels elicited irate protests from the Spanish, above all when, in 1568, the English government ordered the confiscation of treasure destined to pay the Spanish army in the Netherlands. The treasure had been transported in a flotilla that sought shelter in Plymouth, Fowey and Falmouth in order to escape from corsairs in the English Channel. The tone of the protests was so strong that the Spanish ambassador was arrested. To make matters worse, Mary Stuart fled from Scotland to England, where she was imprisoned by order of Elizabeth.

News from the other side of the Channel, such as the cruel repression of the Protestant rebels by Philip's regent in the Netherlands, the Duke of Alva, the public execution of Dutch leaders Egmont and Horn and the outbreak of civil war in France predisposed the people of England to regard Philip II as the 'southern devil'.

The Spanish authorities ordered the embargo of all assets belonging to English subjects and the confiscation of ships flying the English flag in Spanish ports. In 1570, to encourage warships in the capture of corsairs, a law was enacted according to which the royal fifth in the booty shareout would go to the squadron commanders[31] and any goods found belonging to the king's subjects must be returned to their rightful owners.[32]

The tensions did not stop here, however. For, in that same year, Elizabeth of England was excommunicated and news came of the death of Philip II's third wife, Elizabeth of Valois, for which Sebastian, the King of Portugal, blamed Philip. The Black Legend – Protestant-inspired accusations toward the Spanish of authoritarian

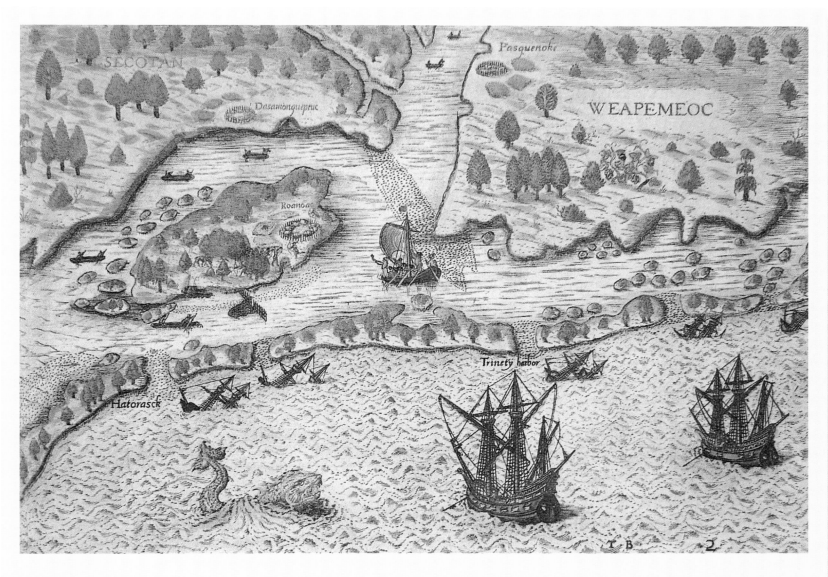

THE VIRGINIA COLONY

After the failure of Gilbert's expedition to North America, Sir Walter Raleigh conceived a new adventure: the establishment of a colony north of those of Spain and beyond the routes followed by fleets from Nueva España and Tierra Firme. To this end, he organised and financed four expeditions known as the Roanoke Voyages, in which the first English colony in America was founded and named Virginia in honour of the Virgin Queen. Elizabeth rewarded Raleigh's courtesy by knighting him.

In 1584 the first expedition was prepared, commanded by Phillip and Barlow, known as Felipe Armadas and Arturo Barlow in the Spanish chronicles. They reached an island known as Roanoke on the coast of Virginia, where they were well received by the natives. Certain of success, they returned to England with the news that they had found lands suitable to be colonised.

In 1585 preparations were completed for the second voyage. This time, seven ships commanded by Richard Grenville and Ralph Lane carried 100 or so colonists determined to settle. Now, however, the Indians were hostile.

The ships proceeded further north and, on their return, the colonists, who had suffered considerable calamities, demanded to be repatriated. The captains refused. Finally the colony was evacuated by Francis Drake, who had reached port after the burning of San Agustín.

The last colonising attempt was made in 1587. John White, a naturalist who had taken part in the previous expeditions, embarked on the enterprise with 112 colonists. Although he knew the area, his leadership qualities were few.

The captain took them directly to Roanoke, where the colonists demanded that White return to England for provisions. On 28 August (Old Style [O.S.] – see 'The Change in the Calendar', p.77) he took to sea, leaving eighty-five men, seventeen women and eleven children, including his granddaughter Virginia Dare, the first Anglo-Saxon to be born in America, on the island.

Having been unable to find funding sources, White did not return for three years. On 17 August 1591 (O.S.) he reached Roanoke, but all he found was a word carved on a tree trunk, 'Croatoa', the name of an island fifty miles to the south. Since the cross was missing that would complete the code they had agreed upon if the colonists had had to flee, White still harboured some hope. The colonists, however, were never heard of again and their fate is still a mystery today.

governement, bigoted religion, and corrupt administration – was beginning to take shape and, after the Victory of Lepanto, the King of Spain emerged as the Paladin of the Catholic Faith.

The Duke of Alva's replacement by Luis de Requesens in 1573 led to a release of tensions, although the balance of powers would no longer be that of previous eras. Elizabeth of England designed a new policy by which to weaken Spanish hegemony and, to this end, she oriented her actions in two directions. On the one hand, she fostered and supported campaigns whose objective was to set up colonies on the west side of the Atlantic from which to embark on more ambitious ventures. On the other, she continued to damage Spanish interests by tolerating piracy (though without official aid), contraband and acts of reprisal.

PUNITIVE EXPEDITIONS

Drake Comes of Age in the Indies

Francis Drake was a man of humble origin. He was born in about 1540 in Crowndale, near Tavistock, the eldest of peasant farmer Edmund Drake's twelve children.

According to some sources, in 1549 a Catholic uprising forced the Drakes to move to Kent, where the family found lodgings in an old abandoned boat on the river Medway and, at the age of fourteen, Francis became an apprentice skipper on a small coaster that often engaged in smuggling. When the coaster's skipper died, Francis inherited the vessel. Determined to try his luck, he sold her and went to Devon, a protégé of the Hawkins family.

The facts are not clear about the first expedition that Drake organised alone. It has been dated to 1570, after the disaster of Veracruz, and it seems that it was motivated by a thirst for revenge and a perceived debt that the Spanish apparently owed the Englishman, although it amounted to no more than the silver he had been unable to steal. His expedition may have been justified as an act of reprisal but there is no documentary evidence of this. It is known that he sailed from England in the *Dragon* and, according to some sources, captured two ships near Chagres. However, other sources have it that he was taken prisoner in Río Hacha and was subsequently set free.

Records exist of a voyage of exploration that took place in 1571, between March and late December, on which Drake restricted himself to exploring the region of Darién and the Isthmus of Panama. It seems that he set up a small base in a port he called Puerto Faisán, from which, aboard the *Swan*, he reconnoitred the coasts of Cartagena and Nombre de Dios, where he made contact with a number of runaway slaves.

What we do know for certain is that Drake returned to England and began to seek sponsors for another voyage. He was refused official aid although, with the support of merchants, he managed to equip two ships. On 24 May 1572 the expedition sailed from London with Drake commanding the *Parcha*, his brother John[33] on the *Swan*, and a combined crew of seventy-three men. They transported three collapsible pinnaces built in Plymouth, with which, as on subsequent expeditions, they planned to sail in shallow waters and up rivers and to make landfall on beaches.

The English sailed straight to Puerto Faisán, where they most probably hoped to take in victuals left by Drake on his previous voyage. Their plans suffered a slight setback, however: someone had made off with the reserves in their absence.

On 9 July they were off the coast of Nombre de Dios, which they attempted, unsuccessfully, to storm. The two versions of the event are very different: the Spanish speak simply of eighteen dead left in the stronghold but Drake tells a fantastic tale in which he took the city and was on the point of making off with the treasure discovered in the governor's cellar, consisting of a pile of silver bars 70 feet long by 10 feet wide and 13 feet high. The truth is that Drake was shot in the leg and the bullet remained lodged there for the rest of his life. In his account, he claims to have received this wound during his strategic retreat to the island of Pinos, after he had failed to secure any booty. When the wound had healed and he had recovered his strength, he sailed for Cartagena, where he captured a 250-ton ship from Seville and made a show of ostentation out of range of the cannons. In order to crew the vessel he was forced to sacrifice his most charismatic ship, the *Swan*.

Now he intended to attack the droves of mules that were crossing the Isthmus with Peruvian silver, but realised that his forces were insufficient. He sought reinforcements, and found them in the jungles between Puerto Caballos and Vallano in Honduras: here he recruited some 200 runaway black slaves. This was in

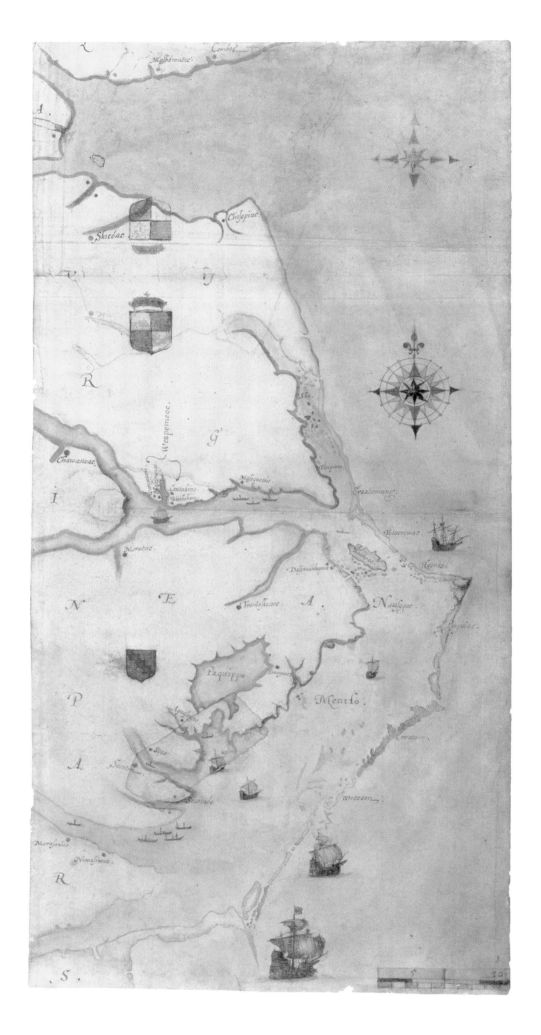

Map of Virginia from about 1600 by John White (active between 1585 and 1603). Preserved at the British Museum, London.

September 1572, and the runaways informed him that the droves would not proceed until January, after the rainy season. Consequently, Drake decided to spend the winter in Puerto Faisán.

During this rest period, in which Drake carried out a number of incursions meeting with varying degrees of success, he was overcome by great misfortune. By January he had lost thirty men, among them his brothers John, in a skirmish, and Joseph,[34] who had died of yellow fever. The English forces were reduced to fewer than fifty.

At last, however, the arrival of the Tierra Firme fleet announced the recommencement of the droves to Nombre de Dios. Determined to capture them, Drake and his men – thirty runaways and eighteen Englishmen – went inland on the Isthmus of Panama. They advanced towards the Camino de Cruces, where they saw the arrival of eight pack mules carrying the treasure and, behind them, two droves of 100 mules. Just as Drake was convinced that the silver was his, a scout sounded the alarm, frustrating the attack. The English were forced to retreat to avoid losses.

Back on board their ships, they sighted a Huguenot vessel[35] commanded by Guillaume le Testu,[36] whom Drake informed of their feats. Le Testu encouraged them in their endeavours and Drake determined to try a new strategy. They sailed to Nombre de Dios, and from there went up the San Francisco river in a pinnace, then proceeded overland to the stretch of the road closest to the Caribbean, just one league from Nombre de Dios. Drake's forces consisted of thirty French and English and some fifty runaways. The strategy worked, the Spaniards were not expecting an attack so near their destination and Drake managed to capture a number of mules.

The spoils were enormous – 100,000 pesos in gold and fifteen tons of silver, much more than they could quickly transport. Furthermore, there were casualties: one negro and one Englishman had been killed and Le Testu was badly wounded. Fearing reprisals, they buried part of the booty and withdrew with bars worth around 150,000 pesos. They left Le Testu with a French cavalier as escort and promised to return to rescue him, but the pursuing Spaniards found the Frenchman and killed him.

Taking advantage of a terrible downpour, the English, who were now surrounded, managed to escape. Drake and Le Testu's men shared the spoils and rapidly set sail in a mood of mutual distrust. The runaway slaves were paid with the metal of the pinnaces, and withdrew.

Drake returned to England on Sunday, 9 August 1573, and his fantastic tales[37] soon became popular, including the capture of Nombre de Dios and the legendary storming of Veracruz. In fact, his conquering feats amounted to no more than the taking of an isthmus town called Venta de Cruces on 31 January 1573,[38] where they took in supplies. Behind the fables, however, there was one indisputable truth: Drake had come to know well the hitherto unexplored region of the Isthmus and it would serve him well in future expeditions.

This time the Queen, who had not been involved with the project, chose not to acclaim publicly Drake's feats, probably to avoid worsening the already tense relations with Spain; unofficially she took advantage of Drake's success by attacking Spanish possessions on the isthmus.

In his correspondence,[39] the Spanish ambassador in London assured his sovereign that '…perpetrators of and accessories after these acts of plunder [were] Captain Juan Aquines and his brother, and Cer-Ullen Huinter [Sir William Winter, superintendent of the Navy] and many others, and the brothers of that Francisco Drac, and Luis Lader'.

The figure of Drake disappeared for a while, although tradition in the Belfast region has it that he was among the Earl of Essex's troops that put down the Irish revolts.

The French Enter the Scene Once Again

The French civil war once again fostered naval expeditions, although this time of minor importance and with few positive results. The leading role in a skirmish that ended badly was played by Pierre Sanfroy,[40] a seaman native of San Vigor, in the service of Captain Pierre Chuetot, who engaged in privateering on his own account. He had sailed from France in May 1570 on a ship bound for Guinea.

Given the presence of Portuguese forces, they decided to cross the Atlantic by following the Santo Domingo route, without touching the African coast. In the island of Cozumel, they took a ship loaded with blankets, wax and honey, on which they embarked, subsequently setting fire to their own vessel.

The fort of San Mateo 1576-1577. The main threat here was an attack from the sea but assaults from inland were not impossible – the degree of menace is reflected in the size of the guns.

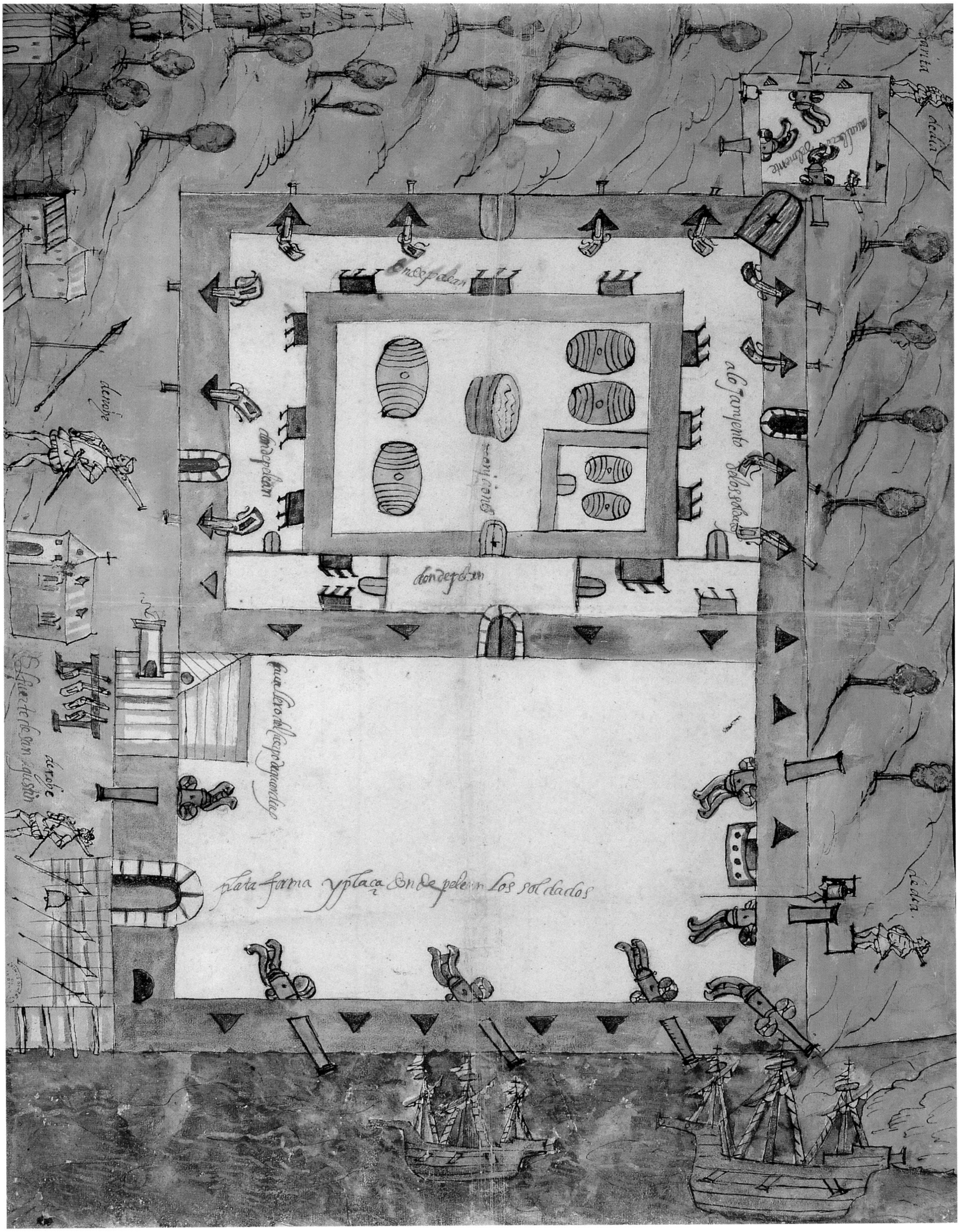
plata forma y placa donde pelean los soldados
donde pelean
alojamiento delos soldados

PATRONATO, 266. Rº 50 — Nº 16

All American strongholds had been warned of the coming of 'el pirata Drake'. Indeed, one of the main obstacles encountered in negotiations over the price to save Cartagena de Indias from destruction was the fact that the English had found a document that referred to Drake in these derogatory terms.

They made landfall on the coast of Yucatan to take in provisions in Hunucmá, a village inhabited by Indians. Once they had occupied the village, they took possession of a silver chalice, a frontal and a red damask chasuble. But finally they were overcome by Spaniards who killed ten of the Frenchmen and took a further ten prisoner, while the rest managed to flee in the ship.

The prisoners were transported to Mérida in Tierra Firme, where four were hanged. A further six, among them Sanfroy himself, were condemned to 'civil death', that is, to serve as slaves. However, their misfortunes did not end here. Summoned by the Inquisition in 1571, they were taken to Mexico where they were tried and handed a variety of sentences.

The next year, Jean Bontemps, at the head of seventy men, attacked the undefended island of Curaçao. His onslaught was met by a *hacendado* named Antonio Barbudo who, with his own troops and a substantial number of Indians, retaliated with cold steel and arrows. Bontemps was killed by an arrow through the throat and Barbudo took his head as a trophy to Santo Domingo.

One of Drake's Disciples Tries his Luck

Two years later, one of Drake's co-religionists, John Oxenham, known to the Spaniards as Oexnam, Ojemkan, Ohemkam or Oxnam, who had seen the treasures of the Indies on the voyage to Panama, decided to engage in privateering on his own account. To this end, he armed a 140-ton ship and sailed for the Isthmus.

He left England in 1575. In Panama, he made contact with a band of runaway slaves led by Juan Vaquero, dismasted his vessel and hid it in Acla Bay. He then set off on foot and followed the river Perenperén to reach the Southern Sea. There he built ships and engaged some seventy men, with whom he lay in wait for the arrival of treasure. They captured a ship loaded with gold, silver and merchandise from Peru and withdrew, hoping to cross the Isthmus and recover their ship before the Spaniards had time to react.

They were too late. The Audiencia of Panama sent Captain Pedro de Ortega with a detachment of eighty well-armed men in pursuit of the plunderers. The Spaniards surprised most of the members of the expedition, capturing almost all of them, including Oxenham. A warning was sent to Nombre de Dios, from whence a flotilla, commanded by General Cristóbal de Eraso, surprised those who were lurking in Acla Bay and captured the ship.

The pirates were taken to Lima. In an *auto da fe* Oxenham, together with Tomás Xeruel and Henry John Butler, was sentenced to take holy orders and was sent to prison for life, after his worldly goods were confiscated and he was forced to work for ten years as an unpaid galley slave. Delivered to the secular arm, the sentence was modified: Oxenham and Xeruel were hanged while Butler was sentenced to life in the galleys.[41]

The following year, Andrew Barker captured a Spanish frigate between Chagres and Veragua from which, among other items, he recovered the four artillery pieces that had been carried by Oxenham's ship.

An Expedition of Reprisal

Andrew Barker's was one of the first privateering voyages to the Indies to be explicitly authorised by the English Crown. His expedition[42] was a measure of reprisal for the damages and losses suffered at the hands of the Spanish Inquisition.

The origins of the story may be traced back to the greed and treachery of one of his fellow countrymen. Andrew Barker lived on Tenerife and, having decided to set up a trade route between the island and Bristol, he returned to England in November 1574, leaving Charles Chester in charge of his affairs.

In March 1575, he chartered the *Christopher of Dartmouth*, commanded by Captain Henry Roberts, to sail to the Canaries. He believed that Chester would have prepared merchandise to enable him to freight the ship for a return journey, but instead he was arrested by the Spanish.

In his absence, Andrew Barker had been denounced by Chester as a Lutheran heretic. The merchandise awaiting dispatch was confiscated, to the loss of some £1,700 for Andrew and his brother John. Roberts managed to sail home in the *Christopher of Dartmouth* thanks to the good offices of a friar, although the payment demanded in return was all the merchandise he had brought from Bristol. Back in England, Barker had to pay the captain £200 in compensation for all the misfortunes he had suffered.

In order to make good their losses, the Barkers obtained a letter of reprisal against Spanish interests, and financed their own flotilla consisting of the *Ragged Staffe*, commanded by Andrew with Philip Roche as skipper, and the *Beare*, captained by William Coxe from Limehouse.

They departed from Plymouth early in June 1575. In Trinidad they made American landfall for the first time and contacted the Indians.

Off the coast of Margarita, they captured a modest vessel from which they took pitch and four or five barrels of Canary wine. Then, in Curaçao, they took in water and victuals. But during the night they were attacked by a group of Spaniards.

Next, near Cabo de Vela, an incident took place that augured ill for the future of the expedition: a dispute arose between Barker and Roche, which marked the beginning of tense relations between both men. Nevertheless, they reached the bay of Tolá, near Cartagena, where they took possession of a frigate transporting gold, silver and emeralds, valued at some £500. One very large emerald mounted in gold was found tied around the thigh of a friar.

After two days in the bay, two Spanish galleons arrived in pursuit of the Englishmen who, although forced to

Sir Francis Drake
Attributed to Marcus Gheeraerts the Younger, 1561-1635.
National Maritime Museum, Greenwich.

abandon the frigate, managed to get away with the booty, which they had already stowed away in their ships.

They passed Nombre de Dios and reached the mouth of the River Chagre, hounded by disease and unable to make contact with runaway slaves. Near Veragua they intercepted a frigate, from which they wrested only insignificant booty, and two Flems joined their crew.

At Veragua a further confrontation occurred between Barker and Roche, which increased tensions. Here, too, it was decided that the *Ragged Staffe*, leaking badly, should be sunk after transferring everything that could be of use to the recently captured frigate.

They proceeded to the Gulf of Honduras, where they plundered a tender carrying victuals and silver valued at around £100. They also captured an important passenger, the notary from Cartagena, for whom they demanded a ransom.

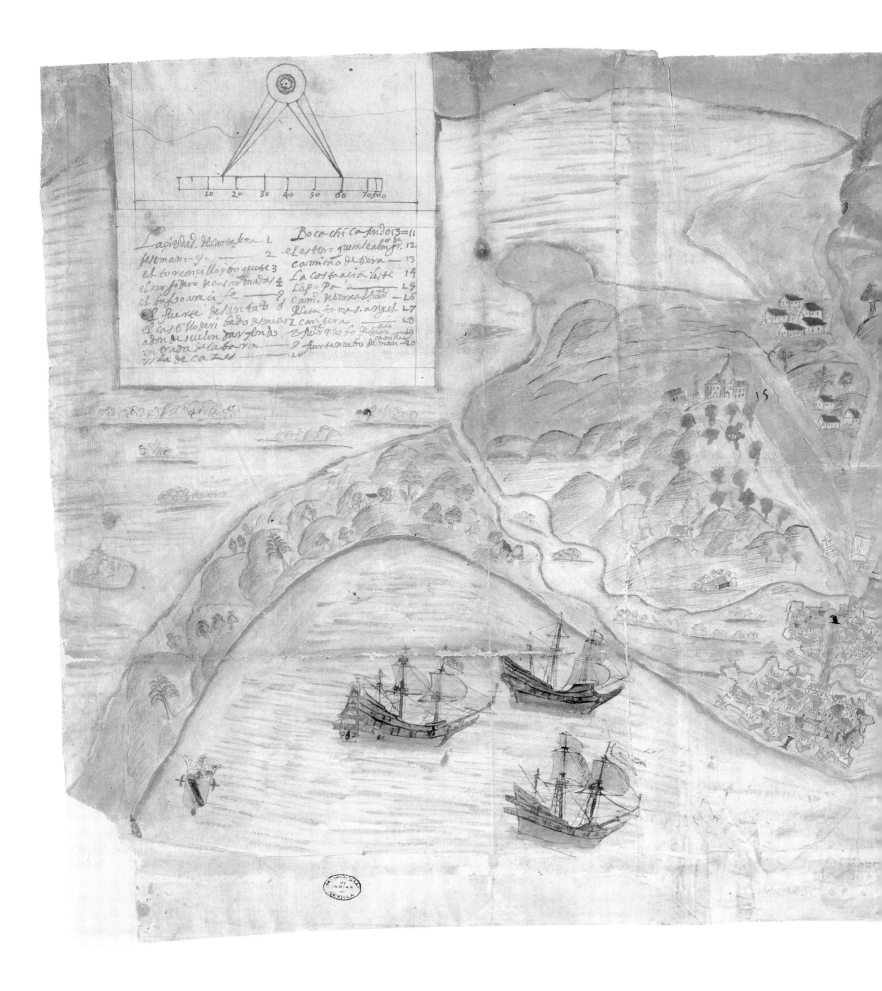

La ciudad de Cartagena — 1
ermani y — 2
el torreoncillo y torreque 3
el surfidero de la armada 4
el baxo are in fe — 5
el fuerte de santa 6
el cayo de los xii deri bados de masa 7
a don de suelen dar fondo
en trada de la barra —
y la de cazes — 10

Boco chi ca fondo 13 = 11
el estero quinta el bacos 12
cam cam no de terra — 13
la costra la seste 14
la po po — 15
cam serra la pan — 16
lata por mas a angel 17
can tera — 18
el puerto de fo roman 19
el puerte nucbo de man 20

15

70

Chart of Cartagena de Indias and its surrounds, 1628.
Cartagena de Indias was one of America's most important cities. Home port of the fleets of Tierra Firme,
it maintained control over trade between the Viceroyalty of Peru and Spain. Drake's assault in 1572 revealed
how weak was the defence of commercial traffic and led the Spanish authorities to redesign the whole defence
structure of the Caribbean.

On the island of San Francisco, William Coxe and a number of followers mutinied, seized command of the expedition and the treasure, and left Barker marooned on the beach with twenty-nine of his corsairs. A Spanish patrol of some sixty men approached under cover of darkness and attacked the stranded men and Andrew Barker was killed alongside others. The rest managed to get back to the ship, still close offshore, and quickly headed out to sea.

They reached an island one league away from San Francisco, where they shared the spoils, including a golden chain that Barker had been wearing on his chest, and separated. On a pinnace captured in San Francisco and a skiff, Coxe and a number of men headed for Trujillo, where, although they managed to storm the city by surprise, they obtained neither gold nor silver.

On the way back to England, bad luck began to prey upon them. The frigate overturned and men and capital were lost, although with material they did manage to salvage, they rebuilt a smaller ship. Misfortunes continued with the death of Philip Roche. But, finally, they reached England with some of the booty, as well as ten demijohns of oil, Oxenham's cannons and other articles.

When they made landfall at Plymouth, they were met by the last of the surprises. John Barker had filed a lawsuit against several members of the crew, accusing them of being accessories in the death of his brother and of leaving him to his fate in the face of the enemy. After a long trial, some were given prison sentences.

A Last Attempt to 'Trade'

On 3 July 1583 a fleet of nine vessels commanded by William Hawkins,[43] John's brother, reached the coast of the island of Margarita. The governor of the island, Juan Sarmiento de Villandrando, went to La Asunción to secure reinforcements, leaving Pedro de Biedma on the island to organise the defence of Pueblo Viejo de la Mar (Porlamar). It seems, however, that the Englishmen only wanted to trade and, after waiting nine days, they withdrew.

Apparently they once again engaged in privateering in English waters for, in 1585 John paid a warranty[44] of £1,000 in favour of his brother William and Humphrey Fones and Company, whose operations in the English Channel would be ratified by a letter of reprisal.

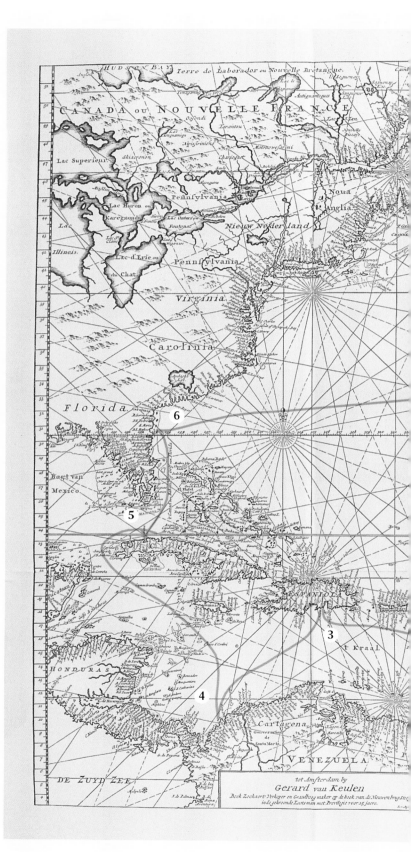

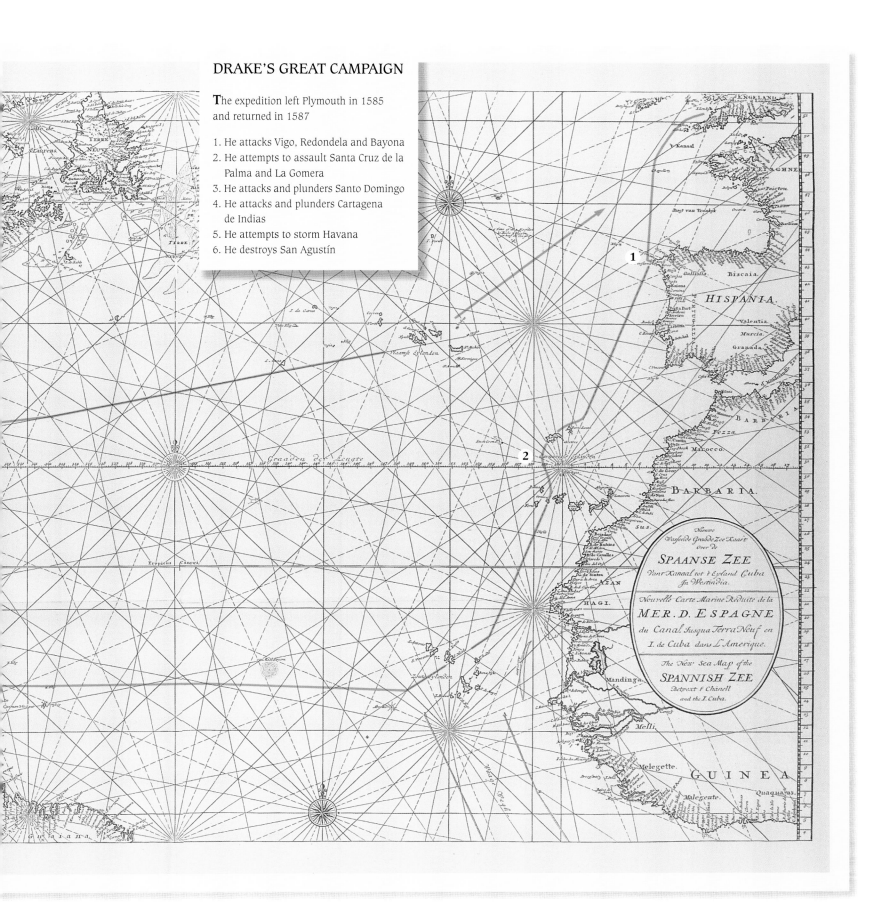

DRAKE'S GREAT CAMPAIGN

The expedition left Plymouth in 1585 and returned in 1587

1. He attacks Vigo, Redondela and Bayona
2. He attempts to assault Santa Cruz de la Palma and La Gomera
3. He attacks and plunders Santo Domingo
4. He attacks and plunders Cartagena de Indias
5. He attempts to storm Havana
6. He destroys San Agustín

THE PRELUDE TO WAR

The 1580s marked further deterioration in Anglo-Spanish relations. Contributing factors were Elizabeth's public homage to Drake after his circumnavigation of the world and the firm support of Antonio of Portugal in her legal battle against Philip II.

For his part, the King of Spain supported the 1579 uprising of Irish Catholics, providing reinforcements for the papal army in the form of volunteers recruited by Recalde in the Cantabrian ports.

In 1584, firm English support of the Low Countries and the expulsion of the Spanish ambassador led to the period of greatest tension between the two countries, aggravated still further the following year by the Treaty of Alliance between England and the rebel provinces, this last was taken to be an official declaration of war and, in reply, all English ships in Spanish ports were seized.

War actually broke out between the two powers in 1586, when an expeditionary force led by the Duke of Leicester was sent to Holland and Queen Elizabeth publicly supported the naval campaign organised by Drake that same year. On the Spanish side, the preparation of the *Gran Armada* was seen by England as an unmistakable declaration of war.

SIR FRANCIS DRAKE'S GREAT CAMPAIGN (1585-1587)

After the great success of his voyage around the world (1577-1580) and enjoying greater prestige thanks to his subsequent knighthood, Drake was in a far better position to secure all manner of support for a new expedition to '…chastise the King of Spain in his Indies…'. Despite initial reticence, fearing reprisals from the Spaniards, the Queen approved the expedition and supplied two well equipped war galleons, the 600-ton *Bonaventure* and the 250-ton *Arot*. Private individuals also provided numerous vessels, outstanding among which were the 400-ton galleon *Leicester*, the *Primrose*, the *Tiger*, the *Minion*, the *Swallow* and others, to form a fleet of twenty-three.

They transported[49] '…two thousand five hundred fighting men…among them five hundred Spanish youths, two cavaliers, and a number of Portuguese troops…'. Drake hoisted his insignia on the *Bonaventure*, while his

THE JEWISH CONVERT CONNECTION

While the activities of Englishmen in the Caribbean are well known, we are not so familiar with English connections with the subjects of the Catholic Monarchy. Most of the inhabitants of Fregenal de la Sierra (Badajoz) – Benito Arias Montano's native town – were of Jewish convert origin[45] and devoted to trade, particularly to black slave traffic. Even the family of the celebrated humanist Pedro de Valencia engaged in traffic, in which it is more than likely that Gómes Suárez de Figueroa, Duke of Feria, Lord of Zafra, Spanish ambassador in London between 1558 and 1559 and staunch protector of subjects of Jewish origin, was also involved.

The presence of the nucleus of Jewish converts in Fregenal extended to the Canary Isles, where one of the governors, Pedro Ponte,[46] was an active convert. Benito Arias Montano himself was in the archipelago during the 1550s, a period of intense commercial exchange with England, although we do not know in what capacity. Hawkins's links with Ponte are well known, as is the participation of the pilot Martínez – whose second surname[47] was characteristic of the Jewish convert community of Fregenal – in his first smuggling operation. There must also have been an extraordinary spirit of mutual trust between Hawkins and Feria, since the Duke was the person behind the 1571 offer to 'change sides'.

Francis Drake also had relations with this community. It seems certain that he was a page at the service[48] of Jane Dormer, the Duchess of Feria, and that as such he would have lived in the early 1560s in Zafra, where he learned to speak and read Spanish. It is possible that he first engaged in the black slave trade while in Extremadura, and that his links with the Hawkins family were established in this way, although others contend that the link was made through family ties with one of John's (Hawkins) brothers. Whatever the case, relations between English smugglers and specific Spanish communities were apparently crucial contributing factors to initial adventures in the Americas.

second-in-command, Frobisher, did likewise on the *Primrose*.

The objective of the plan was to capture Santo Domingo and Cartagena. They would send an expedition overland across the Isthmus to capture treasures in Panama, thence advancing to the silver mines of Honduras. The economic prospects were spectacular: besides the booty, they expected to obtain ransoms for the cities to the astronomical sum of two and a half million gold ducats – twelve times the entire budget of the English government.

The expedition sailed from Plymouth on 24 September 1585, remaining for some time in the Azores to await the

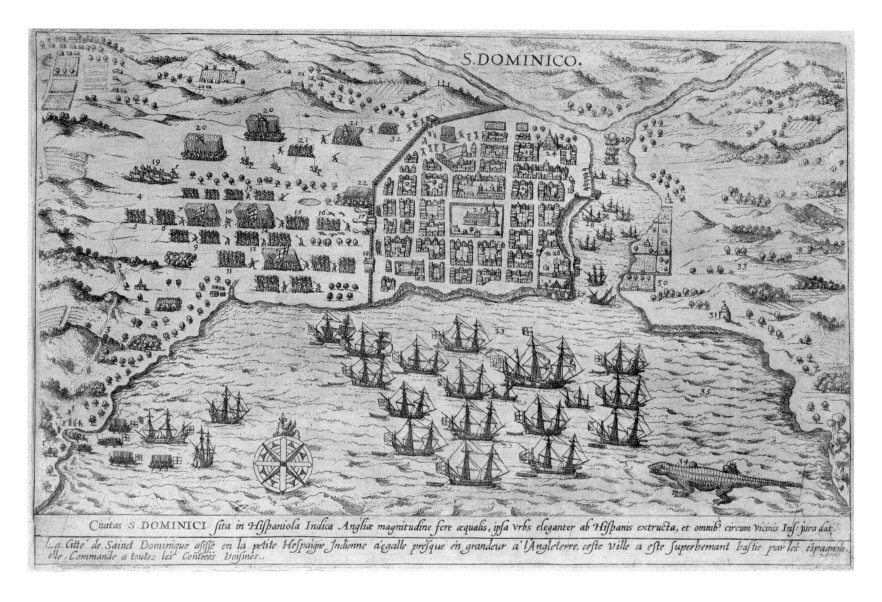

S.DOMINICO.

Ciutas S.DOMINICI sita in Hispaniola Indica Angliæ magnitudine fere æqualis, ipsa vrbs eleganter ab Hispanis extructa, et omnib? circum vicinis Insulis iura dat.

La Citté de Sainct Dominique assise en la petite Hespaigne Jndienne d'egalle presque en grandeur a l'Angleterre, ceste ville a este superbement bastie par les espagnols, elle Commande a toutes les Contrées voisines..

Drake's hopes of making vast profits from his American campaign were dashed after he had taken Santo Domingo. Recently doubts have been cast on the value of the booty he obtained, and it is possible that the citizens managed to deceive the corsair and hide many of the city's treasures.

Indies Fleet, which arrived without incident. Tired of idleness, they proceeded to the coast of Galicia,[50] where they marauded between 7 and 24 October. They attacked Bayona and Redondela without managing to force their surrender; on the other hand, they performed the 'memorable' feats of destroying a hermitage in Vigo and a monastery on the island of San Simón.

In the Canaries, the English fleet was spotted by lookouts and the cities took the necessary precautions. On 11 November the fleet came in sight of Gran Canaria,

but Drake chose not to attack, retracing his steps in an attempt to take Santa Cruz de la Palma by surprise.

Drake's strategy was well planned. The city was protected by forts and militias and a frontal attack would have caused him heavy losses and would have jeopardised his true objective. He therefore divided his forces into two squadrons: the one under his command anchored in front of the city while the other proceeded to Tazacorte.

For five days the English made no move; the defenders relaxed their guard and returned to their everyday agricultural tasks. When he felt that the defences had been reduced, Drake ordered the attack. The Spaniards regrouped and responded by opening fire from the two forts – so accurately that one of the first projectiles made

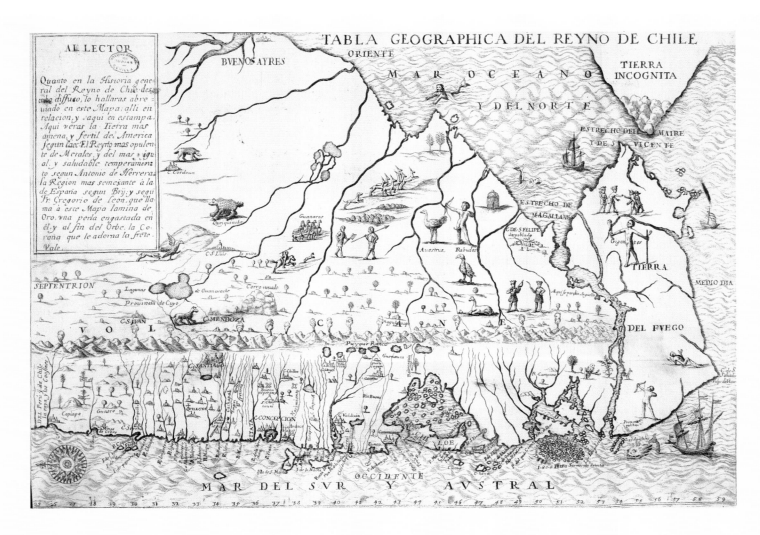

THE CONQUEST OF THE PACIFIC

The conquest of the Pacific was a long-cherished ambition. For years, Spanish ships attempted to make the return voyage by sailing east with the intention of reaching the American coast, but they were unable to find a suitable route until 1565, when Andrés de Urdaneta discovered the way back. From then on, the establishment of a regular shipping line between the Philippines and the port of Acapulco, the Galeón de Manila, made the perilous crossing of the Indian Ocean unnecessary.

The Adventure of the *Golden Hind*

In 1577 Drake prepared one of his famous expeditions. It seems that at first it was intended to be a voyage of exploration to verify trade possibilities on the American coast, but probably after his audience with the Queen he decided to venture to the Pacific coast.

On 13 December four ships and a pinnace sailed from the port of Plymouth. The 240-ton flagship *Pelican* was characterised by an unusually shallow draught – about 10 feet – which allowed it to enter coves and roadsteads, the ideal places in which to find refuge and carry out repairs. The fleet was completed by the *Elizabeth*, the *Marigold*, the supply ship *Swan* and the pinnace *Benedith*, which had been exchanged for a Portuguese ship renamed the *Christopher*. The men totalled 160 and the expedition was generously funded, the Queen herself having contributed 1,000 crowns.

On the way to Cape Verde, they took a Portuguese ship and engaged the services of pilot Nuño Silva, very experienced in the Indies run. They crossed the Atlantic and went in search of the Straits of Magellan. In honour of his protector, Lord Christopher Hatton, Drake changed the name of his ship for that of the *Golden Hind*.

He entered the Straits with the *Golden Hind*, the *Marigold* and the *Elizabeth*, although only the first reached the other end. The *Marigold* sank with all her men while the *Elizabeth* deserted and returned to England.

In the Pacific, Drake took ninety men and decided to try his luck at robbery. To this end he devised a stratagem: he would visit defenceless coastal cities passing himself off as a Spaniard and then making unexpected attacks. In this way he managed to capture a number of ships, including a merchantman in Valparaíso, from which he took 25,000 fine gold pesos and the legendary cross of emeralds, half a finger thick, which he presented as a gift to the Queen.

After several incursions of this kind, he captured the *Nuestra Señora de la Concepción*, which was transporting a substantial cargo from Acapulco to Panama, and two of her pilots, Sánchez Colchero and Martín Aguirre, who bore the letters of the Pacific. Luck was with Drake; with these letters he could make the crossing to the Philippines.

He reached the coast of California, where he anchored in an inlet that he named New Albion. There he repaired his ships and took in provisions for the long homeward voyage. He began the crossing on July 23, finally reaching Plymouth, via the Marianas, Philippines, Moluccas, the Indian Ocean and Africa, on September 26 1580.

The expedition had yielded handsome profits, some £250,000, a sum greater than the annual budget of the British Parliament, which Drake had obtained by assaulting defenceless towns and ships.

Greater still, however, was the prestige he acquired as a hero, although he had done no more than follow the route opened by the Spanish fifty-eight years earlier. English propaganda launched the idea that Drake was the first commander to circumnavigate the world and relegated Elcano to the lowly rank of one of Magellan's lieutenants.

Drake became a man of distinction. He purchased Buckland Abbey in Devon for £3,400, was appointed mayor of Plymouth and came to represent Cornwall in the English Parliament.

Later, other English and Dutch seamen would follow Drake's footsteps in search of the Northern Passage; Cavendish did so between 1586 and 1588, and later Le Mayre, Noort and others attained glory in the icy lands of Cathay.

a direct hit on the *Bonaventure*, causing numerous casualties. Drake missed death by a hair's breadth.

When they had recovered from the shock, the English began to disembark. The launches were received with cannon, musket and harquebus fire; the first was hit full square and sank. Finally, the English gave up and withdrew. They attempted the same strategy in La Gomera, but the results were equally disastrous.

Once in the Antilles, Drake made straight for Santo Domingo, where the first Audiencia de Indias had been established. Its president, who was also governor, Cristóbal Ovalle, was a man of letters with absolutely no knowledge of military tactics.

The defence forces consisted merely of 100 mounted men, 500 harquebusiers and militias formed by '...a few residents with pikes and lances which they had inherited from their fathers or grandfathers, conquerors of the land, and a few harquebusiers, though without gunpowder, bullets or other ammunition...'.[51]

Drake wanted to avoid direct confrontation and so, during the night, he disembarked about 1,000 men armed with harquebuses and muskets. At first light they formed a column that advanced overland, while the fleet remained in sight of the defences concentrated in the port area.

When the English reached the gates of the city, they were faced[52] by '...thirty men on horseback and all the women of the city, although these were armed only with the clothes they wore...'. They all fled, including Governor Ovalle, taking everything he could with him. The presence of the column in the rearguard was enough to force the city to surrender.

In the port, Drake took a ship which he christened *New Year's Gift* and, once inside the city, he entrenched himself in the cathedral.[53] He demanded a tributo de quema of one million ducats, which was not paid. In reprisal he began systematically to destroy the city building by building. He reduced the sum to 500,000 ducats, finally receiving the 25,000 ducats that the citizens had managed to scrape together.

After a sojourn of thirty days in the city, Drake took what plunder he could, including jewels, ewers, clothes and the church bells, and returned to the ships. Once on the high seas, he sent ten galleons with everything he had taken in Vigo, Santiago and Santo Domingo back to Calais. In the meantime, however, Calais had been taken by the Spaniards, who thus managed, in one fell swoop, to recover everything that had been wrested from them.[54]

When Drake returned to England, he learned that Philip II had asked for his head, but Queen Elizabeth had no intention of meeting such a demand. She had sworn revenge on the Spanish king for having sent troops in support of the Irish rebels, and now the opportunity to insult the Spaniard could not have been bettered: Elizabeth received Drake in port and lunched with him, together with her entire diplomatic corps, on board the Golden Hind. *When dessert had been served, she knighted Drake by touching his shoulders three times with the French ambassador's sword, and granting him a coat of arms featuring the globe with the Golden Hind sailing on top. On 1 January 1581 Queen Elizabeth sported the famous cross of emeralds, a gift from Drake, on her breast.*

THE CHANGE IN THE CALENDAR

In 1582 Pope Gregory XIII added ten days to the Julian calendar, which had been in use in Rome since 45 BC, to maintain correct correspondence between the calendar and the seasons, also introducing a new system of determining leap years. Thus the New Style or Gregorian calendar came into existence.

Protestant countries refused to accept Gregory's modifications and continued to use the Julian calendar until the mid 18th century.

Such differences introduced an uncertainty factor in the already complex dating of the 16th and 17th centuries. Thus, for the same event there are two dates, the one given in English chronicles and the one in chronicles by the rest of their contemporaries.

By way of an example, when Morgan took the island of Santa Catalina (Providence) in December 1670, English sources assure us that the event took place on the 15th, while for the French filibusters who fought with him and for the Spanish defenders, the assault was carried out on Christmas Day.

The next objective was Cartagena. News of Drake's mighty fleet had spread to all corners of the Caribbean, and the cities were prepared. Governor Pedro Fernández de Bustos of Cartagena, evacuated all the women and children, hid the treasure and prepared his defences. He requested reinforcements from the surrounding towns and villages, eventually managing to put together a force of 54 cavalry, 450 harquebusiers, 100 pikemen, 20 negroes armed with blunderbusses and 400 Indian archers. The fort of El Boquerón was complete, although construction work of La Caleta was still unfinished. To defend this exposed flank, the governor dug trenches.

The harbour mouth was closed with a chain, although no cannons were sited to block Boca Grande and Boca Chica, the two accesses to La Laguna. The defences were reinforced by a saetta (a three-masted, lateen-rigged vessel of 50-100 tons) and two galleys commanded by Pedro Vique Manrique, stationed between the harbour and the chain.

Drake hove to off Cartagena on 19 February 1586. He had the good luck to capture two slaves who were sailing past in a launch and who described the Spanish defences. To evade them, the fleet entered by Boca Grande and anchored safely in the lagoon.

At 10 o'clock that night the English began to disembark at El Boquerón, but the chains and the defence forces inflicted heavy casualties and forced them back. Next they tried their luck at La Caleta. Six hundred men disembarked at La Punta del Judío, advancing up the beach to avoid traps with poisoned spikes. They were held up from the trenches until the archers and the negroes gave up the fight. Then the defenders dispersed, leaving the city open to attack.

The English took everything of value, amounting to a total of 400,000 ducats – jewels, slaves, eighty pieces of artillery and the cathedral bells. As a tributo de quema, they demanded the exorbitant sum of one million ducats.

The bishop interceded in the negotiations, claiming that it was impossible to put together such an amount. Drake was furious, for among the papers he had found in the city hall was a letter patent announcing the arrival of 'el pirata Drake'. The Englishman attempted to convince the bishop that he was not a pirate but a soldier of the Queen commanding a fleet. Given such circumstances, the bishop's good offices proved to be useless.

Governor Pedro Fernández del Busto managed to reduce the sum to 100,000 ducats but Drake

RICHART ATTACKS HAVANA

Some days before Drake's arrival in Havana, a fleet was sighted on the horizon and the alarm was sounded. Everything seemed to indicate that the ships were an English advance guard, but it turned out to be a French squadron commanded by Richart, consisting of two of his own vessels and a frigate taken from Hernando Casanova, for whom the Frenchman intended to demand a ransom. Richart was unfortunate, however, for Álvaro Pérez de Maya fell upon him, freed the frigate and the prisoners, and captured one of the French ships and eight pirates, Richart among them. They were taken to Bayamo where Captain Rojas ordered them all to be hanged, except for a nine-year-old cabin boy.

Richart's son, who had managed to flee, swore vengeance. He sailed to the south of the island and attempted to take Santiago by surprise. He carried out a first attack on 1 May, but the cannons and harquebuses of Captain Gómez Patiño kept him at bay. Twenty days later French reinforcements arrived in four ships.

A second assault was attempted and, although the French managed to secure their position in the harbour and burned the main church of San Francisco and a number of other buildings, they were eventually repelled, a great many having been killed.

subsequently had second thoughts and demanded a further 100,000 for the monastery of San Francisco and the abattoir. Eventually, the citizens managed to raise 107,000 pesos, which the Englishman accepted. In a display of irony, he issued a receipt[55] worded as follows: 'Agnosco me centenos et septies mille connatos a Gubernatore civibusque, Cartagenae recepisse. 20 die Martii 1586. Fra. Drac.'.

In the confrontations he had lost two-thirds of his men, leaving his military strength drastically reduced. Furthermore, knowing that enemy reinforcements were sure to arrive, that the warning systems had worked and that all the towns and cities of the region knew of his arrival, he decided against the attack of Panama. Instead, on 12 April he set sail, having been at Cartagena for two months.

Havana was expecting an attack, and the city's governor, Gabriel de Luján, prepared his defences. He recruited 230 volunteers to reinforce the garrison, and a further 300 soldiers were sent from Mexico.

On 29 May Drake reached the city with sixteen ships and fourteen launches. He had been lying in wait for the fleet of Nueva España, which did not take to sea. Some 700 Spanish harquebusiers and 300 soldiers came out to meet the English flotilla.

In the face of such a display of strength, Drake again decided to avoid a fight. He set off again with a Spanish flotilla in pursuit to observe his moves.

In Florida, on his way back to Europe, Drake attacked the fort of San Juan de Pinos and burnt the city of San Agustín, which had been abandoned by its inhabitants.[56] On 9 June he made port in the colony of Virginia[57] and evacuated the colonists, reaching England on 28 July 1587.

According to Bernardino de Mendoza,[58] the Spanish ambassador, Drake returned with eighteen damaged ships and losses amounting to 1,000 men. His cargo consisted of leather, sugar and only 200,000 ducats, which was not even enough to pay his crew. Indeed, riots ensued when the money was shared out since some crew members felt that they had been swindled.

From the economic point of view the expedition was an utter failure: dividends were shared out of just fifteen shillings per pound – a loss of 25 per cent. Furthermore, all of Europe questioned the potential profitability and security of trade with the Indies. In the political sphere, such aggression against Spanish possessions overseas played a crucial role in the launching of Philip II's *Empresa de Inglaterra* (the 'Enterprise of England' – the 'Spanish Armada'), which would be a resounding failure the following year.

In 1590 Martin Frobisher was given command of the legendary Revenge *and
served as one of John Hawkins's lieutenants in the blockade of the Fleets.
Despite their best efforts, they attained none of their objectives. Two years later,
Frobisher replaced Raleigh at the head of a squadron designated to sail with
Cumberland's forces in the Azores. The operation was to be a disaster.*

Chapter III

CORSAIRS IN TIME OF WAR
(1588-1604)

THE GREAT ARMADA OF 1588: *FLAVIT JEHOVA ET DISSIPATI*

In January 1586, after news had reached the Spanish Court of Drake's attacks against the coasts of the Peninsula and the disembarkation of Leicester's expeditionary forces in support of the Dutch rebels, Philip II decided to take definitive exemplary action against England.

Some time earlier, Álvaro de Bazán, the Marquis de Santa Cruz, had suggested the idea of forming a Great Armada to carry an army to England and put an end to the arrogance of Queen Elizabeth and her corsairs. The idea gelled and the project[1] was presented. The operation had two objectives: to destroy any enemy formation that attempted to hinder the action, and to transport and disembark troops, artillery and impedimenta to establish a bridgehead from which to penetrate England and force the enemy to accept any conditions the Spaniards cared to impose.

This major enterprise involved the preparation of 510 ships, weighing a total of 110,570 tons, and eighty-six oared boats. The crews would number 16,612, transporting 55,000 infantry soldiers and 1,200 horses. The cost was estimated at three and a half million ducats. But subsequent news of the assault on Santo Domingo propelled the campaign into the forefront.

In the summer of 1587 the original plan was replaced by a combined operation with the Spanish army in the Netherlands, commanded by Alesander Farnese, the Duke of Parma. Santa Cruz would cover the Channel crossing of Parma's troops, helping them establish a bridgehead. But then, in February 1588, Santa Cruz died. The incompetent Duke of Medina Sidonia replaced him.

Early in April the Great Armada was ready, although bad weather delayed its departure. Finally, on 22 July, having been forced to make a stopover in the ports of Galicia, the Armada – a total of 127 ships amassing almost 50,000 tons – sailed for England. Eight days later, the vessels entered the English Channel and sighted the smoke from the innumerable clifftop beacon fires that announced their presence.

The major part of the English fleet, commanded by Lord Charles Howard of Effingham, was at Plymouth. The second division was commanded by Lord Henry Seymour. The vice-admirals – Sir John Hawkins, Sir Francis Drake and Sir Martin Frobisher, among others – were old acquaintances. Despite their numerical superiority (226 ships), they avoided a direct confrontation, relying on prevailing winds and the Channel currents to do part of the work for them. The Spaniards contemplated sailing in to meet them and attempting to defeat the English in the harbour but since this was not the intended objective, the possibility was ruled out.

On 6 August the Great Armada anchored at Calais and waited for Parma. The English dropped anchor across the Channel and held a council of war. Although they knew of the Spanish plans, it would not be easy to thwart them. From the outset a frontal attack was ruled out, but the idea of using fire ships was discussed. During the night, eight burning vessels were launched against the Armada and, fearing that these might be the famous *mecheros del infierno* (fuses of hell), Medina Sidonia fired a cannon ordering the fleet to weigh anchor. The flagship and another fifty vessels responded to the signal, while the rest dispersed and drifted towards the Gravelines bank.

At dawn, the English launched a full-scale attack. At first, the Spaniards merely resisted, until the strong wind allowed them to reform and retaliate on equal terms.

Once again, the English eluded a direct confrontation. Initial losses amounted to the eight English fire ships, a Spanish vessel sunk, two suffering broadsides and a galleass run aground.

There was no significant loss of life, and, having frustrated the Spaniards' objective, the victory on this occasion went to the English.

Seeing that it was now impossible to cross the Channel, the Spanish began to prepare their retreat. They placed the flagship and the best galleons – some six to twelve vessels of great tonnage – in the rearguard and with these managed to keep at bay the 109 English ships, and so avoid entering into combat. On 11 August, the English withdrew.

Six days later the first of a series of terrible storms fell on the Armada, dispersing the ships. Most of the fleet,[2] a total of more than fifty ships, reached Cantabria on

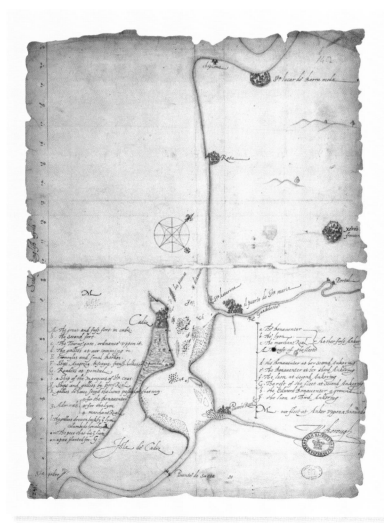

DRAKE'S ASSAULT ON CÁDIZ[3]

When news reached England of preparations for the 'Enterprise of England', they were taken as an official declaration of war. Drake proposed to take a squadron to the Spanish ports and thwart, or at least delay, the preparations.

On 12 April he sailed from Plymouth with seventeen men-of-war and the same number of supply ships. On the 29th he attacked the ships anchored in the bay of Cadiz, sinking a Genoese nao and setting fire to a 670-ton galleon of Santa Cruz's, eight hookers loaded with victuals, and a number of smaller vessels.

The Nueva España fleet, consisting of twenty-five large naos, was anchored in Puerto Real, but fear of the sandbanks and constant harassment by the galleys of Pedro de Acuña forced the English to withdraw. Eighteen Spanish ships had been destroyed and six captured, although only three of these were of any military value.

The arrival of the Duke of Medina Sidonia with major reinforcements forced Drake to sail full speed to Lisbon, where Santa Cruz was waiting. Drake preferred not to engage in any action and Santa Cruz chose not to pursue the Englishman, since he had no infantry and his forces were insufficient.

Drake returned south, with the intention of blocking the passage of the fleets and preventing – or delaying – their provisioning. His assault on Lagos having been repelled, he attacked Sagres and took the castle, which broke off all communication between Andalucía and Lisbon.

Three weeks later he weighed anchor and set sail for England. In the Azores he captured the galleon *San Felipe* on its return voyage from the East Indies, from which he wrested booty estimated at £140,000. This action proved to be ideal for propaganda purposes.

The plan of Drake's assault on Cadiz.

21 September. Then the stragglers began to arrive until a total of ninety-two vessels had anchored – two-thirds of the number that had originally sailed from Spain.

From a military and cost-of-life point of view, the outcome was acceptable. In political terms, however, it was a disaster. Not only had the Spaniards failed to meet their objective, but enemy propaganda magnified a non-existent victory by attributing it to the will of God: *Flavit Jehova et dissipati* (God blew and they dispersed).

THE ENGLISH REPLY

Once it had been confirmed that the Spanish Armada had left the Channel, the English took stock of the situation. The Privy Council[4] was of the opinion that the Spanish capacity to retaliate had been substantially reduced and that the silver fleets and coast of Spain were now ill-defended. The French ambassador in London, Duplessis Mornay, recommended that immediate action be taken, the Venetian ambassador in Madrid was of the same opinion.

Thus, on 7 September Howard was sent a secret message in which he was ordered to devise a plan to intercept the fleets transporting precious metals back from the Americas. In his proposal he counted on the good offices of his second-in-command, Francis Drake.

There was opposition, however. William Cecil, the Lord Treasurer, thought that the Spanish withdrawal was a stratagem to leave the way free for the army in the Netherlands to invade. Howard and Hawkins were of the same opinion, and they insisted that the English objective be to control the Channel and thwart any invasion.

At a meeting held on 10 September, Howard and Drake informed those attending that it was impossible to engage in any action before November, by which time the Indies fleet would be safely back in Sanlúcar. The Spanish, in the meantime, quickly repaired the damage to their ships and were once again ready to defend themselves.

English opinion was that it was now imperative to destroy the Spanish Armada before it had time to reorganise and, to achieve this, there was no alternative but to send a fleet with an expeditionary force that would raze ports and shipyards to the ground. This involved organising 'summer cruises' similar to those that had been so successful in the American campaigns.

THE CAPTURE OF *NUESTRA SEÑORA DEL ROSARIO*

One of the most controversial episodes in the 'Enterprise of England', about which reams of paper have been written, was the capture of the Andalucían flagship *Nuestra Señora del Rosario*.

After colliding with the *Santa Catalina*, the *Rosario* went adrift. And while there is no doubt that its capture was due to this circumstance, the response of its commander, Pedro Valdés, was severely criticised.

The accusations levelled against Valdés were basically two: in the first place, the *Rosario* was transporting treasure that should have been put in safe keeping immediately. Having let off a volley of salvoes to warn the fleet, Valdés sent a boat to inform Medina Sidonia of the situation. In the second place, it seems that Valdés surrendered without firing a single shot. Furthermore, he should have thrown the money, the forty valuable bronze cannons and the gunpowder overboard to prevent them from falling into enemy hands.

Whatever the case, the fact is that they fell into the hands of Drake, and this is the most interesting part of the story. The *Rosario* was discovered adrift by the 200-ton English ship the *Margaret and John*, but seeing that it was impossible even to attempt an attack, the captain went in search of the *Ark Royal* to inform Lord Howard of the position of the Spanish ship.

Francis Drake was the first vice-admiral in Howard's division, and the latter had appointed him commander of the fleet. When Drake heard the news, disobeying orders he changed course and 'chanced upon' the *Rosario*. Drake, on the *Revenge* with Seymour's *Roebuck* in support, threatened Valdés with combat without quarter if he did not surrender.

The Spaniard capitulated. Together with forty others Valdés was taken on board the *Revenge*, where he was treated with the utmost courtesy. It was apparently during supper that Spanish indiscretion provided Drake with the information about the objectives of the Armada that proved to be crucial in subsequent actions.

The jewellery, the treasure and valuable objects were transferred to the *Revenge*. Valdés stayed with Drake until August 11, and throughout the whole of his captivity, until February 1593, he remained under the Englishman's protection.

At the end of the campaign, Drake's conduct came in for sharp criticism. Howard reluctantly accepted his subordinate's excuses, knowing that he could not take drastic action against the corsair due to the latter's fame. The officers of the *Margaret and John* vociferously demanded their share of the booty and other high-ranking officers, such as Martin Frobisher, accused Drake of villainy, irresponsibility and greed.

But worse still was the anger of the Queen when she learned that of the 50,000 ducats wrested from the Spaniards less than half reached London. Drake claimed that they had been stolen from him by both English and Spanish.

His explanations were far from convincing, and further suspicions were aroused when Sir Francis purchased a magnificent mansion, 'The Herbar', from Sir Richard Grenville.

As from that moment and until his death ten years later, Drake's activities were subject to strict surveillance.

The Belem tower dominates Lisbon's harbour. Although few trusted him, Drake was placed in command of the expedition to sink the Spanish fleet Cantabria in 1589. But Drake had another idea in mind, namely the sacking of Lisbon. He had not, however, expected the city to be so well fortified, and the operation ended in resounding failure.

The plan proposed by Drake and Norris, commander-in-chief of the army, was opposed by Howard and Hawkins, who considered it disproportionate in the deployment of resources and men; they advocated a naval blockade instead. They proposed placing six war galleons backed by squadrons of corsairs in the Azores. The other provisioning route, the English Channel, would be blocked by a similar squadron.

However, Drake and Norris prevailed and, on 30 September, Lord William Cecil presented his project, which established three objectives: to destroy the King of Spain's galleons, which were supposedly concentrated in Lisbon and Cadiz; to occupy Lisbon, and from here block communications with America; to take some of the islands of the Azores to complete the blockade.

The main artificers of the victory over the Armada, Charles Howard and John Hawkins, were excluded from the enterprise,[5] and the command was handed to Drake. Norris was put in charge of the land forces, the Dutch

rebels and the King of Morocco supplied reinforcements, and the complicity was secured of the Prior of Crato, pretender to the Portuguese throne.

In February 1589 news reached London that the Spanish warships had sought refuge in the ports of Cantabria. On the 23rd of that same month, Drake and Norris were informed of this and given a new plan of action: they would sail to Cantabria and destroy the ships at anchor. Only after fulfilling this objective would they attack the port of Lisbon. There they would disable all the ships they found and help Don Antonio to recover the throne, provided he had enough supporters. Even in these circumstances, they would remain in Lisbon only until the new Portuguese monarch paid them the sums agreed upon with the queen. They would then proceed to the Azores, where they would take an island to serve as the base for the blockade of the Indies fleets.

The Queen distrusted Drake and she appointed to her military council a secretary of the Privy Council, Anthony Ashley, whose mission was to advise Drake and Norris and to keep a diary of the conduct of both chiefs and officers. Furthermore, before the forces departed, the Queen sent them a letter in which she reminded those in command that their first obligation was to destroy the Spanish vessels in the ports, and that if they disobeyed

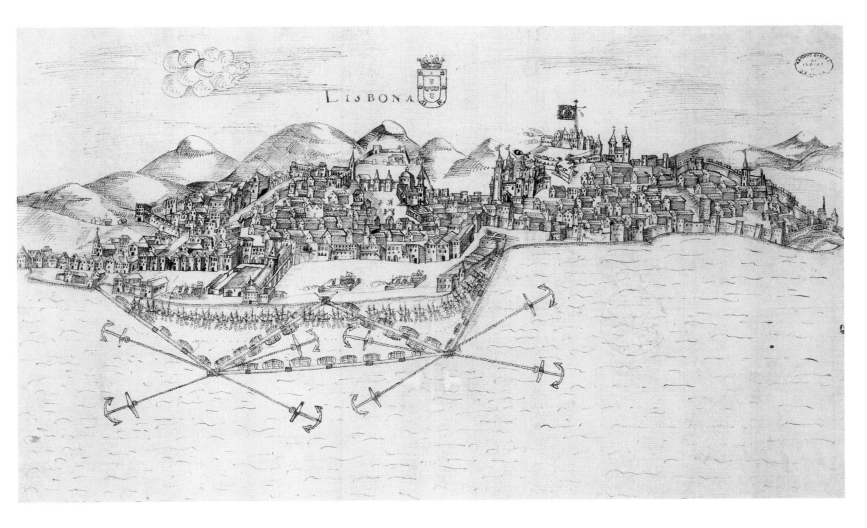

Lisbon in 1596.
The English attack of 1589 had three main objectives to be carried out in order: first the King of Spain's galleons would be destroyed, next the queen's navy would take Lisbon and third, from Lisbon, they would block communications with America.

this order they would be considered traitors and tried as such.

The Spanish spies[6] acted with diligence. Manuel Andrada, one of Don Antonio's secretaries, sent the Spanish ambassador a copy of the agreements reached in London, and Antonio Escobar, Don Antonio's ambassador in France, who had also sold himself to the Spanish, sent all important news he received back to Spain via London.

On 28 April 1589, 150 ships of the English fleet, transporting 20,000 men, sailed from Plymouth bound for the Iberian Peninsula. Before their departure, the first conflicts with Elizabeth had already taken place – Drake and Norris had hidden Robert Devereux, Earl of Essex, a young man of twenty-one who was the Queen's favourite and who had fled from her arms to take part in the venture.

Near the French coast, twenty-four of the fifty Dutch ships that Drake had confiscated deserted, taking almost 2,000 men with them.

At first, Drake considered dividing the fleet, so that one half would satisfy the desires of Elizabeth while he sailed with the remainder to Lisbon to satisfy his own. However, deciding that the division of forces would leave him with too small a contingent, he opted for directly fulfilling his own objective. He dispatched a letter alleging that the wind was against him and, on 4 May, he reached La Coruña. The city was unprepared: news had arrived of the official plans, but not of the maverick Drake's.

After an onslaught lasting fourteen days, Drake ordered his men to re-embark. He had sacrificed 1,300 men and the spoils he had obtained could not possibly offset such losses. Furthermore, ten Dutch vessels had deserted, taking another 1,000 men with them. Drake set a course for Lisbon, presenting all number of excuses, while Norris sent a written request for cannons and thirty companies of veterans with whom to continue the war in Spain.

On 26 May the news reached London. Enraged, the Queen informed the Privy Council that her orders had been disobeyed and she disregarded the explanations of the commanders.

Having disembarked[7] in Peniche and failed in their assault of Lisbon, the English withdrew on 19 July, hounded on their rearguard by Martín de Padilla and the galleys of Alonso de Bazán.

On 5 July Essex reached Plymouth with fifteen ships, and prepared the Court to receive the news that would shortly follow. The main objectives had not been fulfilled, although it was expected that major profits would have been obtained from the sack of La Coruña and Lisbon, or at least this is what they had been led to believe. News of the disaster led to an investigation, and Drake and Norris were ordered to draw up detailed accounts of expenditure and profits.

Protests on the part of the Hansa ports forced the English to return most of the sixty ships captured in Lisbon and, in the absence of this booty, the campaign was a financial disaster.[8] Of the £200,000 invested, only £20,000 were recovered; the losses therefore amounting to 90 per cent. Elizabeth herself lost £50,000.

Riots broke out among the troops when they were demobbed, since their pay amounted to only fifteen shillings per head. Indeed, the protests became so violent that seven men were hanged as an example to the others.

Drake and Norris reached London on 26 August. On the 27th they came before a commission chaired by Richard Hawkins. After several sessions, a detailed report was presented in mid September. The conclusion was that the expedition had been a financial and strategic disaster for which Drake and Norris were directly responsible.

However, since the authorities wanted neither to mete out exemplary punishment in public nor to admit the magnitude of the disaster, Drake was removed from active service and appointed supervisor of the defences of Plymouth, and it was not until 1595, six years later, that he once again formed part of an expedition. John Norris was also removed from service until the spring of 1591, when he joined the English troops stationed in France.

The English strategy of fostering the 'summer cruises' had failed utterly. In Hawkins's words, 'Her Majesty did everything by halves, and through insignificant invasions taught the Spaniards how to defend themselves'.[9]

THE OTHER BATTLE: HOUNDING THE INDIES FLEETS

The assault of Spanish cities in the Americas had so far proven to be undertakings yielding little profit. The costs were high and the risks higher still. Furthermore, in most cases the amount of precious metals deposited in Spain's American cities was small and the places themselves scattered around the Caribbean. It therefore seemed more expedient to wait until the Spaniards had extracted and amalgamated the silver, weighed and minted it, and transported it back to the coasts of Europe where, given a stroke of good luck, it might be wrested from them.

The initiative of Drake and Norris having failed, the Privy Council decided to alter their strategy and foster campaigns focussing on the Azores with the objective of capturing the fleets from the Indies. Several men pursued this objective with tenacity, though nobody did so with the earnestness of George Clifford.

George Clifford, third Earl of Cumberland, had squandered[10] a vast fortune through gambling, and vowed to recover it as quickly as possible. He made his first attempt in 1589 with a squadron of thirteen ships and 450 men. They sailed to the Azores, but the Indies fleet, remembering the incidents with Drake in the Caribbean, did not leave port.

THE CAPTURE OF THE *REVENGE* (1591)

When Marcos de Aramburu came to the island of Flores, the only ship he found anchored there was Grenville's *Revenge*. It seems that some of the Englishman's crew were still on land and their commander did not want to abandon them. Furthermore, he was convinced that the qualities of his ship were sufficient to break through the Spanish blockade without suffering too much damage.

But he was wrong. The *Revenge* was surrounded and her two support ships, the *Golden Noble* and the *Foresight*, chose to remain a prudent distance away. The battle began with the Spanish concentrating their fire on the *Revenge*, which withstood the onslaught reasonably well. Grenville, seeing that his support ships could do nothing to help him, ordered them to withdraw.

Several unsuccessful attempts were made to board the *Revenge*, until finally Aramburu's galleon attacked from the stern and a number of his men managed to get on board and take the English flag.

Despite the fact that on occasions he was attacked simultaneously by four enemy ships, the Englishman refused to surrender and responded firmly to any attempt to board.

During the night the Spaniards granted a truce to the English who, on the following morning, September 11, continued to resist. Grenville received a musket bullet in the leg and was later wounded in the head by an enemy harquebusier. To avoid capture, he ordered the ship to be sunk, but he changed his mind on the strength of opposition from some of the men.

Bazán offered Grenville the opportunity to surrender, assuring him that he would spare their lives and return them to England. A delegation of officers accepted the terms. Grenville was taken on board the *San Pablo*, Bazán's flagship, where he succumbed to his head wound the following day. He was forty-nine-years old.

Some days later the *Revenge* was caught in a storm at sea and sank in the Atlantic.

On 6 September Clifford reached Fayal in the Azores where, determined to make his voyage profitable, he captured seven merchantmen. He then withdrew to reorganise his forces and on the 14th sacked the town, losing men in the process though securing substantial plunder.

John Hawkins[11] took to sea once again in June 1590, accompanied by Martin Frobisher, commanding six ships. Sir John's mission was to observe the movements of Spanish squadrons in the vicinity of the coast of Galicia, while Frobisher, on the legendary *Revenge*, spied on the Spanish fleet near the Azores.

They were discovered, and the Spanish authorities sent word to Havana, where it was decided that the fleets would remain for the winter. The treasure[12] was sent in four frigates to Viana, in the north of Portugal, without being seen. From here it was transported overland on 1,125 mules to Seville.

Tired of waiting, Frobisher returned to England, arriving in Plymouth on 27 September. Hawkins decided to make a move and in mid September sailed to the Azores. The Spaniards took advantage of this by sending 4,000 soldiers to Brittany without encountering resistance of any kind.

Another illustrious personage, Sir Richard Grenville,[13] stationed his squadron near Finisterre, where he confronted a flotilla commanded by Pedro de Zubiaur. Grenville lost seven ships and was forced to withdraw.

In 1591, the Spanish fleet at last set sail, transporting a substantial amount of treasure accumulated over previous years. The English were informed of the movement by their spies and attempted to block their arrival by stationing two squadrons, one of privateers, commanded by George Clifford, in Cape St Vincent, and another, belonging to the Royal Navy, commanded by Thomas Howard, Earl of Suffolk, in the Azores.

Suffolk was in charge of fourteen vessels, among them four large galleons, the flagship *Defiance*, the *Revenge*, captained by Grenville (whom the Spaniards called Campoverde), the *Bonaventure* and the *Nonpareil*. On 9 April they set sail, bound for their patrol area.

Spain responded by making an enormous effort to assemble naval forces.[14] On 30 August the squadron commanded by Alonso de Bazán, which included the forces of Marcos de Aramburu, Antonio de Urquiola, Sancho Pardo and Martín de Bertandona – a total of fifty-five ships and 7,200 men – was sent to the Azores. The

Long Elizabeth's favourite, Walter Raleigh was a controversial figure. After the failure of his colonisation attempts in Terranova and Virginia, he turned his attention to other prizes. From Sarmiento de Gamboa he learned of the legend of a land rich in gold, in the heart of the American jungle near the mouth of the Orinoco – El Dorado.

squadron was reinforced by eight light vessels provided by Portugal and captained by Luis Coutinho. The English withdrew with losses.

The squadron of General Francisco Coloma, consisting of five galleys, was sent to Cape St Vincent. Coloma attacked the Earl of Cumberland's forces near Las Berlingas, where he took a ship of fourteen cannons and a crew of 150, a large zabra and a caravel. Only two Spaniards lost their lives in the operation.

And so the Indies fleets reached Spain. Eleven ships were guided by Antonio Navarro and forty-eight by Aparicio Arteaga. Sixteen of the vessels sank in a storm off the Azores, but the crews and cargo were saved.

Efforts to intercept the fleets were renewed in 1592. This time two squadrons were prepared, commanded by Raleigh and Cumberland,[15] who provided five ships, destined to operate jointly. But when Cumberland fell ill, John Norton took over command of the privateers. The results were both good and bad.

With fourteen vessels Raleigh sailed from Falmouth on 6 May, but at Finisterre he was ordered to hand over command to Martin Frobisher and return. His 'crime' was none other than having entered into a marriage contract[16] in December the previous year without the queen's permission. Sir Walter and Elizabeth Throckmorton, one of the queen's ladies-in-waiting, were sent to the Tower of London for eighteen months.

The outcome was to divide the squadron, since Raleigh's second-in-command, Robert Crosse, refused to obey Frobisher. Furthermore, Norton joined the dissidents, leaving Frobisher with only six vessels. Frobisher was caught in a storm that dispersed his flotilla and was attacked by Pedro Zubiaur, who captured two of his ships and forced him to withdraw.

Borough and Crosse, who were joined by the *Dainty*, property of John Hawkins, near the Azores, took the galleon *Madre de Dios*, which had become separated from the Indies fleet, despite resistance on the part of the crew led by Fernando de Mendoza. The battle lasted one day and one night.

The arrival in Dartmouth of the captured ship aroused enormous expectation. The ship had been plundered without orders and, of the estimated £500,000 booty, only £150,000 were handed over, despite reiterated demands from Elizabeth.

In desperation, the Queen sent Drake to negotiate, but to no avail. Finally, Raleigh managed to recover a further £9,000. The dividends shared out among the promoters of the enterprise were high; Elizabeth reserved for herself a share of the spoils that fetched £70,000 on the market. Raleigh was apportioned only £24,000, and complained irately. But, perhaps with some consolation, was pardoned and at Christmas 1592 he and his wife were released from the Tower.

In 1594 Cumberland prepared a new flotilla of three privateers. He came across Francisco Melo's Portuguese galleon[17] *Cinco Chagas*, and a bitter struggle ensued. Cumberland forced the ship to surrender, although he suffered heavy losses – ninety men, including Admiral William Anthony and Vice-Admiral George Cave, and a further 150 wounded. In reprisal, the English executed all the surviving Portuguese and burned the ship. They also attacked Luis Coutinho's galleon *San Felipe*, but were repelled.

In 1595 and 1596 Cumberland returned to the Azores but this time came home empty-handed.

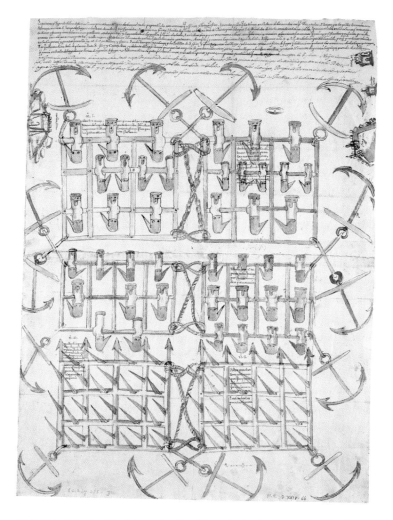

Following repeated English onslaughts, Spain devised a plan of fortifications, which included the American coast. A major architect of this endeavour was Juan Bautista Antonelli, who either designed or modified the defences of the major Spanish strongholds in the Indies.

THE SPANISH RECOVERY

The Spaniards had learned a great lesson from the 'Enterprise of England', namely the imperative need to homogenise the different kinds of ships and to design a vessel specifically for war – the galleon.

To come up with the ideal model, shipbuilders from the north and south of the Peninsula combined in a fruitful operation, creating a vessel that went immediately

Cumberland's final destination was San Juan de Puerto Rico. The garrison had been decimated by an epidemic and offered no opposition to the landing. Several days of bombardment led to the capitulation of the castle of El Morro and the English took control of the city. Their exultation was short-lived, however, for Cumberland and his men also fell victim to the epidemic and had to be repatriated some days before news of their victory reached London.

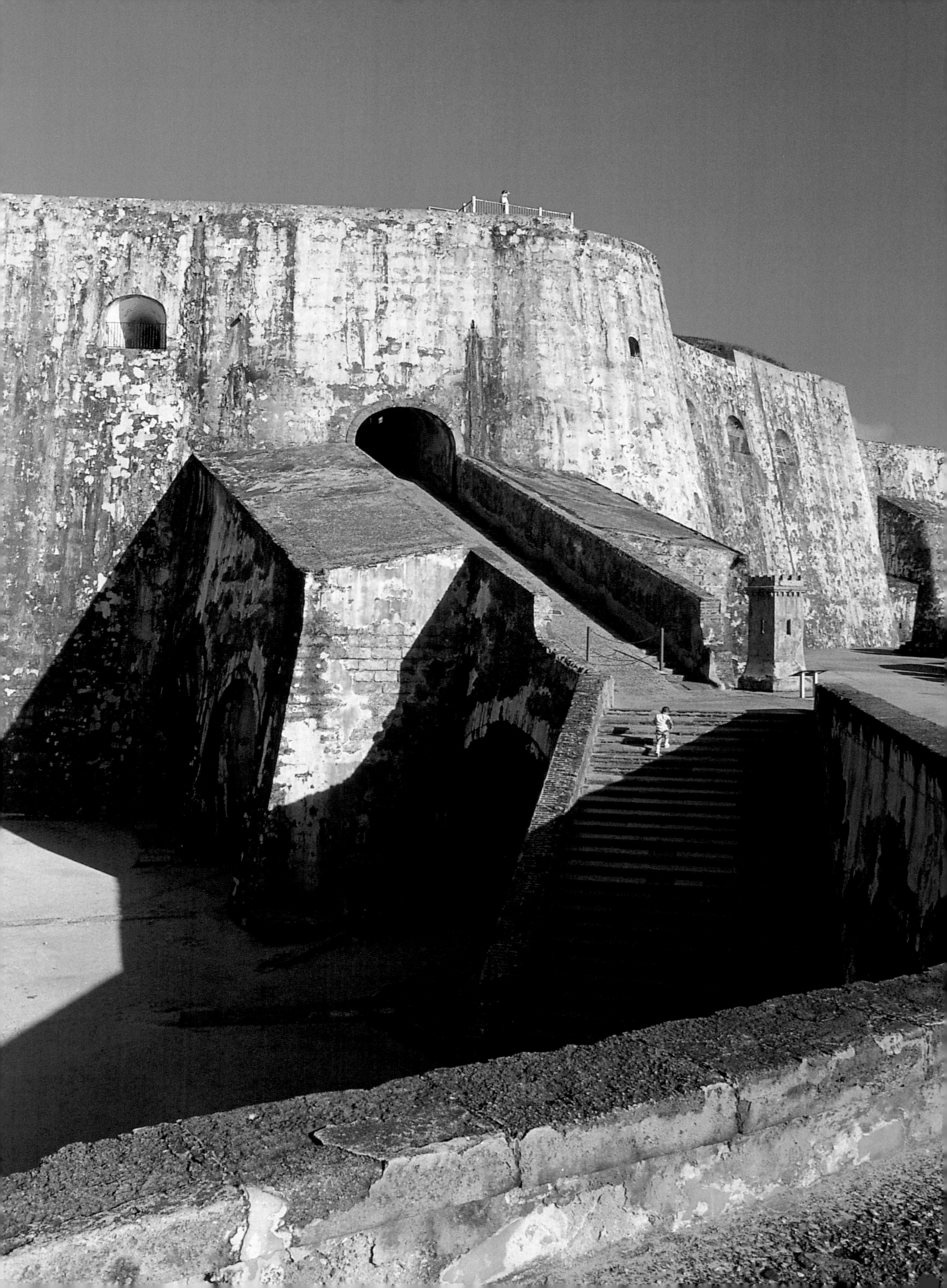

into production, funded by the king himself. By 1592 Philip II's navy was operational again, and consisted of more than fifty galleons fully equipped for war.

Simultaneously, the constant attacks against Spanish strongholds in the Americas had led to a fortification plan directed by Juan Bautista Antonelli and this materialised in the last decade of the century; it was directly responsible for much of the success in the struggle against piracy in the Caribbean.

All these measures, coupled with the taking of Brittany by Spanish forces, intimidated the English who, fearing a new assault, kept their ships between the Azores and the British Isles.

The Expeditions of John Myddelton and Benjamin Wood

During the war between Spain and England, a considerable number of privateering expeditions sailed to the Caribbean. The aim was to repeat past strategies of storming small strongholds or engaging in contraband. The expeditions were not particularly significant, however, and smaller in number than their counterparts of the previous decade.

Captain John Myddelton[18] sailed from England bound for America in a small 50-ton ship, the *Moonshine*, with the aim of assaulting a small stronghold or the pearl-fishing rancherías on the Venezuelan coast. He reached Margarita on 1 June 1592, where his attack was easily repelled by Francisco Manso de Contreras, Governor of Santa Marta, on his way to take possession of his post.

Four ships commanded by Benjamin Wood came across Manso de Contreras, whom they forced to surrender without too much difficulty. They also managed to repel a Spanish counter-attack but, although they were able to plunder the ship, they did not manage to capture it.

Near Cartagena[19] they joined up with Myddelton's flotilla and continued together for some time, without achieving any memorable successes.

James Langton's expedition of 1593 on the other hand was one of the few economically profitable expeditions of the twelve financed by the Earl of Cumberland, thanks to the talents of its commander and the employment of expert pilots who were very familiar with the Indies. He[20] set sail late in June 1593 in command of a flotilla

consisting of the 120-ton *Anthony*, the 100-ton *Pilgrim* and the *Discovery*, a pinnace weighing 12 tons. He was accompanied by seventy men, including Antonio Marrino, a Spanish renegade who had lived in the Indies for years and who acted as pilot. The *Pilgrim* was captained by Francis Slingsby accompanied by another Spanish renegade pilot, Diego Perrus, and fifty-five men.

On Margarita, unopposed they assaulted and plundered a ranchería (see box below), obtaining pearls to the value of some £2,000. The weapons they found were destroyed and they immediately took to sea to avoid counter-attacks.

Later they returned to the ranchería and, knowing that the Spaniards were unarmed, they demanded a tributo de quema amounting to 2,000 ducats in pearls. Having been paid accordingly, they set sail once and for all.

Meanwhile, news of their presence had reached Cumaná, where defences were organised. The Englishmen's attempt to disembark was repelled and a considerable number lost their lives. In Río Hacha they did not even manage to set foot on the beach and, after a number of actions on Hispaniola, they headed for Jamaica, where they captured another frigate, which they sent back to England. They then began their own return voyage, during which they lay in wait for a few days in Cape San Antonio in the hope of capturing a ship.

When they arrived back in England in mid May 1594, their profits amounted to £6,000 excluding the two

THE RANCHERÍAS, A UNIQUE DEFENCE SYSTEM

Pearl fishing was Margarita's main source of income. Located very near the entry to the Caribbean and far from the main settlements of Tierra Firme, the island seemed to be easy prey. Not so, however, for the Spanish had devised a unique defence system. Along the coast, on sites where visibility was excellent, they built six or seven rancherías (pearl-fishing settlements). All in perfect condition, only one would be occupied in a random rotation system. Furthermore, every week the pearls were taken elsewhere for safe keeping, so that there would never be many pearls at a particular ranchería at any given time.

When the lookouts alerted the fishermen of possible attacks, they would abandon the ranchería, taking only the pearls with them. Consequently surprise attacks, which were only possible from inland, were the only way to make any kind of profit, assuming that the attackers were lucky enough to come upon a ranchería with enough pearls to make the effort worthwhile.

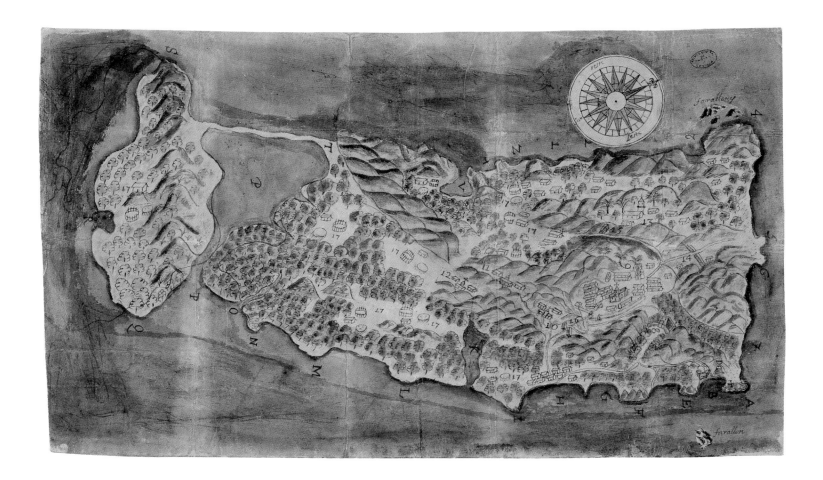

Map of the island of Margarita showing its ports, points, inlets, valleys, hills, roads, salt-water lagoons and trenches on the roads for the defence of the city, 1661.

captured frigates, which were given to the Earl of Cumberland.

Less successfully Sir John Burgh had also sailed from England in 1593. He went with four ships, the *Roebuck, Golden Dragon, Prudence* and *Virgin*. Having sacked a town in Trinidad, he proceeded to Guyana, but we have no knowledge of his feats there. In May he disembarked on Margarita, where he was repelled by Governor Sarmiento de Villandrando, despite the defenders' inferior numbers.[21] The expedition yielded absolutely no profits.

Parker's Expedition (1596)

In November 1596, Parker[22] left Plymouth on what would be his second expedition to the Caribbean. His flotilla consisted of two ships, the 120-ton *Prudence* and the *Adventure*, a tender of 25 tons captained by Richard Hen. The crew numbered 100.

In Caribbean waters he took a pearl ranchería by surprise on Margarita. In Jamaica they met up with Sherley's expedition and continued together into the Gulf of Honduras. They attacked Trujillo on 31 March 1597,

but were repelled. And, although they managed to take Puerto Caballos, they obtained no booty.

They attempted the daring exploit of crossing overland to the Southern Sea, then sailing thirty leagues up the River Dulce in small boats, carrying a dismantled pinnace which they would subsequently reassemble. The operation proved impossible, however, so they returned to the Gulf of Honduras, where they separated.

On 21 September they reached the waters off the coast of Campeche in full daylight in a large ship, a tender and a lighter. Parker pretended to withdraw, while negotiating aid with Juan Venturate to come into the city unseen. In this way, the English took the city unawares by entering via the district of San Ramón. Encountering no opposition, they immediately engaged in disorderly plunder without waiting for dawn.

Francisco Interán, one of the city governors, had taken refuge with a number of men in the Monastery of San Francisco, the established mustering point in case of attacks such as this, where a substantial body of armed men gradually gathered.

In the meantime, Francisco Sánchez, the other governor, began to put together a force from the surrounding villages and made contact with those in the monastery. Together they drew up a joint plan of attack. The strategy consisted in simulating a counter-attack from San Francisco to keep the English occupied while

91

Sánchez blockaded the city streets until the enemy was encircled. The ruse worked, and the English, celebrating their apparent victory, suddenly found themselves surrounded. To escape they used the prisoners as a human shield, tying them together arm-to-arm until they formed a barrier against the Spaniards' bullets. Two hours later, the English gathered their dead, unfurled their flag and retreated. Parker was hit by a bullet 'in the bottom left-hand side of the chest, which has remained encrusted in my backbone ever since'. He and his men retreated to the ships and fled, leaving most of the spoils behind.

The Campechanos vented their fury on the fleeing enemy, killing many and taking others prisoner, Venturate included.

A little further north the English came to the city of Sebo, which they managed to take and plunder, then proceeded to Cape Catoche, where the wind was against them. The Spaniards sent a frigate in hot pursuit, which was joined by another with reinforcements from Mérida, captained by Alonso Vargas Macguca, which caught up with the English. After a bitter struggle, the Spaniards overpowered the *Adventure* and took prisoner Captain Hen and thirteen men, all of whom were executed in Campeche. Parker pursued the frigates to the city but, after remaining there for seventeen days, he eventually withdrew. On 1 July the flotilla sighted the Scilly Isles and two days later entered Plymouth.

In all his voyages Parker displayed great daring. In his expedition[23] of 1601, for example, he attacked Margarita and the whole coast of Tierra Firme, obtaining handsome profits.

Early in November that year, he sailed from Plymouth with two ships, the 100-ton *Prudence* with 130 men and the *Pearle*, commanded by Robert Rawlin, with sixty men, together with a 20-ton pinnace with eighteen men and two small two-masted boats in tow.

At Cape Verde 100 men disembarked to attack St Vincent, which they plundered and set on fire. In Cubagua they attacked a ranchería and, although they were intercepted by the forces of the Governor of Cumaná, they managed to occupy it and obtain a ransom of £500 in pearls.

At Cabo de la Vela they intercepted a 250-ton Portuguese vessel carrying 370 negroes to Cartagena. Due to sailing difficulties, they decided to abandon the negroes in the Bay of Acle while keeping the Portuguese captain hostage. The latter paid a ransom of £500 from his own pocket to save them all.

THE UNLUCKY FATE OF THE RENEGADE VENTURATE

During the retreat from Campeche, one of those attempting to escape was the renegade Venturate.

Venturate was caught in the water as he swam towards one of the boats. Subsequently, his conduct aroused suspicion, so he was imprisoned as a precautionary measure.

During their interrogation, several of the prisoners confessed that it was Venturate who had facilitated their entry into Campeche. His treachery thus having been revealed, the renegade was condemned to death. He was publicly executed in the cruellest possible way: pieces of flesh were ripped from his body with red-hot pincers until he expired.

Parker's major objective was Portobelo. After the destruction of Nombre de Dios the city had been rebuilt behind the bay and was now defended by several castles and bulwarks.

On the night of 7 February, in the light of a full moon, the English entered the mouth of the Portobelo river. Those manning the castle of San Felipe challenged them, demanding to know where they came from and what their intentions were. Some of Parker's men spoke good Spanish, and managed to deceive the watch into believing they had came from Cartagena.

They were given the order to anchor until dawn, which they obeyed unquestioningly. One hour later, thirty men in the small two-masted vessels sailed upriver to the castle of Santiago. They were ordered to halt, made landfall and ran to take the village of Triana, where the alarm was sounded for the first time.

They proceeded up a rivulet to Portobelo, where they disembarked opposite the Casas Reales. Here they surprised a detachment of soldiers with two bronze cannons and forced them to retreat. They then turned the cannons against the Spaniards.

Pedro Méndez, Governor of Portobelo, had put together a force of sixty men and proceeded to block the Englishmen's passage at a bridge, but he was wounded in both arms. The Spaniards took the governor to a house where they entrenched themselves, waiting for the morning to be able to assess the English positions and forces.

Finally, the house was taken and the governor captured, having received eight wounds more. In the Casas Reales they took the Royal Scribe prisoner together

THE ASSAULT AND SACKING OF CADIZ IN 1596[24]

Robert Devereux, Earl of Essex.

After his flight from the Peninsula, Antonio Pérez, Philip II's former secretary, wanted for his involvement in shady affairs, travelled from London to Paris, betraying state secrets to anyone who cared to listen. Among other things, he revealed the precarious situation of the defences on the coast of Andalucía and the lack of organised troops to repel disembarkation by enemy forces.

The news reached the ears of Robert Devereux, Earl of Essex, one of Queen Elizabeth's favourites and a fortune seeker. He managed to persuade everyone of the expediency of a bold attack against Cadiz, from whence he would attempt to organise an overland campaign. When the war was at its height, he put together a formidable Anglo-Dutch fleet consisting of almost 160 ships, twenty of which were provided by the Dutch, and an expeditionary corps with all the impedimenta necessary for a major campaign. Charles Howard, Lord High Admiral of England, was put in charge of the operation, with Essex leading the expeditionary corps and Thomas Howard, Walter Raleigh and Francis Vere as subalterns.

They sailed from England and in early June reached Lisbon. As the city was very well defended, they proceeded to their main objective. On June 30 they came in sight of Cadiz, where between forty and fifty vessels belonging to the Tierra Firme fleet and eighteen galleys of the Escuadra de España were anchored. Defences were prepared with the support of the artillery of the forts, but once again the incompetence of the officers, captained by the Duke of Medina Sidonia, whom the poet Góngora dubbed 'God of the Nitwits', tipped the balance in favour of the English.

The city was assaulted, sacked and burned. On 16 July the English left, taking a handsome booty with them. Sailing along the Portuguese coast, they landed at Faro, but obtained nothing. Finally, after a raiding excursion at La Coruña, they set sail for England.

The expedition had been highly profitable in fiscal terms, and from the propagandist point of view very detrimental to Spanish interests.

The English stole two frigates and re-embarked at nightfall, having been masters of Portobelo for one day. They set sail under artillery fire from the forts of San Iago and El Oriental and constant musket fire from the beaches. Parker himself was hit in the elbow and wrist.

Finally they entered the Bahamas Channel on 31 March 1601 and reached the Azores without incident. Here they stayed for two months during which time they took in provisions. Parker set sail for Plymouth, arriving there on 6 May 1601, while his flotilla remained in the Azores ready for further operations.

The Last Voyage of John Hawkins and Francis Drake

As previously mentioned, since 1592 Elizabeth's Royal Navy had remained near the coasts of England without risking engagement in major campaigns that would leave the country defenceless against the constant Spanish threat. But, in 1595, with European conflicts developing in a way unfavourable to England, it was decided to take the initiative and once again organise the 'summer cruises', which operated on three fronts: Cadiz, the Indies and the African coast.

A major fleet, composed of twenty-seven large ships, twenty-five smaller ones and 2,500 men, commanded jointly by John Hawkins and Francis Drake, had set sail from England in mid 1595. Thus, Drake had returned to sea, but although he had sponsored the enterprise, the Queen authorised the expedition provided that John Hawkins was co-leader.[25] Relations between the two men, strained since Drake's flight in San Juan de Ulúa, had become insupportable after Hawkins presented the report that led to Drake's being grounded. However, the importance of the mission forced them to bury the hatchet and together they drew up a plan[26] that contemplated plundering the main cities of the Americas, the assault of Nombre de Dios and Panama, and the establishment of an English colony on the Isthmus.

Despite efforts on the part of both men to simulate amicable relations, the adventure was destined to end in failure. Hawkins was nearing seventy and had become slow and whimsical. Thomas Maynarde,[27] an army captain involved in the campaign, wrote that 'Sir John was so slow to get down to business that the others had already eaten their meat before he had even begun to roast his over the fire'.

with a host of other important people, as well as 9,000 or 10,000 ducats which Parker pocketed as his own personal booty. The rest of the plunder was shared among his men. He decided not to raze the city to the ground and, as a tribute to the courage of Pedro Méndez, who had been wounded ten or eleven times, he set him free without demanding a ransom.

RICHARD HAWKINS IN THE PACIFIC[28]

The Hawkins expeditions had by no means terminated, for by 1593 a new generation had come onto the scene. Richard, the only son of John Hawkins and Katherine Gonson, received every support from the family clan in the preparation of his expedition to the Pacific.

He sailed from Plymouth on 22 June on the 300-ton, 20-cannon galleon *Dainty*, accompanied by a second 100-ton, 8-cannon ship and the 60-ton tender *Fantasy*.

His first objective was the Canary Isles, but a storm drove him away from the archipelago. A second storm battered his flotilla during the Atlantic crossing and, four months later, he reached the Brazilian coast. His misfortunes did not end here, however, for the second ship was lost on the coast and the tender deserted, leaving Hawkins to continue alone on the *Dainty*.

In the Southern Sea he assaulted Valparaíso, where he captured five cargo ships, for which he was paid a ransom of 25,000 ducats. He kept one for himself, together with the pilot, Alonso Pérez Bueno.

When the news reached Viceroy García Hurtado de Mendoza, he sent three well-armed 500-ton galleons commanded by Beltrán de Castro y de la Cueva. Three tenders joined the flotilla, each one with thirty men, and dispatch boats were sent to Panama and Nueva España as well as packet boats to the coastal towns. On 3 June a reinforcement flotilla sailed from El Callao.

News that Hawkins was in Chincha put Beltrán de Castro on his trail. One day later he came across the English and attempted to capture them, but the Spanish flagship broke its masts and the *San Juan* suffered

the same contretemps. The chase continued with the vice-admiral's ship and the tender, but Hawkins lightened his cargo and escaped.

On 30 June, in the Bay of Atacanes, the first battle was fought, from which Hawkins came out worse. Beltrán de Castro continued the pursuit and, on 2 July, came alongside and fired a broadside. The English sustained considerable damage and, although the Spaniards offered them the chance to surrender, Hawkins refused.

The Spanish fired another broadside and then boarded. Many Englishmen were killed; indeed, there were only ninety survivors, among whom there were several wounded, Hawkins himself sustaining two bullet wounds.

Hawkins was taken on board Beltrán de Castro's ship. In Panama he disembarked prisoners and took those of highest rank to El Callao, which he entered triumphantly on 8 May.

De Castro's victory was jubilantly celebrated in Lima, and his feats were immortalised in the *Poema de Santa Rosa* by the Count of La Granja:

Calderón y Castilla, eterna fama
logra, matando ingleses a montones.
Un mar de sangre sobre el mar derrama
hecho un león, el león Quiñones.
Lezcano, el hierro convertido en llama
ilustra a hazañas cántabros blasones
Luján, Rivera y Avalos el fuerte
En cada amago vibran una muerte.

Since the event was considered an incident of war, Hawkins was treated as a corsair. Having healed his wounds, Beltrán de Castro had him as a guest in his own home and prevented him from falling into the hands of the Inquisition.

Finally Hawkins was transported to Spain, where he was jailed for a year. Freed in 1602, he returned to England. His ship was incorporated into the Squadron of the Southern Sea, under the name of *La Inglesa*.

The Queen provided the recently constructed ships[29] *Garlande* and *Defyance*, and the galleons *Bonaventure, Hope, Foresighte,* and *Adventure*, as well as regular troops under the orders of Sir Thomas de Baskerville. Privateers[30] also joined the expedition, leading to a total of twenty-eight ships and men from all walks of life, totalling 1,500 seamen and 3,000 soldiers. The fleet also carried dismantled disembarkation launches designed by Drake himself, probably based on the pinnaces he had used in previous campaigns.

Preparation of the fleet was held up[31] due to the attack by a Spanish garrison on the town of Blavet, in Brittany. Four hundred harquebusiers also disembarked from four galleys in Cornwall and, meeting no resistance, they plundered several towns and villages. Panic spread throughout England and, fearing a large-scale disembarkation, defence measures were adopted. However, the fleet preparations were resumed when it was realised that this had been merely an isolated incident.

On 7 September 1595 Drake hoisted his insignia on the *Defyance*, while Hawkins raised his on the *Garlande*.

Shortly after they had put to sea, the first disagreements arose. Drake demanded victuals from the rest of the fleet, claiming that he was carrying 300 more men than anticipated, but Hawkins refused to comply.

Later Drake proposed attacking the Canaries to obtain provisions and to raise the morale of the expeditionary forces. Hawkins dissented, claiming that if they did so the element of surprise would be lost and reminded Drake that the true objective was the Indies. Baskerville supported Drake's plan, convinced that his troops would take Las Palmas in a matter of three or four hours. Hawkins eventually gave way.

They reached Las Palmas at dawn on 6 October. The alarm was sounded and, in a short space of time, almost 1,000 men had been mobilised. Furthermore, 400 reinforcements were expected from Tenerife.

Concerning the defences, differences arose between the Spanish officers. Governor Alonso de Alvarado advocated impeding the disembarkation, while Regidor Antoni Arias preferred to fight the English on land. The chiefs of the companies of militiamen supported Alvarado, and preparations were made to prevent the English from landing.

The Dutch fleet, commanded by Pieter van der Does, attacks Las Palmas de Gran Canaria in 1599.

The English began their attack in twenty-seven launches carrying 500 men, protected by three ships, while a further twelve ships approached land, opening fire against the Spanish defences.

After a battle lasting an hour and a half, with the loss of forty English lives, four launches and damage to five of the ships, Drake ordered his men to retreat. Given the situation, Baskerville reckoned that four days would be needed to take the city. Drake admitted that Hawkins had been right and gave up the attempt.

In the Bay of Arguineguín, 500 Englishmen went ashore to take in water. The Spaniards captured one of the launches that had gone astray and learned of Drake and Hawkins's intentions. They immediately sent warning to the Indies.

Finally, on 9 October the English decided to head for the Antilles. They reached the Caribbean to learn that the flagship of the Tierra Firme fleet, carrying a treasure of two million pesos, had anchored at Puerto Rico and been dismasted. Sancho Pardo Osorio was in command of the vessel, manned by a force of 300.

When news of this reached Spain, there was considerable fear that the English would attempt to take the treasure, and a flotilla of five frigates commanded by Pedro Tello de Guzmán was sent to transport it back. The flotilla reached the Caribbean, where it captured the *Francis*, an English ship that had fallen behind the others. The Spaniards learned that the English fleet was in Guadeloupe, assembling disembarkation launches and taking in provisions.

The Spanish sailed full speed to Puerto Rico, where they arrived on 13 November. The defences were quickly prepared. The governor sank Sancho Pardo's galleon in the channel and set up a barrier of tree trunks and a chain. Inside the bay Tello de Guzmán's frigates were lined up and, on land, numerous forces were deployed: 1,500 soldiers, 300 of Sancho Pardo's seamen, 500 of Tello's and 9,000 armed civilians. Using some of these men, the governor formed a company of lancers under his command and all the possible landing points were covered by armed detachments.

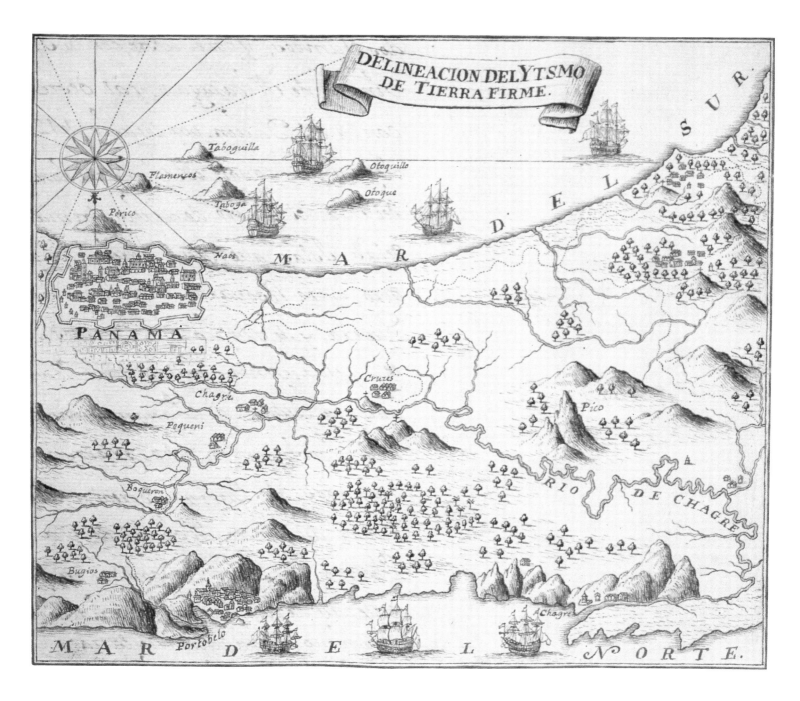

DELINEACION DEL YTSMO DE TIERRA FIRME.

Map of the Isthmus of Tierra Firme showing Panama on the Pacific coast and Portobelo on the Atlantic coast where Drake was rebuffed.

On 22 November Drake was sighted off Punta Escambrón, and the Spaniards immediately opened fire. One shot made a direct hit on the dining room of the *Defyance*, where Drake was having supper with his officers. Captains Nicholas Clifford and Brute Brown, together with five others, were killed. Drake came out unscathed.

Spanish chroniclers describe the event thus: 'While an English gentleman, a lieutenant-general, was dining, an artilleryman on the hill saw a light on the table and aimed so well that his shot swept everyone from the table and others in the near vicinity, a total of fifteen…'.[32]

The following day, the English sought a suitable disembarkation area, eventually attempting to make landfall at the southern end of the Islas Cabras. The water was not deep enough to anchor the ships, however, so they decided to attack from the launches. But the manoeuvre backfired. Fire from incendiary devices lit up the attackers and they were swept by artillery and musket fire. Nine launches were destroyed and 400 Englishmen killed.

On 24 November (12 November O.S.), Drake attempted a second attack. Seven launches advanced towards El Boquerón, to be met by musket fire. Realising that he could not carry off the attack without suffering enormous casualties, Drake decided to retreat, weighing anchor on the 28th (the 16th, O.S.). The citizens were jubilant, and their jubilation increased when they learned that Hawkins had apparently been killed in the battle. In fact, he had died of a fever on

Nombre de Dios, 1541
On 6 January 1596 Drake attacked Nombre de Dios, meeting with practically
no resistance. He then prepared to attack Panama, but the accesses were too
well defended and Drake was forced to retreat, having incurred substantial
losses. As an act of reprisal, he razed Nombre de Dios to the ground. The
inhabitants moved to Portobelo in search of more easily defended terrain.

20 November (12 November O.S.) between Guadeloupe and Puerto Rico. On 20 December Pedro Tello de Guzmán set sail for the Peninsula, the holds of his frigates loaded with treasure.

In Río Hacha the English burned a number of buildings and entered Santa Marta, where they did the same. At Cartagena Drake decided not to risk losing more men, and finally they reached Nombre de Dios[33] on 6 January 1596 (27 December 1595, O.S.).

The city had been evacuated and was defended by sixty men led by Governor Diego de Amaya. Drake had secured the collaboration of a renegade, the mulatto Andrés Amador. In the face of the superior numbers of the English, and after only brief resistance, the defenders retreated to the mountains, after which the attackers entered and plundered the city.

Having consolidated his position, Drake began preparations for his final objective, the assault of Panama. To this end, he attempted unsuccessfully to secure the services of runaway slave guides in a nearby village.

The President of the Audiencia de Panamá was ready for Drake, having prepared numerous defences, organised by Juan Bautista Antonelli, both in the River Chagres area and on the overland route. Drake disembarked and began his attack from the river, while Baskerville took the land route. At dawn on the 8th the battle began at the fort of San Pablo de la Victoria, on Loma Capirilla, where seventy harquebusiers under orders from Juan Enríquez Conabut were defending the position.

The Spaniards managed to hold the English at bay with heavy harquebus fire, inflicting many casualties. Sotomayor sent fifty soldiers as reinforcements, commanded by Captain Hernando Lierno Agüero, who approached sounding trumpets and drums, simulating a column. The English were taken in by the ruse and retreated to the coast pursued by a contingent of negroes who cut many of their throats. Baskerville's losses amounted to some 500 men.

COLD STEEL

Until portable firearms were perfected, the fact that it was impossible to fire consecutive shots in a short space of time severely restricted their usefulness in hand-to-hand combat. Several kinds of pistols were used that fired a single shot, but after this being armed with cold steel was essential.

There was a wide variety of steel weapons each with its own specific use. The most important was the sword, in all its different variations. Besides its purely military use, it was a symbol of rank and not everybody could possess one.

There was a form of fencing in which the sword was used simultaneously with the *daga de vela* or left-handed dagger, the function of which was to deflect blows and stab the adversary at close quarters.

In wartime different types of lances were used, which varied in length. On ships, given the limited room for manoeuvre on deck, short pikes were the most common form of lance. Some kinds of lances, such as the halberd, the partisan or the spontoon, also symbolised leadership or rank, when borne either by the commanders themselves or by their escorts.

During boarding and in man-to-man combat on deck, the weapon par excellence was the boarding axe. Each of its sides had different functions: the axe was used for inflicting blows and cutting the running ropes, while the pike served as an auxiliary element which allowed boarders to gain a stronger foothold on the ship's timbers.

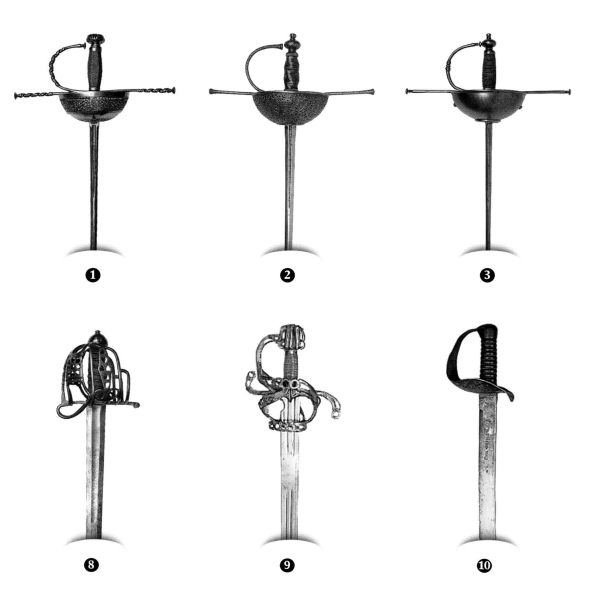

1. Sword with handguard
2. Toledan sword with handguard
3. Solingen rapier
4. German sword with handguard
5. Tomás de Ayala sword with handguard
6. Sword with handguard and flamboyant blade
7. Swept-hilt rapier
8. Claymore or Scottish sword
9. Swept-hilt rapier
10. Boarding sabre
    from the 18th century
11. Swept-hilt rapier
12. Swept-hilt rapier
13. Toledan sword
14. Left-handed dagger
15. Left-handed dagger
16. Left-handed dagger
17. Left-handed dagger

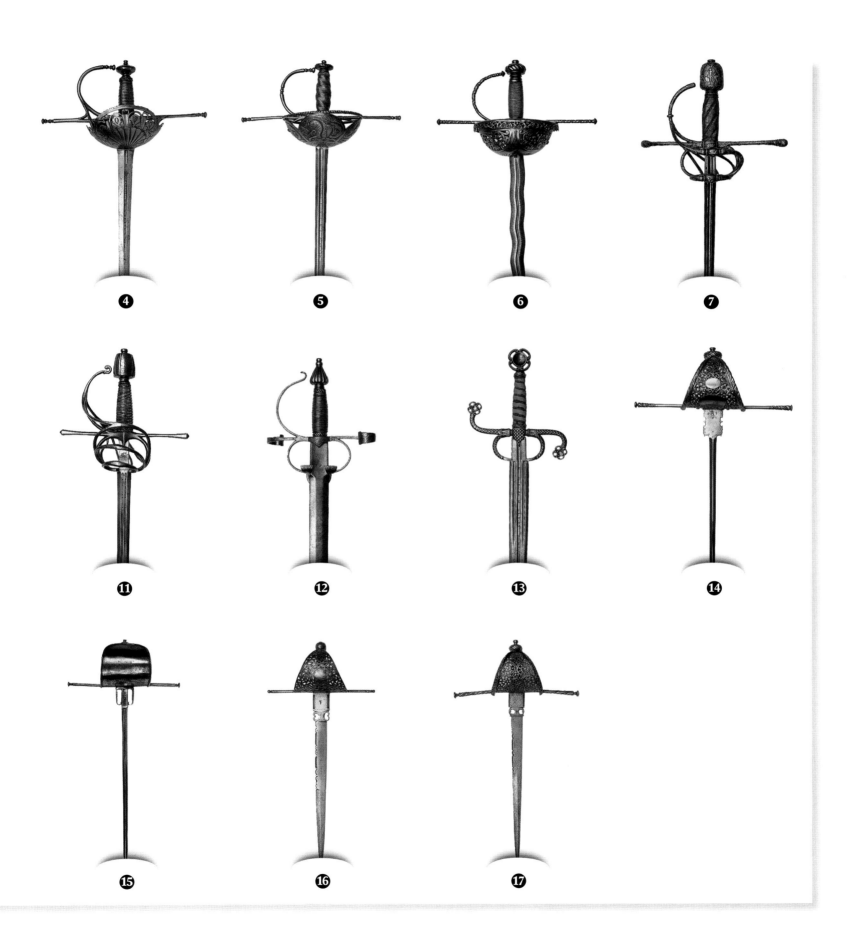

❹
❺
❻
❼

⓫
⓬
⓭
⓮

⓯
⓰
⓱

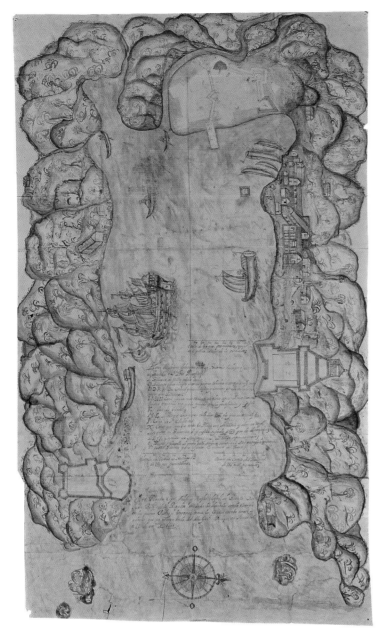

Chart of the bay and inlet of Portobelo, 1688. The Archivo de Indias, Seville.

Drake felt obliged to help Baskerville and withdrew to Nombre de Dios, ordering men to disembark to cover the retreat. As an act of reprisal, on 12 January (N.S. – New Style) he burned Nombre de Dios to the ground and on the 15th set sail with seven large galleons, twenty-four warships and the same number of launches. The people of Nombre de Dios refused to rebuild the city.

The highly demoralised English sought refuge in Veragua and Drake, who was suffering from dysentery, locked himself in his cabin. On 27 January (O.S.), while the fleet was on the high seas, he fell into a state of delirium and demanded to be dressed in full dress uniform and armour. Early in the morning of 28 January, when the fleet was eight or nine leagues from Nombre de Dios, Drake passed away. Baskerville took over the command.

The English fleet anchored to pay their last respects to their commander. His body was placed in a lead coffin and two small boats were launched on either side of the *Defyance* to be set on fire when the coffin was lowered overboard.

The news soon reached Portobelo, where it was received with great rejoicing. Word went around that Drake had died of grief at his unsuccessful attempt to take the city.

Utterly defeated, Baskerville burned several damaged ships, freed prisoners and regrouped his forces into fourteen units, setting sail for the Bahamas Channel.

His flight would not be uneventful, however. In Spain a fleet of eight galleons, thirteen smaller ships and 3,000 men had been prepared to defend the Indies. It had set sail from Lisbon on 2 January 1596 (23 December 1595, O.S.), commanded by Bernardino Delgadillo de Avellaneda and Admiral Juan Gutiérrez Garibay. At the head of the infantry was Joanes Villaviciosa.

On 11 March Avellaneda, commanding only thirteen ships, came face to face with the English at the island of Pinos. Garibay, who was sailing in the vanguard with three galleons, decided to attack without waiting for the rest. Although the English were taking in fresh water, they reacted immediately. The outcome of the battle was the capture of an English ship with 300 men on board and a tender with thirty-five. Furthermore, in their retreat the English abandoned the launches. On the Spanish side a ship was lost and, between the dead and wounded, around eighty men were left hors de combat.

The English managed to flee by lightening their load, even throwing artillery overboard. Only eight of the twenty-seven ships that had sailed from England returned to Plymouth, in April 1596, to bitter disappointment at Court.

Sir Anthony Sherley's Expedition (1596)

Parallel to Drake's and Hawkins's expedition, another expedition was organised, commanded by Sir Anthony Sherley[34], whose mission was to harass Portuguese settlements on the coast of Africa, specifically Sao Tomé. Nonetheless, he eventually headed for the Caribbean, partially because of his lack of success in the venture and partially because of a hostile climate.

He sailed from Southampton on 23 April 1596 at the head of nine ships, a frigate powered by oarsmen and a pinnace, which transported 900 men with provisions for

THE DEATH OF DRAKE

Drake died off the coast of Nombre de Dios, his health shattered by fevers, having been delirious for several days. The Spaniards were convinced that his demise was due to mortification over his defeat.[35]

According to some chroniclers, 'when Drake's men saw their leader so sick, they decided to poison his food to relieve his suffering. But the corsair refused to touch anything that had not been tasted first by someone else. So they eventually decided to add poison to an enema they administered to him....'[36]

Drake's body was buried at sea in a lead coffin[36] 'a little to the east of the castle of San Felipe, beneath a rock'.[37]

Funeral of Admiral, Sir Francis Drake by Thomas Davidson.
Plymouth City Museum and Art Gallery.

a ten-month campaign. On 29 April they reached Plymouth, where they found the Earl of Essex preparing his attack against Cadiz. Sherley placed three ships and 500 men at Essex's disposal.

Six days later they reached the Spanish coast and from there they continued along the coasts of Barbary and the Canaries.

They expected to encounter the Sao Tomé fleet near the island of Mayo but they were disappointed. They therefore continued their voyage to Cape Verde, where they arrived on 5 July. Sherley ordered the course to be changed for the Indies to flee from the hostile African weather and because the '…water that fell from the heavens stank and in six hours became transformed into larvae…'.

On 30 August they sighted the coast of America and having sailed past Guyana they disembarked in Praia, which they took without encountering much resistance. Sherley decided to launch an assault on Santiago, six miles away, with 260 men. Santiago was strongly fortified and access to the city was very difficult. Sherley and his men reached the first buildings, where a strong contingent of pikemen was expecting them. Nevertheless, the English were astute

enough to kill their captain with accurate shots, and the Portuguese retreated, leaving the two lower forts unmanned.

On 3 August Sherley and his men entrenched themselves to face the tremendous onslaught of the Portuguese who, thanks to their superior numbers, killed eighty among the English forces. Seeing that his situation was desperate, Sherley devised a strategy to deceive his enemy and carry out an orderly retreat.

The English pretended to attempt to storm the castle, forcing the Portuguese to fall back and, taking advantage of the confusion, they managed to reach the port and take to sea. They set a course for the Caribbean and, on 17 October, reached Dominica, where they rested until 25 November, after which they set sail once more.

Since they did not have an expert pilot among their crew, they were unable to find the pearl rancherías on Margarita and Cumaná. On 12 December they sighted Santa Marta, disembarked two leagues from the city, and took it practically unopposed. Thanks to the good offices of Martín de Castilla, who managed to convince Sherley of the local inhabitants' poverty, the Englishman decided not to burn the city, restricting himself to taking the artillery and rescuing an English prisoner who had been held captive there since Drake's assault.

On 31 March they attempted to storm Trujillo by combining their forces with those of William Parker. However, the city was very well fortified and all Sherley achieved was the death of a number of his men in the defenders' gunfire.

They assaulted Puerto Caballos hoping to obtain some booty, but what they found was '...the poorest, most miserable place in the entire Indies...'.

They attempted to accede to the Southern Sea by sailing in dinghies up the River Dulce, but to no avail. Once again stricken by disease and lacking victuals, they decided to return to England.

On 13 May they were off the coast of Havana, intending to sail to Terranova to take in provisions, renew the crews and sail south to India. However, the fleet dispersed and its ships ended up at different destinations, having failed to make any profit.

George Clifford Attempts to Recover his Fortune in the Americas (1598)

The Earl of Cumberland still dreamed of restoring his squandered fortune. Having decided against capturing another Indies fleet he prepared an expedition to the Antilles.[38] To this end, he managed to put together a fleet of twenty ships and 2,000 men. He embarked on the *Malice Scourge*, captained by Sir John Berkeley, at the head of the troops on the *Merchant Royal* and on Vice-Admiral Robert Filch's *Ascensión*, a ship captured from the Spanish.

They sailed from Portsmouth early in March 1598, bound for Lanzarote. In mid April they reached the island and 500 men disembarked at Puerto Naos. The new governor, Sancho de Herrera, decided to slow the English advance towards the capital by organising constant skirmishes. Meanwhile, the city's inhabitants had time to take their riches to the caves for safe keeping and to abandon Teguise.

When the invaders arrived, they were offered a show of resistance from the castle, but the defenders withdrew when they saw the English deploying their artillery. The English remained on the island for one week, during which time the only spoils they managed to obtain were the church bells, a number of pieces of artillery and 150 tons of malvasia grapes, which were sent to England.

George Clifford (1558-1605), Third Earl of Cumberland by William Rogers (1545-1610). Private collection.

On 22 April the English fleet began the Atlantic crossing. Cumberland had led his men to believe that they were bound for Brazil to attack Pernambuco and that, during the voyage, the lack of fresh water had forced him to change his tactics. His new destination was Puerto Rico; his objective, Panama.

Puerto Rico had suffered a terrible epidemic and its garrison had been reduced to 134 soldiers and 24 artillerymen, reinforced by a further 200 men who had recently arrived.

The English fleet anchored in the Ensenada de los Cangrejos on 15 June. Seven hundred men disembarked and advanced towards the city, hounded by the Spanish cavalry. They had to cross a bridge over the channel of San Antonio, defended by ten soldiers and eighty armed civilians. The defenders managed to hold back the English at this point, killing fifteen; the Spanish officers also died, however. In view of the difficulties, the English re-embarked.

On the following day, they landed near Punta Escambrón and entered the city unopposed. At the castle of El Morro Governor Antonio Mosquera entrenched himself with 400 men and refused to surrender.

For days the fort was bombarded by cannon fire from the ships and a number of batteries set up on land. Their provisions having run out, the Spaniards were forced to accept an honourable capitulation. They came out with their flags unfurled and embarked on two English ships, who abandoned them near Cartagena.

On 14 September news of the exploit reached Spain and the order was given to prepare an expedition force to recover the city. The garrison stationed at Blavet in Brittany had been repatriated after the Peace of Vervins (see box overleaf), and they now embarked on the fleet commanded by Pedro de Zubiaur. Two additional squadrons were prepared, one in Lisbon led by Diego Brochero and the other the Armada de la Guarda de la Carrera de Indias. When everything was ready for departure, news arrived that the English had withdrawn. The epidemic that had decimated the Spanish garrison had also afflicted the English, added to which harassment by patrols stopped them from getting provisions. Cumberland quit the island on 14 August, taking everything he could with him: the church bells, the cathedral organ, 1,000 crates of sugar, 2,000 quintales of ginger, one ship with a cargo of negroes and another with a cargo of pearls. He set sail with most of the fleet and left Berkeley in charge of the garrison.

In mid September Cumberland reached England and told of his plans to establish a trading post from which to undertake new ventures. In the meantime, on 24 August, Berkeley had blown up part of the Castle of El Morro after having attempted to obtain a ransom for the city, and set sail with what was left of the expeditionary force. Between 700 and 1,000 Englishmen had perished, mostly as a consequence of the epidemic.

Despite the withdrawal of the English, a fleet from Spain was sent carrying 400 reinforcements, commanded by Francisco Coloma, and transporting the new governor, Alonso de Mercado. When the expedition arrived in April 1599, 250 of the local inhabitants had returned and begun to build new strongholds in case of further attacks.

The Legend of El Dorado

The legend of a land rich in gold in the heart of the American jungle has its origins in a tale told by a Chioca Indian to Captain Luis de Daza, who accompanied Sebastián de Benalcazar. The result was that for almost 100 years the Spanish organised expeditions to discover this fantastic land.

The English heard of the legend from Pedro Sarmiento de Gamboa who, on his return to Spain in 1586, was

George Clifford had squandered a vast fortune through gambling. Inspired by the examples of Drake and Norris he determined to recover his wealth as quickly as possible by attacking the Indies Fleets as they returned to Spain laden with Caribbean treasures

captured by English corsairs and taken to London. Sarmiento told the story to Raleigh, assuring him that he had heard it from Antonio Berrio, Governor of Trinidad and Guyana. As from this moment the dream of establishing a colony in America became geared towards the discovery and conquest of El Dorado, and to this end several expeditions were organised.

Robert Dudley[39] sailed from Southampton on 6 November 1594, beginning his voyage with the clear intention of exploring the American coasts, the preliminary step to the creation of an empire with its base in Guyana. England intended to set up a major trading post from which to launch a sustained anti-Spanish campaign, hoping to involve the Indian *caciques* (local chiefs)[40] in the cause.

PEACE WITH FRANCE AND THE TREATY OF VERVINS

In 1598 the Peace of Vervins at last put an end to the war with France, which had been officially declared on 20 January 1595. When the respective delegations met to establish the terms of the agreement, the French proposed that a secret clause be introduced that 'annulled the papal interdiction west of the meridian of the Azores and south of the Tropic of Cancer'.

To the surprise of the French, the Spanish accepted the clause, believing that it was of only minor importance. In practice, however, it annulled the bulls of donation by which Spain could exercise her rights over the West Indies, or at least annulled the subsequent intervention of the Pope in the settling of conflicts.

Having seen his demands satisfied and on the understanding that subsequent interpretations of the clause would lead to permanent confrontations, Henry IV declared that 'peace does not exist beyond the Tropic'.

As the clause became public knowledge, all countries considered that they were free to sail the waters of the Indies.

Dudley's expedition was a resounding failure. From the very outset bad luck plagued his flotilla, consisting of the 200-ton *Beare*, the *Beare's Whelp*, commanded by Captain Munck, and two pinnaces called the *Frisking* and the *Earewig*.

The expedition sailed to the Canaries, where they arrived late in December and stayed twelve days waiting for Munck.

On 1 February 1595 they sighted Trinidad and, having explored part of the island, proceeded to Paracoa, or Parico, where they built a small fort near the beach, manned by a contingent of fifty. Subsequently Antonio Berrío arrived from Margarita with 300 men.

The English reconnoitred the entire island, putting up in Indian villages without making a truce with the Spaniards, who outnumbered them significantly.

For sixteen days they explored the Orinoco, where the Indians told them of a 'rich nation where men powdered their bodies with gold until they seemed to be made of the precious metal, and beyond a great city called El Dorado…'.

At this point George Popham's expedition arrived[41] on a pinnace that had departed from Plymouth on 6 February. Dudley awaited the arrival of Walter Raleigh, who had financed the expedition, until, on 12 March, he left Trinidad together with Popham.

A few leagues north of Grenada they took a Spanish pinnace laden with wine and continued with the intention of selling the vessel into San Juan de Puerto

Rico. There they were unsuccessful, so they decided to try their luck on Hispaniola.

Dudley set a course bordering the bank of Abre Ojos, or Los Abrojos, now Banco de La Plata, and then proceeded to Bermuda, where he hoped to come across a ship that might have gone astray from the Spanish fleet recently sailed from Havana.

However, storms and the lack of victuals persuaded him to give up the venture and return to England. On his homeward voyage he encountered a 600-ton Spanish galleon and the ships bombarded each other for two days. Eventually Dudley allowed the Spaniards to escape, since he lacked sufficient forces to board the enemy ship and suspected that its cargo may merely have been fish.

Dudley finally reached St Ives, Cornwall, late in May 1595, having sustained heavy losses and obtained no spoils whatsoever. Meanwhile, Popham engaged in actions on Margarita and Cumaná, but the Spanish forces defeated the English on both occasions.

The Expedition of Preston and Sommers (1595)

Onb 12 March 1595, two months later than originally planned, a flotilla, destined to operate in conjunction with Popham's fleet, sailed from Plymouth. The commander of the expedition was Preston,[42] on the *Ascension*, and his lieutenant was Sommers on the *Gift*, with a total of 300 seamen and soldiers. A pinnace completed the flotilla.

They had been waiting almost a month for the arrival of Captains Jones, on the *Derling*, and Prowse, on the *Angel*, who were supposed to act as escorts. Eventually Jones and Prowse followed them a week late.

Having overcome a series of slight mishaps, on 8 May they reached Dominica, where they exchanged objects for food with the Indians, rested and tended their sick.

On the island of Coche they took prisoner a number of Spaniards and their black fishermen, and obtained pearls. Having been paid the corresponding ransom in Cumaná, on 27 May they arrived at Guaira, where they disembarked and captured the governor of the fort.

They studied the best way to cross the hill and attack the city of Caracas (Santiago de León). They knew that the

King Philip II of Spain by Antonio Moro. Real Monasterio de San Lorenzo de El Escorial, Madrid.

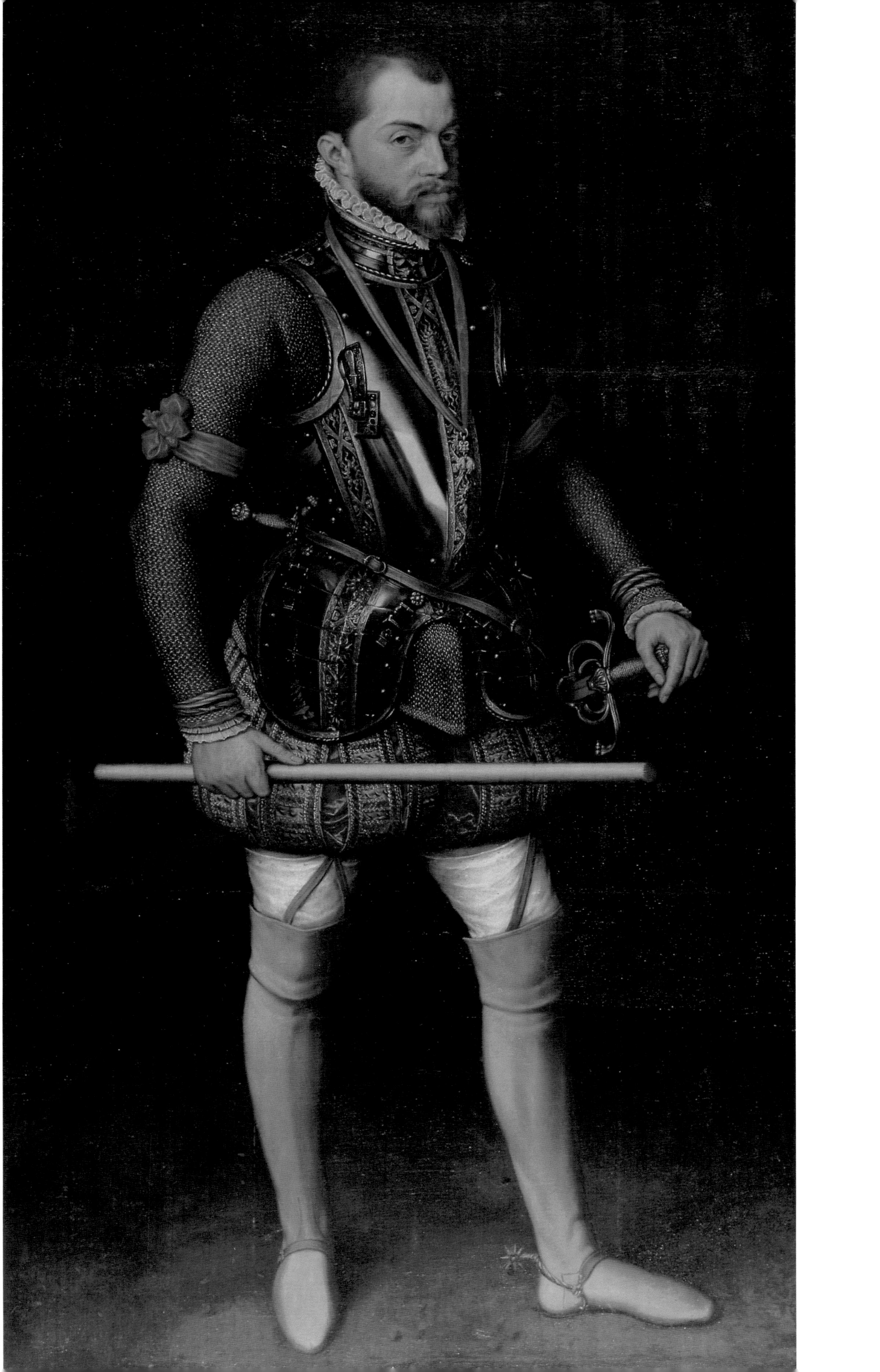

MILITARY ACTION AGAINST THE CANARIES

Holland had managed to put together a formidable fleet during the last years of the century. Organised in 1576 under the auspices of William of La Marck, the Dutch ships had taken part in military campaigns alongside the English, and now prepared to engage in warfare alone.

In 1599 a fleet of seventy-two ships commanded by Pieter van der Does sailed from Holland between 15 and 25 May. It ventured south and attacked Gran Canaria, obtaining a handsome booty and causing considerable damage. The fleet then continued to Brazil, where it obtained a consignment of sugar, and returned to Holland on 10 September, half the ships having been lost in the meantime.

William of Nassau 'The Taciturn', Prince of Orange (1533-1584). Attributed to Johann Andreas Thiele. Roudnice Lobkowicz Collection.

The expedition served to consolidate a navy that, by the next century, would have become the most powerful in Europe.

Spaniards had positioned defences on the road and that the hill was insurmountable. A Spanish officer informed them that there was an old Indian path, but that the defenders would most probably have blocked it. In Cumaná they captured a Spaniard who knew this path, and negotiated his freedom in exchange for acting as their guide.

After a skirmish with a cavalry detachment sent to intercept them, the English decided to advance along the Indian path. At nightfall, they rested beside a river. As the Spanish officer from the fort had suspected, the path was blocked with fallen trees and other obstacles; consequently, the ships' carpenters had to work hard to open the way.

Having negotiated the blockade, the men grouped on a hilltop from which they could see the city a short distance below. They prepared to attack, unfurled their banners and fired two musket shots to dissuade the Spaniards, who were waiting for them on horseback. After a number of skirmishes, the Spanish retreated, leaving the city at the mercy of the Englishmen. Around three in the afternoon they entered Caracas, where all they found was wine, iron and other goods difficult to transport.

On 1 June a Spanish emissary arrived to negotiate a tributo de quema fixed by the English at 30,000 ducats.

The following day he returned and lunched with Amias Preston to negotiate the ransom. The Spanish offer was just 3,000 ducats, a figure that Preston considered ridiculous.

The Englishmen razed the surrounding villages to the ground and took a number of Indians prisoner. From the captives they learned that the governor had asked for reinforcements, and came to realise that the Spaniards were playing for time. Preston ordered the city to be burned and the men to depart immediately thereafter.

The withdrawal took place on 3 June and proved to be as arduous as the advance. They climbed the hill on the Camino Real, reaching the summit that night. Here they found a great barricade blocking their way although, fortunately, it had been abandoned. Considering this to be a safe place, they spent the night here and the following morning continued on their way back to the sea.

Towards midday they reached the fort of La Guaira and began to make their preparations. They loaded hides and sarsaparilla and took in victuals and fresh water, sailing at nightfall. But, not wishing to depart without leaving a last souvenir of their presence, they set fire to the fort and surrounding Indian houses.

On 9 June they reached Coro. Since there was nobody with them who was familiar with the area, at nightfall they anchored two leagues from the coast and sent patrols to reconnoitre the territory. Around eleven o'clock on the night of 10 June, they made landfall and advanced towards the city.

The road was blocked by a strong barricade that the Spaniards staunchly defended, but the Englishmen's superior numbers forced them to retreat. They spent the night at the barricade and continued to advance the following morning, during which they were ambushed at several points by small Spanish detachments.

Around midday they entered Coro, where they found neither resistance nor booty. Consequently, the English set fire to the city and returned to their ships.

They explored the Bay of Laguna (Lago Maracaibo) for the space of two days and one night but, not daring to venture too far inland, they returned to sea and, on 16 June, set sail for Hispaniola. Five days later they anchored off Cabo Tiburón, having lost eighty men who died of 'loose bowels, a common condition in this country'.

On their return voyage to England they made port in Jamaica, and on the morning of 13 July encountered

ONCE AGAIN IN THE PACIFIC

While the Dutch engaged in major actions in European waters, navigation in the Pacific soon became an objective of strategic importance. The Dutch organised several expeditions to explore those waters and discover routes by which to establish trade relations.

On 27 June 1598 Admiral Jacques Mathu sailed from Rotterdam at the head of five ships and 547 men, with the aim of establishing settlements in Chile that would subsequently serve as trading posts. By 6 April the following year they were sailing the Straits of Magellan, but they stopped in Bahía Grande for a period of five months.

In the southern spring they engaged, with losses, the Southern Sea Armada. They unsuccessfully attempted to flee into the Pacific, and all the ships and men were lost.

In 1598 a second expedition was prepared in Rotterdam by Oliver van Noort. Four ships and 248 men departed on 13 September with the intention to trade without engaging in acts of hostility.

Fourteen months later, after a highly eventful voyage, they reached the Straits of Magellan and entered the Pacific on 29 February 1600. They attacked a ship off the coast of Valparaíso, as a result of which they were pursued to the Philippines, two of the ships reaching the Straits of San Bernardino on 14 October. Here a confrontation took place with Morgan's *San Diego*, with losses sustained on both sides. Finally, on 26 August 1601 the *Mauricio* and eight survivors reached Holland, marking the end of a thoroughly unprofitable voyage.

Walter Raleigh, who was returning from Guyana. During the night of the 20th the two flotillas lost contact and, after a number of attacks on strongholds and isolated ships, were forced to retreat.

At last, on 10 September 1595, they reached the Welsh port of Milford Haven. Despite the 'military victories', the expedition had been financially unsuccessful.

Lawrence Keymis's Expedition (1596)

Lawrence Keymis[13] was an experienced sea captain who, in 1595, had taken part in Popham's expedition in command of an oar-powered frigate. On 26 January 1596 he sailed from Portland on the *Darling of London* accompanied by the *Discoverer*, a pinnace from which he became separated after a few days. Sir Walter Raleigh had financed the expedition, the objective of which was to explore Guyana.

By the end of March, Keymis had arrived at the mouth of the River Arrowari. During the following five months he explored Trinidad and Guyana, establishing contact with the indigenous population and meticulously noting his observations. From a monetary point of view, however, the expedition yielded absolutely no profits.

The Expedition of Leonard Berry (1596)

Leonard Berry,[14] one of Walter Raleigh's lieutenants, sailed from Limehouse on 14 October 1596 on the pinnace *Watte*. On 28 January 1597 he touched the Barbary coast where he encountered Benjamin Wood, who, with a flotilla of three ships, was sailing to China.

Having rested and taken in provisions on the island of Mayo, Berry set off on his ocean crossing to Guyana and separated from the Chinese fleet. He caught the current that flows from the Cape of Good Hope to the coast of Brazil on 20 February, and seven days later sighted America.

He and his men explored the coast of Guyana until the beginning of May, when Berry decided to sail to the Caribbean. On 28 June 1597 Berry's fleet passed the Lizard and that same night arrived at Plymouth. On his voyage to Guyana, Berry maintained contact with a tender, the *John of London*, commanded by Charles Leigh, whose intention was apparently to trade.

PEACE WITH ENGLAND

The deaths of King Philip II and, later, of Queen Elizabeth gave rise to a new era in the relations between Spain and England. In 1604 the new King of England, James I, and Philip III of Spain signed a peace treaty that at last put an end to twenty years of undeclared war.

Only one front remained open for Spain, that of the Dutch rebels, with whom Philip negotiated a truce in 1607. Thus a period of peace began that would last until 1621, when smuggling once again became the main activity in the Americas.

The Somerset House Conference by Pantoja de la Cruz. National Maritime Museum Picture Library.
After the death of Queen Elizabeth, a conference of Spanish and English delegates was convened at Somerset House in The Strand to discuss peace terms.
The meetings would last from May to August 1604 and result in the Treaty of London signed on 28 August 1604 – the end of an undeclared war that had been
waged for more than thirty years. The delegates were seated in a strict hierarchical order. On the left from Spain and Flanders, from the top of the table:
Juan de Velasco, Duke of Frias, Corregidor of Castille; Juan de Tassis, Count of Villa Mediana; Alessandro Robido, Senator of Milan; Charles de Ligne, Count of
Aremberg; Jean Richardot, President of the Consejo Privado; Louis Vereyken, Principal Secretary. On the right the English delegates, from the top of the table:
Thomas Sackville, Earl of Dorset, Lord High Treasurer; Charles, Lord Howard of Effingham, Earl of Nottingham; Charles Blount, Earl of Devonshire;
Henry Howard, Earl of Northampton; Robert Cecil, Earl of Salisbury, Lord Treasurer.

CHAPTER IV

A PERIOD OF PEACE
(1604–1621)

PEACE AT LAST

In 1598, after the death of King Philip II, his son, Philip III, a man of pacifist leanings who longed to put an end to three decades of conflict in Europe, was proclaimed King of Spain. Five years later, the death of Elizabeth and the Stuarts' ascent to the throne of England created conditions favourable to change in Anglo-Spanish relations.

A conference was convened in London to reach agreements that would lead to the end of hostilities. Queen Elizabeth's former counsellors, headed by Charles Howard,[1] proposed that in order for the armistice to be acceptable, England should be allowed to trade freely with the Indies and to set up bases in the Caribbean from which to do so. Robert Cecil supported this proposal, although he knew that Spain would never accept it. Eventually the English moderated their demands, above all because King James wished to begin his reign without foreign conflicts.

For her part, Spain needed peace as a preliminary step towards achieving the isolation of Holland and to be able to concentrate all her military efforts on subduing the rebels. Consequently, Philip III was prepared to make concessions.

The 'Peace of London' was at last signed in 1604. Spain agreed that the English could engage in trade anywhere except the Americas and secured King James's commitment to punishing by death any of his subjects who sailed to the Indies.

In the conflict with Holland, the fall of Ostend and the withdrawal of English aid tipped the balance in favour of Spain, but the economic recession of 1606 halted the campaign. Weary of the conflict, Spain sought a truce with the States General, which was signed on 9 March 1609 for a period of twelve years.

Article IV of the treaty[2] allowed the Dutch to trade with Peninsular ports as far as the line of Tordesillas. To trade further west they needed the express permission of the King of Spain. However, the article included a proviso, namely that this restriction would not be valid in those countries 'that chose to grant permission, even beyond the stipulated limits'.

The interpretation of this proviso would give rise to subsequent conflicts, in that the Dutch equated the colonists' readiness to accept smuggling with the permission granted by third countries to trade. Basing themselves on this interpretation they attempted to set up a trading post in Esquivo in 1613 and, in 1615, in Cayena, Oyapoc and the Amazon.

Having solved her main problems, Spain gained breathing space in which to launch an aggressive campaign against pirates, illegal traders and colonists who collaborated with them. As an incentive, Philip III authorised the colonists to keep the merchandise confiscated from illegal traders and even to execute them after expeditious trial.

PERSONAL INTERESTS, REASONS OF STATE

In December 1602 two prominent English merchants, John Eldred and Richard Hall, began to trade in the Antilles and became directly involved in contraband.

They decided to embark on this venture because of the positive results obtained by rival companies. The Dutch firm of Moucheron, the property of Balthasar Moucheron,[3] had opened an establishment in London, opposite which Balthasar's brother Peter had opened his own. The Genoese firm of Cataneo had been operating on a regular basis in the Antilles for some time.

The Cataneos had made handsome profits from trade with Hispaniola, to the extent that the *Prosperus*, an English ship chartered by the company, had remained for three years in the port of Guanahibes with absolute impunity. On another occasion, Pompilio Cataneo had managed to load eight vessels in Manzanillo as well as a Dutch ship, the *Angel Gabriel*, with a cargo valued at 30,000 ducats.

Eldred and Hall[4] decided to embark on an expedition in December 1602. Other individuals interested in direct trade were Thomas Middleton and Richard Hawkins,

closely linked to the circles of Sir Robert Cecil and charterers of the *Vineyard*.

Charles Howard, Cecil's partner in smuggling operations, was involved with several enterprises in the Caribbean and even maintained trade relations with Spain during the war.

To counteract the personal interests of Howard and Cecil, the English delegation at the London Conference demanded the right of free trade with the Indies. Reasons of state came to prevail, represented by the king himself who, though in favour of free trade, forced the

London in the 18th century

delegates to adopt a more flexible stance and reduce their demands with a view to putting an end to a war that favoured only those engaged in smuggling.

At the same time, drastic measures were taken to transport whole populations who protected smugglers and to devastate entire regions of America. The naval system was restructured and the main American strongholds were fortified as evidence of Spain's resolve to protect her monopoly at all costs. The measures proved effective: the activities of smugglers decreased, but the price was very high.

HISPANIOLA, A LAND OF REDEEMERS

If there was one Caribbean island characterised by the goodwill of its authorities towards smugglers, then that island was Hispaniola. This had been the first American

land to be populated by Spaniards, but it lacked the major natural resources of the continent and soon became a second-class region.

At the northern end of the island stood a number of ports with only a small Spanish population from which the dispatch of products from the Vega, the main productive area of the island, was controlled.

Leather, a Profitable Business

During his term of office, Governor Nicolás de Ovando, ordered the import of cattle[5] to supplement the scant food resources on the island. The cattle adapted well to the local climate and reproduced rapidly, soon becoming one of the mainstays of the colony's economy.

PRICES

One negro	50 or 60 hides
One *vara** of fine cloth	2 or 3 hides
Four or five *varas* of Rouen fabric	1 hide
Five or six *varas* of *angeo* (coarse linen)	1 hide
One pipe of wine	20 or 25 hides

* *vara = 83.59cm*

On Hispaniola trade in contraband reached epidemic proportions.
To try and combat the practice, drastic measures were adopted, such as
grouping the island's northern communities around Santo Domingo.

Indeed, the livestock became so abundant that only the hides were exploited, the meat being left for scavengers.

The difficulties involved in transporting the hides, or even the herds themselves, from the production areas in the Vega, Santiago and Cotuy to Santo Domingo led to the search for easily-accessed ports from which to export the products.

Puerto Plata, Montecristi and La Yaguana became the main ports on the north coast of the island, although official ships could not reach them. The presence of corsairs limited navigation, and they became the true masters of the ports, from which it was easy for them to engage in smuggling, exchanging hides for negroes, cloth and wine.

The first smugglers were Portuguese, although by the 1560s the English and French had come to dominate. Both Hawkins[6] and Jean Bontemps made important connections that led to highly profitable business. After 1565, when the officers who traded with Hawkins were duly punished for doing so, the *tangomangos*,[7] the name given to middlemen, came onto the scene. These were normally individuals working alone who, in return for substantial commissions, received orders, transmitted them to the smugglers and put together the products. When caught red-handed, they paid fines, never challenging the sanctions imposed.

In order to control smuggling in 1573 it was proposed that controls[8] should be made on salt, as on mercury, so that only enough to produce a specific amount of leather would be supplied. Sale of the leather would subsequently be controlled. Furthermore, it was proposed that the population of the north coasts be moved inland.

By 1577 the whole island had come to collaborate in the export of leather beyond the control of the capital.

The Policy of Depopulation

Smuggling increased to such an extent that the entire population became involved. In 1598 Baltasar López de Castro[9] denounced the fact that contraband was ruining the legitimate economy and suggested that the herds of cattle be moved to areas close to the capital or at least to places where the Audiencia could control their exploitation.

By then the Dutch had cornered part of the market and, with the connivance of the Banda del Norte, extended their branches to Cuba, Jamaica and Venezuela. The upper classes also became involved in the business:[10] Luis Colón, Columbus's grandson, and Aldonza Manrique placed their fiefs in Jamaica and Margarita at the disposal of smugglers as a way to cover up their operations.

Late in 1601 the Spanish authorities, thoroughly disgruntled with the situation, ordered the immediate formation of a squadron of coastguards known as the *Armada de Barlovento* (Windward Fleet), but peace negotiations took precedence over the project, which was postponed. In 1603 López de Castro's presence at the Spanish Court was instrumental in persuading the Junta de Guerra del Consejo de Indias to depopulate Puerto Plata, Bayajá and Yaguana.

In August 1604 López de Castro returned to the island, bearing decrees ordering Governor Osorio to carry out the depopulation. The fact that the archbishop of Santo Domingo[11] denounced the revelation that, through the

THE TWO SPAINS[12]

Two conflicting attitudes to politics, economics and Spain's role on the world stage existed side-by-side in the Spain of the Philips.

On the one hand, there were those who believed that Spanish involvement in one armed conflict after another would lead the nation to ruin, and they advocated a pacifistic policy based on diplomacy and negotiation. Those on the other side favoured making Spain the world's dominant power, stepping up the arms race and interfering with the affairs of other states.

In company with a militant policy, went a view that trade with foreign countries should be restricted, and the Spanish economy converted into a series of monopolies. This would have the side-effect of intellecutally isolating the Spanish people from the emerging new schools of thought and new ideas. Opposed to this view were the advocates for the economics of free trade and commercial companies.

The philosophy of free trade and peaceful foreign policyprevailed during the reign of Philip III, in which figures such as Lorenzo Suárez de Figueroa, Second Duke of Feria, and his co-religionists, with strong connections with the Jewish convert sector, were highly influential.

The militant group came to dominate during the reign of Philip IV and eventually managed to totally isolate Spain.

The City and Port of Seville by Alonso Sánchez Coello. The Museo de América, Madrid. See detail opposite.

smugglers of the Banda del Norte, protestant bibles were being introduced into the island was crucial to the operation's being set in motion.

The order for eviction was given and was met by waves of protest. Late in January the Dutchman, Paulus van Caerden,[13] who had anchored in Guanahibes, offered military aid to those inhabitants wanting to resist.

In mid February Osorio set off with armed men to carry out the orders. To prevent the evicted inhabitants from returning, everything was burned to the ground. Montecristi, Puerto Plata, Bayajá and Yaguana were depopulated and the inhabitants regrouped in two newly created enclaves,[14] Monte Plata and Bayaguana, near Santo Domingo. It was forbidden, under pain of death, to settle further north or west of Santiago or further west of San Juan de la Maguana and Azua.

The consequences[15] were terrible. It proved possible to transfer only 8,000 of the 110,000 existing head of cattle, and the rest ran wild. Meat became extremely scarce when, because of the lack of suitable pasture, only 2,000 head survived. A third of the population of Bayaguana died from starvation and disease and, in 1609, the town was burned to the ground. Having become homeless, many people turned to cattle rustling to survive.

In 1608 Antonio Osorio was replaced as governor of the island by Diego Gómez de Sandoval, who attempted

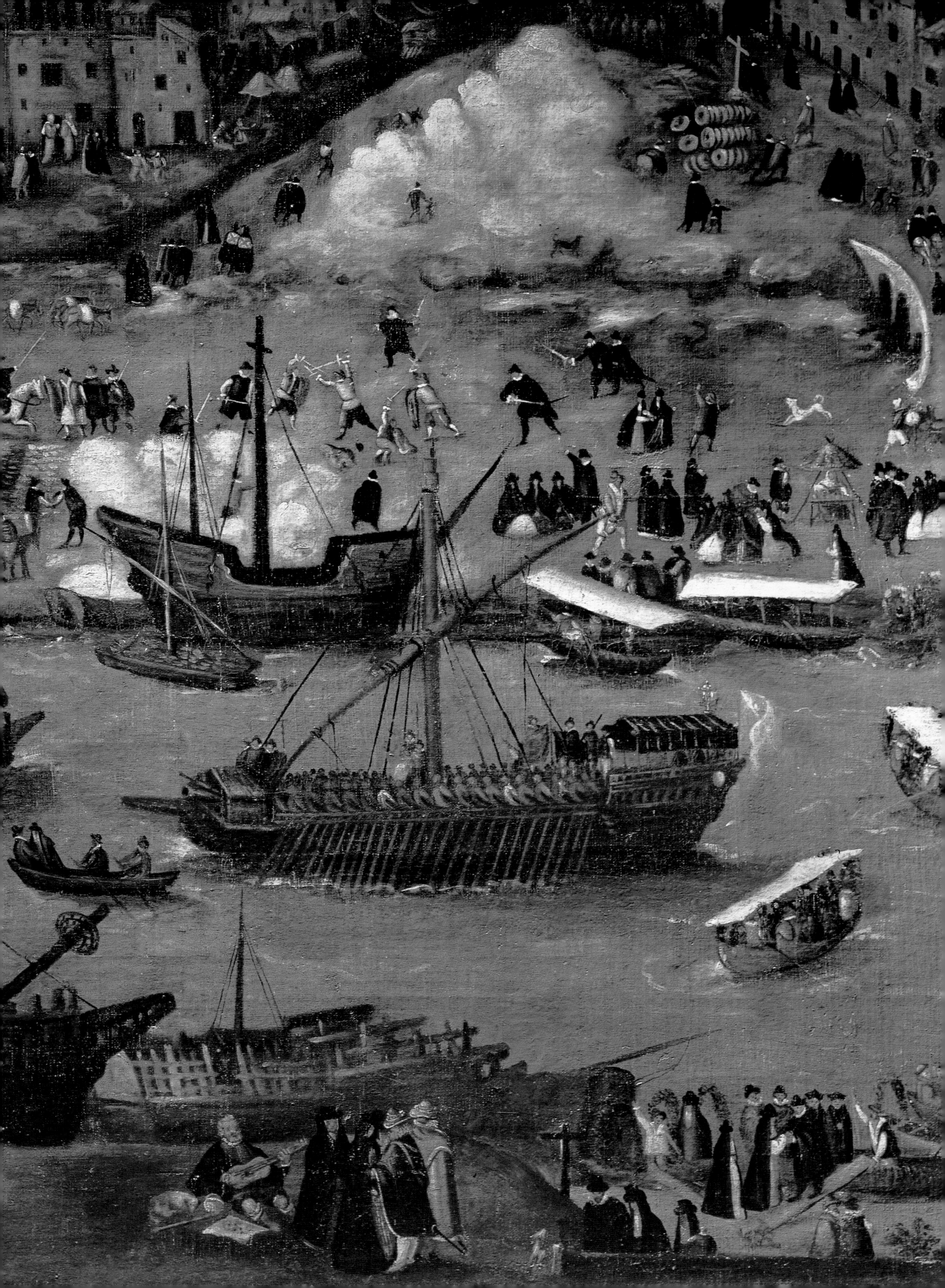

COMPLICITY, A
COMPLEX PROBLEM

If any one was particularly responsible for smuggling at the northern end of Hispaniola, then that man was Francisco Ceballos, an alderman of Puerto Plata and governor of the fortress.

Ceballos was the rich, powerful owner of a large sugar plantation. Furthermore, he had marital ties with the *oidor* (judge) Grajeda, with Christopher Columbus and with the Licenciado Ortegón, thanks to which he used the Audiencia of Santo Domingo as a cover-up for his illicit activities. Puerto Rico and Florida also depended on this same Audiencia, so that Ceballos was practically immune from any action taken against him in any of these places.

Ceballos employed over 250 negroes, acquired illegally from the Portuguese, the French and from none other than Hawkins, whom he had befriended during the Englishman's voyage of 1562. Hawkins was a partner of Pedro Ponte who, in turn, had commercial links with Bernáldez,[16] who was sent to block illicit dealings by his brother-in-law Angulo,[17] a 'diabolical man' who was the son and grandson of Jewish converts. Formally accused of illegal trade, Bernáldez was exonerated thanks to the influence of his cousin Alonso Bernáldez de Quirós, Governor of Venezuela. In 1566 Jean Bontemps came to Puerto Plata and stole three ships in connivance with Ceballos. Fêted during his stay, Bontemps was able to trade in hides and sugar and managed to establish commercial relations, promising to return the following year.

The beginning of these relations coincided with the arrival in Florida of the forces of Pedro Menéndez de Avilés, who sent a detachment to Puerto Plata commanded by Juan de Garibay y Aguirre,[18] who reached the port on 1 January 1567.

Everything seemed to be going well until, in February, two French ships belonging to Hugo Guorguesio's expedition entered the port with their war banners flying and trumpets and drums sounding, while from the forecastle, swords raised, the Frenchmen threatened to put all the inhabitants to the sword.

They had not reckoned on the presence of Garibay, however, who organised effective defences and began to bombard the flagship from the fort. Using the tender, the French managed to capture a Spanish vessel called *La Pintadilla* and were preparing for a second attack when their ship was sunk by a direct hit. They salvaged what they could and attempted to recover their position. An attempt was made to disembark, but the French encountered such fierce opposition that they were forced to retreat.

Ceballos prevented Garibay from setting off in their pursuit by staving in his launches, having informed the French that he also intended to hide the Spanish gunpowder and ammunition.

When Garibay returned to the fort, the gunpowder had disappeared. When he demanded it back from Ceballos, the latter began to shout, a pre-arranged signal that formed part of the plan.

The French resumed the offensive. Ceballos withdrew with most of the inhabitants to the mountains, leaving Garibay to face them alone and without gunpowder. Even so, he managed to repel the onslaught with harquebus fire.

Seeing that they were insufficient in number to take the fort, the French proceeded to Montecristi to procure reinforcements. But since they were unable to persuade their compatriots to join them, they gave up their attempt to take Puerto Plata.

In the meantime, Ceballos had gone to La Isabela and prepared to trade without further impediments, sending a French ship to Puerto Plata to keep Garibay occupied. He also provided Gourguesio with a pilot, Mezina, to guide him to Florida.

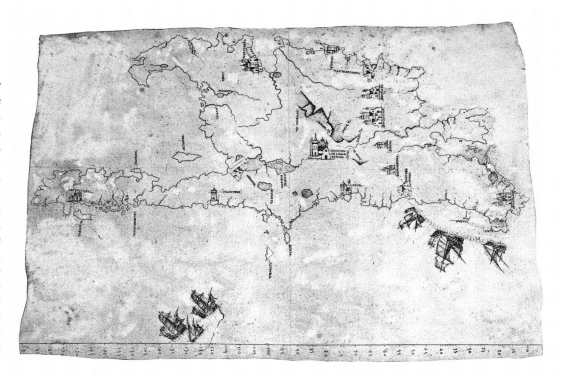

Map of Hispaniola, 1568

Garibay captured a negro called Caramanzana, the brother of the woman who lived with Ceballos, and sent him to the Audiencia as the person responsible for the smuggling operations. However, Ceballos had sufficient influence in Santo Domingo to have Caramanzana released and returned to Puerto Plata.

In May Jean Bontemps returned, to be warned by a cannon shot fired by Ceballos. Bontemps withdrew to Montecristi, as previously agreed with Ceballos, where he spent four months dealing in hides.

The Audiencia's support of illicit operations reached such extremes that Garibay had no option but to abandon the fort, allowing Ceballos to transfer its artillery to his own estate. Protests from Puerto Rico were to no avail, and conflicts worsened until Garibay's troops abandoned Hispaniola on 12 November 1568.

Total calm by Van de Velde the Younger, 1633-1707.

to restore livestock raising. He forbade the sacrifice of cows and calves and hunts were organised to eradicate the packs of wild dogs that decimated the herds. However, the rise in prices brought economic ruin to the colony.

The worst outcome of the devastation was that vast areas of the island were abandoned, later to be occupied by French and English evicted from other places. This in turn gave rise to the emergence of buccaneers and filibusters.

SEEKING THE ROUTE TO THE WEST

In 1602 the *Oost Indische Kompanie* (East India Company) was founded in Amsterdam to secure the Dutch trade monopoly with the East Indies and to earn the right to found colonies, appoint governors, establish treaties, declare war and mint currency.

Eight years later, in 1670, Holland created a central administrative body in order to control the colonies and expeditions were organised to seek alternative routes to and from Europe. To this end, two major expeditions set sail, commanded by Wilhelm von Scoutten and Joris van Spielbergen.

Le Mayre's Expedition

Isaac Le Mayre, an important and influential merchant from Hoorn, organised an expedition in 1615 to locate a passage south of the Straits of Magellan that would allow him to break the monopoly of the East India Company.

He prepared two ships, the *Hoorn* and the *Concordia*, commanded by Wilhelm von Scoutten.

FREEDOM OF THE SEAS[19]

In 1602 Admiral Heemskerk, in the service of the Dutch East India Company, captured the Portuguese carrack the *Catalina*. Back in Holland, he was required to share the booty among the shareholders, but a major group of them, who were Mennonites, considered the gains to be ill-gotten.

The directors of the Company commissioned a twenty-two-year-old jurist, Hugo Grocio, to draw up a report that would persuade them otherwise. The outcome was the *De iure praede commentarius*, which Grocio compiled between 1604 and 1605, although for a number of reasons it was not published in its entirety until 1868.

In 1608 the Company asked Grocio to publish Chapter 12 of his report, *Mare liberum*, which appeared in Leiden the following year. This request was in response to two factors: on the one hand, negotiations of the Twelve-Year Truce were at their height and Holland was determined to safeguard its rights in Indian waters; on the other, there was a pressing need to contest King James's May 1609 decree restricting fishing rights in waters off the coast of England.

In the words of García Arias, *Mare liberum* was written against Portugal, published against Spain and used against England. Its sources of inspiration being the Spanish School of International Law, specifically the thinking of Vitoria and Vázquez Menchaca, the document proclaimed the right to visit and trade with other nations and denied that any particular nation could be granted exclusive navigation rights.

Reactions were immediate. England rejected the document and produced her own, which culminated in Selden's *Mare clasusm, seu de Dominio Maris Libri Duo*, published in 1635. The controversy, replies and counter-replies, lasted until 1645.

Venice rejected Grocio's theses by virtue of its conflict with Spain over

Marina by Adam Willaerts, 18th Century.

control of the Adriatic. Spain, for its part, delayed any rejection that might momentarily be favourable to its interests, although its replies came after the outbreak of war.

The controversy was finally resolved in about 1703, when *Dissertio de Dominio Maris*, by Cornelius van Brynkershoek, imposed the principle of the freedom of the seas, each nation being allowed exclusive dominion over its immediate territorial waters only.

Chart of the Straits of Magellan, 1671

CHANGES IN THE NAVAL STRUCTURE

The ships involved in the Carrera de Indias may be divided in functional terms into cargo and escort vessels. The fleets of Nueva España and Tierra Firme consisted of a considerable number of armed merchant ships, carrying infantry for their defence, and two escort galleons, the *Capitana* and the *Almiranta*, of greater tonnage, better armed and with larger crews. The naval structure was completed with the *Armada de la Guarda de la Carrera de Indias*, more popularly known as the *Galeones*, consisting of a variable number – generally eight – of heavily armed ships whose mission was to bring silver back to the home country, although they also transported other high-value goods.

The merchant vessels were conceived exclusively as transport units and made no concessions to military use. Their weight was restricted to some 500 tons to allow them to sail over the sandbanks of Sanlúcar and San Juan de Ulúa, although their average weight was usually around 400 tons. In fact, the restriction was established in relation to maximum breadth, which was determined at seventeen cubits.

The escort vessels were a more interesting case. *Capitanas, almirantas* and *galeones de plata* were conceived for combat, although strictly for defence purposes. The galeón de plata, or 'silver galleon', was in fact a huge strongbox for silver, designed to repel enemy attacks and of a structural strength capable of withstanding any contretemps.

The galeón de plata, conceived as a three-decked ship – two ordinary decks and the *puente corrida*, with its half and quarter decks – was designed, in theory, to transport merchandise as if it were a regular merchantman; hence the fact that its hold and deck of *baos vacíos* (empty beams) were set aside exclusively for this.

The upper deck, normally used for heavier calibre artillery on warships, accommodated the infantry employed to defend the galleon. The lower deck was for the artillery, which would, to save weight, be of a lighter calibre than that of the ships of the Armada. Man-to-man fighting on board was the final outcome of naval battles, and the galeón de plata was designed to make this practically impossible.

Manoeuvre of the galleon was controlled from the *puente corrida*, which constituted a kind of parade deck on which fighting took place if necessary. A major characteristic of this deck was the use of *jarretas de firme* to close the bridge so that the smoke from the artillery would not accumulate in the 'tween decks.

Above the bridge, the cabin superstructures for the captain and officers and the bunkrooms for the pilots enormously increased the volume of the *obra muerta*.

1. The pilot's cabin. The pilot was assigned his own cabin at the top of the vessel's superstructure. Aided by a second pilot, pilotines and a coast pilot, he was responsible for correct navigation.
2. The officers' cabins.
3. The tiller housing. The helm was encased in a kind of drawer in which the pinzote moved according to orders from the pilot.
4. The *Santabárbara*: this accommodated the artillerymen and the cannons protecting the helm.
5. The quarterdeck and forecastle: essentially areas used for handling the rigging and manoeuvring.
6. The second deck.
7. The *fogón* or kitchen, where the sailors' and soldiers' rations were prepared.
8. The heads – the sailors' toilets.
9. First deck.
10. The *baos vacíos* deck, where soldiers were accommodated on escort vessels.
11. Munitions store or powder bunker, where the gunpowder and arms were stored. Aft was the place where the artillerymen loaded the cartridges with gunpowder and then passed them up to the Santabárbara through a hatchway.
12. The stern crutch store, often used as the place in which to load cartridges or to store emergency provisions.
13. The baling pump.
14. The bullet store.
15. The hold.
16. The rigging store.
17. The launch and lifeboat.
18. *Falconetes*, or small artillery, to be used at short range.

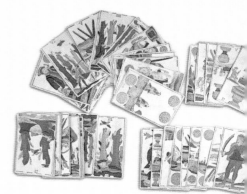

During the Atlantic crossing there were long periods during which the crews had very little to do. Since occupying their time was no easy task, games of chance became part of their everyday activities. Gambling was penalised but if anything this provided a greater incentive to play.

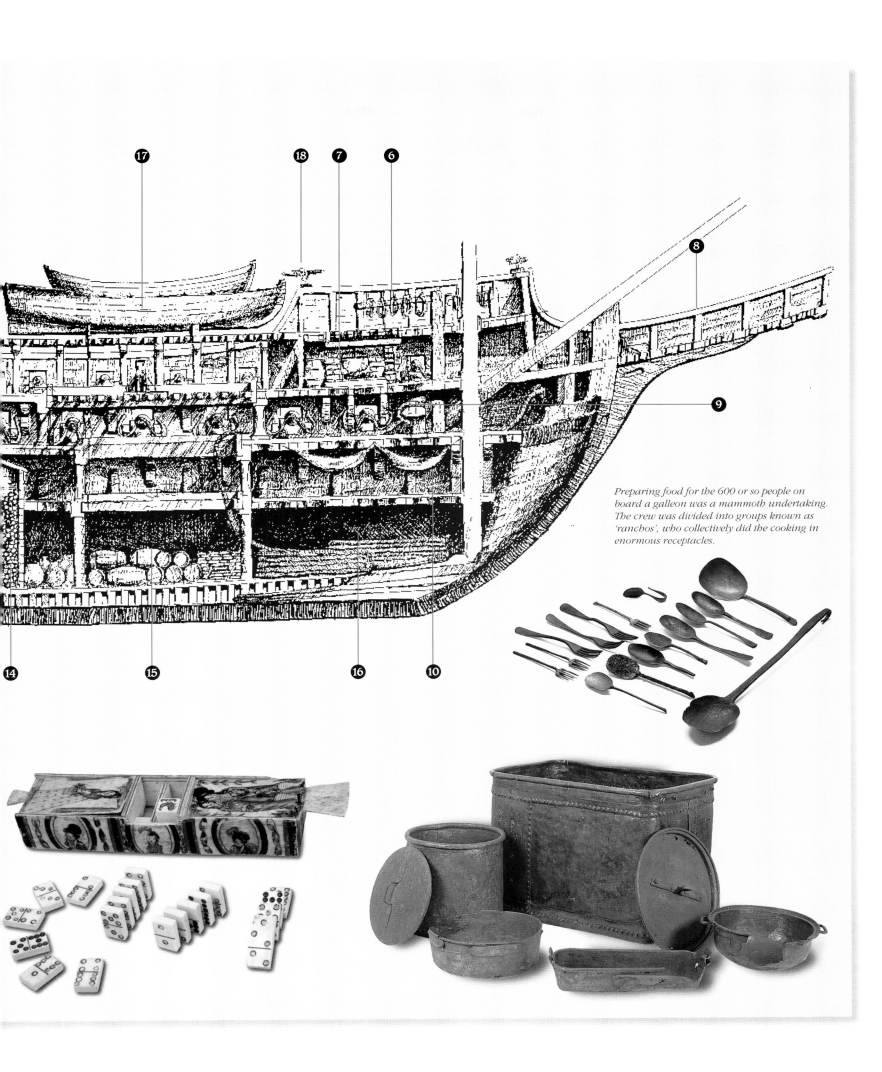

Preparing food for the 600 or so people on board a galleon was a mammoth undertaking. The crew was divided into groups known as 'ranchos', who collectively did the cooking in enormous receptacles.

AMSTERDAM

On 4 July the flotilla set sail with Jacob, Isaac's son, as purser. In Patagonia the *Concordia* was lost. The *Hoorn*, on the other hand, achieved its goal on January 24 1616 when it discovered a passage which they called Le Mayre. In honour of the ship and their native city, they christened America's southernmost point *Kaap Hoorn* (subsequently known to the English as Cape Horn and to the Spanish as *Cabo de Hornos*).

In October the Dutch reached the Moluccas. At Batavia (today Djakarta), the *Hoorn* was captured and its merchandise confiscated by the Governor of the East India Company, basing his action on the exclusive navigation rights that had been granted by the Dutch authorities. They finally returned to Holland in 1617 having been authorised to join Spielbergen's expedition. Le Mayre died during the voyage.

The Expedition of Joris van Spielbergen (1614-1617)

Spielbergen, an expert German sailor employed in the service of the Dutch, set sail on 8 August 1614 at the head of 800 men with the aim of establishing a trading post on the coast of Chile or Brazil that would serve as a stopover on the route to the East Indies. His flotilla consisted of five ships built specifically for the expedition: the 600 ton, 28-cannon *Grote Zoon* and *Grote Maan*, the 400-ton, 22-cannon *Neuew* and *Eolus*, and the tender, *Morgenstern*, weighing 150 tons and carrying eight cannons.

In February 1615 they reached the Pacific coast, where they began to engage in plunder. The Viceroy of Peru, the Marquis of Montesclaros, sent a six-ship escadrille of which only the flagship *Jesús María*, carrying 22 cannons and 400 men, and the 12-cannon vice-admiral's ship *Santa Ana*, carrying 200 men, were equipped for war.

The encounter took place on 17 July off Cañete, south of Lima. The Spanish escadrille had dispersed, leaving only the flagship, the vice-admiral's ship and a tender to face the Dutch; many Spanish lives were lost. At dawn

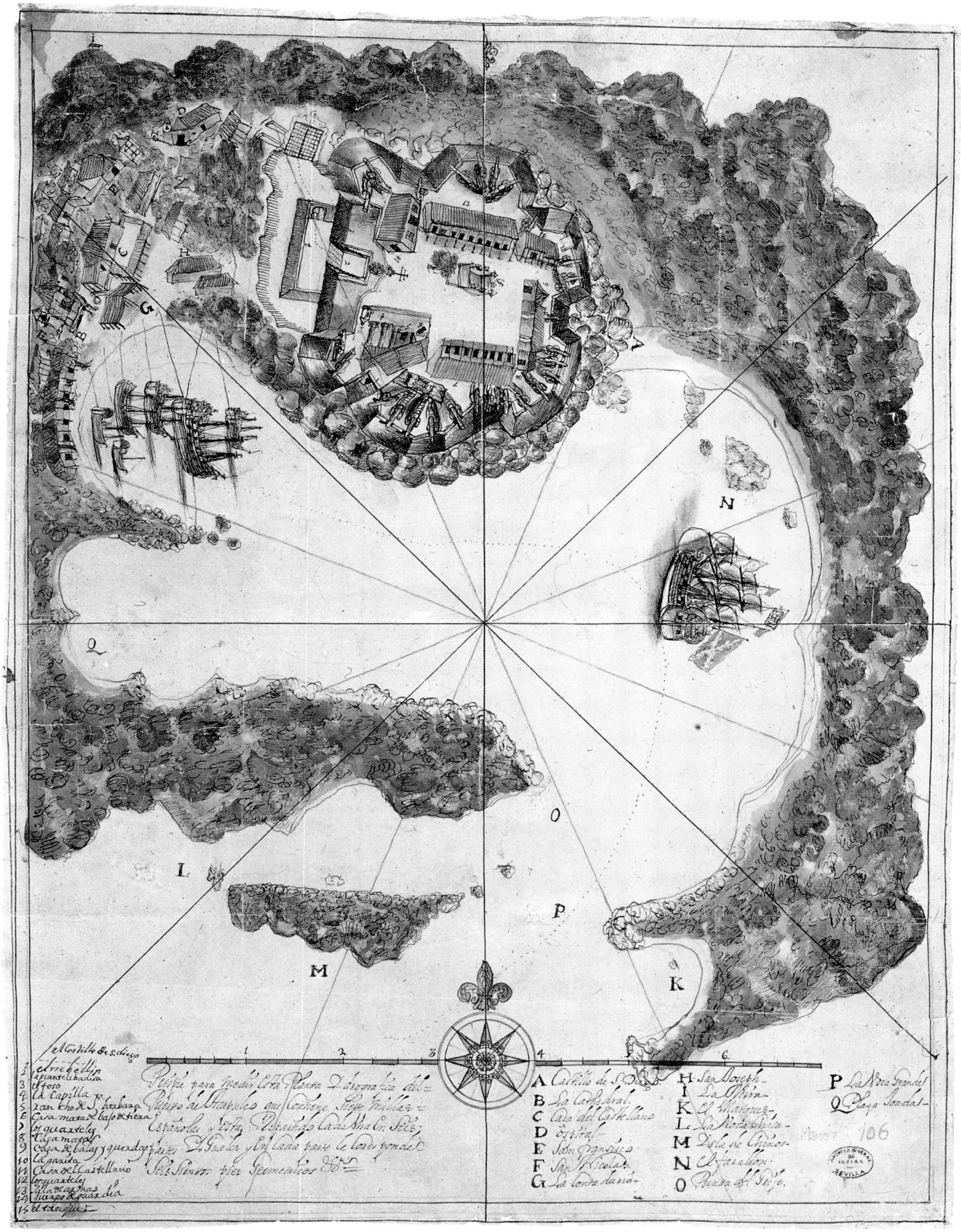
N
O
P
K
L
M
Q
1
2
3
4
6
A Castillo de S. Diego
B La Cathedral.
C Casa del Castellano
D ospital
E San Fransisco
F San Nicolas
H San Joseph
K El Marques
L La Boca Chica
M Isla de Chinos
N El Farallon
O Punta del Grifo
P La Boca Grande
Q Playa Sondas
Castillo de S. diego
1 el rrebellin
3 el foso
4 la capilla
6 Casa mata de baso de tierra
7 los quarteles
8 Casamatas
10 la garita
11 Casa del Castellano
12 los quarteles
13 Sala de armas
14 querpo de guardia
15 el tanque
106
ARCHIVO GENERAL DE INDIAS SEVILLA

the following morning, the Spanish flagship withdrew leaving the vice-admiral's ship to face five enemy vessels. Eventually she was sunk.

The news spread like wildfire and defences were hastily prepared. On 21 June Spielbergen began to bombard El Callao. The response was gunfire from two large cannon positioned in the stronghold, manned by a Franciscan friar, Father Gallardo,[20] who had been an artilleryman before taking holy orders. The friar made a direct hit on both the mainmast of the *Grote Zoon* and the hold of the *Morgenstern*, forcing the Dutch to withdraw.

On 8 August the Dutch were in Payta, where four companies of musketeers landed. Here they were confronted by Paula Giraldo, wife of the corregidor of Piura who, commanding a force of local inhabitants and Indians, managed to resist for a time.

In Acapulco the Dutch exchanged prisoners for victuals and then proceeded unmolested to the Philippines and the Moluccas, where a number of ships joined the flotilla. After an unfortunate encounter with Juan Ronquillo's squadron, on 25 April 1617 they finally reached the coast of Holland.

THE *SANTA ANA* IS SUNK[21]

Having engaged in combat with the Spanish flagship, the Dutch squadron next became involved in an artillery duel with the vice-admiral's ship, the *Santa Ana*, which lasted from dawn until eight o'clock in the evening, when the vessel was finally sunk.

Only four surviving crew members were rescued by the Dutch. To their astonishment, they discovered that one of them was a woman dressed as a soldier, namely Catalina de Erauso, the famous *monja alférez* (nun sub-lieutenant).

RAPID AID[22]

On January 20 1618, two soldiers from the garrison of Santo Tomé were ordered by the Cabildo to go urgently in search of reinforcements to counter the attack by English forces commanded by Keymis.

The envoys sailed up the rivers Orinoco, Meta and Casanare until they reached Pauto. From here they set off for Santa Fe de Bogotá, arriving there on April 9.

Having learned of the situation, president Borja sent a platoon of twenty-five soldiers, who made the same journey in reverse, reaching Santo Tomé on August 19. But there were no English; they had left Guyana six and a half months earlier.

The New Riches of America

Early in the 17th century the economy of the coastal settlements in Tierra Firme had changed. There was practically no demand for sugar, pearl production was decreasing rapidly and hides were becoming more and more scarce.

New products emerged as viable alternatives, foremost among which was tobacco. Its consumption had begun to be popular in England in 1580 and, between 1590 and 1600, the English and Dutch engaged in large-scale smuggling of the product.

With the publication[23] of *A Counter-Blaste to Tobacco* in 1604, King James contributed to increasing its popularity among the upper classes. It served to guarantee perfect harmony among guests, to the extent that refusing to share a pipe of tobacco was tantamount to an insult. The demand grew, and colonists in Venezuela, Trinidad and Guyana became the main suppliers, particularly from the port of Cumanagoto.

In 1606 tobacco production[24] was prohibited in Venezuela, Margarita and the Windward Isles, and in February the Governor of Cumaná, Pedro Suárez Coronel, was ordered to depopulate Cumanagoto.

After the truce with Holland, many of the corsairs who were still active redirected their activities towards contraband in Trinidad and Santo Tomé.

Given the magnitude of the problem, in February 1610 the Governor of Trinidad, Antonio Berrio de la Hoz, was ordered to take exceptional measures to persecute smuggling. Berrio himself was a smuggler,[25] and to cover up his own activities he made some arrests among newcomers to the business. The following year Berrio was replaced by a judge and the situation would be brought under control.

New Colonisation attempts by the English in America

Despite the fact that the peace treaty with Spain had imposed a trade ban with the Indies, England aspired to establishing colonies in America in which to set up trading posts that would serve as bases for commerce.

Two attempts were made, the first in Virginia, where the legend of Pocahontas was born. And in the second, an old acquaintance, Sir Walter Raleigh, revived the myth of El Dorado and sailed for Guyana in 1617. Only the first expedition was successful.

Don Fadrique de Toledo's 1621 victory of the Dutch in the Straits of Gibraltar.

Voyages to New England

In 1607 a second phase of colonisation began along the coast of Virginia, this time in the region of Chesapeake Bay. Of particular importance on the expedition was Captain John Smith, a twenty-six-year-old man who, in his book, *The Generall Historie of Virginia*, published in London in 1624, told the story of Pocahontas (or Matoaka), daughter of Chief Powhatan, who was born in about 1596.

Smith[26] was taken prisoner by the Indians in 1607. Sentenced to ritual sacrifice, he was rescued by the twelve-year-old Pocahontas. In response, Powhatan adopted him, naming him Nantaquod. Smith returned to Jamestown where, in October, Captain Newport ordered him to ceremonially crown Powhatan on behalf of the Virginia Company. The ceremony did not go well and Powhatan forbade Pocahontas from returning to Jamestown; the hostilities between Indian and colonialist continued.

In July 1609 Sir Samuel Argall arrived in Jamestown where he announced that the colony was now subject to the authority of The Treasurer and Company of Adventurers and Planters of the City of London for the First Colony in Virginia. Wounded in an explosion and thoroughly tired of the situation in the colony, in October Captain John Smith returned to England.

In May 1611 Sir Thomas Dale arrived in Virginia to replace Sir Thomas Gate as supreme commander. He built the city of Henrico, near Apamatuk, a village he ordered to be burned at Christmas to avenge those of his men who had been killed by the Indians.

PIRATES OF THE CARIBBEAN, 1493-1720

Argall kidnapped Pocahontas[27] in 1613 in order to compel Powhatan to sign a peace treaty. Placed in the custody of the preacher Alexander Whitaker, in Jamestown, she was converted to Christianity, was renamed Rebecca and met John Rolfe, whom she married in April 1614. Dale attempted to marry Powhatan's younger daughter, but was rejected. In compensation, he was allowed to make an alliance with the Indians, thus guaranteeing the safety of the colony.

When King James heard the news, he accused Rolfe of high treason because of his marriage to the daughter of a 'king of savages'. Nevertheless, in June 1616 the couple and their son sailed back to England, where they were received with honours. The Virginia Company took advantage of the situation to obtain more funds to extend the colony and Smith wrote to the queen requesting that she receive 'Lady Rebecca'.

In March 1617, when preparations were being made to return to Virginia, Pocahontas died in Gravesend, probably from smallpox.

Walter Raleigh and his Last Adventure

In 1595 Walter Raleigh had published his book *Discovery of the Large, Rich and Beautiful Empire of Guiana, with a Relation of the Great and Golden City of Manoa (which the Spaniards Call El Dorado)*, in which he told his version of the legend of El Dorado. Since then he had attempted to gain permission to return to America, but the peace treaty with Spain complicated his plans.

As an element representative of the regime of Elizabeth, in 1613 he found himself in the Tower of London, accused of conspiracy against King James. And, although he tried hard to convince the king of the attractiveness of his proposal, he achieved no success until 1616. Once again at liberty, he was authorised to make the voyage, although he was strictly forbidden to engage in piracy.[28]

The following year he set up a company[29] in London to raise funds, and he eventually set sail with fourteen ships, led by the *Destiny*, and 2,000 soldiers. Spain received warning of the expedition from their ambassador in London, the Count of Gondomar.

On 7 November the fleet reached Trinidad, where Raleigh put his plan of attack into practice. At the head of six vessels, Sir Walter sailed to take San José de Orduña, the capital of the island, while his son and Lawrence Keymis sailed up the Orinoco with a flotilla of light ships to storm Santo Tomé.[30]

While Raleigh was successful, his son was not, losing his life in the confrontation with the local inhabitants, who put up fierce resistance. The Spaniards retreated into the jungle and sent two soldiers to request aid from Bogotá. On 29 January Keymis ordered the retreat, having been hounded for nine days, during which the inhabitants, reinforced by Indian bowmen, applied guerrilla tactics and inflicted many casualties.

Back in Trinidad, Keymis reported to Raleigh that he had lost 250 men, including his son. In despair over the outcome, Keymis shot himself, although it is probable that it was Raleigh himself who pulled the trigger.

Sir Walter then attempted to persuade his captains to take the Indies Fleet, but they all opposed him and some even deserted. In April, he ordered the fleet to set sail with a small booty consisting of tobacco and a number of jewels stolen from the church. His misfortunes did not end here, however. His captains continued to desert and by the time he reached Bermuda, only two of his ships remained.

Back in Europe he attempted to dock in France,[31] but a mutiny forced him to sail on to Plymouth. Once more in London, he was arrested and jailed in the Tower, accused of piracy on the basis of evidence presented by the Spanish ambassador.

He escaped twice, but on both occasions was recaptured. Finally, on 29 October 1618 he was hanged as a pirate and conspirator.

A 17th-century galleon based on studies and drawings by José Monleón in the 19th century.

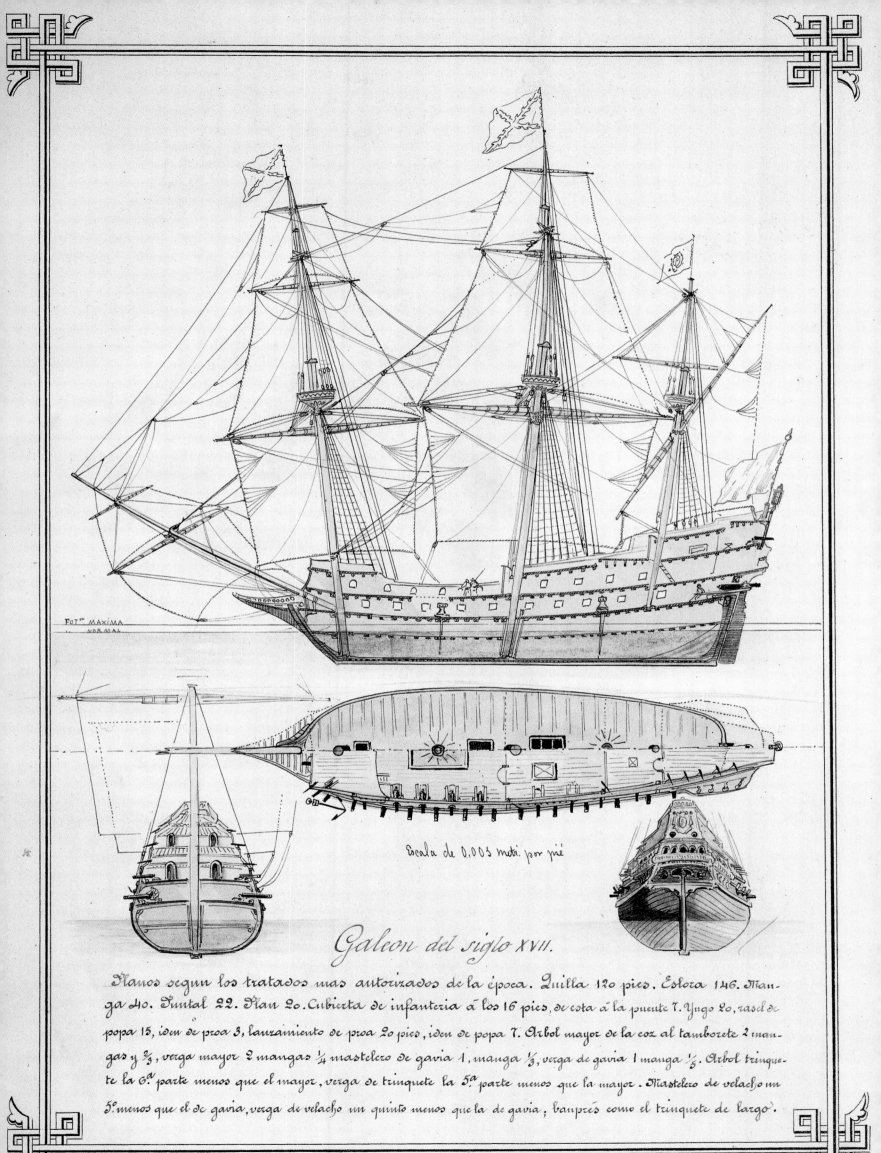

FOT.ª MÁXIMA NORMAL

Escala de 0.005 metr. por pié

Galeon del siglo XVII.

Planos segun los tratados mas autorizados de la época. Quilla 120 pies. Eslora 146. Manga 40. Puntal 22. Plan 20. Cubierta de infanteria á los 16 pies, de esta á la puente 7. Yugo 20, rasel de popa 15, idem de proa 3, lanzamiento de proa 20 pies, idem de popa 7. Arbol mayor de la coz al tamborete 2 mangas y ⅔, verga mayor 2 mangas ¼ mastelero de gavia 1, manga ⅓, verga de gavia 1 manga ½. Arbol trinquete la 6ª parte menos que el mayor, verga de trinquete la 5ª parte menos que la mayor. Mastelero de velacho un 5° menos que el de gavia, verga de velacho un quinto menos que la de gavia; banprés como el trinquete de largo.

The defence of Cadiz against the English by Francisco de Zurbarán (1598-1664). Prado Museum, Madrid.
Following the death of King James, hostilities once again broke out between Spain and England.
In 1625 a fleet was sent to Cadiz in an unsuccessful attempt to storm the city.

CHAPTER V

THE EXPANSION OF THE TRADING COMPANIES AND THE FIRST FILIBUSTERS (1621-1654)

The End of the Truce

Philip III died in the spring of 1621, shortly before the Truce of Antwerp was due to be signed. Determined to continue hostilities, on 3 June Holland granted the Dutch West India Company a trade monopoly. The Company, 'whose first obligation was to wage economic warfare against Spain and engage in large-scale corsair piracy', was constituted with the aim of consolidating commercial exchange that had been earlier established, supported by contraband activities.

With an initial capital[1] of more than seven million florins provided by wealthy traders from Amsterdam, Middleburg, Rotterdam and Groningen and distributed in the form of 1,200 shares, the Company headquarters were set up in Amsterdam. The seventy-four delegates elected a council of nineteen members, the *Heerem XIX*, to be responsible for decision-making and managing the Company.

A period now began in which a succession of wars and revolts on the Peninsula, beginning in about 1640, led to a neglect of American affairs and, at least, toleration of settlements on the small Caribbean islands.

The Dutch became the leading naval power. Financial support obtained from major company investments gave rise to a spectacular increase in the number of vessels sailing under the colours of the House of Orange. Now they attempted to sweep all competition from the seas.[2]

Through the Company Holland mobilised her corsairs, who served as the country's main weapon in the fight against Spanish interests. The States General provided sixteen ships and four yachts; these were matched by an equivalent number belonging to the Company and privateering was thus propelled into being one of the main sources of income. Prior to 1647 two-thirds of Holland's profits came from plunder, while the remaining third was obtained from commercial activities that included contraband and the salt trade. The Prince of Orange received ten percent of the profits, while a further ten percent was distributed among the crews. The remaining eighty percent went into the Company's coffers to be passed along to shareholders once expenses had been discounted.[3]

Their main operations consisted of attacking the black slave-trading colonies in Africa, seizing the Portuguese share of trade with America, and engaging in contraband in the Caribbean.

To this end, three initiatives were undertaken at enormous expense: the establishments of colonies in Brazil, Saint Martin and La Tortuga, off the coast of Venezuela. Over the first a battle was fought in which Holland and Spain matched their naval might.

The Company began to decline, when the Dutch were expelled in 1625. In order to re-establish the balance in 1632 Holland decreed Freedom of Contraband, by which any ship could engage in smuggling in American waters without the Company's authorisation. In 1646 privateering became subject to regulations and, one year later, the Company was authorised to engage in the slave trade. These new activities prolonged its life until 1674, the year in which its enemies' assault of African trading posts led to its definitive bankruptcy.

England and France by no means remained on the fringe of these expansionist policies. Trading companies were created in the attempt to gain footholds on the small Windward Isles from which to participate in contraband and the tobacco and leather trades. Adventures on Providence, San Cristóbal (St Kitts) and La Tortuga opened up new prospects for trade relations in Caribbean waters.

Finally, a progressively debilitated Spain, chastised on all fronts, was forced to find a way out of her dilemma. Through the Peace of Westphalia (1648) and the Treaty of Münster, Spain '…not only recognised the free trade and navigation of the East Indies and West Indies Companies in their respective areas of influence, but also officially accepted Dutch rights of possession in Brazil and the Caribbean, among many other things…'. According to Article V of the Treaty, the Caribbean became a *Mare Clausum*, since the territories that each of the parties would occupy were fixed, and trade was forbidden in the domains of the others.

The First Operations: Ambition and Prudence

At the end of 1621 Holland's States General had planned a pillaging expedition to Peru, inviting the recently constituted Dutch West Indies Company to take part.[4] The objective of this campaign led by L'Hermite was to sack the Viceroyal of Peru. To this end it was to sail '…to this kingdom and set fire to all the ships of the South Seas and sack the cities of Lima and El Callao, destroy Panama by fire and cause as much licit damage as possible as acts against people contrary to their religion…'.[5]

Spain had been forewarned, although it was thought that L'Hermite's fleet would sail to the Caribbean and, in 1623, as a counter measure, she sent General Larraspuru with a squadron of fourteen galleons to protect the return voyage of the fleet of Nueva España.

L'Hermite was killed during the siege of El Callao, and his exploits were continued by Schapenham, with equally unfavourable results. Either the prudence of the recently constituted Company, or the fact that it was planning a large-scale campaign in the Caribbean after the end of the Truce, saved it from complete failure. But the Spanish Pacific was strengthened, and the Dutch did not attempt to attack it again until ten years later.

The Company conducted its own expedition and, as had been expected, sailed to the Caribbean. Led by Pieter Schouten, the objective was to compile as much information that may be of use to subsequent operations as possible: ports, salt pans, fortifications and garrisons, watering and fruit-supply places, routes of dispatch boats and fleets, possible shelters and any other details of a strategic nature. The flotilla sailed around the Caribbean, the Gulf of Mexico and the Greater Antilles. Besides gathering information, the Dutch engaged in some pillaging, attacked Sisal in the Yucatan and captured a number of ships. In February 1625 they returned to Zeeland loaded with spoils.

The Search for Salt

Holland had the ships and funds to undertake their explorations of trade and plunder but this was not enough. The ships had to be crewed, and the crews' staple diet was meat and fish, which, to be preserved, had to be salted. The salting industry was one of the mainstays of the coast economy of the United Provinces, and it depended on an abundant supply at low prices. Butter and cheese production was also influenced by the availability of salt. The salt pans of Araya on the Venezuelan coast had, since 1585, been one of the main sources of supply, although during the Truce the Dutch salt supply came from Setúbal and Araya was ignored.[6]

Once the Truce had been broken, the Dutch attempted to return to Venezuela for supplies. The first incident occurred in September 1621 when Diego Arroyo Daza,[7] the Spanish Governor of Cumaná, prevented the Dutch from getting water supplies in Araya. The Dutch reply was to attack with ten vessels – they were repelled.

In 1622, in order to secure control of the salt pans, the Spanish began construction of the Castle of Santiago del Arroyo de Araya on the Cerro de Daniel hilltop, named after the Dutchman Daniel Moucheron, who had earned the dubious privilege of being hanged on its summit. The castle[8] was equipped with artillery and a garrison of 100 soldiers.

The fortifications at Araya were built to protect the salt industry and were the idea of the Governor of Margarita, Andrés Rodríguez de Villegas. From the end of the 16th century, the Dutch, having been expelled from their traditional places of supply on the African coast, sought new areas to exploit. Araya had a huge salt pan, the working of which was carried out clandestinely by the Dutch, and many conflicts took place there.

The fight for salt had only just begun, however. Late in November 1622, forty-three Dutch cargo ships bombarded the fort and 1,000 men disembarked. Arroyo forced them to retreat, inflicting many casualties and destroying three ships. Nevertheless, on the following day reinforcements came in the form of sixteen merchant vessels and permission was requested to load salt. The Spanish refused and, seeing that the enemy was preparing defences, the Dutch withdrew.

Things were quiet for only a month. In January 1623 a new fleet of forty-one ships positioned itself off the coast of Araya. They bombarded the fort for two days and then withdrew.

Six Dutch cargo ships were captured in the vicinity by a fleet of fourteen galleons captained by Admiral Tomás de Larraspuru, and a number of others engaged in smuggling in the Sisal area were forced to flee in haste.

A further 106 ships from several places in America attempted to obtain provisions in Araya, and received an identical response from the Spanish authorities. No further attacks were made.

But salt was still a vital concern, and the Dutch devoted themselves to seeking sources of supply.

The main Dutch settlements were La Tortuga and the River Unare on the Venezuelan coast, and the island of

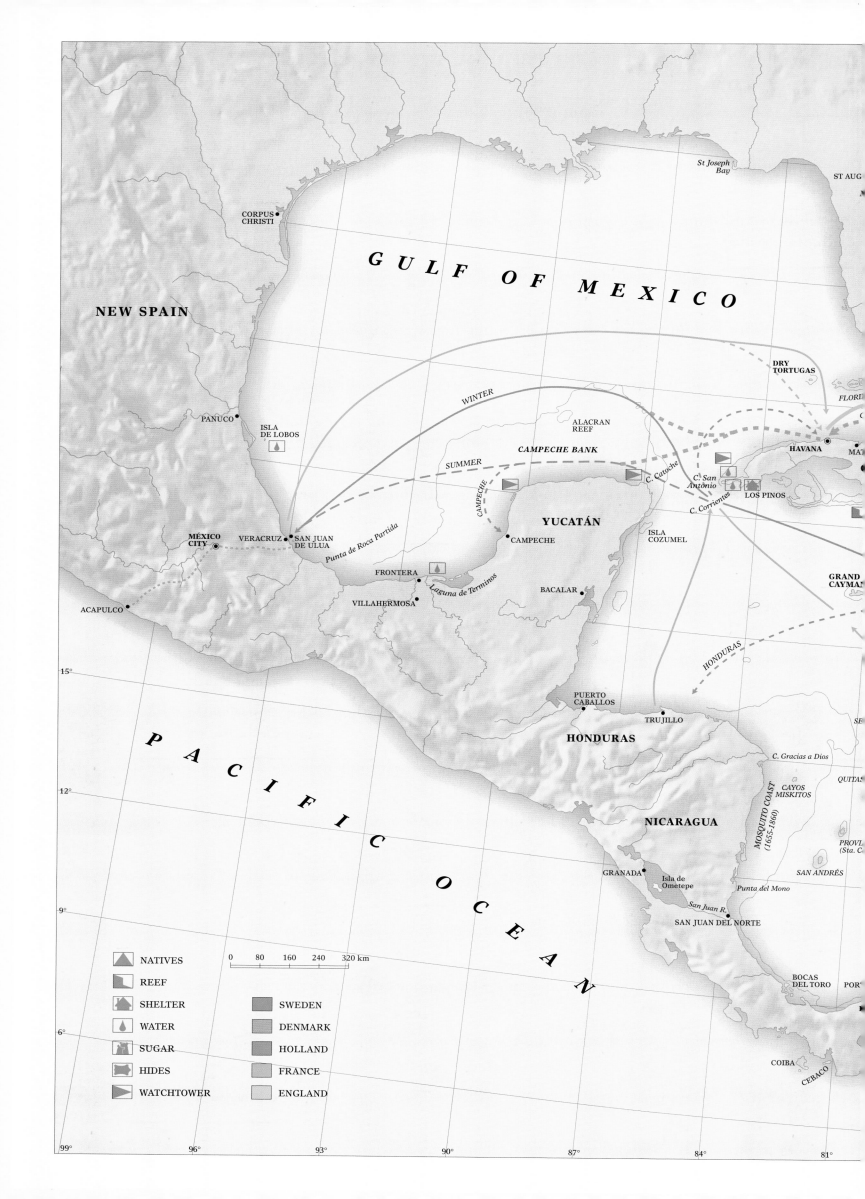

GULF OF MEXICO

NEW SPAIN

St Joseph
Bay

ST AUG

CORPUS
CHRISTI

DRY
TORTUGAS

FLORI

WINTER

PANUCO

ISLA
DE LOBOS

ALACRAN
REEF

CAMPECHE BANK

HAVANA

MAT

SUMMER

C. San
Antônio

C. Catoche

LOS PINOS

MÉXICO
CITY

VERACRUZ

SAN JUAN
DE ULUA

Punta de Roca Partida

CAMPECHE

YUCATÁN

CAMPECHE

ISLA
COZUMEL

C. Corrientes

FRONTERA

Laguna de Terminos

VILLAHERMOSA

CAMPECHE

BACALAR

GRAND
CAYMAN

ACAPULCO

15°

HONDURAS

PUERTO
CABALLOS

C. Gracias a Dios

QUITAS

SE

TRUJILLO

P A C I F I C

12°

HONDURAS

CAYOS
MISKITOS

MOSQUITO COAST
(1655-1860)

NICARAGUA

PROVI
(Sta. C

O C E A N

GRANADA

Isla de
Ometepe

SAN ANDRÉS

9°

Punta del Mono

San Juan R.

SAN JUAN DEL NORTE

BOCAS
DEL TORO

POR

6°

COIBA

CEBACO

△ NATIVES

0   80   160   240   320 km

▱ REEF

⌂ SHELTER

◈ WATER

SWEDEN

🏭 SUGAR

DENMARK

▱ HIDES

HOLLAND

▶ WATCHTOWER

FRANCE

ENGLAND

99°   96°   93°   90°   87°   84°   81°

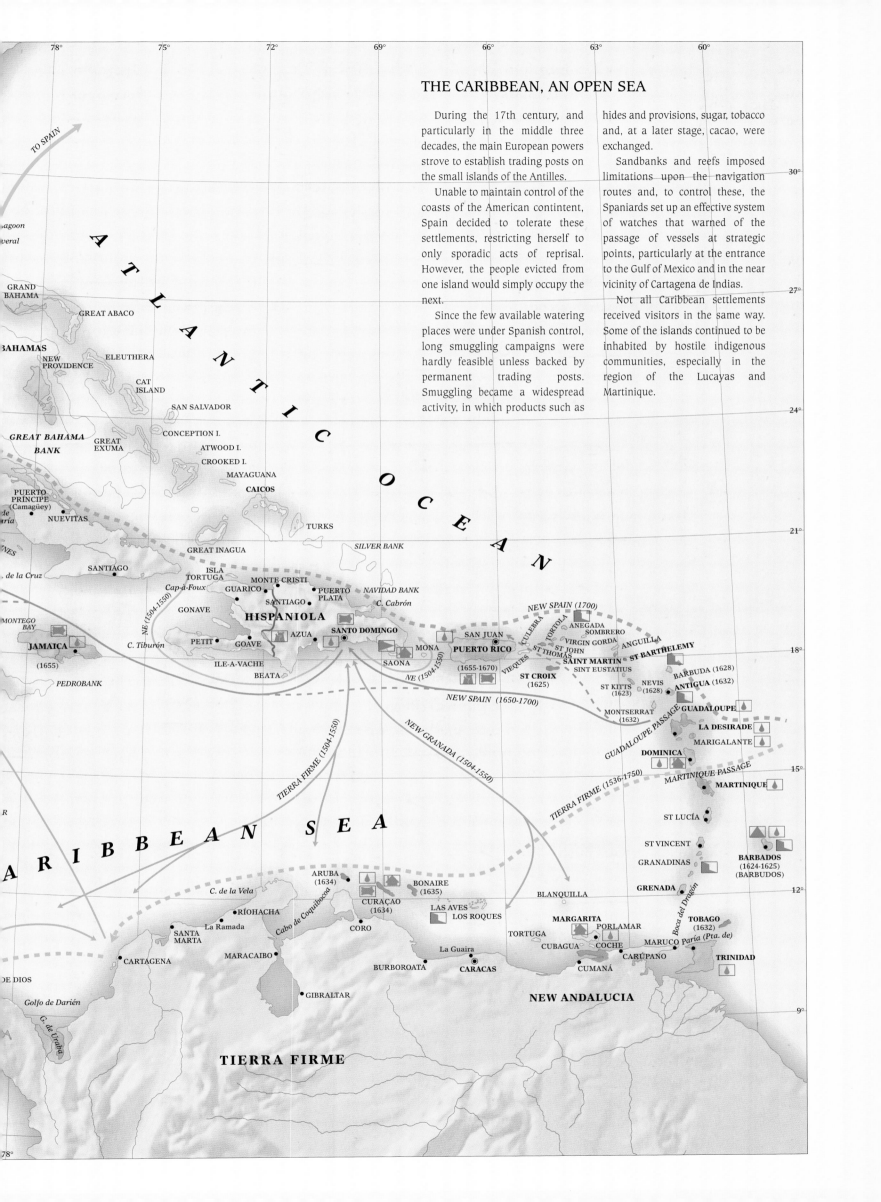

THE CARIBBEAN, AN OPEN SEA

During the 17th century, and particularly in the middle three decades, the main European powers strove to establish trading posts on the small islands of the Antilles.

Unable to maintain control of the coasts of the American contintent, Spain decided to tolerate these settlements, restricting herself to only sporadic acts of reprisal. However, the people evicted from one island would simply occupy the next.

Since the few available watering places were under Spanish control, long smuggling campaigns were hardly feasible unless backed by permanent trading posts. Smuggling became a widespread activity, in which products such as hides and provisions, sugar, tobacco and, at a later stage, cacao, were exchanged.

Sandbanks and reefs imposed limitations upon the navigation routes and, to control these, the Spaniards set up an effective system of watches that warned of the passage of vessels at strategic points, particularly at the entrance to the Gulf of Mexico and in the near vicinity of Cartagena de Indias.

Not all Caribbean settlements received visitors in the same way. Some of the islands continued to be inhabited by hostile indigenous communities, especially in the region of the Lucayas and Martinique.

ATLANTIC OCEAN

CARIBBEAN SEA

TO SPAIN

GRAND BAHAMA
GREAT ABACO
BAHAMAS
NEW PROVIDENCE
ELEUTHERA
CAT ISLAND
SAN SALVADOR
GREAT BAHAMA BANK
GREAT EXUMA
CONCEPTION I.
ATWOOD I.
CROOKED I.
MAYAGUANA
CAICOS
PUERTO PRÍNCIPE (Camagüey)
NUEVITAS
TURKS
GREAT INAGUA
SILVER BANK
SANTIAGO
de la Cruz
ISLA TORTUGA
Cap-à-Foux
MONTE CRISTI
GUARICO
SANTIAGO
PUERTO PLATA
NAVIDAD BANK
C. Cabrón
GONAVE
NE (1504-1550)
C. Tiburón
HISPANIOLA
AZUA
SANTO DOMINGO
MONTEGO BAY
JAMAICA
(1655)
PETIT GOAVE
MONA
SAN JUAN
PUERTO RICO
(1655-1670)
CULEBRA
VIEQUES
ST THOMAS
ST JOHN
TORTOLA
VIRGIN GORDA
ANEGADA
SOMBRERO
ANGUILLA
SAINT MARTIN
SINT EUSTATIUS
ST BARTHELEMY
PEDROBANK
ILE-A-VACHE
BEATA
SAONA
NE (1504-1550)
ST CROIX
(1625)
ST KITTS
(1623)
NEVIS
(1628)
ANTIGUA (1632)
BARBUDA (1628)
NEW SPAIN (1700)
NEW SPAIN (1650-1700)
MONTSERRAT (1632)
GUADALOUPE PASSAGE
GUADALOUPE
LA DESIRADE
MARIGALANTE
DOMINICA
NEW GRANADA (1504-1550)
TIERRA FIRME (1504-1550)
TIERRA FIRME (1536-1750)
MARTINIQUE PASSAGE
MARTINIQUE
ST LUCÍA
ST VINCENT
GRANADINAS
BARBADOS
(1624-1625)
(BARBUDOS)
GRENADA
ARUBA (1634)
C. de la Vela
CURAÇAO (1634)
BONAIRE (1635)
LAS AVES
LOS ROQUES
BLANQUILLA
MARGARITA
PORLAMAR
TOBAGO (1632)
Boca del Dragón
RÍOHACHA
La Ramada
Cabo de Coquibocoa
CORO
TORTUGA
CUBAGUA
COCHE
MARUCO
Paria (Pta. de)
SANTA MARTA
MARACAIBO
La Guaira
CARÚPANO
TRINIDAD
CARTAGENA
BURBOROATA
CARACAS
CUMANÁ
DE DIOS
Golfo de Darién
G. de Urabá
GIBRALTAR
NEW ANDALUCIA
TIERRA FIRME

Saint Martin. On La Tortuga things went well. A Dutch fort was built and salt production prospered. Benito Arias Montano reported that there were more than 1,000 piles of salt ready and that, in the space of only one week, they had managed to load 2,940 carts.

In 1631 a punitive Spanish expedition captured two hookers and destroyed the installations, although the following year production had reached 12,000 fanegas (55.5 litres) per week. Arias Montano put an end to it in 1638. As interim governor[9] of Cumaná since 1633, he attacked La Tortuga, destroyed the fort and flooded the salt pan.

The history of the River Unare settlement was even less successful. In 1633 the Dutch had built another fort on the Unare, from which they were almost immediately expelled by Arias Montano. A new settlement was established but in 1640 the attempting colonialists were again thrown out by Juan de Orpin, the Spanish Governor of Cumanagoto. During this operation, eight hookers and 700 men were located, 100 of whom were killed by Orpin and his troops, who destroyed the settlement buildings and flooded the salt pan. A timber fort that had been transported piece by piece from Holland and assembled in just seven days was preserved as a shelter for the Spanish garrison.[10]

In 1633, the Spanish Junta de Guerra decided to intervene and ordered the expulsion of the intruders. To this end, they commissioned the fleet of Tierra Firme,[11] commanded by the Marquis of Caldereyta, which reached Saint Martin late in June, took the island and left a garrison of 250 men, appointing Cebrián de Lizarazu as governor. However, Lizarazu was faced with poor supplies. They were supposed to come from Puerto Rico or Santo Domingo, but did not arrive with any regularity. They lacked gunpowder and carriages for the artillery, water if it did not rain, and food if they did not fish. In 1635 a mutiny broke out, triggered off by the constant privations suffered by the men and, in 1644 a large Dutch fleet, commanded by Peter Stuyvesant, invited the demoralised garrison to surrender. After brief resistance, that served merely to save the defenders' honour, the Spaniards were expelled.

The Dutch occupied one half of the island, sharing territories with the French, who populated it later.

Ever searching for safe productive havens, in April 1634 the Heerem XIX had decided '…to approve the taking of the island of Curaçao in order to secure a place from which to obtain salt, timber and other products…'.[12] The

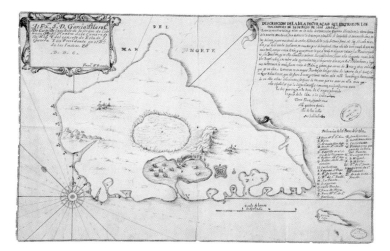

In the opinion of the Heerem XIX, the higher council of the Dutch West India Company, Curaçao was a potential source for salt, timber and other products. In April 1634, they planned an operation to take and colonise the island – this they successfully did in late July.

operation was carried out by Joannes van Walbeeck and Pierre Le Grand, who encountered little resistance from Governor Lope López de Morla.

The occupation extended to Aruba, where the Dutch had been exploiting a low-quality salt pan for the past ten years, and one year later to Bonaire.

In Saint Martin a rock-salt mine of excellent quality was discovered. The Dutch began occupation in 1630 leaving thirty men behind to build a fort and four artillery pieces. By the following year, the island had become one of the main loading centres, annually supplying approximately 400 ships. Problems of logistics were solved with the construction of the fort and the supply of water from the Company's trading post on the nearby island of St Kitts.

A Large-Scale Operation: the Brazil Campaign

The States General proposed that the Company undertake a new enterprise, the establishment of a Dutch colony in Brazil from which to efficiently conduct their trading activities. A fleet of thirty-five ships and 3,000 men, commanded by Jakob Willekens with Pieter Pieterszoon Heyn as his second – Heyn would later become the Company's most famous admiral.

The cost was enormous: two and a half million florins which would have to be reimbursed with the annual eight and a half million they expected to obtain from the new colony. They sailed early in 1624, took reinforcements in

The Dutch retreat from San Juan de Puerto Rico (1625) by Eugenio Caxes (1572-1634). The Prado Museum, Madrid.
In 1625 a large Dutch fleet commanded by Boudewijn Hendrijks was sent to take Bahía. It failed but, on its return voyage, the fleet laid siege to San Juan de Puerto Rico. Despite inferior numbers, the garrison resisted.

Cabo Verde and then proceeded directly to San Salvador (Bahía), which they took on March 8 having encountered practically no resistance.

When King Philip IV got news of this, he ordered the city to be recovered immediately, since the prestige of Spain as a major naval power was at stake.

A huge combined fleet was prepared: twenty-six Portuguese ships commanded by Francisco de Almeida and thirty-seven from the Armada del Océano reinforced by other regional squadrons commanded by Juan Fajardo de Guevara. The combined command was given to Fadrique de Toledo, who was thus in charge of a total of sixty-three ships, 945 cannons, 3,200 sailors and 7,500 soldiers.

The fleet came in sight of Bahía, reconquering the city in May 1625 with the capture of 3,000 prisoners, and expelling the Dutch from Brazil.

The Dutch attempted to recover Bahía, sending Boudewijn Hendrijks (whom the Spaniards called Balduino Enrico) with thirty-four ships and 6,500 men. He arrived too late, however, the city was already lost.

Hendrijks set sail northwards and divided his fleet into two. Seventeen ships commanded by Vermont set off for Africa, while he set sail for the Greater Antilles with a further seventeen ships and 1,500 men. The Heerem XIX had been considering taking Puerto Rico for some time, since its position at the entrance to the Caribbean was ideal as a base for contraband. As an alternative, they could attack the Indies treasure fleet or even attempt to assault Havana. Meanwhile, spies had reported the Dutch

The imposing fortress in San Juan de Puerto Rico.

The Naval Battle between Holland and Spain by Juan de la Corte.
After the battle of the Downs in 1639, the Dutch became Europe's leading
naval power. Despite this, Spain was still strong enough to control her sea
lanes to the Americas.

intentions, and sent the attack plans to San Juan. The report also mentioned an alternative plan to attack Matanzas, fortify the city and prepare a subsequent assault on Havana.

In San Juan, Governor Juan de Haro had prepared the defences. The castle was equipped with artillery and garrisoned by 350 soldiers. However, Haro made a mistake; he thought that Hendrijks would attack by El Boquerón, but the Dutch sailed straight up the river, passing practically unscathed beneath the Castle of El Morro. Diego de Larrasa described the operation as follows: '...he entered with such self confidence as if he were in Holland or Zeeland, due to the poor or non-existent dexterity and low number of the artillerymen. The artillery was in such a sorry state that many pieces

became jammed at the first firing, since the carriages were so old and some of them had been loaded four years earlier...'.[13]

Hendrijks bombarded the Point of San Lázaro and then proceeded to sack the city. The governor made a stand in El Morro, but the Dutchman took the fortress and then besieged the castle.

On 27 September the assault was prepared and Haro was sent an ultimatum to surrender, he refused to accept. To break the blockade he arranged a sortie of eighty men, which achieved some success. Captain Botello, with a group of defenders, managed to embark and assault the fort of El Cañuelo, thanks to which the Spaniards were able once again to take control of the bay.

On 21 October Hendrijks again demanded that Haro surrender, threatening to burn the city if he did not. Haro replied: '...I have studied the paper you sent me, and if all the powers of Holland were here today in Puerto Rico, I would rejoice, for then they would witness the courage of the Spanish. And if you burn the city, we have courage enough to build new houses, for there is still timber in the hills and materials on the land. And today I am in this fort with enough men to burn all your ships. So send me no more missives, for I shall not reply to them...'.[14] San Juan was set on fire.

The besieged then received reinforcements from Santo Domingo and, seeing that his efforts were fruitless, Hendrijks decided to raise the siege. He set sail on 1 November. As he departed, rounds of artillery fire from

The attack on San Salvador de Bahía on 9 May 1624
by Andries van Eertvelt (1590-1652).
National Maritime Museum Picture Library.

the castles seriously damaged his fleet. During the affray, one of the Prince of Orange's ships, the *Mendeblinck*, was beached. Desperate to recover her, the Dutch sent five launches against the six Spanish launches sent to capture her – four commanded by Captain Santiago de Villate, two by Amézqueta. With no time to save the ship, the Dutch mined her and withdrew. But the fuses were too long and Amézqueta[15] had enough time to board *Mendeblinck* and defuse the explosives.

The city was recovered with heavy losses. Ninety-six buildings, including the fort, had been burned, along with a further forty-five stone buildings; the churches were pillaged; slaves, archives and jewels were stolen; Bishop Balbuena's library was sacked.[16] Hendrijks lost a

warship and a launch, some 200 soldiers, and fifteen of his men were taken prisoner. The punishment meted out by Haro was exemplary. He informed the Governor of Santo Domingo, on whom he depended, that he would send them '…straight to hell, unless they choose to go to heaven…'.[17] The difference was a matter of nuance: they were all hanged – eleven having converted to Catholicism, which assured their passage to heaven, the remaining four preferring to go to hell.

Sailing via Santo Domingo, Hendrijks proceeded to Margarita, where he took and abandoned a number of cities. He went to Coche, Cumaná and Araya, where he attacked the Castle of Santiago with cannon fire and engaged in a skirmish with the twenty-five men who were defending the position. He then continued north, making a number of captures on the way, and finally came in sight of Havana. Having attempted nothing, he withdrew to Matanzas.

SANCT SALVADOR

In 1627 Piet Heyn was ordered to recover the city of San Salvador de Bahía. The assault was a success, and major profits were made from the subsequent pillage. Heyn was unable to consolidate his victory, however.

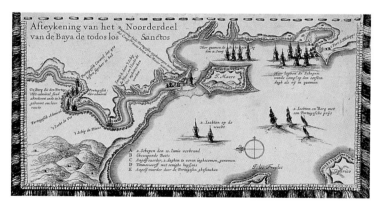

He took fresh water and some beef in Cabañas. While making landfall, he suffered a defeat and decided at last to set off on the return voyage to Holland. Boudewijn Hendrijks died of a fever on 2 July 1626 in Cabañas. Of his 6,500-strong expeditionary force only 1,500 men remained, of whom a mere 200 were soldiers. After sixteen months of vicissitudes, the final balance was decidedly negative.

Pieter Heyn, a Man of Good Fortune

Pieter Pieterszoon Heyn was born in Delfshaven in 1578. He began his successful career as a corsair in 1593 and, after being a prisoner of the Spanish between 1619 and 1623, he was appointed vice-admiral in the Brazil campaign.

After the defeat of the Spanish in Bahía in 1624, Heyn returned to Holland, where the Heerem XIX placed him in command of a new fleet – nine ships and five yachts with a number of alternative objectives: the first to reinforce Hendrijks in his punitive expeditions; the next to capture the enemy fleet; the final, if possible, to assault Bahía.

He set sail in mid May 1626, reaching Barbados in June and then proceeding to Havana. Off the island of La Tortuga he sighted the forty-strong fleet of Tomás de Larraspuru, but decided not to attack.

He returned to Cabo Verde and thence sailed to Bahía, which he assaulted by surprise, sacking the port and capturing a number of ships, although he was unable to secure the city. By virtue of his success, however, he was received with honours on his return to Holland in 1627.

The return of the Dutch East India Company fleet
by Andries van Eertvelt.
National Maritime Museum Picture Library.

One year later the Heerem XIX placed him in command of a mighty fleet of thirty-six sailing ships, with 2,300 sailors, 1,000 soldiers and 679 cannons, of which 120 were of bronze. His mission was to attack the fleet '…that brings to Europe the golden rod that chastises and demoralises the whole of Christendom, a rod whose might may be defeated by twenty-four well-armed warships and twelve dispatch boats provided with cannon and munitions, crewed by valiant soldiers…'.

On reaching Cuba, he awaited the arrival of the Spanish fleet. The Governor of Havana sent dispatch boats to Veracruz, Cartagena and Honduras in an attempt to prevent the ships from sailing. But Heyn was familiar with this strategy and intercepted the dispatches. He captured six boats, sank one and forced the other to return to Havana. Only the dispatch to Cartagena reached its destination. Consequently the fleet of Tierra Firme did not set sail, but the Honduras squadron and the fleet of Nueva España departed as planned.

THE PROBLEM OF PRISONERS

One of the main problems facing colonial authorities was what to do with prisoners. During the reign of Philip II,[18] it was ordered that the ships' crews captured in the Indies be sent to the galleys and the captains and first mates thrown overboard. But those were other times.

During the second quarter of the 17th century, the situation in the Indies was one of total war and, on most occasions, the conflicts were resolved by capitulations in which prisoners' lives were spared.

In 1634 twenty or so Frenchmen were captured by the Governor of Puerto Rico and sent to Seville, where they were held prisoner in the Casa de Contratación. Their upkeep generated expenses and, not knowing what to do with them, the president[19] asked the king how he should proceed. The reply was that '…these men be allowed the opportunity to *oir* (hear), but on no account must they be released…'.

Uncertain about the meaning of the reply, the president wrote back to the king, saying that '…in order to execute your orders with all diligence, I note the word "oir", which from the context of your instructions might be interpreted as *"huir"* (flee). Thus we inform Your Majesty and await your instructions as to the execution of your order…'.

Philip IV's laconic answer, in his own handwriting, was '…the word is "huir", and the order will be thus executed'.

Early in August the Honduras flotilla put into port, escorted by two warships. It was attacked by nine Dutch ships and, after a bitter struggle, the flagship was captured.

Heyn lay in wait for the Nueva España fleet and, on 5 September, an advance guard of twelve sailing ships arrived and was immediately captured. A few hours later the rest of the fleet appeared, eleven sailing ships escorted by four galleons commanded by Juan de Benavides and his admiral, Juan de Leoz.

The fleet was taken by surprise and quickly prepared for attack. Their safest move was to enter the port of Havana, which Heyn was blockading, or even to run the ships aground in the vicinity of the harbour and attempt to unload the silver and defend it on land.

The Dutch were to the windward, allowing them to manoeuvre with advantage. Benavides attempted to flee to Matanzas, which lay ahead and where the defence was being prepared, but the manoeuvre was inefficiently executed. From Havana, the Spaniard sent the following report to the king: '...I sailed from San Juan de Ulúa on 8 August, after the *arribada* in which the flagship was dismasted. It took me thirty days to reach the Havana coast, which I sighted on 8 September at dawn near the port of Matanzas, and at the same time I saw a Dutch armada of thirty-two hookers bearing down on me. Seeing that I was determined to proceed and resolved to die in the attempt, my men urged me to avoid the risk and save Your Majesty's silver...and heeding the advice of those in a position to give it, I agreed to seek refuge in the port, thinking that by leaving the enemy little room for manoeuvre I could save the silver, or at least the men, and burn the ships, the treasure remaining where it might be saved. I reached the bay when night had fallen, although it was as light as day. Although there the wind usually drops at night, on this occasion it freshened, and the enemy came so close that I had to disembark the men as fast as I could, planning to defend myself on land and burn the ships. But the men fled in disorder when I was still at my captain's post giving orders. When I set foot on land, I was alone. The enemy immediately boarded our ships, firing many rounds. And thus they seized everything...'.[20]

Heyn captured the ships unchallenged, transferred the silver to his own vessels and torched those of the enemy, except for the four galleons. Almost all the prisoners were freed and, on 17 September, he sailed from Matanzas for Europe. Knowing that he risked attack in the English Channel he entered Falmouth, and from there, duly escorted, he reached Holland on 9 January 1629.

The booty was estimated at eleven and a half million florins. Once expenses had been deducted, there remained a net profit of seven million, to be shared out among the interested parties. The Prince of Orange received his ten percent, the crews another ten – equivalent to seventeen months' pay – and just over five million went to the Company who, that year, paid their shareholders dividends of fifty percent.[21]

With the profits thus obtained, an armada of sixty-one ships and 7,300 men was formed, under the command of Hendrick Corneliszoon Loncq, to capture Pernambuco in 1630, and thus establishing the colony of New Holland that would survive until 1654.

Pieter Heyn was given a hero's welcome: fifty rounds of cannon, fireworks, medals and triumphal parades celebrated the return of a man who was rewarded with the title of Lieutenant Admiral of the Dutch Navy. The States General were congratulated by the ambassadors of France, England, Venice, Denmark and Sweden and by Pope Urban VIII, whose relations with Philip IV were far from cordial.

In Spain, the news caused uproar. Benavides and Leoz were arrested and imprisoned in the Castle of Carmona, awaiting trial. The accusations were extremely harsh, and the punishment exemplary. Benavides was beheaded in Seville on 18 May 1634, despite opposition from the entire Spanish nobility, and Leoz died in an African prison having unsuccessfully tried to achieve reinstatement.

Other Actions by the Company

Heyn soon had a great number of imitators, the first of whom was Cornelis Corneliszoon Jol (Cornellius Goll), better known as Peg Leg thanks to the wooden member that replaced the left leg he had lost in a sea battle at the age of twenty.

He sailed from Holland in command of a fleet of twenty-seven hookers and galleons, reaching Havana in 1629. However, his operations became restricted to minor acts of pillaging after his dream of capturing either the fleet or Havana faded.

ARIAS MONTANO
AND LA TORTUGA

Benito Arias Montano began his life in the Caribbean as a privateer.[22]

In 1631, leading forty soldiers and a number of Indians, he sailed on several canoes to the island of La Tortuga, off the Venezuelan coast, where he came across and managed to capture two Dutch hookers taking in salt, the larger a 600-ton, 22-cannon vessel and the smaller a 300-ton, 6-cannon ship.

He destroyed the installations, wharves and machines used to extract salt and both killed and captured a considerable number of Dutchmen, achieving a memorable victory.[23] As a reward for his services, he was appointed Interim Governor of Cumaná.

In March 1638, Arias learned that eight Dutch vessels were working the salt pans sheltered by a fort that had recently been built on the island. He requested aid from the governor of Margarita, who provided him with fifty soldiers, the same number of Indians, and six canoes.

A chart of the island of La Tortuga and the Dutch fortress, 1628.

On 4 April thirteen canoes, 150 soldiers and 200 Indian archers and oarsmen took to the sea. They were sighted by a lookout ship and the alarm was sounded. Arias and his men disembarked and attacked the fort, which surrendered after the Spanish had managed to break through its defences. The victors beheaded forty of the defenders while the rest fled to their ships. The fort was razed to the ground, the wharves and their installations destroyed and the salt pans flooded. Arias Montano came away with a booty of eight artillery pieces.

Equally thwarted was Johann Adrian Hauspater (Adriano Juan Pater to the Spanish), who attacked St Thomas of Guyana. He attempted to build a fort to defend a settlement, for which he offloaded bricks and other construction materials. However, resistance from the local inhabitants, who employed guerrilla tactics, led to the loss of 200 of Hauspater's men in the space of a few days.

Bitterly frustrated, he attempted to assault Santa Marta, which he reached on 26 February 1630 with 3,000 men. The city was evacuated and an 'imposing' Spanish contingent[24] prepared to defend it: fifty men in three trenches and in the fort, and four soldiers and fifteen unarmed men to fire the artillery. The fire power of the fort artillery was equally strong: four bronze pieces and two small iron ones, six quintals (600 kg) of gunpowder and a few bullets, with which they were able to fire twelve shots in the two hours of the artillery duel.

When the gun battle was over, Hauspater decided to disembark. Governor Quero ordered his men to fall back. They abandoned the trenches, deserting the defenders of the fort. Behind the wall, Cristóbal Matute and four soldiers confronted the 3,000 Dutchmen.

Hauspater ordered those in the fort to surrender. Matute accepted, provided that the city was not burned. After the capitulation, Matute abandoned the fort and, carrying his weapons and walking stick, followed by his four unarmed men, he marched out to meet his astonished attackers.

The Dutch seized what little remained in the city, including the artillery and the bells. On 5 March Hauspater sailed for Brazil where, on 12 September, he was dealt a severe blow by Oquendo. When his ship caught fire, Hauspater jumped overboard clinging to a commander of the *Prins Willem*, but his strength eventually ran out and he drowned.

THE TRIAL AND EXECUTION OF JUAN DE BENAVIDES[26]

When news reached Philip IV of the disaster of Matanzas, the monarch ordered Juan de Solórzano, of the Consejo de Indias, to formulate accusations against Benavides and Leoz. The lengthy report recommended that, though they be absolved of negligence, they should be punished with utmost severity.

Benavides was imprisoned in the castle of Carmona, where he spent five years, and Leoz, having been released by the Dutch, was sent to solitary confinement for four years.

On 18 January 1633 Benavides was sentenced to death in Madrid. Protests on the part of the nobility managed to postpone his execution for eighteen months, but the order was finally given in secret for the sentence to be carried out, a decision of which the Royal Tribunal of Seville was not informed until 15 May 1635.

Transferred to Seville, Benavides was informed of the sentence and given a black coarse woollen tunic to wear over his prison uniform. He was forbidden to wear the habit of Santiago or to bear any emblem indicative of his rank.

On the morning of 18 May he was taken to the scaffold on the back of a mule, an honour granted only to knights. Outside the gates of the High Court, the sentence was read. '…This is the sentence dictated by His Majesty the King and his Royal Counsellors against this man for his part in the loss of the fleet of Nueva España, which the enemy captured in the year of 1628. May God have mercy on his soul….'[27]

The scaffold stood in Plaza de San Francisco and, to avoid incidents with the nobles, the entrances to the square were blocked, impeding the passage of carriages and mounts. If any noble wanted to create a commotion, he would have to do so on foot.

Benavides climbed up to the scaffold, kneeled beside the chair and conversed with a friar, who delivered absolution. Then he rose and sat on the chair, clutching the cross of Santiago. He told the executioner to proceed.

His feet, arms and trunk were tied to the chair and he was blindfolded. The executioner stood before him, as befitting his rank, and delivered three consecutive blows to his neck.

His body was then untied and left on the scaffold, covered with a black cloth. The nobles assumed responsibility for his funeral, which was conducted with utmost solemnity, and he was buried in the main chapel of the Monastery of San Francisco in a niche provided by the Marquis and Marchioness of Ayamonte.

The following year Peg Leg Jol returned to the Caribbean. His operations were unsuccessful, even though he managed to capture a number of smaller vessels after lying in wait for the Spanish fleet. He attempted to secure reinforcements in 1633[25] by striking an alliance with the Cuban pirate, Diego Reyes, known as Diego the Mulatto or Diego Lucifer, in order to attack Campeche.

On 11 August he reached the Mexican city with eleven warships and two sloops. With 500 men he managed to capture Campeche, and demanded payment of 40,000 pesos in return for not setting fire to the city. Since the defenders claimed not to have such a sum, the city was torched.

On 15 March 1638 Peg Leg set off once again. The Governor of Havana, having been warned of the presence of the Dutch pirates transmitted a warning to Veracruz and Portobelo. The alarm reached Veracruz in time, but not Portobelo. Carlos de Ibarra had already set sail with the Tierra Firme fleet and, on 30 August, saw Peg Leg anchored in Pan de Cabañas.

The attack was unsuccessful and, although Peg Leg made a second attempt on 3 September, he lost a great many men without managing to capture a single ship. His proposal for a third attack was rejected by his men, and he was forced to withdraw without having attained his goal. Ibarra went back to winter in Veracruz, where he arrived on 24 September. Meanwhile, Peg Leg's fleet was severely damaged during a hurricane.

The fleets of Nueva España and Tierra Firme having regrouped, they set sail for Spain along an unusual route – avoiding both Havana and The Azores – and reached Cadiz on 15 June 1639 to great jubilation throughout the entire kingdom.[28]

In 1640 Peg Leg once again attempted to take Havana but lost four hookers without achieving his aim.

St Kitts, a Land of Fraternity

After the end of the Truce, the small islands of the Caribbean attracted the attentions of bands of French, English, and Dutch adventurers who had discovered, in the cultivation of tobacco and contraband, a way to escape abject poverty.

In about 1622 Sir Thomas Waernard or Warner[29] had set up a small tobacco colony on the tiny island of St Kitts. At first, the colony was attacked by Indians, who caused heavy losses. But having recovered, the English massacred the indigenous population, saving only the young men who were put to work as slaves on the plantations.

Three years later, a brigantine with forty men and four cannons sailed from Dieppe, commanded by Pierre Belain d'Enambuc, Captain of the Royal Navy, with Urbain du Roissey de Chardouville as his second.

They sailed to the Island of Pinos, where it seems they had been engaged in piracy since the beginning of the

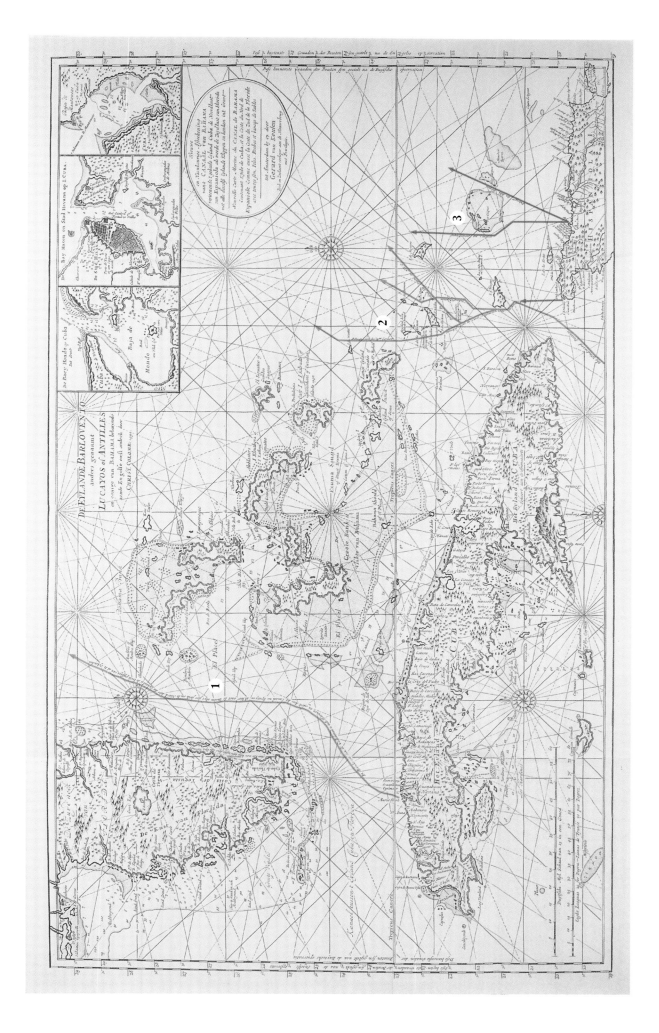

A Dutch chart marking the routes out of the Caribbean Sea followed by the Spanish (1), the English (2) and the French (3)

AVAST THERE!

The constant presence of the enemy at sea meant that everyone on board had to be prepared to defend the ship as best they could. So that every man would be aware of his mission, the *Consejo de Guerra* (War Council), formed by the officers, established a plan of combat and assigned each man his post and function.

The sailors were required to furl the yards with chain stoppers, to prevent them from falling if the halyards were broken during combat. The most skilful would go to the helm and auxiliaries were ready if the tiller broke.

The gunners were assigned to the artillery pieces, each of which was attended by an expert and two assistants, except those on the quarterdeck and forecastle, which were attended by two men only.

The infantry was deployed throughout the ship, commanded by the officers and each man assigned a mission.

1. Bow watch (three gunners)
2. Second watch (three gunners)
3. First piece or *mura* (three gunners)
4. Second piece or *mura* (three gunners)
5. Third piece or *mura* (three gunners)
6. 'Pump dale' piece (three gunners)
7. Crosspiece of the main mast (three gunners)
8. Third quarter (three gunners)
9. Second quarter (three gunners)
10. First quarter (three gunners)
11. Stern 'chaser' (three gunners)
12. First forecastle gun (two gunners)
13. Second forecastle gun (two gunners)
14. Third quarterdeck gun (two gunners)
15. Second quarterdeck gun (two gunners)
16. First quarterdeck gun (two gunners)

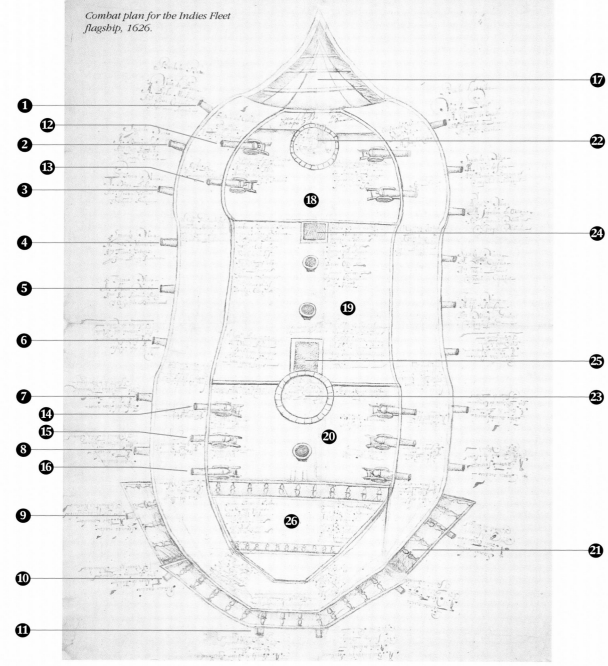

Combat plan for the Indies Fleet flagship, 1626.

17. Beak head. A number of men armed with harquebuses and muskets would stand on the beak head. Their function was to shoot into the enemy portholes in order to prevent them from firing at will.
18. Forecastle. The first mate would stand at the forecastle assisted by two sergeants, one on either side, and several men armed with harquebuses and muskets. If a boarding operation was being prepared, the infantry was provided with boarding axes, sabres, swords and other cold steel.

19. Half deck. Here most of the infantry would be positioned, along with reserve sailors armed with pikes, boarding axes, sabres and swords. Their function was to resist any attempt to board the ship and, when necessary, to assault the enemy. Here, too, carpenters, shipwrights and their assistants waited to meet any emergency.
20. Roundhouse. This is where the pilots and the chiefs of staff would assemble to assist the commander, although they might also do so from the quarterdeck (26). They

would often be accompanied by passengers, who would have no role to play in the battle.
21. Covert way. Men armed with harquebuses would be positioned in the covert ways at the stern.
22. Foreyard. A captain and two men would be positioned on the foreyard, armed with grenades and other projectiles, which they would throw onto the enemy deck.
23. Main topsail. Men would be positioned here as on the foreyard, given cover from the top platform by men armed with harquebuses.

24. Forward hatchway. One captain with three men, three lieutenants and a sergeant would be positioned here to 'extinguish fires' and 'provide the infantry with ammunition and withdraw the wounded'.
25. Main hatchway. The *cirugía* or hospital would be beneath the main hatchway, where the wounded would be taken.
26. Quarterdeck. The *cabos* (captains) would stand on the quarterdeck, giving orders to the artillerymen on either side.

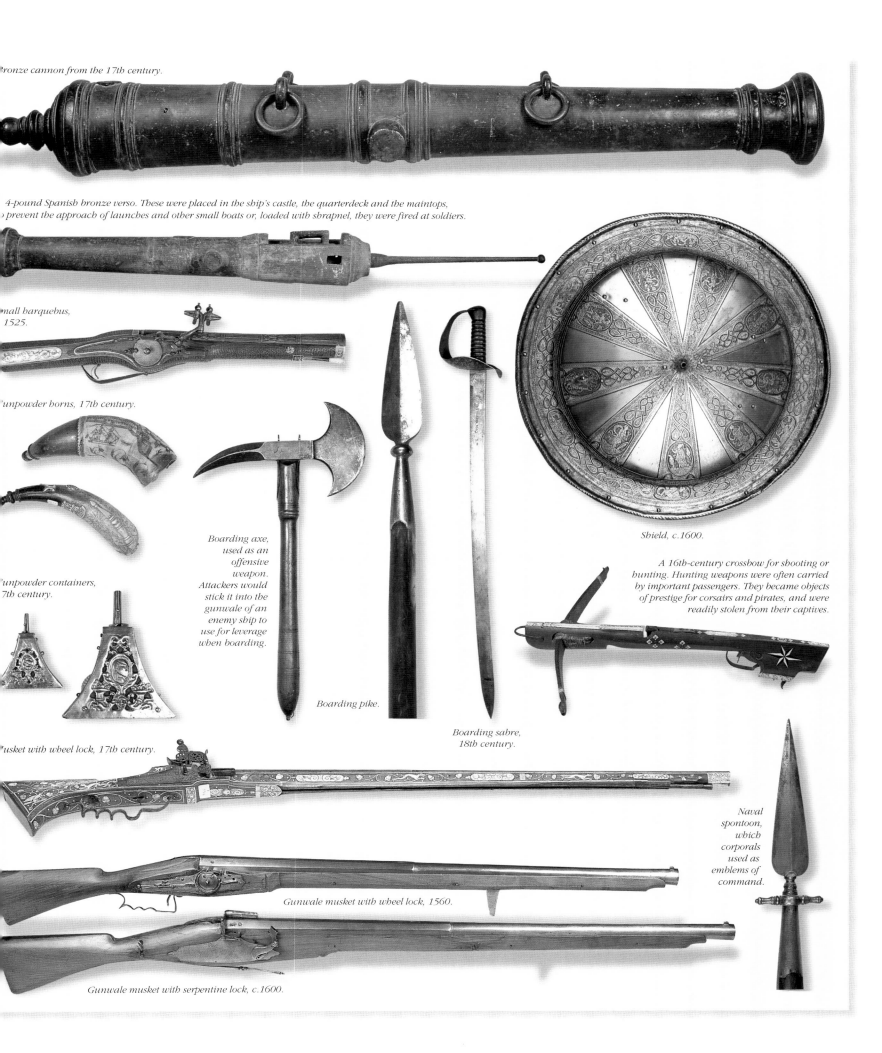

Bronze cannon from the 17th century.

4-pound Spanish bronze verso. These were placed in the ship's castle, the quarterdeck and the maintops, to prevent the approach of launches and other small boats or, loaded with shrapnel, they were fired at soldiers.

Small harquebus, 1525.

Gunpowder horns, 17th century.

Gunpowder containers, 17th century.

Boarding axe, used as an offensive weapon. Attackers would stick it into the gunwale of an enemy ship to use for leverage when boarding.

Boarding pike.

Shield, c.1600.

A 16th-century crossbow for shooting or hunting. Hunting weapons were often carried by important passengers. They became objects of prestige for corsairs and pirates, and were readily stolen from their captives.

Boarding sabre, 18th century.

Musket with wheel lock, 17th century.

Naval spontoon, which corporals used as emblems of command.

Gunwale musket with wheel lock, 1560.

Gunwale musket with serpentine lock, c.1600.

The Recapture of Bahía, Brazil by Juan Bautista Maino (1578-1649).
The Prado Museum, Madrid.
In 1624 the Dutch fleet, with thirty-five ships and 3,000 men commanded
by Jacob Willekens and Pieter Piet Heyn took the city of Bahía practically
without resistance. In a counter-attack, Spain prepared a formidable
Spanish-Portuguese armada commanded by Fadrique de Toledo.

1620s and, near Gran Cayman, they suffered severe damage due to an encounter with a Spanish galleon. They were forced to anchor off St Kitts, where they met Levasseur, with a number of slaves, and made contact with the English. Some sources claim that d'Enambuc had been on the island between 1620 and 1623 with Henry de Chantail and Levasseur and that he had good contacts

there. Whatever the case, relations between the French and English communities were so good that Warner and d'Enambuc agreed to travel back to their respective countries and obtain funds to consolidate the colony, which they would share as comrades. Having sealed their agreement, they sailed back to Europe with a cargo of tobacco and timber.

In October 1626 Cardinal Richelieu had been appointed Superintendent General of French navigation and trading. D'Enambuc gained an audience with him and received his support for the project. On the last day of October, the St Kitts Company was constituted, a privileged company known as the West India Company or Association of the

The Recapture of the Island of St Kitts by Eugenio Caxes (1572-1634). The Prado Museum, Madrid.
News of the of French and English settlers on St Kitts produced a quick reaction from the Spanish authorities. Fadrique de Toledo, who had commanded the fleet sent to Brazil, was ordered to expel the colonists from the island, which he did.

Lords of the Company of the American Isles,[30] with a capital of £40,000, of which £10,000 had been provided by Richelieu himself. The Company granted d'Enambuc and du Roissey permission to set up colonies on the Isles, between 11° and 18° North.

On 8 May 1627 300 Frenchmen reached St Kitts. Warner had arrived shortly before, leading 400 men, with authorisation from an English company constituted in London by Lord Karlay.[31]

Five days later, a frontier treaty was signed which apportioned the centre of the island to the English, the north-west and south-west remaining under French control.[33] Fortifications were built, Fort Charles in the English zone, with twenty-two cannons, Fort Richelieu in the north, with fourteen pieces, and Basse-Terre in the south, with eleven.

When news of this development reached Madrid, Fadrique de Toledo was ordered to expel the colonists from St Kitts on his way to Brazil. Having got wind of the Spaniards' plans, Richelieu sent a flotilla composed of nine ships, commanded by Francis Rotondy, with the intention of reinforcing the settlement. The French arrived very early and, believing that the Spanish fleet had already passed by, withdrew to San Eustaquio, where they built a fort.

In mid September the Spanish squadron[33] arrived – thirty-five galleons, fourteen merchant vessels and eight English ships captured in Nevis. The Spaniards landed at Basse-Terre, defended by Du Rossey, who was sent reinforcements in the form of 900 men. Having resisted for some time, however they surrendered after securing an honourable capitulation.

The Spanish continued their offensive by attacking Fort Charles and finally capturing Fort Richelieu. Some 2,300 prisoners were taken along with 129 cannons and 42 stone mortars, 1,350 muskets and harquebuses and much ammunition. The fort was burned and the prisoners released on condition that they go back to Europe, never to return to the Indies.

The French set sail for Antigua, but a storm forced them to seek shelter on Saint Martin, where they suffered many calamities due to lack of water. Du Rossey returned to France and reported to Richelieu, who had him imprisoned in the Bastille as punishment for his lukewarm defence of the colony.[34] Other Frenchmen dispersed, founding colonies on Montserrat, St Barts and Anguilla.

The English were more fortunate. They agreed upon a more orderly retreat but were threatened that should the Spanish return from Brazil to find they had not in fact quit the island they would be put to the sword. Needless to say, as soon as the Spanish weighed anchor, the English set about rebuilding their settlement. In 1630 d'Enambuc returned to St Kitts, the pact between the two communities still in force.

Others of the expelled population sailed to the north coast of Hispaniola, where they became buccaneers, while some settled on La Tortuga, devoting themselves to tobacco cultivation and engaging in trade with the Dutch. The Dutch West India Company offered them protection and '...promised not to allow them to perish, providing them with everything they needed in exchange for leather obtained from hunting livestock...'.[35] Thus, the consequences of the St Kitts expulsions were wholly unexpected: not only did the settlement remain but some of the other islands were also colonised.

This experience encouraged others to undertake similar projects. In 1630 admiralty rights were granted to the English Company of Providence,[36] authorising it to issue letters of marque. The Company managed to maintain the colony until its expulsion in 1641. In 1635 Richelieu reorganised the French Company of the Indies and d'Enambuc established new settlements on Martinique and Guadeloupe.

La Tortuga, a Free-Trade Market

Since its foundation beneath Dutch protection, the colony of La Tortuga had suffered a number of setbacks. In 1635 Ruy Fernández de Montemayor,[37] commanding 250 men from Santo Domingo, evacuated the island, beheaded 195 colonists, took thirty-nine prisoners and thirty slaves. He did not leave a garrison, however and, before long, a new French colony was established by people from Tierra Grande, the name by which the north coast of Hispaniola was then known.

One year later it would be a detachment of Englishmen from Nevis who fell upon the island, killing forty Frenchmen who had settled there permanently.

The Spanish were not prepared to tolerate the settlement, and sent the Windward Fleet, commanded by Carlos de Ibarra, to put the colonists to the sword. The operation took place in 1638, and those who managed to escape found refuge once again on Hispaniola.

On 14 February[38] that same year Philippe de Loinvilhiers de Poincy, Knight of the Order of St John of Jerusalem and Squadron Leader of the Royal Armada was appointed Captain General of the American Isles to replace d'Enambuc, who had died on St Kitts in late 1636. At the same time, the King of France appointed him Lieutenant General of the Isles.

Prepared to occupy his new posts, de Poincy reached St Kitts in February 1639. He was accompanied by Levasseur, now his lieutenant. Levasseur's presence on the island caused the first problems. He was accused of being a Huguenot and, to avoid having to expel him, de Poincy decided to send him to regain control of La Tortuga, which had been re-populated by 300 men freed by Roger Flood,[39] the former functionary of the English Company of Providence.

At the end of May 1640 Levasseur[40] embarked with fifty men, all of them Huguenots from Normandy, and sailed to Port Margot, a small island close to Hispaniola. During a period of three months he established contact with the

THE ASSASSINATION OF LEVASSEUR[42]

In his despotic actions as governor, Levasseur was aided and abetted by two godsons, Tibaut and Captain Martin, whom he had designated as his successors. Tibaut's relationship with a prostitute, renowned for her beauty, was the cause of such constant reproach on the part of his godfather that the godson hatched a conspiracy.

One morning, when Levasseur went down to inspect the warehouses, he was attacked by seven or eight men armed with muskets. The shots hit their mark, although this was not the governor himself but his image reflected in a mirror. Preparing to defend himself, he turned to his black sword-bearer, but before he could react he was stabbed by Tibaut.

THE INHABITANTS OF LA TORTUGA[43]

Once the colony of La Tortuga had come under the jurisdiction of the American Indies Company, work was organised in such a way as to ensure the harmonious co-existence of filibusters, buccaneers, inhabitants and *engagées*.

The filibusters were seafaring adventurers who engaged in pillage and smuggling. Some of the booty thus obtained supplied the colony with part of its necessary resources.

The buccaneers, who settled on the north coast of Hispaniola, devoted themselves to hunting the wild cattle that roamed the large areas depopulated during the devastation that took place early in the century. They kept the hides and smoked and salted the meat. They worked in hunting cycles of six or twelve months, and then went to La Tortuga to sell meat and tallow. The hides were for export, in exchange for which they obtained weapons, gunpowder and ammunition.

The inhabitants cultivated the tobacco plantations and made a living from trade, although they also took part in defence and, occasionally, set off on adventures on the high seas. The hardest tasks were performed by black or Indian slaves.

During a second phase, the Company supplied engagées – free

men who signed a three-year contract obliging them to work as servants in conditions similar to those of slavery. During the first two years of the contract, their work conditions were good, but often during the last year of their

The shorelife of a buccaneer.

commitment they were treated so badly that they were forced to sign another contract in order to improve their situation.

buccaneers and swelled his forces by fifty men. On 31 August he began his assault on La Tortuga, which he eventually managed to capture.

Initially he submitted himself to de Poincy's authority, signing a covenant with him by which, in the name of the Company, he was appointed governor. The first article of the covenant, dated 2 November 1641, guaranteed equality to the two religions and set down the regulations by which the island would be governed.[41] Special attention was paid to the division of profits, one tenth being reserved for the king and the remainder divided into two halves, one for the Company and the other for the governor and his officers. In turn, this latter half was shared among three parties: Governor Levasseur, Lieutenant General de Poincy, and the officers.

However, Levasseur did not really intend to abide by the covenant. Now over forty and highly experienced in the art of war, he chose the most suitable site and built a fort there, La Roca,[44] in which he set up his headquarters. He ignored de Poincy's orders and repelled a detachment of forty men who had been sent from St Kitts under the command of Seigneur de Lonvilliers, de Poincy's nephew, to oversee his actions. He imposed the Huguenot religion as the official form of worship, burned the chapel and persecuted Catholics. Furthermore, the impenetrability of La Roca was revealed in 1643[45] when

THE ASSAULT OF LA TORTUGA[46]

At dusk on 10 January 1654, the Spanish forces sighted La Tortuga. Among the rank and file, Juan de Morfa Giraldino, an Irish fugitive who had been a filibuster, advised the officers as to the best way to plan the assault. However, the initial plan to land unobserved, under cover of darkness, failed, and the fleet had to pass beneath La Roca under fire from the French artillery.

The Spanish ships sailed to the west coast of the island and anchored in a cove where many men disembarked. The troops assaulted a town, consolidated their position and reformed beneath the protection of the armada. Before nightfall, they reached the foot of the mountain and made camp.

On 12 January the ships approached La Roca, which they began to bombard with cannon fire. Meanwhile, the infantry advanced and placed their artillery. On the following day they were reinforced by two bronze pieces, and they fired on the fort during the whole afternoon and night.

During the night the French made an attempted sortie, but they were taken by surprise and repelled. They were offered quarter for the first time, but the French refused.

Finally, at ten in the morning on 18 January, Fontenay capitulated, agreeing to '…leave the fort and the island with his men, clothing, and banner…and to sail for France in the ships assigned to them with thirty of their slaves…'.

Levasseur resisted an attempted assault in which the Spanish, with 1,000 men and ten ships, were forced to retreat having lost a tenth of their soldiers.

The fortification of the island favoured its prosperity. A point of reference had been created in which it was safe to trade, the buccaneers sold their hides and purchased merchandise brought there by smugglers. Tobacco plantations, warehouses and depots were set up. Levasseur collaborated with the corsairs and, although he did not openly support privateers, he allowed them to sell their merchandise without asking questions about their provenance.

While Levasseur was governor, La Tortuga became a kind of free-trade republic. And, while formal dependence upon the Company authorities did exist, in practice the only laws in force were those dictated by the governor. He obtained enormous profits by levying extortionate taxes on trade agreements made on the island and enforced his law by imposing a reign of terror. He built a prison in La Roca[47] which he called Purgatory, from which convicts descended into Hell, a machine of his own invention in which he tortured his victims until they were maimed and crippled for life.

Such abuses could not go unpunished, however. In 1652 the Chevalier de Fontenay[48] reached St Kitts aboard a frigate armed with twenty-two cannons. He was hoping to recruit men to replace his exhausted crew.

For some time de Poincy had been looking for a man capable of leading an action against Levasseur in order to regain control of La Tortuga, and Fontenay seemed to fit the bill. He had gained considerable experience in the Mediterranean campaigns and, with the Malta galleys, had taken part in the battle between the Turkish fleet and the forces of General Neufchesés on 28 September 1644. Thus, on 29 May 1652 Poincy and Fontenay signed a covenant similar to that by which, years before, Levasseur had been appointed Governor of La Tortuga. An assault force was assembled and sailed straight to the island. When they arrived, however, it was to hear of Levasseur's assassination[49].

La Tortuga was now governed by the conspirators who, having no loyal forces with which to oppose Fontenay, agreed to surrender in exchange for permission to keep the former governor's worldly goods and the promise that his death would never be investigated.

Having thus taken possession of the island, Fontenay reinstated the Catholic religion and submitted himself to the authority of the Company. The change of governor encouraged many people to return to the island and rules on harmonious co-existence were re-established.

Fontenay concentrated his efforts on consolidating the colony. In order to forestall problems with the Spanish, he refrained from colonising Tierra Grande; on the other hand, he fostered privateering, taking its Mediterranean version as his model.

News of the changing situation on the island reached Hispaniola through the interrogation, early in May 1652, of English and French prisoners from La Tortuga. Late in August, the prisoners were transferred to Santo Domingo, where they were interrogated again.

A report was sent to the King Philip IV, in which it was concluded that '…the English and French enemies, with over 1,000 men, made landfall on the north side of the island, in twenty-two towns on the best sites. Unhindered they went from place to place stealing cattle and the fruits of the island, taking much meat and many pelts from the people in villages close to the north and in particular from La Tortuga, where the islanders have their fort…'[50].

On 18 August the following year Andrés Pérez Franco, Captain General of Hispaniola, died, and was temporarily

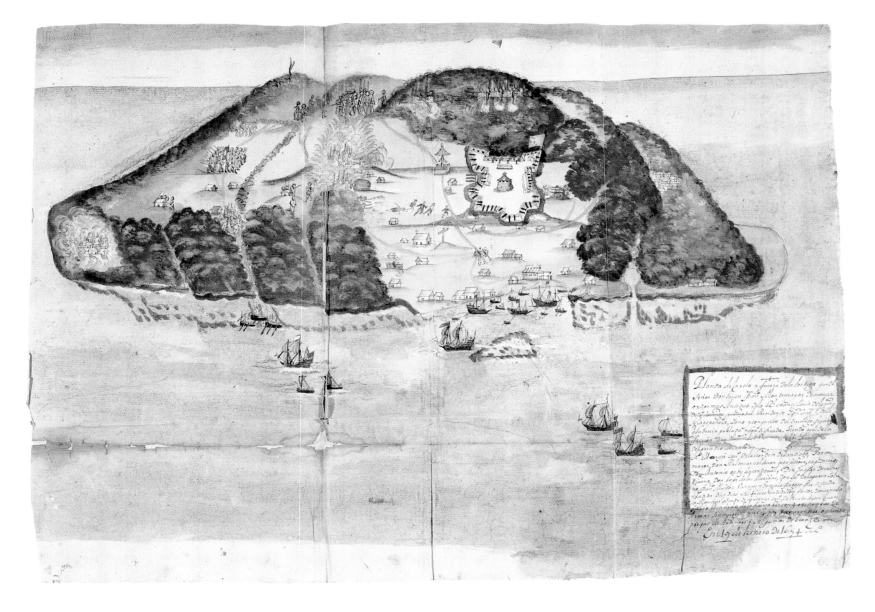

In January 1654 La Roca, the famous fortress defending the island of La Tortuga, was stormed. The French were eventually expelled after unsuccessful attempts to recover the fort. Due to the political situation of the time and, above all, the lack of foresight on the part the new Governor of Hispaniola, Montemayor Cuenca's efforts to retake possession for Spain proved ineffective.

succeeded by Juan Francisco Montemayor Cuenca, a thirty-three-year-old who swore to resolve the situation.

He convened a number of Juntas de Guerra y Hacienda, through which he proposed to intervene and made due preparations to this end. On 8 December Montemayor wrote to the king, informing him of the need to immediately expel the French and indicating the appropriate measures by which to achieve this aim.

Without awaiting the king's reply, Montemayor and his men set sail and reached the coast of La Tortuga on 10 January 1654. Eight days later the French capitulated –

330 men, without women or children, surrendered, and twenty-five soldiers were released from the prison. A total of 500 people were sent from the island under safe-conduct, while Thomas de Fontenay, the governor's brother, was held as hostage. Seventy pieces of artillery, of which four were bronze, were taken, and Indian slaves were found. The final balance of the operation was the deaths of two Spaniards and between twenty-five and thirty defenders, and profits of 20,000 ducats, without counting the value of the artillery.

To secure control of the island, a detachment of 150 men was left behind under the command of Baltasar Calderón Espinosa who, in August, repelled two counter-attacks by the French.

Despite Montemayor's efforts, however, following the arrival of Bernardino de Meneses Bracamonte y Zapata the new Captain General and President of the Audiencia of Santo Domingo, on 8 April 1655, the island was evacuated.

New settlements would give rise to the new island of La Tortuga – destined to become a den of filibusters.

Sir William Penn by Sir Peter Lely, 1618.
National Maritime Museum Picture Library, Greenwich.

Chapter VI

THE SUN SHINES FOR ALL.
BUCCANEERS, FILIBUSTERS AND CORSAIRS
(1655-1671)

Oliver Cromwell's victory and his transformation of England into a republic broke the fragile balance of the Peace of Westphalia. He considered Spain his most important enemy and, after the Anglo-Dutch war was over, he fostered an anti-Spanish policy. In 1653 he signed a trade treaty with Portugal and joined France in an alliance against Spain. The following year he attacked Spanish interests on two fronts. He sent a twenty-five-ship squadron commanded by Admiral Blake to the Mediterranean, transporting an army under the orders of General Montague. To Latin America he sent thirty-eight ships under Sir William Penn, transporting 3,000 men commanded by General Venables.

The Mediterranean fleet achieved some success off the coast of Cadiz and the Canary Islands, but the American squadron suffered an embarrassing defeat at the gates of Santo Domingo. To compensate for this, Venables seized the island of Jamaica, then owned by the Duke of Veragua, and inhabited by a small colony of farmers and shepherds. This incident would change the history of piracy in the Caribbean and, from 1655, Jamaica would become a hideout for filibusters and smugglers.

THE DESIGN OF THE INDIES. *THE WESTERN DESIGN*

Two months after Blake's departure from England, on 24 December 1655, Penn and Venables sailed from Portsmouth. The campaign did not get off to a good start. The crews almost mutinied in protest against the poor quality of the food and because they had no knowledge of their destination. Indeed, Penn and Venables were almost as disheartened as their men. They had instructions from the Protector not to open their orders before they reached Barbados, only then would they learn their objective. Thus, thirty-five days later they reached the islands, read the orders and were joined by 3,500 men headed for Hispaniola.

The Spanish were aware of the English intentions but the news was not taken seriously at first. Spain believed that Cromwell would not initiate hostilities without previously declaring war. Nevertheless, several warning notices were sent to the Americas to organise the defence.

Two hundred soldiers and harquebuses, gunpowder, ammunition and other provisions arrived from the Peninsula, along with the new Governor of Hispaniola, Bernardino Meneses y Bracamonte, Count of Peñalba, who would take over from Montemayor Cuenca. The regular forces of Santo Domingo were made up of 700 men reinforced by 1,300 lancers recruited from around the island – an insufficient number to face 6,000 English soldiers with all their impedimenta.[1]

On 23 April (N.S.) the English squadron arrived at the gates of Santo Domingo. Although the goal was clear, the English could not agree on their assault plan. It seemed that the fortress might succumb if all the forces

CHRONICLE OF AN INDISCRETION

In Portsmouth the vessels that were to be sent to the Indies were rapidly being prepared, and meanwhile their destination was the best kept secret in England.

The news of their course came by chance. A French priest living in London named Stoupe, who acted as Cromwell's agent, unexpectedly entered the Protector's office one day.

Cromwell was examining a nautical chart and estimating distances. With just one glance Stoupe realised it was a chart of the Gulf of Mexico and he memorised the name of the publisher.

As soon as he could, he went to the printer and asked for a copy of the chart, but to his astonishment, was told that such a chart did not exist.

'But I've seen it!' said Stoupe.

'In that case,' responded the printer, 'it must have been in the hands of the Protector because the number of copies is limited and he has forbidden me to sell any without his permission.'

The Spanish ambassador, Alonso de Cárdenas, came to hear of the incident and contacted Stoupe. He offered him £10,000 in exchange for the secret but, instead of revealing it, Stoupe lied.

Stoupe sent the true information to France, where it reached the ears of the Prince of Condé. Condé passed the information on to John of Austria, who put it down to false rumour.

Nevertheless, when Blake's squadron set out, the alarm had been raised among the Spanish authorities and was rapidly transmitted to the Indies.

landed in the same place near the city and attacked immediately, but Penn, Venables and the attaché, Edward Winslow, who was the civil commissioner, disagreed.

Finally, the men were divided into two forces. A small party led by Colonel Buller landed in Haina and the main group made landfall in Nizao under the direct orders of Venables. The English intended to divide the defenders.[2]

The strategy failed. By the time Venables was due to join up with Buller, his soldiers were in very poor shape. They had been marching for three days through dense jungles and over dry sandy terrain under a scorching sun with no water to quench their thirst and eating such bad food that most had developed severe dysentery.

On 25 April 6,000 regrouped soldiers began to move. The 3,500 soldiers who had boarded in Barbados were undisciplined and the officers recognised the low morale of the men. It was then that the Spanish launched a first attack with 150 lancers, who seemed like 'the kind of vagabonds who manage to escape from Spanish galleys',[3] armed with catapults for slaughtering cattle.

Nevertheless, after an initial setback and suffering many casualties, the English managed to advance and reach the walls, where they encountered very strong resistance. The number of casualties rose and they decided to retreat to prepare a second attack with the aid of the fleet that had yet to take part.

Taking advantage of the confusion, the Spanish launched their main attack from the rearguard, using forces that until then had remained hidden in the fort of San Gerónimo. The English ranks fell into disorder. Overcome by fright, they took refuge behind the cavalry that had remained in the rearguard, itself retreating to join the main group headed by Venables's own regiment. Had it not been for the bravery of General Heane,[4] who laid down his life for the sake of his officers, the Spanish would have exterminated the English army completely. Even so, more than 600 Englishmen died and more than 1,000 others were wounded. Venables dismissed his chief of staff and ordered a number of men who had abandoned their positions to be hanged. Commissioner Winslow fell ill and died.

A third attack was planned but the Barbadians refused to fight.[5] On 12 May the commanders ordered the forces on board. At a meeting of the Council of Officers it was considered impossible to return to England without a victory to justify the expedition, and so they headed for Jamaica.

On 18 May they landed and took the city, the small Spanish population fleeing to the mountains. Nine warships and four converted supply ships formed a coastal station under the orders of Commander Goodson.[6] The squadron withdrew at the end of July and set off for England, where it arrived between 9 and 18 September. Penn and Venables were received with an order for their arrest and imprisoned in the Tower of London. They were prosecuted, but set free again soon afterwards.

Spain declared war and the seizure of British interests; in a very short time hundreds of English merchant vessels were confiscated.

Blake began his campaign against Spain. He stationed himself in front of Cadiz but, running out of water he soon had to retreat to Lisbon, leaving Stayner with seven vessels lying in wait to make a capture. Stayner attacked the Spanish fleet, capturing two boats and treasure valued at two million pieces of eight.

When Montague reached Portsmouth with the treasure, he was showered with favours by Cromwell and paid tribute by Parliament. Richard Stayner was knighted. The silver was 'loaded onto thirty-eight wagons accompanied by guards and was slowly driven through the cities and countryside of southwest England to the Tower of London, where the metal received the national die'.[7]

ENGLISH JAMAICA

The main Jamaican objective between 1655 and 1664 was the island's consolidation as a colony. After the main body of the squadron had withdrawn, Goodson became head of the naval station and d'Oyley, a lieutenant colonel from Venables's regiment, became governor of the newly constituted colony.

Governor d'Oyley[8] believed that the best strategy for consolidation would be to implement an aggressive policy and he established the system of granting letters of marque as a means of defence, turning Jamaica into a den of privateers of all nationalities in exchange for handing over part of their gains to England – first the Republic and then the Crown. Simultaneously he promoted the creation of plantations and the settlement of smugglers in order to achieve economic prosperity. Finally, he took the initiative and launched a campaign against Tierra Firme. Goodson attacked Santa Marta, sacking the city and burning it to the ground. Not daring to do likewise against Cartagena, for fear that his forces would be insufficient, he returned to Jamaica in mid November.

In April 1656 he returned to Tierra Firme with the intention of taking one of the Spanish fleet's vessels. He attacked Río Hacha but desisted once again in the face of Cartagena's defences, returning home at the end of June. To make the most of the trip, 1,400 planters were boarded in Nevis and taken to re-populate Jamaica.

In January 1657 Goodson returned to England and was substituted as Commander in Chief by his deputy Christopher Myngs.[9] Myngs took up d'Oyley's strategy and continued his aggressive policy, organising defences and coastguard patrols, achieving considerable success against Dutch vessels.

In May 1658 Spain finally reacted by sending a squadron. During one patrol on the north coast Myngs discovered four troop transporters landing 550 soldiers from Nueva España.[10] The troops headed for Cagway, the island's former capital, and placed artillery among the

Much of the filibusters' booty was squandered on wine, women and song.

JAMAICA, A PLACE OF LEISURE

When they returned to Jamaica, the filibusters would spend the product of their looting faster than it had taken them to obtain it. Taverns and whores were the final destination of the Spanish silver.

The most famous taverns in Port Royal before their destruction during the earthquake in 1692 were known by names such as Black Dog, Blue Anchor, Cat and Fiddle, Chesire Cheese, The Feathers, Green Dragon, Jamaica Arms, Kings Arms, The Salutaçon, The Ship, Sign of Bacchus, Sign of the Mermaid, Sign of George, Sugar Loaf, Three Crowns, Three Mariners, Tree Toons and Windmill.

The main products consumed were brandy, beer and rum. Drunkards, flypados or grogyes would indulge in all sorts of excesses and lose their money through gambling.

The brothels, known as punch houses, were filled with prostitutes of all nationalities. Some of them ended their days very sadly indeed. The most famous whore on the island, Mary Carleton, known as the German Princess, was hanged in Tyburn in 1673.

Morgan blamed the prostitutes for the state of poverty in which his men lived, and some believe this is the reason why he returned to sea in 1670.

port defences seeking to consolidate a position from which to begin the recovery of the island.

Myngs went in search of reinforcements and returned north with ten vessels and troops provided by the governor. He established a beach head and, after a bloody battle, the English position was recovered and the Spanish troops annihilated.

In an act of reprisal Myngs sailed to Tierra Firme attacking Santa Marta and Tolú, capturing three merchant vessels that were sailing from Cartagena to Portobelo, and triumphantly returned to Jamaica six weeks later. Back in Jamaica he sold the captured ships to the buccaneers:[11] 'the largest eight-cannon vessel was sold to Robert Searle who renamed it the *Cagway*; the second with four cannons and weighing 50 tons was sold to the Dutchman Laurens Prims who renamed it the *Pearl*, and the third went to John Morris who renamed it the *Dolphin*'.

FLAGS AND BANNERS

A vessel at sea was identified by a set of symbols which included standards, flags, streamers and broad pennants. Standards represented the maximum authority of a state, kingdom or republic. In general they were only used on the flagship of a fleet or squadron, and it was obligatory to salute them when they passed.

Flags served to identify the nationality of a vessel. Additional flags known as 'jacks' were frequently placed on the bow of the ship indicating the squadron, fleet or service to which she was assigned.

Streamers served as an additional reference and were visible at the top of the masts or hanging from the yardarms.

The rank of the vessel's commander, or the division to which the ship belonged within the squadron, was generally indicated by broad pennants or smaller pennants.

Pictured are the flags of the countries involved in this history, including a few other contemporary Mediterranean flags by virtue of their importance.

Flag of France

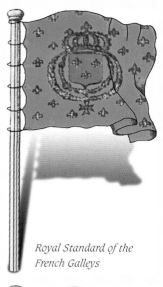

Royal Standard of the French Galleys

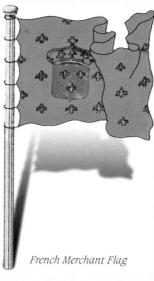

French Merchant Flag

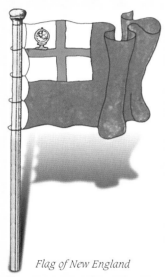

Flag of New England

Union Jack

Spanish Royal Standard

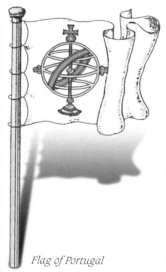

Flag of Portugal

Portuguese Battle Flag

Portuguese Merchant Flag

Swedish Royal Flag

Flag of Malta

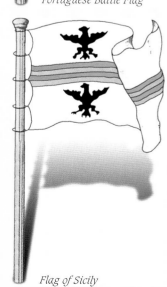

Flag of Sicily

Flag of Genoa

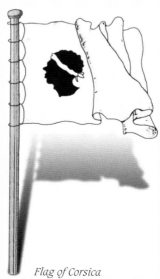

Flag of Corsica

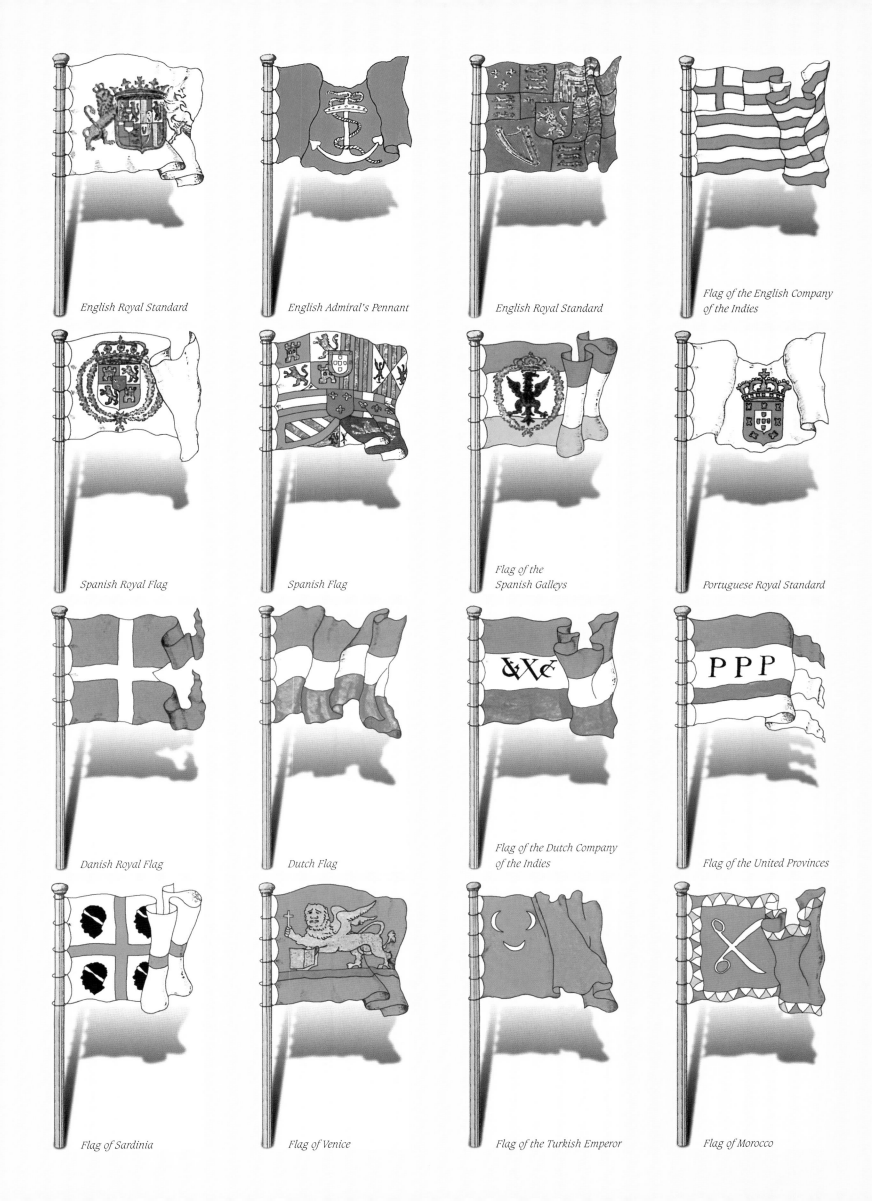

English Royal Standard

English Admiral's Pennant

English Royal Standard

Flag of the English Company
of the Indies

Spanish Royal Flag

Spanish Flag

Flag of the
Spanish Galleys

Portuguese Royal Standard

Danish Royal Flag

Dutch Flag

Flag of the Dutch Company
of the Indies

Flag of the United Provinces

Flag of Sardinia

Flag of Venice

Flag of the Turkish Emperor

Flag of Morocco

The English Offensive against Tierra Firme

D'Oyley's strategy was successful and many buccaneers adopted Jamaica as their base of operations, considerably reinforcing the English military forces. The situation allowed England to recover the initiative and, presenting his first trip as a warrant, Myngs decided to return to the fray.

Strengthening his three-frigate squadron with numerous corsair vessels that joined up, he attempted to repeat the strategy: fast surprise attacks and several consecutive objectives far from his previous area of operation. He attacked and sacked Cumaná, destroying its port; then came Puerto Caballo and Coro. In Coro he seized twenty-two chests belonging to the King of Spain that were being transported to the home country in a Dutch vessel; their value was £50,000.

After a four-month campaign Myngs triumphantly returned to Jamaica. Upon entering Port Royal, however, he realised that the chests had been plundered[12] during the return voyage and a considerable part of the spoils had been stolen. Myngs tried to take the law into his own hands and discover the plunderers among his men. But, before he could move a finger, d'Oyley made him responsible for the losses, accusing him of appropriating 12,000 pieces of eight[13] 'without provision for the rights of the State' and sent him back to England as a prisoner.

But England had more important matters to attend – the restoration of Charles II. Myngs declared himself a loyal supporter of the king and was soon found innocent and reinstated. In a fit of revenge he accused d'Oyley of receiving more money than he should, and the governor was replaced.

King Charles II (1630-1685) by Pieter Nason, 17th century. Sociedad de retratos históricos.

Jamaica's Institutionalisation

In 1661 d'Oyley's policy underwent an important shift and the following year a convoy set out from England transporting Lord Windsor, the new governor, appointed by the Committee for Foreign Plantations. Christopher Myngs travelled aboard HMS *Centurion*, a 46-cannon frigate. He arrived in Barbados in July and sent letters to the Governors of Puerto Rico and Santo Domingo asking them to admit trade with English vessels.[14] Although Madrid had made peace with England three years earlier, the authorities refused to acknowledge the settlements in the Indies and, for fear of endangering the trade monopoly, did not accept English claims.

On 21 August Windsor and Myngs arrived in Port Royal and the process of institutionalising[15] the colony began immediately. The governor offered lands for settlement to all those who were at least twelve years old and established a Local Assembly, a Court and an Admiralty which would allow him to issue letters of reprisal. In relation to military affairs, he completed the fort built to defend the port and named it Fort Charles. He raised the salary of the armed forces and replaced the five regiments of soldiers distributed around the island. He finally received an answer from the Spanish governors rejecting his requests. Windsor had received secret instructions that 'if the King of Spain refuses to admit trading with our subjects then we must secure trade with his subjects everywhere by force'.[16]

Applying his orders, he would grant letters of marque to all who landed in Jamaica, 'in order to subdue our enemies on land and at sea, along the entire coast of America'.[17]

Over a few days, Windsor called on the people to voluntarily join a great expedition against the Spanish under the orders of Commander in Chief Commodore Myngs. In three days he gathered 1,300 men, two thirds of whom were filibusters. Several vessels belonging to the king joined the venture and among the officers was a twenty-seven-year-old named Henry Morgan.

The Attack on Santiago de Cuba

With the excuse that it served as a point of departure for Spanish expeditions intending to recover Jamaica, Myngs planned a reprisal campaign against the city of Santiago de Cuba.[18] The English fleet left Port Royal on 1 October 1662 and headed for Punta Negril, Jamaica. In order to avoid the Spanish watch, Myngs dropped anchor east of his objective near a key where Sir Thomas Whetstone's vessel was already waiting to join the expedition.

Myngs had already obtained espionage information about the layout of the Spanish defences and, after holding council aboard the *Centurion*, it was decided to launch a direct attack against the port in an attempt to surprise the Spaniards. Reinforced by another seven Jamaican pirates who had joined the expedition, he set off for Santiago. They sighted the castle lights during the night and decided to attack at dawn on October 16, but were confounded by unfavourable winds.

Around noon they changed their plans and profiting from the offshore wind headed towards the nearby town of Aguadores, at the mouth of the River San Juan. At nightfall they landed 1,000 men who began advancing. At daybreak they reached a plantation three miles from the city, and paused to rest and replenish their water supplies.

They continued their march until they sighted Santiago, surprising the Spanish, who knew of their movements but had not expected them so soon. Nevertheless, at the entrance to the city, Governor Pedro Morales was awaiting them with 250 men and two orderlies. In reserve, a former Governor of Jamaica and good friend of the English, Cristóbal de Isasi Arnaldo, had another 500 men under his command.

Myngs began the assault on Morales and took control of the city with the aid of Isasi,[19] who betrayed his own. The booty included seven vessels anchored in the port.

Some defenders took refuge in the castle while others fled to the mountains. The English spent five days persecuting the fugitives while the filibusters sacked the city. There was scant booty and the filibusters proposed attacking the castle, but Myngs refused to submit the stronghold to a long siege and decided instead to blow up the castle walls.

Five days later 700 barrels of gunpowder were indeed used to blow up the castle, the cathedral, the governor's

OTHER MINOR ACTIONS

The new associations that emerged from the recently created colony of Jamaica did not restrict sporadic actions by independent filibusters.

In 1662 Bartolomeu Portugués[20] appeared in Manzanillo, Cuba, where he stole a small vessel which he armed with four cannons and used to travel around the south of the island.

One year later, on July 7, he captured a merchant ship near the Cape of Corrientes with the aid of thirty men. To his surprise he obtained a booty of 75,000 escudos and 100,000 pounds of cacao.

With the captured boat he set out for Campeche, where he arrived at the end of the year. He attempted to avoid the defences by sending people to land, but he was discovered and taken prisoner. El Portugués was put on trial and sentenced to death, but managed to escape. He walked along the beach for 70 leagues (more than 100 miles) until he ran into a group of pirates who were replenishing their water supplies. He joined the group and managed to convince them to attempt new robberies in Campeche.

Making the smuggler's sign, he approached a Spanish merchant vessel in the port and knifed everyone on board. Then he set sail for Jamaica, but was shipwrecked in the Jardines de la Reina.

residence, the hospital and main households – everything was razed to the ground. This was followed by more sackings and an ordered retreat taking the bells and cannons with them. It took the citizens of Santiago ten years to repair all that had been destroyed.

On 1 November Myngs returned to Port Royal with a list of twenty-six casualties, six of whom fell during the battle. The rest were due to illness or accident. One tenth of the booty was set apart for the king and one fifteenth for the Duke of York.

Three days earlier Windsor had departed from the island, leaving Sir Charles Lyttelton as the provisional governor, having appointed Myngs[21] member of the Council of Jamaica.

The Sacking of Campeche in 1663[22]

The consolidation of La Tortuga as a safe hideout and centre for smuggling in the early 1660s caused the buccaneers, not for the first time, to threaten to abandon Jamaica. The situation required a positive action that would bring the dissenters back into the support of the island's militia. Once again the man chosen for this vital operation was Myngs who, emboldened by his success at Santiago de Cuba, decided to lead a squadron composed of the 40-cannon *Centurion* and the *Griffin* with a crew of 100 men under the command of Captain Smart. The regular forces were joined by Mansfield and his 4-cannon brig and other captains such as William James, totalling several dozen vessels. On 21 January 1663 they set sail, but soon lost contact with one another.

An advance group led by Myngs reached the coast of Yucatan and landed 1,000 men on a beach four miles west of Campeche during the night of 8 February.

The alarm was raised at daybreak. A group of small vessels supported by two larger ones headed for the beach. But it was too late: the simultaneous attack by land and sea was too much for the city, which surrendered at 8 o'clock in the morning.

Despite having been taken by surprise and regardless of their inferior number, the 150-strong militia of Campeche offered strong resistance. Aided by the city's intricate defences, they inflicted casualties on the English troops, including Myngs himself, who was wounded while leading the attack and taken aboard the *Centurion*.

Mansfield took charge and at the battle's end there were thirty dead among the English, and fifty dead, 170 taken prisoner, among the defenders.

On the morning of 10 February Antonio Maldonado de Aldana entered the city to surrender and request that the prisoners be treated well. The man he spoke to was Mansfield and from then on the Spanish would refer to this action as the Mansfield attack.

The filibusters remained in the city until 23 February, obtaining substantial spoils which they loaded on to three 300-ton merchant vessels. Upon departing the city they encountered foul winds and the fleet was dispersed. The *Centurion* arrived in Port Royal on 26 April 1663 with a booty of 150,000 pesos. Myngs retired to England, where he was knighted by Charles II.[23]

The Resurrection of La Tortuga

Just as the 'Western Design' changed the fate of Jamaica, events were shaping the course of the island of La Tortuga. In the face of imminent attack on the city of Santo Domingo from the forces led by Penn and Venables, in March 1655 the Governor of Santo Domingo, the Count of Peñalba, ordered the evacuation of La Tortuga, in order to deploy all his forces for the defence of the city.[24]

With no soldiers now on station, it seems that, shortly after the evacuation, a few families of French settlers from Hispaniola returned to the island. In December 1656 the new governor, Félix de Zúñiga,[25] wrote to the king

criticising the Count of Peñalba's inefficient operations and asking permission to evacuate the island once again, leaving only 100 men behind.

But things had changed in France. Louis XIV had re-adopted Richelieu's old project and, in December 1656, appointed Jeremie Deschamps,[26] Seigneur du Rausset, Governor and Lieutenant General of La Tortuga. By 1659 du Rausset had obtained the necessary resources for his venture and departed from La Rochelle with thirty men.

He sailed straight to Jamaica where d'Oyley appointed him Governor of La Tortuga on behalf of England. He dropped anchor in Port à Margot and engaged between 500 and 600 men to re-populate the island. Thanks to his skill and diplomacy, du Rausset had become representative of all the island's inhabitants, appointed governor by both France and England and well received by the Fraternity of the Brothers of the Coast. He managed to rebuild the defences and consolidate the colony, which would soon become a den of filibusters.

In about 1662 du Rausset sailed for France to convalesce after suffering a disease that continued to undermine his health. He left the government in the hands of his nephew M. de la Place. But things did not turn out well – du Rausset ended up in the Bastille.[27]

D'Ogeron or the Golden Years of La Tortuga

In 1649 the Company of the Isles of America had sold all its colonies, which were now in private hands. In July 1664 the executor of Louis XIV's centralist policy, Colbert, founded the French Company of the Indies[28] and recovered the possessions that had been sold to provide profits for the king.

On 15 November a sales contract was signed at the Bastille between du Rausset and the Company of the Indies,[29] in which du Rausset sold the isle of La Tortuga to the Company for £15,000. Giving very precise instructions on the new colonial policy, the Company appointed Bertrand d'Ogeron its governor.[30]

D'Ogeron arrived in La Tortuga on 6 June 1665 and gained the acknowledgement of the Fraternity, initiating a policy to attract filibusters back to the island.

With this in mind, he wrote to Becharmet, secretary of the State Council, informing him that 'between seven and eight hundred French had settled along the coast of this island [Hispaniola], in inaccessible places...in groups of

WOMEN ON LA TORTUGA

D'Ogeron believed that the fastest way to make the buccaneers settle down was to provide them with the means to set up a family. In France he managed to procure one hundred prostitutes, whom he transported to La Tortuga and proceeded to sell.

Couples were not forced to marry, but they had to establish a pact which included three conditions:

a) Each man must pay the cost of transporting his partner.

b) The women would be well treated: they were partners not slaves. If a woman was abused (ill-treated, battered) she could turn to the governor and he would dissolve the links between her and the guilty man.

c) If a woman's companion died in action or did not return after a few months, she was free to look for another partner.

The arrival of the first contingent in 1666 was described as follows: '…The men had formed a semicircle on the beach; many had shaved. The women were brought to land in

In the late 1670s, the arrival of women and children did much to brighten the lifestyle on La Tortuga.

groups of ten. When the canoe reached the beach, the women stepped into the water with their skirts lifted half way up their thighs and there they waited for the rest of their companions. Everyone remained silent until the last woman had stepped onto land. They

did not dare look at the men straight in the eye, and the men seemed indifferent. Suddenly, one of the brothers stepped out and, leaning on his rifle, began a long ceremonious, grandiloquent speech. He spoke of good behaviour, of honesty, of loyalty and even of

redemption. He ended by telling the women that since they had chosen this line of conduct they should continue at all costs and correct their bad instincts. The sale took place without incident….'

three or four or six or ten…living like savages, acknowledging no one, with no leaders elected among them and committing all sorts of misdeeds. It is therefore imperative that Your Majesty order all these people off Hispaniola…and send them to La Tortuga, where they would go anyway if the island were fortified'.[31]

Fortunately for the interests of La Tortuga, the authorities of Hispaniola now ordered an exceptional measure by which they intended to eradicate buccaneering – they slaughtered all the livestock that had returned to the wild. They also reinforced their attack against the settlements by increasing the number of Cincuentena patrols who forced the buccaneers to retreat.

Many retired to La Tortuga and engaged in the cultivation of cacao, wheat, tobacco, cochineal and

coffee. For these trades it was necessary to introduce a large labour force and, over the next two years, 2,000 engagées arrived on the island. Among them was the French surgeon Alexander Oliver Exquemeling,[32] who arrived on 7 July 1666. To make La Tortuga even more attractive d'Ogeron waived the governor's special rights and so increased the people's profits; he also organised a market and, in 1666, he promoted the arrival of European women.[33]

The success of his policies encouraged d'Ogeron to become ever more ambitious. In 1667 he undertook to achieve cohesion between buccaneers and filibusters under his command. The Spanish actions had resulted in many casualties and he believed that a reprisal campaign against one of the island's cities would be well received. The target chosen was the city of Santiago de los Caballeros.[34]

The operation's leadership was entrusted to Delisle who arrived first in Puerto Plata. He landed 400 filibusters and advanced overland towards Santiago, upon which he fell at dawn on Holy Friday. He sacked the city and, to celebrate his victory, organised a great orgy.

Next the invaders attempted to reach the coast with hostages but their passage was blocked. Delisle threatened to kill the governor and the citizens capitulated – not to preserve the governor's life but to defend their own possessions. The French were allowed to pass and retreat to La Tortuga.

D'Ogeron Returns to France

With such success behind him, d'Ogeron planned a large-scale attack and asked the Company for more resources and people in order to 'attack the town of Santo Domingo and become master of the island'.[35] With this in mind he travelled to France in 1668, where he remained until the middle of the following year seeking support for his campaign.

Meanwhile, the buccaneers began to leave La Tortuga and establish new settlements in Cul de Sac and around Yaguana, renamed Leogane. Taxes had been reduced but, nevertheless, those levied by the Company were still very burdensome and the smugglers attempted to avoid them by trading directly with the Dutch in the new coastal settlements. The Company in turn imposed a prohibition of direct trade and, encouraged by Holland, the coastal inhabitants revolted against La Tortuga. It was to such a situation of unrest that d'Ogeron returned and, indeed, things became so bad that, in August 1670, d'Ogeron almost lost his life[36] trying to put down the violent demonstrations against prohibition.

A French squadron helped to pacify the coastal area, but the problems persisted inland. The colony now facing serious danger, in October 1671 d'Ogeron proposed its transference to Florida. During the same month Louis XIV offered a general amnesty to those who had taken part in the revolt. The proposal was rejected and the colonisation of the north coast of Hispaniola began with the cultivation of tobacco.

By 1674 the La Tortuga colony had been so neglected by the Indies Company that d'Ogeron himself stated 'the poverty of some of the inhabitants of La Tortuga and the coast of Santo Domingo is so great that they do not have

the means with which to buy arms or gunpowder'.[37] Finally Colbert dissolved the Company, its properties being incorporated into those of the Crown, and free trade was decreed.

D'Ogeron decided to seek new support and travelled to France, leaving his nephew de Pouançay as the provisional governor. D'Ogeron died unexpectedly in Paris at the end of January 1676 and de Pouançay was appointed Governor of La Tortuga in mid March.

El Olonés

One of the buccaneers most active during d'Ogeron's term of office was Jean-David Nau. Notorious in Spanish eyes as *El Olonés*, he reached the Antilles as an engageé around 1660. Having served his term he bought his freedom and became a buccaneer. He began trading in La Tortuga and received a vessel from the then governor, de la Place, with twenty men aboard, but only eight months later he was already the leader of eight vessels and 400 men.

He attempted an attack on Campeche[38] but was shipwrecked. Despite this setback, he assaulted the city with those of his men still surviving. He ran into the defences, lost most of his forces, and saved his own life by playing dead, camouflaging himself with blood and sand.

He managed to flee to Campeche, where he rose a few slaves to revolt; they stole a canoe and he was able to return to La Tortuga.

Nau was near Key Fragoso,[39] Cuba, when he sighted a Spanish frigate heading full sail in his direction. It had been sent by the Governor of Havana to search for him and on board was the man appointed to execute him.

The buccaneer lay in ambush and prepared his artillery. He launched the attack forcing the Spanish to surrender and taking over the vessel. He was especially brutal with the negro who would have been his executioner.

Back in La Tortuga, Nau became the associate of Miguel el Vasco[40] and other Frenchmen who had lived on the coasts of Venezuela, and who now proposed what promised to be a profitable venture: the assault of two cities very close to one another, Maracaibo and Gibraltar.

In August 1667 they mobilised 1,000 men and attacked Maracaibo.[41] They entered the bay by night and surprised

The Cruelty of Lolonois
LOLONOIS

During his Central-American campaign, El Olonés was ambushed several times on his way to San Pedro. He took a number of men captive and demanded that they show him the defenders' positions and a safe alternative route. When they refused to cooperate, he became enraged and 'cut open a prisoner's chest with his sabre, tore out his heart and bit into it. He then threw it into the face of the others, shouting 'Show me another way or the rest of you will get the same treatment!''

the sentinels, although the alarm had been raised and the inhabitants were able to flee to Gibraltar. The raiders obtained a small booty of about 20,000 reales, furniture, other goods and a dozen prisoners, who were tortured until they confessed where they had hidden their possessions.

From Maracaibo they went on to Gibraltar, which was now fortified and entrenched and fought back, inflicting many casualties on the buccaneers. Even so, the city fell and the governor was beheaded. A tributo de quema was imposed but not satisfied, and the city was razed to the ground.

Back in Maracaibo Nau obtained a tributo de quema of 20,000 reales and then sacked the city, stealing the bells and icons from the church. After this adventure he set sail for the Isla Vaca where he divided the booty – 260,000 reales and another 100,000 in fabrics and other goods. They celebrated their victory in La Tortuga and all the profits were spent in two weeks.

In order to recover his losses Nau took to sea again and launched a campaign against Nicaragua, first attacking Puerto Caballos. Then he moved away from the Gulf of Honduras arriving in Cape Gracias a Dios and settling in Cape Las Perlas. He spent the following ten months taking his vessel apart in order to build another smaller one.

He then set out towards Rio San Juan and headed inland, but many of his men deserted. He decided to go south and, when he reached the Darien, he attacked a native village in search of food. The buccaneers were defeated by the natives and all were eaten alive except one, who was able to flee and tell the story.[42]

MODYFORD OR THE SURVIVAL OF JAMAICA

At the end of May 1664 Edward Morgan arrived in Jamaica to take up his post as Lieutenant Governor to Sir Thomas Modyford. The subsequent arrival of Sir Thomas on 4 June marked the beginning of a new era in the history of Jamaica. Sir Thomas had been recommended by George Monck, Duke of Albemarle and his mission was to eradicate piracy.

On his arrival he issued an edict – 'as from today all hostilities against the Spanish must cease'.[43] Almost at once many filibusters left for La Tortuga.

The protests of the settlers soon began to be heard. The planters and merchants argued that their prosperity and defence depended on the buccaneers. With the very real possibility that 1,000-1,500 filibusters with fourteen or fifteen vessels who used Jamaica as the base for their operations would withdraw to La Tortuga, it was decided that Sir Thomas's edict would be relaxed somewhat.[44] Soon afterwards, a letter was received from London repeating the ban on attacking the Spanish and ordering that all seized goods be returned. Modyford now became ambivalent in his actions: while not actually fostering filibustering, he nevertheless turned a blind eye.

The singularity of Jamaica, one of the most vulnerable points of the English colonial structure in the Caribbean, had ever made it expedient for the Crown to transport to the island all those criminals who had not been sentenced to death. Now, the unravelling situation required reinforcements and the king ordered that 'all prisoners sentenced to capital punishment…should be reprieved and sent to the colonies'.[45]

Sporadic Actions: Raids in Tabasco

Despite the prohibitions, some filibusters continued to act against Spanish interests. Captains Henry Morgan, Freeman, Kackman, Morris and David Martien left Jamaica in January 1665 with a few vessels and 200 men.

They reached the coast of Tabasco[46] and made landfall in Santa María de la Frontera. They climbed towards the capital, Villahermosa de Tabasco, bordering the Grijalbo river, and reached the outskirts of the city on February 24.

At four in the morning they began their assault, surprising the defenders in their sleep: they took command of the city and sacked it.

During their return voyage they stopped in Santa Teresa, where they demanded a ransom of 300 head of cattle in exchange for a few men they had captured. When they were boarding they sighted three Spanish frigates sent by Antonio Maldonado, lieutenant to the Governor of Campeche, under the command of José Aldana.

Surprised and stranded on land and outnumbered by the Spanish, they fled, leaving their booty and ships behind. Morris, Morgan and Martien headed north where they captured a few boats with which to continue their actions, now at Trujillo on the coast of Honduras, from

The lake and city of Maracaibo, 1699
The cities of Maracaibo and Gibraltar on Lake Maracaibo were favoured targets for the filibusters in the second half of the 17th century.
El Olonés and Morgan stole substantial spoils from here in August 1667 and March 1669 respectively.

JAMAICA, CURAÇAO AND SLAVE TRADING[47]

From the mid 17th century, slave trading in the Caribbean was organised through storage and distribution companies.

Holland obtained its supplies from San Jorge de Mina, Santo Tomé and the mouth of the River Zaire, transporting the negroes to their company in Curaçao under the monopoly of the Dutch West India Company.

On the other hand, the English kept their negroes in Barbados and Jamaica. The complete circuit was carried out through the Company of Royal

TO BE SOLD on board the Ship *Bance-Island*, on tuesday the 6th of *May* next, at *Ashley-Ferry*; a choice cargo of about 250 fine healthy

NEGROES,

just arrived from the Windward & Rice Coast. —The utmost care has already been taken, and shall be continued, to keep them free from the least danger of being infected with the SMALL-POX, no boat having been on board, and all other communication with people from *Charles-Town* prevented.

Austin, Laurens, & *Appleby*.

N. B. Full one Half of the above Negroes have had the SMALL-POX in their own Country.

RECIEN LLEGADOS DE EUROPA, procedentes de las más selectas prisiones: condenados a la pena capital, enganchados franceses y reos de *muerte civil*, salvaban la vida a cambio de la esclavitud, los trabajos forzados y la venta como siervos. Estos fueron métodos utilizados por los tribunales para redimir los delitos de muchos desgraciados enviados a tierras americanas como mano de obra.

Adventurers of English Commerce with Africa founded in 1660 by the Duke of York, brother of King Charles II. Incapable of withstanding the impetus of the Dutch, the Company went bankrupt in 1667.

Between the English, La Tortuga and the main Spanish colonies, major smuggling trade took place. Apparently, English planters maintained correspondence with the Dutch despite the Royal Adventurers. The Anglo-Dutch wars were in reality the fight for trade in the Caribbean and slave trading was one of the main points of friction.

Corsairs such as John Petersen, who operated under Jamaican letters of marque, systematically attacked the slave vessels of the Dutch Company. With his 30-ton ship *Kastel Fergat* and a

Portugal's struggle for independence from Spain meant that the country ceased trading in slaves for some time. In 1696, when independence had at last been recognised, a formal asiento was established allowing the Portuguese to resume their activities in the trade.

crew of French, English and Germans, in November 1659 he attacked the *Sant Jan*, a ship belonging to Adriaen van der Veer which was transporting ninety negroes.

He was responsible for a number of other robberies and, once the war was over, the Dutch protested before the Jamaican authorities. He was accused of behaviour inappropriate to his mission and branded a pirate.

The links between slave trading and piracy continued to be very tight. Many filibusters began their careers in slave

trading and some governors such as Modyford had been agents of the Company of Royal Adventurers in Jamaica and later in Barbados.

In 1663 official traffic of Spanish

possessions was granted by *asiento* to Grillo and Lomelín from Genoa. Genoese businesses were permanently immersed in controversy. Their ships, built specifically for the asiento, did not meet the characteristics demanded by the regulations, and all their transactions were permanently under suspicion.

The inhuman treatment of slaves was typified by the corporal punishment meted out to those who refused to accept their lot. Flogging, torture and punishments of all kinds marked a slave's day-to-day existence.

The need for a large labour force to work the fields and mines was the original impetus for the massive importing of black slaves.

But the most serious accusation against them came after Morgan's sack of Panama. A memorandum drawn up by the Comercio de Lima assured that Grillo had granted powers to military men and engineers to inspect the defences and had established relations with an Englishman living in Jamaica named Roger Reyt. Reyt had supposedly been in Portobelo and returned with documents containing precise data about the defences.

As evidence, it was contended that Grillo's agents had been warned and had fled from Panama; also that Grillo's possessions had been respected during the attack.

The carimba

The Spanish procedure for receiving a slave was completed with the *carimba* or marking. It consisted of marking the subject on different parts of his body, usually the breast, back or upper arm, with a red-hot metal carimba.

All slaves received two marks: the monogram of the *asentistas*, indicating their place of origin, and the *coronilla real*, which indicated they had been legally introduced and the corresponding taxes had been paid.

The coronilla was not stamped on the subject until after thirty days, to avoid payment of taxes for those who died or were rejected during the period.

It seems that some monograms were associated with diseases and other supplementary data that the buyer might need to know.

Various monograms used for branding slaves in the last three decades of the 17th century.

whence they proceeded to Costa de los Mosquitos. Nine native guides led them south up the River San Juan and to Lake Nicaragua. Crossing the lake by night and resting during the day, on 29 June they attacked Granada, taking more than 300 prisoners. To avoid pursuit they sank the Spanish boats, freed their prisoners, crossed the lake and returned from the southwest to Jamaica.

JAMAICA AT WAR

Meanwhile, in the spring of 1665, news had reached Jamaica of the beginning of the Second Anglo-Dutch War. The filibusters became Jamaica's army and the order to cease hostilities was revoked.

Vagabonds were now rioting in the streets of Port Royal and, in November, Modyford[47] gathered them all in the Bay of Bluefields to persuade them to carry out a campaign against the Dutch colonies of Curaçao, Saba and San Eustaquio. At the head of these forces was Edward Morgan as chief of the Jamaican militia.

It was believed that the booty would pay the costs of the campaign and the filibusters were told that 'if there is no booty there will be no pay, and the king cannot be burdened with any considerable cost, except for gunpowder and mortars'.[48]

More than 600 reformed prisoners took to sea in ten vessels. As soon as they had set sail, the lack of discipline became evident and the men demanded that the method for dividing the booty be altered in their favour. In July they reached San Eustaquio, took the island, and from there went on to Saba, Martín and Tórtola. The filibusters refused to continue until the booty had been shared out – 900 slaves, arms, cattle and cotton.

They chose Mansfield as their representative before Modyford and accepted his proposal to set out for Curaçao, but the project was finally rejected due to the bad weather conditions and the corsairs' opinion that if they attacked the Spanish colonies they would obtain greater profits.

In Cuban waters they sighted and captured a vessel with twenty-two men on board, whose throats were cut. Later they arrived in the port of Júcaro, south Cuba, where they attempted to buy provisions but were rejected because of the people's fear of attack. Some 200 or 300 filibusters marched forty-two miles inland to take possession and set fire to the city of Sancti Espíritus,

taking 200 horses and numerous prisoners for whom they were paid a ransom of 300 fat cows. These raids were justified with the argument that a substantial number of corsairs were Portuguese under licence from the French governor of La Tortuga.

They later arrived in Bocas del Toro where they split up: seven of the squadron's vessels set out for Costa Rica and the remaining eight headed towards the city of Nata in the province of Veragua.

In January 1666 France unenthusiastically followed the terms of the treaty it had with Holland and declared war on England.

One month later the Council of Jamaica[49] presented a document containing twelve reasons for the colony to be interested in issuing letters of marque against Spanish interests. Modyford gave support to the proposal and defended it by pointing out the local confrontations and the need to respond to the violent acts of the Spanish coastguards. He opened negotiations for the return of the filibusters to La Tortuga, whose only incentive was economic. From then on he handed out licences to corsairs of any nationality to attack Spanish strongholds and piracy became widespread. Mansfield was the main beneficiary of these protests and soon became leader of the filibusters.

On 8 April 1666 the expeditionaries arrived in Portete. They managed to capture the coastguards before they could land and give warning, and anchored in Punta del Toro with the intention of taking the capital, Cartago, by surprise.

They fell on the nearby city of Matina where they captured thirty-five Spaniards. But an Indian named Esteban Yaperi,[50] from the town of Teotique, ran to warn the Governor of Costa Rica, Juan López de Flor. By mid April hundreds of militia were combing the jungle and taking up positions in the nearby mountains of Turrialba, ready to block the way of the invaders despite a serious lack of arms.

Mansfield's men were no better off. The jungle caused the filibusters great suffering, and hunger and exhaustion caused fights to break out over the small amount of wheat they had stolen from the Indians.

Aware of the difficulties that Mansfield's men were facing, de Flor ordered an advance, forcing the filibusters to retreat. On 23 April the exhausted and famished survivors reached their vessels in Portete and retreated to Bocas del Toro.

Two vessels deserted and Mansfield found himself in an uncomfortable situation and unable to return. In an attempt to gain credibility he decided to attack the island of Santa Catalina.

Mansfield and the Dream of the Divine Providence

Mansfield was attempting to establish a filibuster base far from the influence of the French and English and to constitute a free republic. The place chosen was the island of Santa Catalina (Providence).[51]

With two frigates and three tenders he arrived on the island on 25 May, landing on the north coast without being seen. Near midnight 200 corsairs advanced over the island, among them 100 English, 80 French from La Tortuga and a few Portuguese.

The sleeping inhabitants were guarded by a reserve of just eight soldiers. Mansfield guaranteed their personal safety and ordered the French troops to prevent the church from being sacked. Ten days later he took to the sea with 170 prisoners. He left Captain Hatsell in command of the island with thirty-five corsairs and fifty negroes under his orders, waiting for Mansfield or any other English authority to return.

On 11 June he anchored in Punta de Brujas on the north coast of Panama to land the prisoners and continue his journey to Jamaica. Eleven days later he reached Port Royal with two vessels and discovered that fortune was awaiting him there in the form of pieces of gold. With the changes introduced in February by the Council and the governor, attacks on Spanish possessions were prized so that Mansfield's capture of Santa Catalina was rewarded, after an initial reprimand for not having achieved the entrusted objectives. Four days later the news of Mansfield's victory was sent by Modyford to Secretary of State Lord Arlington.

Mansfield offered to submit Santa Catalina to Jamaican jurisdiction,[52] but this proposal was rejected by Modyford. He then addressed La Tortuga but was met by the same response. He set his last hopes on the Governor of New England, but died suddenly before setting off on the voyage in 1667.

Meanwhile, the Governor of Panama, Pérez de Guzmán, reacted with celerity sending José Sánchez Ximenez at the head of an expedition. His objective was to recover the island before the position was consolidated by reinforcements sent from Jamaica. The success of the operation increased Perez de Guzmán's prestige and the dream of 'Providence' vanished into thin air.

Henry Morgan enters the Scene

In May 1667 the First Treaty with Madrid was signed to end the constant friction between England and Spain, who were in a permanent state of small scale war. At the end of that year Modyford announced that he had received information of Spanish plans to invade Jamaica and he appointed Cuba as the place from which to launch a campaign.

Some time later, in February 1668, the governor's brother, James Modyford, substituted Edward Morgan as Chief Justice of Jamaica. James entrusted Henry Morgan, head of the local militia, with the mission of 'gathering all the English corsairs'[53] and discovering the place from which the Spanish intended to invade Jamaica.

In agreement with the governor, Henry Morgan chose the isle of Cuba as the objective. He organised an expedition to destroy the preliminaries and, in April, set sail with a dozen vessels and 700 men. It seems that the initial plan was to take Havana but the idea was rejected upon seeing their defences. Morgan entered Los Jardines de la Reina to reach the Gulf of Ana María, left his boats there and went inland to assault the city of Puerto Príncipe (now Camagüey). He took 50,000 pieces of eight and a few hundred head of cattle, which he salted and then made the locals transport to the coast. Thus his booty was handsome enough to allow him to continue his misdeeds, but during his retreat he was attacked by militia on horseback and lancers on foot, and 200 of his men were wounded.

The Sacking of Portobelo[54]

Upon his return to Jamaica Morgan told Modyford that his information regarding a Spanish invasion had indeed been correct and the governor subsequently gave unconditional support to all new actions.

Morgan then planned another attack, this time without the cooperation of the French filibusters who had retired after disagreeing with the way the booty had been shared out after the Puerto Príncipe campaign. With four frigates, eight tenders and fewer than 500 men he sailed to the Isthmus of Panama and dropped anchor in Bocas del Toro. He boarded his men on twenty-three canoes and small boats and sailed northeast along the coast, taking four nights to cover the 150 miles to Portobelo, where he arrived on 10 July 1668.

They landed at night and walked the distance to the city. The attack was launched at dawn and in order to spread panic the English opened fire on anything that moved. It took them very little time to take the city. They reached the fort of Santiago and blew up the arsenal with its garrison inside. Later they reached the outskirts of the fort of San Gerónimo where the defenders had taken refuge without suffering a single casualty.

The assault was carried out in stages, using the nuns and priests of the city as a shield. After a determined defence, the fort capitulated with a toll of forty-five dead among the attackers and five Spanish soldiers.

Soon outrageous actions were taking place. Morgan adorned the castle with a red flag and its walls with the bodies of the fifty beheaded soldiers who had been taken prisoner. The civil population was no luckier and many inhabitants were tortured until they confessed where they had hidden their possessions; all sorts of abuses were committed.

Informed of the assault, the Governor of Panama reached Portobelo with reinforcements and attacked Morgan's positions but was unable to defeat the holders of the fort. After negotiating he paid a tributo de quema of 100,000 pesos and retreated to allow the English to leave. Morgan recovered his vessels and sailed to Port Royal, which he entered triumphantly on July 27.

But the attacks did not cease here. From Panama the French filibuster, Picard,[55] extended the offensive to the province of Veragua where he pillaged in the main cities capturing a few prisoners and gold pounds from the mines in the area. It seems that he crossed the Isthmus to reach the Pacific in the area of Nata but the authorities had already been alerted and he was forced to return to the Caribbean.

The Spanish response was aggressive. The regent for the young Charles II of Spain, Queen Mariana de Austria,[56] ordered the issue of letters of marque and fostered indiscriminate attacks on British interests.

The Attack on Maracaibo[57]

In order to recover lost time and without waiting to re-arm his forces, Morgan decided to raid Trinidad or Margarita with eight vessels and 500 men. But one of his French followers proposed that they attack Maracaibo as Jean-David Nau had done two years earlier.

The proposal was accepted and in February they set sail. After stopping in Aruba to obtain provisions they headed to the Gulf of Venezuela[58] and came in sight of Maracaibo on 9 March. Since Nau's raid the bay had been defended by a small castle armed with eleven cannons. It was assaulted during the night and taken without resistance. One officer and eight soldiers in charge of its defence ran to give warning to the city when they saw the column advance.

The aggressors fired their cannons, then boarded and sailed to the city that had now been abandoned by its people. Without caring how long it took them to do so, Morgan organised groups and sent them to chase down the inhabitants, especially the priests and friars. They employed persuasive methods to make the poor wretches confess where they had hidden their possessions and valuable objects.

Morgan had been collecting for almost a month when Alonso de Campos y Espinosa, Admiral of the Windward Fleet,[59] reached the sandbank of Maracaibo with three vessels: the flagship *Nuestra Señora de la Magdalena* with thirty-eight cannons and weighing 412 tons; the 26-cannon, 218-ton *San Luis*, commanded by Mateo Alonso Huidobro, and a 14-cannon, 50-ton tender named *Nuestra Señora de la Soledad*, alias *Marquesa*.

They dropped anchor blocking the sandbank and sent forty harquebusiers to land, who restored six cannons on the fortress. After closing the way out several letters were sent to the nearby villages asking for reinforcements.

When Morgan heard of the Spanish action he prepared his men to emerge from the trap and prepared his thirteen vessels for combat. The Spanish ships had the advantage, however, the river mouth was so narrow that Morgan's men could not manoeuvre and were forced to fight from the bow against the sides of the anchored vessels, which were also being reinforced from land.

FOOD AND DRINK

The diet of the filibusters was based on the combination of certain basic products. The drinks consumed by the English stationed in Jamaica consisted mainly of beer and liquors, especially brandy and rum.

The meat, which was usually beef or pork, was smoked and mixed with lard and cooked to tenderise it for stewing or roasting. Fresh meat was grilled.

Some of the most typical drink and food combinations received curious names such as:

SIR CLOUDESLEY, a jocular name given by the English to a typical drink of the 17th century made of brandy mixed with a little beer, frequently sweetened or spiced, with an added touch of lemon juice. The same drink without lemon was known as flip. The name of the drink was in honour of Sir Cloudesley Shovell (1650-1707), famous for his services against the corsairs in the Mediterranean.

MUM: The original name of this drink was *Mumme* and its place of origin was Brunswick (Germany). It was very popular in the 17th century and was a strong beer made of wheat and oat malts and flavoured with herbs.

KILDUIJVEL: Literally *Kill-Devil*, a euphemism for rum used by the Dutch during the 17th century.

RUM: Alcoholic beverage distilled from molasses obtained from grinding sugar cane. Widely consumed around the Caribbean, this drink substituted other more expensive alcoholic beverages such as brandy. The origin of the term is unknown although it could stem from the archaic English adjective 'rum', used to designate something of excellence. In order to preserve water on English vessels, it would be mixed with rum, giving rise to a drink known as *Grog*. In 1688 the British Admiralty ordered that rations of rum be handed out instead of brandy to all those stationed in Jamaica.

SALMIGONDIS or SALMAGUNDI: A French term for a very spicy stew made of a mixture of meats, vegetables and a number of other ingredients. The mixture of meats was frequently rolled into balls or cylinders, while the rest of the ingredients served as an accompaniment. It became very popular among buccaneers, becoming the subject of a great variety of recipes.

Sir Cloudesley Shovell – an English seaman of the 17th century, famous for his jocular nature – gave his name to a popular drink consumed on English ships.

Alonso de Campos challenged Morgan to surrender but the latter refused and demanded a war tribute. He sent forth a fire ship disguised as a war ship by placing dummies and wooden cannons on board. The Spanish artillery opened intense fire, but the flagship and the vice-admiral's ship became entangled, blocking their way. The filibusters set fire to the ships and the Spaniards burned to death. Taking advantage of the situation, Morgan captured the tender.

Campos and Huidobro took refuge in the castle with their crew opening heavy fire against those who attempted to leave the bay. With the wind against him and no cannons on the bow with which to attack the Spaniards, Morgan tried to reach an agreement. He offered to free his prisoners in exchange for being allowed to pass, but Campos refused and Morgan was forced to return to Maracaibo.

On the following day the Englishman attempted to attack the fortress by land but he met with the fire of the harquebusiers and the resistance of the crews, reinforced by seventy men from the local militia.

After realising that the fortress had only six cannons, Morgan found a way out. As darkness fell he sent people out in boats so that the Spanish would think an attack was going to take place at night, simultaneously on land

In early April 1669, when Morgan and his men had been in Maracaibo for almost a month, Alonso de Campos y Espinosa, commanding three vessels from the Windward Fleet, appeared at the entrance to the lagoon. When all seemed lost for the bucaneers, the Welshman's cunning broke the blockade. By sending a fire ship into the enemy flotilla, he set fire to the Capitana, Nuestra Señora de la Magdalena, *and the Almiranta* San Luis *and, taking advantage of the confusion, managed to capture the tender,* Nuestra Señora de la Soledad.

and from the boats. To reinforce their defences they changed the placement of the cannons to receive the assault from land.

Morgan had won. He had managed to take his crews out aboard the vessels; sheltered by the darkness they began their retreat without giving the Spanish time to situate their artillery. Morgan abandoned his prisoners on the sandbank and continued towards Port Royal where he arrived on 27 May with a handsome booty.

The Viceroy of Mexico opened proceedings[60] against Campos and Huidobro, sending them to prison in Seville. The War Council heard their case and considered they had proceeded boldly during the defence, for which reason they were exonerated.

The end of hostilities with Spain was proclaimed again one month after Morgan reached Jamaica. Modyford expressly ordered him not to take to sea.

To make up for this, Morgan bought lands for cultivation and remained inactive for one year.

The Spanish Counter-Attack

As a consequence of the intense attacks on Spanish strongholds, in April 1669 Queen Mariana de Austria authorised the issue of letters of marque in the Indies.[61]

THE CAPTURE OF THE *MARY AND JANE*

One of the most popular freebooter captains among the English in Jamaica was the Dutchman Bernard Claesen Speirdyke. Known as Captain Bart or Barnard, he commanded the *Mary and Jane*, a small six-cannon vessel with a crew of eighteen.

In January 1670 he was sent on a conciliatory mission to Cuba to temper relations with the Spaniards. Having dropped anchor in Manzanillo Bay to the southwest of the island of Cuba, he observed the arrival of a vessel with an English flag.

He sent a boat out with two men to welcome the newcomer, the *Fama* commanded by Rivero Pardal. The two men were captured when the crew on the ship learned that they were Jamaicans.

The *Fama* then hoisted a Spanish flag and assaulted the *Mary and Jane*, arguing that they possessed a letter of marque against English interests. Yelling 'Defend yourself, dog!' Rivero boarded the Dutchman's vessel and, in the ensuing uneven combat, Bart and all his crew were killed.

Many slave traders, smugglers and adventurers decided to serve the Spanish governors and an attack began against the filibuster bases in Jamaica.

One of the most notorious corsairs was the Portuguese Manoel Rivero Pardal, who obtained a letter of marque from the Governor of Cartagena. In early 1670 Rivero Pardal sailed from Cartagena[62] on his ship *San Pedro*, alias *Fama*, armed with fourteen cannons and a crew of seventy. His destination was Point Morant where he expected to obtain a few negroes, but the weather conditions sent him somewhere near the Cayman islands. To make the most of this circumstance, he attacked and set fire to several fishing villages in Gran Cayman, capturing a ketch and a canoe, as well as four children whom he took to Cuba.

The actions of the Spanish corsairs were successful and Modyford was forced to attempt to improve relations by sending a conciliatory mission to Havana. The man chosen to travel was Captain Bart aboard the *Mary and Jane*, carrying letters addressed to the Governor.

Meanwhile, Rivero had taken to sea again and came across the *Mary and Jane*. The vessels engaged in combat,[63] which ended with the death of all the filibusters and the capture of the ship.

At the end of May Rivero was to be found in Cartagena from where he left with the reinforcement of the *Gallardina*, a vessel captured from the French two years

earlier. He approached the coast of Jamaica hoisting English colours, one of his usual tricks. On 11 June he confronted William Harris and captured one of his tenders after sacking and setting fire to the colonies of Montego Bay.

He received reinforcements from Santiago de Cuba and used this advantage to carry out other forays, giving rise to calls for revenge among the inhabitants of Jamaica. When he received news that Morgan had taken to sea Rivero decided to go after him, and ran into John Morris instead, a lieutenant to Morgan, aboard his *Dolphin*.[64]

A terrible storm hurled both vessels towards the Cuban coast where Rivero sought refuge in a bay. Morris had arrived first and Rivero manoeuvred in an attempt to block his way out. But the Englishman foresaw the move, boarded the *Fama* and captured it. Rivero was killed by a shot through the throat.

Other Filibuster Attacks: Laguna de Términos

Simultaneous to Morgan's campaign, a group of filibusters led by Brasiliano, Joseph Bradley and Lecat sought to try their luck. Having decided to join forces they entered the Gulf of Mexico[65] in the spring of 1669. With forty men, of whom thirty-four were Dutch and the rest English, Brasiliano and Bradley blocked Campeche while Lecat stayed behind to patrol, not obtaining a single capture.

Upon attempting to land, Brasiliano lost two of his men. Tired of waiting they retreated to Laguna de Términos to careen their ships and recover their strength. When they returned to the blockade Brasiliano captured three fishermen and tortured them to obtain information. Thus he came to know that a merchant vessel was expected with the new governor on board.

On 18 December 1669 the Spanish set out with three ships forcing Brasiliano and Bradley to flee. The wind hurled Brasiliano towards the southeast; there he attempted to take refuge in the Yucatan, but was stranded on the beach. A few prisoners managed to flee and raise the alarm among the Spanish authorities, who decided to take the initiative. But Lecat arrived very conveniently and rescued them. Brasiliano boarded Bradley's frigate and they returned to Jamaica. Lecat stayed behind with Juan Erasmus Reyning and together they captured a Spanish merchant ship which they renamed *Sevillian*.

Upon their return to Jamaica they discovered that the Portuguese corsair Manoel Rivero Pardal had sacked the island.

A New Reprisal Campaign

The influential George Monck died in July 1670 and the most important advisers around King Charles II advocated ceasing hostilities against Spain; a second Treaty of Madrid was signed, proclaiming the establishment of good relations. This had repercussions on Jamaica and Modyford, accused of fostering piracy, was replaced as governor by Sir Thomas Lynch.[66]

Apparently, Rivero Pardal's sackings[67] of Jamaica sparked off actions of reprisal massively supported by the filibusters and led by Henry Morgan. Other sources assure that Morgan decided to return to sea because the filibusters had squandered their fortunes on drinking and whoring.[68] The fact is that a Council was organised on the Isle of Vaca on 28 October during which the filibusters studied different proposals: attacks on Cartagena, Veracruz and Panama were considered. It was decided to assault Panama. As the promoter and leader of the campaign Morgan would keep one per cent of all goods obtained for himself.

On 18 December 1670 eight vessels and more than 2,000 corsairs sailed from Port Royal for Panama. On their way they captured the island of Santa Catalina where they took 450 prisoners and freed the convicts who were serving jail sentences. Meanwhile, they sent a small advance squadron ahead with three ships and 600 men under the command of Captain Bradley. Brasiliano and Reyning set out to the castle of San Lorenzo at the mouth of the River Chagre to prepare for the arrival of the rest of the expedition. But the operation was not easy and the result was 250 casualties among the defenders and 400 among the filibusters.

The Sacking of Panama[69]

Morgan arrived with the rest of the expedition at the beginning of January, leaving 500 men behind to protect the castle and vessels while the rest went up the river advancing in two columns: one on land and the other in seven small boats and thirty-six skiffs. They went very hungry during the seven days it took to reach the outskirts of the city, because they had expected to obtain provisions from the farms along the way but these had been evacuated by the Spanish.

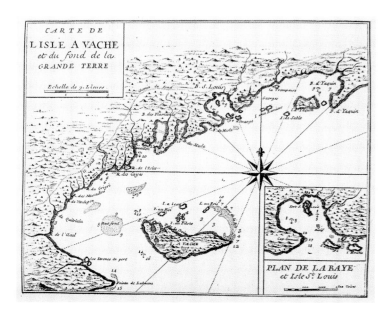

Isla Vaca (today Île-à-Vache), south of Hispaniola, became a place for filibusters to take in provisions and organise themselves before engaging in a campaign and, after a successful ambush, a place in which to share out the spoils of their actions. It was used as a hideout by Morgan and El Olonés, among others.

On 27 January they reached a hill known from then on as *Loma de los Bucaneros* (Buccaneer Hill). Guided by the convicts set free in Santa Catalina they surrounded the city to attack from the forest, disconcerting the inhabitants whose strategy was to attract them to an area where the cavalry could spur forward effectively. The defence was commanded by Juan Pérez de Guzmán with 1,200 infantry and 200 cavalrymen who had been reinforced with troops from Nata, Penonomé, Villa de los Santos. Nuns, women, children and the king's silver were evacuated to Peru aboard the *Trinidad*.

The infantry was very inexperienced. After battling for two hours and disobeying the orders of their leaders, they abandoned their positions falling under Morgan's fire: almost 600 men were killed. They continued the defence from their houses in a disorderly manner, their main preoccupation being to save their ranches. At noon the city was evacuated, the arsenal was blown up and the Spanish retreated to Penonomé. By three in the afternoon the city was in the hands of the filibusters.

The booty was enormous although not as large as expected since the silver and the most valuable objects had been sent away on the *Trinidad*. In revenge, the cannons were spiked and their trunnions cut off, the fortifications were razed to the ground, as was the port, and all other valuable objects left behind were destroyed.

In January 1671 Morgan's forces, which included Rok Brasiliano, Lecat, Prins and Reyning, attacked and destroyed Panama, despite staunch Spanish defence. The buccaneers' cunning and the incompetence of the Spanish infantry were crucial to the success of the operation.

The city was set on fire and devastated to the extent that it had to be rebuilt elsewhere.

On 24 February the filibusters returned to the River Chagre with their booty, taking 600 prisoners whom they intended to torture in order to obtain information of their hidden riches.

After sharing out the booty Morgan set out for Jamaica in mid March, liberating the prisoners after being paid a ransom. He obtained a benefit of 400,000 pesos, a fortune which allowed him to retire and buy his nobility, living as an affluent member of the Jamaican community. On the other hand the filibusters received only 200 pieces of eight (10 silver pounds) and felt betrayed.

Upon his return, Pérez de Guzmán found his home had been vandalised: seventy beds, looking-glasses, furniture and paintings had been destroyed and his personal library containing over 500 volumes was torn to shreds. He was dismissed from his job on 9 October 1671 and after the arrival of inspector Francisco de Marichalar, he was submitted to the routine procedure of imprisonment and trial which lasted from 17 November 1661 to 20 February 1672. Eventually Pérez de Guzmán was acquitted but by then he was a shadow of his former self. He returned to Madrid and died in 1675.

Betrayals and Desertions

After the sack of Panama, Reyning and Lecat continued to patrol the Gulf of Mexico. They were harassing a Spanish coastguard when they ran into HMS *Assistance*

DISCIPLINE AND PUNISHMENTS

MAROON: Derived from the Spanish term *cimarrón*, this name was given to the man who was abandoned on a desert island. The act of abandoning someone on a desert island was known as marooning.

KEELHAULING: Extremely cruel punishment used by the English and Dutch at sea. The actions that most clearly reflect its cruelty took place in 1673 during the Dutch recovery of the colony of San Eustaquio from English hands. The Dutch squadron commanded by commodore Cornellis Evertsen *(Kees the Devil)* took the island and, after some investigation, learned that during the English occupation three Dutch sailors had treacherously murdered the previous governor of the stronghold, Jan Symonsen de Buck.

To set an example, the sailors were submitted to public trial and condemned after being found guilty. It was decided to separate the men into two groups: one of them would be hanged while the other two would be keelhauled, beaten and marooned on a desert island.

On the day of the execution, all three were taken to the gallows to feel the rope around their necks but only one of them was hanged. The other two were led to the ships anchored in the bay. First they would be keelhauled and this required special preparation. A heavy rope was passed from the deck to a yardarm on the mainmast down into the water, under the hull, up to the yard arm on the other side of the mast and thence back down to the deck. To the bight of this rope the culprit would be tied by his feet and hoisted to the yardarm where he would be suspended for a few seconds before being plunged into the water while a group of seamen on the far side of the ship would heave on the rope to haul the man beneath the hull and up to the yardarm above their heads. The operation was repeated three times and then the rest of the sentence was carried out. The agony of this asphyxiating punishment was exacerbated by the fact that the guilty man was dragged beneath a hull and keel that were covered in molluscs and nail heads, which cut into the poor wretch's body. To prevent the convict from drowning, his nose and mouth were daubed with grease.

It was normal for officers on war ships to apply cruel punishments to pirates and those accused of exhorting the others to mutiny. Among these tortures, keelhauling was common practice.

under the command of Lynch. The Englishman needed to ingratiate himself with the Spanish and, under orders, his crew accused the filibusters of piracy and attempted to capture them. Recognising their opponents' greater strength Reyning and Lecat fled and took refuge in Campeche.[71]

Here, however, they were arrested, severely punished and threatened with death if they did not agree to obey the orders of the Campeche authorities. The pirates accepted and even came to embrace Catholicism.

They abandoned their English crew on the Isle of Tris and became coastguards. During their first patrol on Laguna de Términos they captured four British vessels. During the following months Reyning remained on land attending to his business while Lecat continued to work as a coastguard.

On 28 April 1672, while Lecat patrolled in a captured tender, Reyning sailed from Campeche aboard the *Sevilliano*, transporting the retired governor Fernando Francisco de Escobedo to Tabasco. They arrived on July 18 with a hold full of cacao and brazilwood from Campeche. From there they travelled on to Veracruz and then to Campeche to careen. In August Reyning learned of the war between England, France and Holland and took to sea with an unknown destination. Upon his return Lecat found himself alone and set out in an attempt to find Reyning, but neither was ever heard of again.

Morgan's Arrest

The Spanish ambassador to England considered the assault on Panama an act of piracy and protested vociferously. When he arrived in Port Royal, Morgan found that Lynch had taken over as governor and a radical change had taken place in English policy towards Spain. Morgan was arrested and taken to England, although his arrival was delayed until April 1672 due to his poor state of health. He arrived in London in August[72] but, as a consequence of the ever changing Anglo-Spanish political situation he was never put on trial. Charles II knighted him and appointed him Lieutenant Governor of Jamaica.

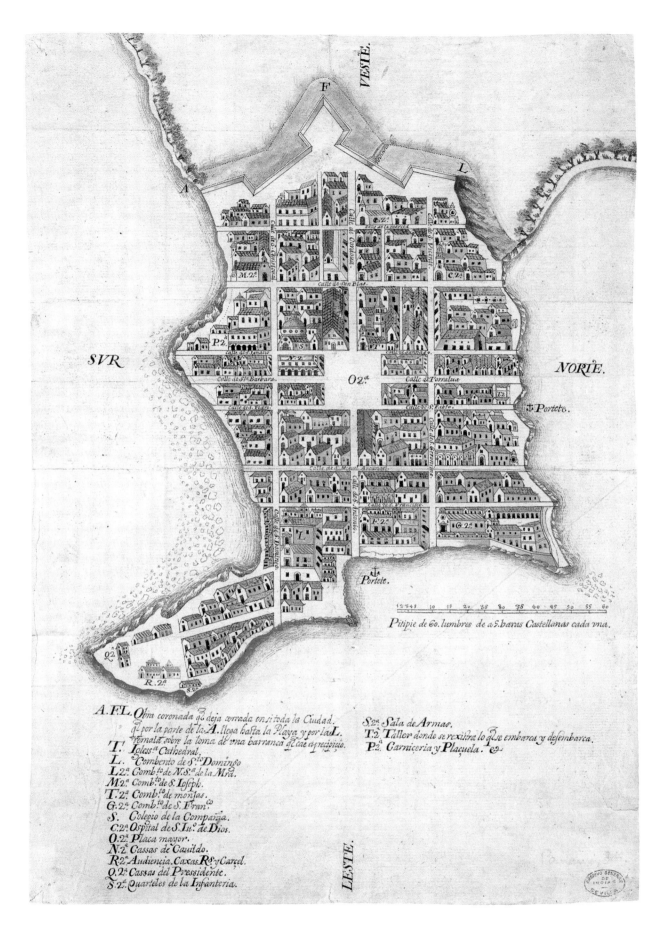

Plan of the new city of Panama, 1673
The destruction of Panama City in January 1671 at the hands of Morgan's filibusters made it expedient to relocate the city to a safer place.
A peninsula oriented west-east, with steep cliffs and a suitable bay for a port was the chosen site. The western side of the city was heavily fortified
against attack from the land and was fortified, cutting off access from inland, and the city was built on a grid of streets running parallel
and perpendicular to the sea with a large square – the Placa Mayor – in the heart.

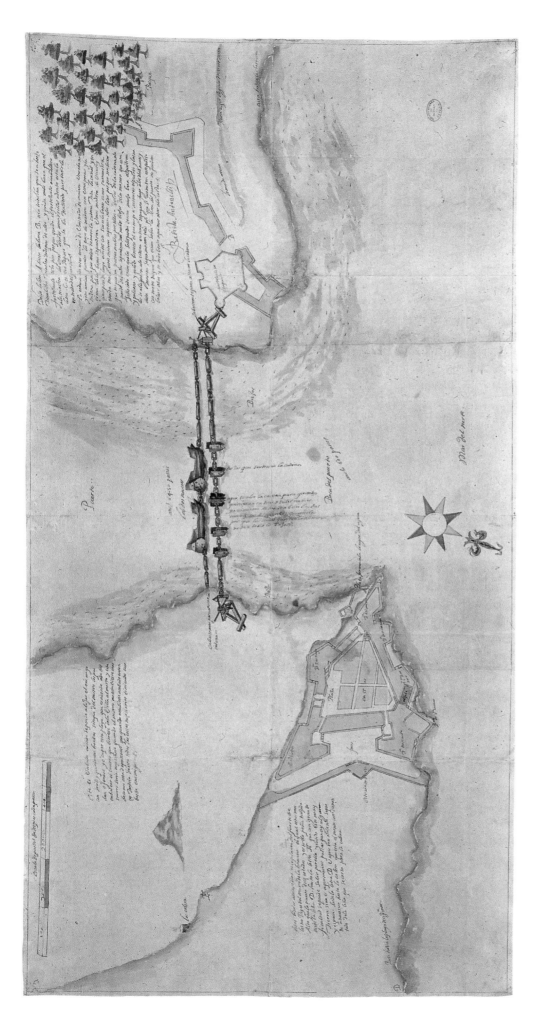

The defences of Havana, 1612.

CHAPTER VII

THE END OF A GOLDEN ERA
(1672-1700)

In 1670 the Second Treaty of Madrid between Spain and England marked the beginning of the end for the filibusters. Spain ceded the island of Jamaica to England, renouncing subsequent claims, and a radical change took place in English policy regarding relations with the Hispanic colonies. As an initial measure Modyford, the Governor of Jamaica famous for his defence of filibusters, was replaced by Thomas Lynch, whose policies were geared towards reaching agreement with the Spanish. On 1 July 1671 Lynch took over his post and ordered the immediate revocation of letters of marque. Modyford was arrested, accused of fostering piracy and, six weeks later, was sent back to England as a prisoner.

In mid August, by royal proclamation, the King of England offered amnesty to all filibusters,[1] with the alternative opportunities of joining the Royal Navy or receiving assistance in settling on the island as colonists. This offer was echoed in the colonies of New England, Bermuda, New York and Virginia. However, the authorities in London had failed to take into account that the filibusters were too rebellious to accept such offers, preferring to migrate en masse to the island of La Tortuga and leaving Jamaica unprotected. Some remained behind, in the belief that the proclamations were mere propaganda, as had been the case with previous changes of governor. This time, however, things were different and some who disregarded the new orders ended their days on the scaffold.

After months of hesitation, in April 1672 Henry Morgan was sent back to England as a prisoner. Once more, fate was on his side – his arrival coincided with the outbreak of the third Anglo-Dutch war. France supported England, and Spain, allied with Austria against the French, was once again at war with the British. One year later William Beeston was appointed Commissioner of the Admiralty in Jamaica – maritime affairs and, in particular, control of privateering were once again handled with a degree of permissiveness.

WAR RETURNS TO THE CARIBBEAN (1672-1678)

Spain's entry into the war revived the systematic filibuster attacks against Spanish interests. With their base on La Tortuga and with Jamaica as port of landfall, major contingents of adventurers were organised to supplement the regular forces. But on this occasion Spain was not alone. Holland sent Admiral Ruyter in command of a squadron whose mission was to impose order on the troubled waters of the Caribbean. He was accompanied by Jacob Binckes, in command of the frigate *Nordhollandt*, with forty-six cannons and 210 men.

In May 1672 Binckes reached Martinique, where he made alliances with Cornellis Evertsen and Hurriaen Aernouts. From the Dutch colony of Curaçao, Governor Jan Donker began to issue letters of marque for privateering activities against the English and French. A group of corsairs, among them Aernouts, set a course for North America intent on assaulting English positions and, in July, they took New York (after the subsequent peace treaty the city would be returned to the English). Back in Europe, Ruyter reached Cadiz in December 1673, presenting a balance of thirty-four English and French ships captured and over 150 destroyed.

The French Offensive Fails

News of the outbreak of war reached the Caribbean during the second half of 1672. France launched an offensive led by de Baas-Castelmore, Governor of St Kitt's, aimed at the Dutch positions in Curaçao. Once more the filibusters were summoned to assist, and 400 of them voluntarily answered the call. On the 50-cannon *Ecueil* and the *Petit Infant*, they reached La Tortuga on 18 February 1673, where they were reinforced by over a dozen small privateers. Finally they set sail for Curaçao, commanded by Bertrand d'Ogeron.

On the night of 25 February, an error on the part of the pilot aboard the *Ecueil* caused the ship to be wrecked near Arecibo, northwest of Puerto Rico,[2] with the loss of many lives. The survivors sent word to de Pouançay and to the island authorities. Although Spain was neutral and obliged to provide assistance, the local militias attacked the shipwrecked sailors – ten militiamen were killed and twelve wounded in the fray, while between forty and fifty of d'Ogeron's men lost their lives. Nor was anything done to prevent bands of local people from plundering the remains of the vessel and murdering a number of Frenchmen.

The Governor of Puerto Rico, Gaspar de Arteaga, ordered their arrest and summoned two officers from Santo Domingo to examine 460 prisoners, who were transported to the prison of San Germán escorted by sixty Spanish soldiers. Months later, while some of the captives had fallen victim to local epidemics, another group was exchanged.

D'Ogeron managed to escape with a number of companions,[3] reaching Hato de Arriba, where they stole a small fishing boat after murdering its two crew members

THE PRIVATEERING REGULATIONS OF 1674[4]

On 22 February 1674, in response to the virulent attacks by filibusters, the first regulations were decreed for privateering in America.

The document consisted of nineteen articles, which together covered the following:

- Booty would be shared out three ways, according to the tradition of Vizcaya.
- Pirates would be punished as such.
- To make privateering a more attractive proposition, it was the charterers who would receive the former Quinto Real.
- It would be compulsory to hand over prisoners.
- No colonial authority, fleets or squadrons could benefit from part of the booty.
- Booty could be sold exempt from excise and other duties.
- To all effects, services rendered by privateers would be considered as rendered by the Royal Navy.
- Privateers would enjoy the privileges of the militia.
- The use of small pistols during the act of boarding was authorised.

and throwing their bodies overboard. A few days later they reached first Cabo Rojo, and then the Bay of Samaná – they had survived so many calamities that their contemporaries looked upon d'Ogeron's return to La Tortuga as nothing short of a miracle.

Reprisals Against Puerto Rico

In October, d'Ogeron put together a force of 500 filibusters and sailed to Puerto Rico to help his men. He engaged reinforcements in Samaná and made landfall in Aguada, with the intention of freeing the prisoners who were still in San Germán. He attempted to negotiate with Arteaga hoping to persuade the latter to hand over the prisoners but, having failed to do so, he disembarked 300 men and they advanced upon the castle. The Spaniards, however, were prepared, and time after time the efforts to storm the castle were repelled.

In order to exert pressure on his enemies, d'Ogeron sacked Hato de Arriba. In retaliation Arteaga, far from being intimidated, ordered the immediate execution of forty of the prisoners and placed the rest in strict confinement. Over the following two months the French made sporadic attacks, none of which were successful, finally returning to La Tortuga on 29 December. There, d'Ogeron requested permission to return to France.

The wish to gain supremacy over Caribbean trade brought European powers into confrontation on more than one occasion. Holland and France engaged in bloody conflict to control the trading posts on the islands close to Tierra Firme. England sought, in particular, to expand her colony in Jamaica, and to achieve this did not hesitate in forming an alliance with Spain in 1670.

As for the prisoners, in the spring of 1674 some 131 were still engaged in forced labour on the fortifications of Puerto Rico,[5] but they were eventually evacuated to Havana for subsequent deportation.

Neutral England

In 1674 England signed a peace treaty with Holland and adopted a neutral stance in the war with France. This new scenario propitiated changes in Jamaican policies aimed at fostering good relations with the island's neighbours. In January the Duke of Carlisle was appointed governor, although he did not occupy his post until five years later.[6] In the meantime, the position was held by Lord Vaughan, who reached Jamaica in mid March accompanied by Henry Morgan as his second-in-command.

One month later, the new authorities offered a general amnesty, ordered all privateering to cease and began to persecute piracy. Lynch, who had fallen into disgrace, left Jamaica for England on 24 May.

Vaughan's term of office went through difficult times. Morgan obstructed the application of measures against piracy through both his passivity and his conduct, continuing to drink and gamble in the taverns just as he had in his heyday. In 1677, Beeston was elected Speaker of the Jamaican Assembly and began to introduce a series of increasingly important reforms. In March 1678 Vaughan left his post and was replaced by colonel Samuel Long until the Duke of Carlisle arrived in May 1679.

Carlisle's policies clashed with the interests of the Assembly, which led to the latter's dissolution in August of that year. In July 1680 Beeston was deported back to

In the last quarter of the 17th century the French advance was monitored from Santo Domingo, capital of Hispaniola.

England by order of Colonel Long, the chief justice. But his luck improved – just fourteen weeks later the roles were reversed: Carlisle and Long were deported to England.

The Second Caribbean Campaign

For Spain and Holland the war with France continued. Once more, the scenario was transferred to the colonies, where the warring powers did everything they could to eliminate competition in the flourishing trade with the Indies. The Dutch West Indies Company went bankrupt and France set up the Senegal Company to engage fully in the black slave trade.

Early in 1674 Aernouts,[7] who had joined Binckes in the Dutch actions, returned to North America. In New York he found that the Treaty of Westminster had converted the English colonies into neutral territory, so, in order to profit from his journey, he decided to attack French possessions north of Maine. He took control of Penobscot, San Jean River, Jemsec and named his new territories New Holland. As governor he appointed Pieter Roderigo, who had to settle a number of disputes with the English over fishing rights.

Holland prepared a large-scale attack, choosing as leader a man who was very familiar with the Americas – Jacob Binckes.[8] Promoted to vice-admiral in March 1676,

Binckes took command of an squadron consisting of three ships of the line carrying between forty-four and sixty-six cannons, six frigates with between twenty-four and thirty-six cannons, a fire ship and numerous troop transporters. His mission was to evict the French from and occupy their colonies in the Caribbean.

In May he occupied Cayena, Mariagalante and San Eustaquio, and then sailed south beyond the Lesser Antilles in search of new objectives. On 16 June he sighted Guadeloupe, but, having ascertained the strength of its defences, decided not to attack. A few days later Binckes and his men disembarked in San Martín, where they killed the French governor and captured 100 negroes. Finally, in mid July, he reached his main objective, Tobago, which according to his instructions, was the ideal place to set up a permanent fortified base. He attacked the island unopposed, took possession, evicted the French population and left his second-in-command, Pieter Constant, as governor. From Tobago he launched a campaign to incite the buccaneers of Santo Domingo to boycott the taxes levied by the French West Indies Company and to abandon the French colonies in the Caribbean.

France reacted immediately and put together a major fleet commanded by Jean Conde d'Estrées,[9] who, by December, was operating in Caribbean waters. He recovered Cayena, made port in Martinique where he recruited volunteers, and continued to Tobago, which the Dutch had converted into a great fortress. In mid February he and his contingent of 4,000 men anchored off the coast of the island.

On 21 February the French landed 1,000 infantry soldiers and blocked the port with fourteen light vessels. On the morning of 3 March a simultaneous attack was launched against the port from land and sea. The numerical superiority of the Dutch proved to be decisive, and they forced the French to retreat, but not before they had caused considerable damage: ten of the thirteen Dutch vessels anchored in the port were irreparably damaged by artillery fire.

The French took refuge on Grenada and Martinique, their dead numbering almost 1,000, and d'Estrées returned to the old continent in search of reinforcements. Early in July he was received by Louis XIV in Versailles, and the king granted him additional forces. They sailed on seventeen ships from Brest on 27 September 1677.

De Pouançay, Governor of La Tortuga

Meanwhile, in March 1676, de Pouançay was appointed the new governor of La Tortuga. At the beginning of May the following year, aware of the need to strengthen French positions in the Caribbean, he sent a report to Colbert, informing him that it was imperative to adopt two immediate measures:[10] to fortify La Tortuga and to foster settlements on Hispaniola where he would create a new colony with its capital in Petit Goave.

Some months later, d'Estrées reached the Caribbean and requested that de Pouançay form a filibustering squadron of twelve ships and 1,000 men, which he placed under the orders of Grammont. In Tobago, the Dutch had managed to rebuild their artillery defences, but they were desperately short of men – fewer than 500 in any condition to fight – partly as a result of casualties in the first battle and partly due to tropical diseases. Furthermore, they had been sent no reinforcements and they lacked ships and provisions.

On 6 December the French fleet reached the island and prepared its attack. Despite torrential rains, which hindered his manoeuvres, d'Estrées disembarked 1,000 men and installed his artillery. The port was not a strategic priority since the two Dutch ships remaining there were no threat to the forces of the Sun King. The attack began with heavy, highly accurate artillery fire that destroyed the Dutch defences at the third volley. In the ensuing assault, the French killed 250 defenders, Binckes among them.

The French Fleet Founders off the Islas Aves

Having recovered Tobago, the French now moved on to the offensive. Reinforced by a dozen filibusters and their vessels recruited on St Kitt's, d'Estrées went west to Curaçao. The fleet sailed parallel to Tierra Firme, but the pilots were unfamiliar with the waters and guided the ships into a danger. At nine o'clock in the evening of 11 May 1678, the crew of one of the filibusters' ships fired a musket and cannon shot to warn of the perilous sand banks of the Islas Aves. Seven ships of the line, three transporters, three filibuster vessels and 500 lives were lost.

The survivors sought refuge on Santa Dominica (Haiti) and, in July d'Estrées returned to France. From now on, the filibusters determined to embark on their own adventures.

Grammont Attacks Maracaibo

Having come out from under the protection of the French fleet, and now under the command of Grammont, the filibusters entered the Gulf of Venezuela, where they took the Spaniards by surprise. At the beginning of June 1678, 2,000 men on six large ships and thirteen smaller ones headed for Maracaibo. Grammont disembarked half his men and marched over the Peninsula of San Carlos towards the fort that guarded the outskirts of the city. The defence forces were led by Francisco Pérez de Guzmán[11] who, sensing that attack was imminent, placed 100 harquebusiers outside the walls. The filibuster artillery responded by bombarding the defenders' positions.

Grammont made it past the bar, blockaded the harbour mouth with his six large ships and entered the lagoon with the thirteen smaller vessels. Governor Jorge Madureira Ferreira, who had been in the post for just one week, did not inspire confidence in the population and, not knowing whom to support, the citizens fled in panic. On 14 June the city fell into the hands of the filibusters. Those unfortunate enough to be captured were tortured to death unless they confessed where their treasure was. After fifteen days in the city, by which time nothing of value was left unfound, the filibusters abandoned Maracaibo and sailed for Gibraltar.

The city had been evacuated and was defended by a reserve detachment of twenty-two soldiers who withstood the bombardment as long as they could before surrendering. With the road clear, Grammont went fifty miles inland as far as Trujillo. This city had also been evacuated, and its inhabitants had fled seventy-five miles inland, to Mérida de la Grita. Here the defences were more solid, consisting of 250 soldiers with four pieces of

PEACE REACHES CABALLO[12]

In the spring of 1680, the filibusters of Tortuga learned of the end of the war in a highly unusual way: Jan Willems and his men were on a beach near Puerto Plata when they were sighted by a Spanish patrol from Santiago. The patrol withdrew and, shortly afterward, a cavalry company arrived on the scene bearing a white flag. The officer in charge bore a copy of the Royal Decree that ratified the Nimega Peace Treaty, bringing the Franco-Spanish war to an end. Willems received a copy of the decree and took to sea to deliver it to Pouançay.

SPANISH PRIVATEERING

From the colonies, the Spaniards engaged in intensive privateering against French interests. The most active of the many Spanish corsairs was Juan Corso, known to the English as Corsair John, a man feared and hated by his victims. One of Pedro de Castro's subordinates, Corso was the arch enemy of Governor Lynch.

The first accounts of him date from April 1680, when he led an action against an English detachment in Laguna de Términos. After their successful assault, Corso and his men proceeded in two canoes to the coast of Yucatan, getting as far as the Bay of Honduras. Near the island of Cocinas, they sighted a small frigate and a large vessel lying at anchor. They boarded both and put the crews to the sword. The large ship was the *Laurel*, later renamed the *León Coronado*.

After committing a number of outrages, de Castro went to Veracruz, while Corso took a canoe to Campeche. During one of his operations he captured another ship, which he renamed the *Nuestra Señora de Hon Hon* and incorporated into the Windward Fleet in 1682.[13] De Castro eventually tired of privateering and handed his command over to Corso, who engaged in confrontations with the French and the English, even in peacetime.

In April 1683 Lynch wrote to the Governor of Havana, complaining of the activities of Corso and of the fact that the Governor of Santiago had ignored his protests.[14] Lynch accused Corso of piracy – stating that he had captured two of his ships and put their crews to the sword – and of regularly committing such acts of barbarism as cutting off a man's head simply because he did not row as strongly as Corso wanted.

Corso was known for his violence. Typical were such acts as when he himself tried and executed a number of French pirates; he came across Captain Prenar in a bay, put his entire crew to the sword, and sent the captured sloops to Santiago; Captain van den Klaus and his crew suffered the same fate, after being cruelly tortured; Corso once captured a boat manned by a crew of four, one of whom he killed with his own hands because the man was sick.[15] In another letter written in August, Lynch compared Corso to de Graaf and Grammont.

In the spring of 1685, Corso and de Castro joined forces once again and together they stumbled across a secret French colony established in Mexico by René Robert Cavelier, seigneur de Lasalle. The Spaniards destroyed the settlement in the knowledge that such an act would be much to the liking of the Madrid authorities.

Fortune finally turned its back on Corso when, in May 1685, he was caught in a storm in the Bay of Apalache. He and his men were shipwrecked and drowned

---

artillery in a fort reinforced by others on nearby hilltops. Although the filibusters maintained their bombardment for several days, the hill defenders controlled their positions. On 1 September, achieving little by their attack and knowing the risk of a counter-offensive, the filibusters withdrew.

On their way back to the lagoon, they burned Gibraltar to the ground as revenge for their failure in Mérida de la Grita. On 3 December Grammont and his men left the Lagoon of Maracaibo with their ships laden with captives and a substantial booty, estimated at 150,000 pesos.[16] On Christmas Eve they reached Petit Goave and were welcomed as heroes.

PEACE AT LAST (1679-1683)

The Peace of Nimega marked the beginning of a period in which the belligerent European powers began the reconstruction of their commercial structures, severely damaged after five years of conflict. Spain entered the 1680s in a major economic recession, which she attempted to mitigate by bringing consignments of silver from America. Cultivation of anil dye (indigo) began, requiring greater manpower and the black slave trade controlled by privileged companies rapidly increased, though not without opposition from traditional traders. France and England suffered from the fall in tobacco prices, which had particular repercussions on the colonies. However, this same in the price of tobacco forced many filibusters who had settled down to devote themselves to agriculture to take to the seas once more.

The Filibusters Assault Caracas

After a year and a half of peace and quiet, Grammont returned to Tierra Firme and led his filibusters on a sensational attack on La Guaira and Caracas. On 26 June 1680, forty-seven corsairs stole into La Guaira,[17] while the inhabitants were sleeping soundly in their beds. When the city and its 150 defenders awoke, they found that Grammont and his men had already occupied the stronghold.

Captain Juan de Laya Míjica[18] managed to escape and warned Caracas before the filibusters had time to take the city by surprise. The royal treasures were evacuated inland on a heavily guarded mule train while the militia, under orders from Governor Francisco de Alberro, prepared the defences.

Finally Grammont arrived. While the militia held back the attackers, Laya made a sortie in which he killed some of the filibusters and wounded others, including Grammont, who received a cutlass blow to the neck. Eventually, however, the attackers prevailed and made off with a handsome booty. Caracas lost its reputation as an impenetrable city and Grammont became a legend by virtue of the boldness of his feat.

MORGAN, GOVERNOR OF JAMAICA

During the Duke of Carlisle's term of office as governor,[21] the issuing of let passes reached its zenith. Felling brazilwood in Campeche, especially in the region of Laguna de Términos, was an alternative to traditional

In December 1679 an alliance was struck between Alliston, Cornelius Essex, Thomas Magott and Sharp who,[19] led by Coxon, set off to take Portobelo. They sailed from Port Morant, Jamaica, on 17 January 1680 and, just twenty miles from the coast, encountered the French brig *Flibustier*, which joined the venture.

They fell on Portobelo, sacked the city, shared the booty and withdrew to Bocas del Toro, Panama. Their aim was to assault the Pacific ports but, instead of sailing south to attempt the difficult passage around Cape Horn, they planned to cross the Isthmus of Panama and capture a ship from which to carry out their exploits.

They returned to Isla Dorada and, in Darién, captured an Indian who showed them the way across the Isthmus. In April, 332 filibusters set off for the Pacific coast.

They reached the ocean after an uneventful voyage and, on the first night after their arrival, Sharp, together with 135 men, managed to take a ship. With this new acquisition they formed a small flotilla and carried out attacks along the coast of Panama.

The Spaniards reacted by sending out patrols in their pursuit. One night a Spanish platoon came across the pirates and inflicted many casualties. Coxon decided to abandon the venture, and returned to the Caribbean with seventy men.

Those who remained chose Sawkins as their commander and embarked on the 400-ton *Santísima Trinidad*. Near the city of Remedios, Sharp took over command after the death of Sawkins. But the crew was dissatisfied with Sharp as a leader and a number of men deserted. As a consequence, John Watling took command. But Watling was murdered during the assault of Arica and Sharp once again became master of the situation. They reached the Atlantic by rounding Cape Horn and arrived in St Thomas in the Virgin Islands, where the men dispersed.

In March 1682 Sharp reached Plymouth. On June 10 he was arrested, accused of piracy and taken before the high court of the Admiralty. After a controversial trial that raised protests from the Spanish ambassador,[20] he was absolved for lack of evidence and received a four-cannon ship called the *Bonito*. When he was subsequently relieved of command, he decided to return to the Caribbean on his own ship. Having received a letter of marque from the Governor of Nevis in January 1684, Sharp continued to engage in privateering for some time afterwards.

forms of cultivation, but the region could be reached only by sea. Carlisle issued documents addressed to the Spanish authorities, requesting that the holders be allowed unmolested passage to their destination – abuse of the let pass served as a cover-up for many activities that bordered on piracy.

But pirates were persecuted with firmness; several filibusters, including Essex and twenty of his companions, were tried and condemned as pirates; after the assault of Portobelo, Carlisle ordered the attackers to be pursued, even reaching the extreme of commissioning Coxon to do so. Morgan took part in the hunt and managed to arrest three of the culprits.

In January 1681 a sloop commanded by Captain Jacob Evertsen reached Jamaica.[22] Morgan was now interim governor of the island after the Duke of Carlisle had been deported, and the arrival of Evertsen – in Morgan's words a 'well-known pirate' – gave him a golden opportunity to show how seriously he took the mission of combating piracy.

The sloop was boarded by port officers and Evertsen and twenty-six others were arrested and taken to Port Royal. Six of the crew were Spaniards and Morgan exchanged them for some of his men held in Cartagena. The rest of the crew was English. In March the 'pirates' were taken before the Court of the Admiralty and eventually hanged. In the meantime, Evertsen and a number of others had managed to escape.[23]

Two months later, on 28 July (O.S.), Lynch was once again appointed Governor of Jamaica to satisfy constant pressure from the Spanish ambassador in London.[24] By May of the following year, Lynch was in his post, with Hender Molesworth as vice-governor. His first undertaking was to settle accounts with his 'old friend' Henry Morgan by opening proceedings against him for his activities while interim governor, basing his prosecution on the many complaints received during Morgan's term of office. But Lynch was confounded by a lack of collaboration from other governors of English colonies in North America. He filed a protest and, in March 1684, the king issued a proclamation demanding collaboration.

In Pursuit of the Fleets

The filibusters of La Tortuga wasted no time and returned to their former patrol zones. In July 1682 several squadrons, among whom were such illustrious names as Grammont, de Graaf, Pierre Bot and Jean Willems, lay in wait for Spanish ships off the coast of Cuba.

In other latitudes, Captain Manuel Delgado,[25] commanding the frigate *Princesa*, part of the Spanish Windward Fleet, was transporting 120,000 silver pesos from Puerto Rico and Santo Domingo in the vicinity of the Canal de la Mona. The frigate had been captured from the French, who renamed her the *Dauphine*, although she was commonly known as the *Francesa*.

Since he needed provisions, Delgado headed for La Aguada de Puerto Rico, where de Graaf, on board his ship, the *Tigre*, took him by surprise. During the bloody battle one fifth of all Delgado's 250 men were killed and the rest were taken prisoner, later to be freed on the

island of Cuba. The crew of the *Tigre* received 700 pieces of eight each and the *Princesa* became de Graaf's new ship.

Two months later the fleet led by Grammont – eight ships that had remained in the vicinity of Punta Icacos without obtaining any booty – decided to return to Santa Dominica. Having careened and repaired the ships, they sailed for the Pasaje de Barlovento, in The Bahamas, where they had made major captures.

In November, news of their movements reached Santo Domingo just as Nicolas van Hoorn was arriving with a shipment of 300 slaves from Cadiz.[26] Governor Francisco de Segura requisitioned the ship and, when he discovered artefacts stolen from Cadiz herself, arrested van Hoorn. The Dutchman assured Segura that he had taken no part in de Graaf's action and accused the governor of acting against him in reprisal. Seeing that he would obtain nothing, he escaped in early 1683 with twenty of his men and a quarter of his cargo. He reached

Petit Goave, where he joined the filibusters and obtained a letter of reprisal.

Van Hoorn sailed with Grammont to join forces with de Graaf and Andrieszoon in the blockade. Having captured no ships of any great value, they headed for Cartagena. On the way they came across two large Spanish merchant ships, the *Nuestra Señora de la Consolación* and the *Nuestra Señora de Regla*, anchored off the coast. The ships had sailed from the Bay of Honduras bound for Havana from where they would return to Spain with the fleets. Now they were attacked and, having surrendered, incorporated into the squadron.

Some weeks later Grammont and van Hoorn joined up with de Graaf and Andrieszoon.

The Sacking of Veracruz[27]

The blockade of Cuba, ongoing through the winter of 1682-1683, did not yield the expected profits, but it was nevertheless decided to keep a major force in the area: two large ships, one sloop, a boat and 500 men. Now, aware of their strength, the filibusters agreed to wait no longer and to go to the very harbour where the fleet of Nueva España was anchored and to take the consignments of silver before it was loaded on board. To ensure the success of such a coup, they retired to the island of Guanaja to await reinforcements from the north of Yucatan and to allow time for all the units to come together. Once all was ready, the squadron sailed for Veracruz.

THE CANOE,
A WEAPON OF WAR

During the latter half of the 17th century, many Spanish corsairs used canoes as an effective weapon, often escaping pursuit by heading into shallow waters.

About 90 feet long, between 16 and 18 wide and with a depth of hold of only 4 or 5 feet, the canoe was armed with a 6-pound cannon at the prow and four stone mortars at the stern. Built entirely of mahogany, it was propelled by either two sails or between thirty-six and forty-four oarsmen depending on the wind conditions.

Capable of transporting 120 men, the canoe had a draught of 1 foot 6 inches, thanks to which it could land on the beach or enter rivers and lagoons.

Canoe, after a French drawing from the 17th century.

On 17 May, when Governor Luis de Córdova and other city dignitaries were together at a meeting, two of de Graaf's and Willems's ships were sighted. They anchored at the entrance to the harbour even though the wind was favourable for them to enter the port, and this aroused the suspicions of Mateo Alonso de Huidobro. The captain requested permission from the governor to take 400 men with him to the Windward Fleet to see what was happening, but his petition was rejected – the authorities believed there was no danger.

Under cover of darkness the following night, 800 filibusters stole into the city. At dawn simultaneous attacks took place, taking both the garrison and the sleeping inhabitants by surprise. The swiftness of the attack and the defenders' lack of ammunition made the filibusters' task much easier. By morning the Governor's Palace, the last nucleus of resistance, was under attack and Huidobro and many others died in the fight. Each house was systematically sacked in an operation that lasted four days. Until, at last, the filibusters withdrew to the island of Sacrificios with 4,000 captives, for whom they demanded an astronomical ransom from Mexico.

While they were waiting for news, the victors shared their spoils, which Spanish officers estimated at 800,000 pesos in coins, 400,000 pesos in silver, and 200,000 in jewels. Two weeks later the coveted ransom was paid and they freed the prisoners, keeping a group of 1,500 negroes and mulattos as slaves, before taking to the sea in their thirteen ships.

As they departed, the fleet of Nueva España, commanded by Diego Fernández de Zaldívar, arrived at Veracruz. Zaldívar had the wind behind him and he was in an excellent position from which to attack. But he decided against it and the filibusters escaped. With no further obstacles in their way, they took in water in Coatzacoalcos and then left Yucatan. They returned to the southern Cuban islands, where they sold their booty and occupied their time smuggling their ill-gotten gains past the Jamaican customs.

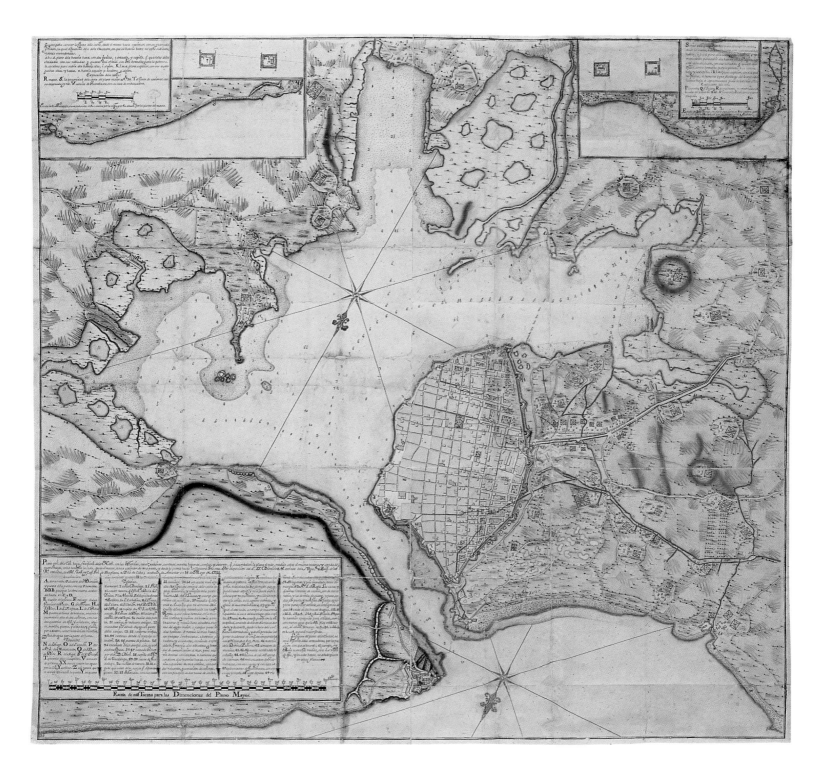

By the late 1600s Havana had become one of the most important cities in the Americas. The point of encounter for armadas and fleets, it developed major shipbuilding and munitions industries, thanks to which, in the early 1700s Havana was able to undertake an ambitious construction project of naval vessels.

War Breaks Out Again between Spain and France (1683-1684)

The assault on Veracruz triggered new hostilities between France and Spain. On the last day of September 1683, de Cussy was appointed, in France, Governor of La Tortuga. In April the following year he occupied his post and launched a campaign against Spanish interests.

Two months later, Andrieszoon organised another campaign in Tierra Firme, with the intention of attacking Cartagena.[28] News of a number of assaults alerted Juan Pando Estrada, governor of the city, who took the initiative by seizing three merchant vessels anchored in the port: the 40-cannon *San Francisco*, the 34-cannon *Nuestra Señora de la Paz* and a 28-cannon galliot. Preparations having been completed on Christmas Eve, 800 soldiers and sailors, under orders from Andrés del Pez, set sail to intercept the filibusters.

But things did not turn out as the Spaniards had planned. The small ships of the filibuster fleet swarmed among the Spanish merchant ships, forcing the latter to defend themselves with no order of combat. In the confusion, the *San Francisco* ran aground and, after a fight lasting four hours, was captured. Willems took the *Nuestra Señora de la Paz* after ninety Spaniards and only twenty filibusters had lost their lives.

The ships were shared out equally. Having been refloated, the *San Francisco* was given to de Graaf, who renamed her the *Fortune*; Andrieszoon received the *Nuestra Señora de la Paz*, renaming her the *Mutine (Scoundrel)* and Willems received de Graaf's ship, the *Francesa*, formerly the *Princesa* or *Dauphine*.

All resistance having been eliminated, on Christmas Day the filibusters blocked the port of Cartagena with an old ship. In the middle of January, a consignment of slaves arrived on English ships, which the filibusters, respecting the English neutrality, let pass. A few days later the blockade was lifted and the filibusters set sail for Hispaniola.

They made port in Roatán and then continued to the south of Cuba, where they received news of the outbreak of war between Spain and France since the attack on Veracruz. De Graaf took advantage of the situation by sailing to Petit Goave to request new French letters of marque, leaving Andrieszoon and Willems to patrol the coasts of Cuba.

The Blockade of Cuba

Once more the filibusters used a blockade of Cuban waters to impede traffic with the Peninsula. On 18 May in an area close to Havana, they sighted two large ships and went to intercept them. The ships were sailing under the Dutch flag and identified themselves as the *Stad Rotterdam (City of Rotterdam)* and the *Elisabeth* belonging to the Dutch East Indies Company.[30] (England and France had, by now, reached a secret agreement to hinder the passage of Dutch ships and thus prevent their trade with Tierra Firme.)

Despite Holland's neutrality, Andrieszoon ordered the cargo to be inspected and boarded the ships with ninety men. The search revealed that, at Cartagena, they had taken on board substantial merchandise and people of importance hoping to elude the blockade under the

ENGLISH FILIBUSTERS EMIGRATE NORTH

Unrelenting proclamations by the English Governors of Jamaica and the action of coastguards forced English filibusters to seek new hunting grounds.

In August 1684 the ships of Andrieszoon and Willems were identified. Although Governor Cranfield informed London that the presence of the filibusters contravened the king's order to provide pirates with no assistance, it was difficult to execute the order because they brought great quantities of silver to the colony, thanks to which it was possible to acquire highly select commodities.

In New Providence, the Bahamas,[29] Governor Robert Clark issued new patents, but so strong were the protests from Jamaica that he was replaced by Robert Silburne. A similar situation existed in Carolina, which Lynch reported. The Spaniards preferred to solve the problem by sending three galleys from San Agustín to sack estates near Charleston. The English prepared acts of reprisal, but the arrival of Governor James Colleton put paid to these plans.

The pirates who operated on the River Delaware were protected by Governor Markham, who belonged to the Quaker community of Pennsylvania, while those of New York received support from Governor Fletcher.

In Jamaica, despite protests from the colonists, Albemarle embraced a policy of permissiveness, from late 1687 until his death in 1689, when the new governor, Sir Francis Watson, once again pursued the filibusters.

protection of the Dutch flag. Andrieszoon demanded half the 200,000 pesos and all the Spanish passengers be handed over. Despite initial opposition, the demands were satisfied and the Dutch were allowed to continue their voyage.

The Spanish immediately protested. In their defence, the Dutch alleged that they had been the victims of a surprise attack and, if they had been aware of Andrieszoon's intentions, they would not have allowed him access. However, the truth of the matter was that the Dutch kept the other half of the cargo, alleging that the filibusters had taken everything – they obtained handsome profits from their action.

De Graaf Seeks Pardon

In the spring of 1684, having lifted the blockade, de Graaf came across a 14-cannon Spanish ship flanked by another, unidentified vessel. During the night he boarded the Spanish ship and took its cargo of quinine and forty-seven pounds of gold. The following morning he discovered that the other ship was an English vessel that had been captured by the Spaniards near Cuba.

Seeking to to improve his relations with the English, de Graaf returned the ship and its crew to Lynch.[31] The freed captives reached the Bay of San Felipe on May 6, bearing a letter in which de Graaf paid his respects to the governor and noted that he had returned the ship, done the crew no harm and had nothing against the British nation.

Lynch thanked him for his gesture and, above all, for having treated the crew well.[32] Later he interceded on de Graaf's behalf so that the Dutchman was pardoned for his attacks against English interests and was even naturalised as an 'Englishman'. Furthermore, the British authorities provided the necessary credentials and safe conducts to the Spanish authorities so that de Graaf's wife might join him.

In the meantime, through the English ambassador at the court of Madrid, attempts were made to negotiate de Graaf's pardon on the part of the King of Spain but, while negotiations were taking place, the attack on Veracruz led to a declaration of war.

New Attacks in Tierra Firme

In January 1685 the Cuban blockade was on-going: Willems on the *Mutine* and de Graaf on the *Neptuno* (the ex-*San Francisco)* continued in the area while Andrieszoon sailed with a small fleet to Nueva España. Other captains, among them Rose, Vigneron and Le Garde, joined the expedition and de Graaf, seeing that he had been relieved from command, sailed south to join Andrieszoon.

Other captains supported his manoeuvre, but they reached Andrieszoon before de Graaf. On the night of 17 January a lone ship was spotted. Just before daybreak it was challenged, and the answer came in French. The ship appeared to be Spanish and the filibusters were taken aback but Rose did not hesitate: he opened fire and set off in pursuit. As the new day dawned the ship's true identity was revealed – it was the *Neptuno*, de Graaf's ship. Rose was suitably reprimanded and de Graaf re-assumed his leadership and ordered the flotilla to sail to Curaçao, where it arrived on 20 January. They sought permission from

---

DE GRAAF TO THE SOUND OF GUITARS[33]

The figure of Laurens de Graaf became highly popular among Spanish sailors, who celebrated his major exploits – Campeche and Veracruz – and even his failures – Havana – in song. Traditional songs also made reference to his Lutheran religion, the fact that he betrayed his king after having served as an artilleryman on Spanish vessels, and his nature as a renegade – although this might also refer to his origins in Zeeland, one of the rebel Dutch provinces.

Dime Lorençillo ai
te tentó el demonio
pues con nueve velas, Marita
diste vista al Morro

el caso que hicimos ai
de tus nueve velas
fue poner cuidado, Marita
en las zentinelas

Tiene esta ziudad
para su defensa
el Morro la Punta
y tambien la fuerza

Del Morro y la Punta
no se meda nada
que una fuerza vieja
no estorva la entrada

Viendo no havia nada
te hiziste a la mar
siguiendo tu viaje a desembocar

Saqueaste a Campeche
perro luterano
no temes a Dios
no eres christiano

Si a la Vera Cruz
saqueaste dormida
a la bana no
que esta prevenida

No soi levantado
ni menos traidor
soi un leal vasallo
al rei mi Señor

estrivillo

estas son las oras
y este el estrivillo
viba el rei despaña
y muera lorenzillo

Governor van Erpecun to make a number of repairs, but the request was denied, among other reasons because the Dutch had still not forgotten the assault on the 'Indiamen' in Cuban waters.

De Graaf continued along the coast to the Gulf of Honduras, while the others sailed to Isla Dorada, where they encountered other filibusters who proposed penetrating the Isthmus to the Southern Sea and attacking the Spanish colonies. A group of sixty-four men led by Rose decided to scuttle their ship and join in the venture. Another contingent of 118 men belonging to Andrieszoon's squadron also joined the adventurers, while Andrieszoon himself, seeing his forces diminished, returned to Santa Dominica.

At the beginning of May, he went back to sea and returned to the keys of south Cuba, often flanked by

TREASURE HUNTING EXPEDITIONS

During the last three decades of the 17th century, English and French adventurers engaged widely in the retrieval of treasure from sunken Spanish vessels. Several expeditions were organised, some by illustrious personages, and met with varying degrees of success.

Phips's Expedition (1686-1687)

On 12 September 1686 Phips's flagship the *James and Mary*, together with the *Henry*, sailed from the Downs, England. Although the official purpose of the expedition was to trade with the Spanish, its true objective was to seek the remains of the *Nuestra Señora de la Pura y Limpia Concepción*, the flagship of the Nueva España fleet that had been sunk in 1641.

The Spanish authorities had jealously guarded the secret of her whereabouts, but after a few days' search, Phips found the remains on the sandbank of Abre Ojos.

Retrieval work lasted until 2 May 1687, when Phips sailed home to England with over £200,000 worth of silver. On his arrival, in June, he was welcomed as a hero, although a detachment of soldiers were sent to guard the *James and Mary* while she was anchored in Deptford, among other reasons to prevent Phips from evading taxes with part of the treasure.

Narborough's Expedition (1687-1688)

After Phips returned to England, and in the knowledge that some silver still remained among the wreckage of the *Concepción*, a second expedition to Abre Ojos was organised. Strong, who had taken part in the first campaign, was given command of the *James and Mary*. The flotilla was completed by three more large vessels. Narborough captained the king's frigate, the *Foresight*, while Phips was placed in command of the 400-ton *Good Luck and Ahoy*.

The flotilla set sail from the Downs on 3 September 1687, but they soon encountered bad weather that caused considerable damage to Phips's vessel, forcing him to return to port. Strong lost contact with the rest of the fleet off Finisterre and failed to join up with Narborough in Barbados in mid November, although this had been the original plan.

In mid December they reached Abre Ojos, where they found fifty-or-so ships working among the wreckage. Five months later, having managed to retrieve very little, they set sail for England. Narborough died during the return voyage and he was buried at sea.

When the legendary Spanish galleons were sunk, many lives were almost invariably lost. The depths of the sea and the lack of suitable diving equipment severely hampered rescue operations.

On their return, Strong and four other officers were arrested and accused of having appropriated £1,200 worth of silver from the first voyage to evade taxes. The charges were later withdrawn.

Laurens de Graaf's Expedition

In 1689 a Spanish tender was captured by filibusters. From its captain, they learned of the existence of a Spanish vessel that had sunk on the bank of La Serranilla, and de Cussy proposed that de Graaf be sent to retrieve the treasure. De Graaf prepared four small ships and set sail early in March.

The English Governor of Jamaica, William Watson, reported that a considerable number of Frenchman had left the island for an unknown destination but, as France was at war with the League of Augsburg, few gave credit to the news, believing it to be a subterfuge.

De Graaf sailed to La Serranilla, found the remains of a galleon and, after several weeks' diving, managed to recover four cannons and three stone mortars. Such was the importance of the find that he sailed on his biggest ship to Saint-Domingue for reinforcements and more divers. Contrary winds delayed his return, and de Graaf was forced to seek provisions in the keys of southern Cuba. He did not reach La Serranilla until two and a half months later.

At the beginning of November Watson reported that de Graaf and 250 of his men had arrived in Montego Bay, Jamaica, in search of provisions and that the population had fled on learning the name of the visitor.

O'Byrne's Expedition (1693)

After twenty years in the service of the King of Spain, Admiral Arturo O'Byrne, was granted a licence in 1692 to retrieve Spanish vessels sunk off the coats of America.

Phips's success encouraged sixty-eight English investors to prepare for the expedition, for which they counted on the experience of Strong, among others.

However, the delays caused by the war against France, in which Spain and England were allies, and the attacks perpetrated by the French Company of the Indies, meant that the expedition did not leave England until August 1693.

In February 1694 the ships reached La Coruña, where Strong succumbed to an illness. Having lost its main guide, the expedition was a resounding failure.

Quicksilver was an essential element in mining. It was used to amalgamate precious metals and both its transport and supply were taxed.

The waters of the Greater Antilles and the Bahama Channel were the final resting place of many treasures, some of which have been retrieved thanks to modern diving equipment. Pictured are several items salvaged from the galleons Nuestra Señora de la Pura y Limpia Concepción, Guadalupe *and* Tolosa.

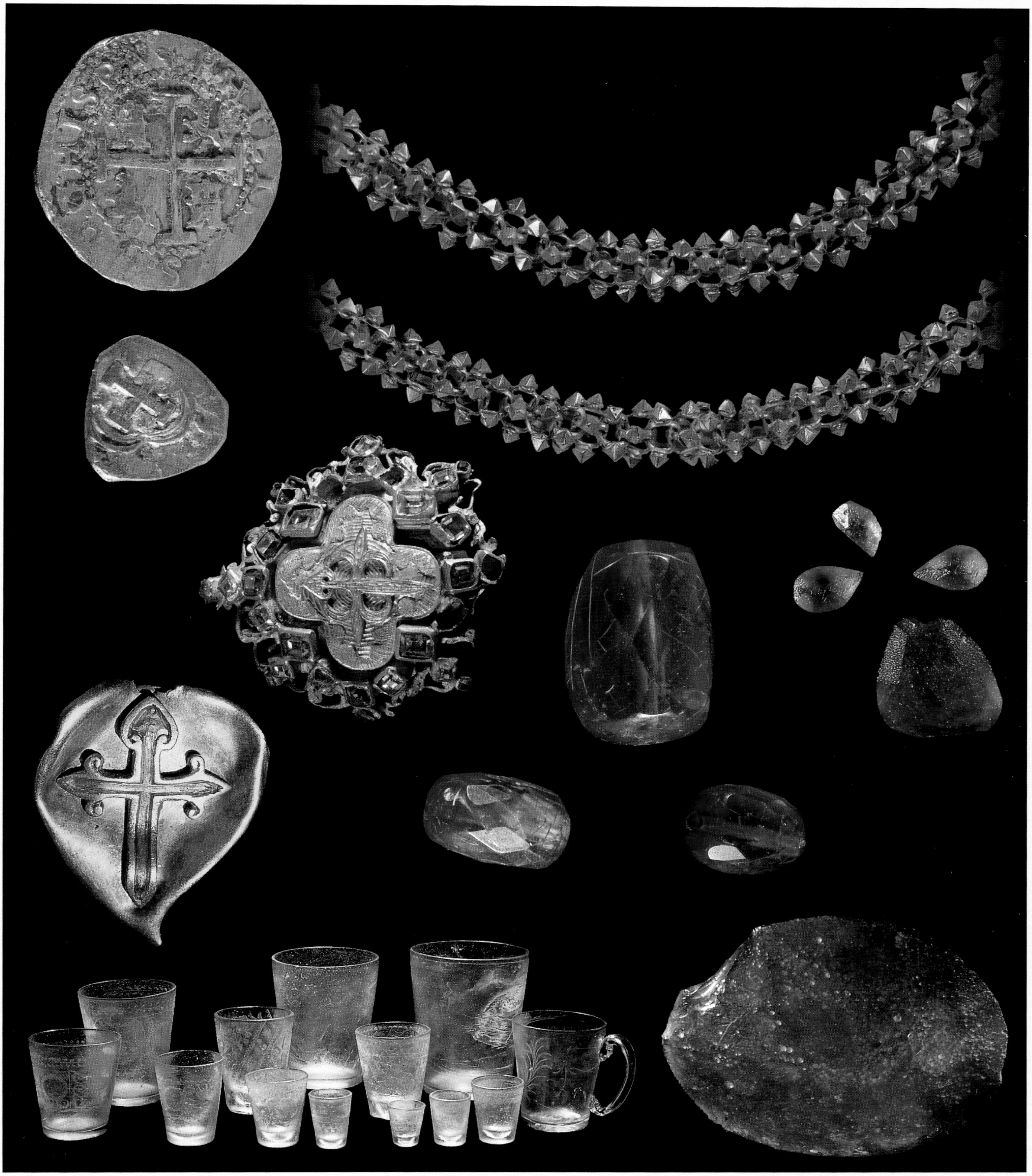

Jamaican patrol ships. It is possible that he took part, together with de Graaf and Grammont, in the Campeche operations and met with them on the island of Pinos to organise the expedition.

De Graaf Sacks Campeche[34]

One of the boldest actions ever conducted by filibusters took place in July 1685 in Campeche. Led by de Graaf and with Grammont as second-in-command, 700 men on six large ships, four smaller ones, six sloops and seventeen canoes lurked in the vicinity of Cape Catoche for almost one month, putting a force together for the assault.

Yucatan lookouts had detected these movements and warned the Governor of Campeche, Felipe de la Barrera y Villegas, who prepared the city's defence. At the end of June news reached him that an attack was imminent, and he closed the port.

The filibusters came within six miles of the coast on the afternoon of 6 July. First a landing party took boats and headed for Campeche. The Spaniards were prepared, however: four companies of militiamen – a total of 200 men – were stationed on the beach and thwarted the manoeuvre, forcing the invaders to retreat.

The following morning, a new attack was prepared. The first wave managed to land on the beach and consolidate their positions. The plan was to divide their forces into four squadrons: 100 would form the advance guard, under the command of Captain Rettechar; 200 would march with de Graaf straight for the city; 200, with Captain Foccard, would advance parallel to de Graaf; a further 200 would follow Grammont in a circular manoeuvre to attack the rearguard.

In desperation and to avoid her capture, the defenders decided to sink the *Nuestra Señora de la Soledad,* a coastguard frigate captained by Cristóbal Martínez de Acevedo that had been prepared to repel a direct attack against the port. The ship was blown up and the Spanish took refuge in the fort, leaving the city at the mercy of the filibusters. Over the next few days, the invaders devoted themselves to plundering.

On 12 July the assault on the fortress began with heavy bombardment. Simultaneously, two columns of militiamen from Mérida arrived in the city to strengthen

the defence and immediately engaged in fierce combat with the intruders. The skill of Grammont, who managed to catch the militia in a crossfire, was decisive in the eventual victory.

As the evening fell, so, too, did all hopes of receiving external aid and the fort defenders requested a truce in order to negotiate the terms of capitulation. The Spanish militia mistrusted the French and, fearing that they might come under attack even as negotiations were underway, they evacuated the fort. Their suspicions were justified: that night a last assault on the fort did indeed take place – nobody offered any resistance.

The filibusters lived a life of ease for two months, while they waited to make a handsome profit from ransom for the prisoners. However, the governor of Yucatan, Juan Bruno Téllez de Guzmán, refused to pay. Irritated by the delay and knowing that the Spanish were preparing an assault to recover the city, Grammont organised a mass execution in the square. When the first two captives had been hanged, Felipe de la Barrera y Villegas and other citizens approached de Graaf saying that they had thought the French to be more humanitarian. They had chosen well: the Dutchman was against the executions and placed himself between the prisoners and their executioner, with whom he engaged in a bitter argument. Eventually, given the imminence of the Spanish attack Grammont gave in and the filibusters re-embarked.

By the end of August 1685 de Graaf had quit Petit Goave on the *Neptuno,* followed by Pierre Bot on the *Nuestra Señora de Regla* and a further three ships. On 11 September they encountered a strong contingent of the Windward Fleet[35] commanded by Andrés de Ochoa y Zárate and, though they attempted to flee, the *Nuestra Señora de Regla* and a sloop were taken.

The rest of the ships managed to escape and soon sighted the frigate *Nuestra Señora de Hon Hon* and the vessel *Jesûs María y José,* alias *El Sevillano,* which seemed easy prey. They set off in pursuit, unaware that the ships were two fast dispatch boats serving as decoys to lure them towards the main body of Ochoa's forces. At four in the afternoon of 13 September the *Santo Cristo de Burgos* and the *Nuestra Señora de la Concepción,* the vice-admiral's ship of the Armada, appeared. Realising the danger, de Graaf tried to flee, but the dispatch boats turned and four ships bore recklessly down on him; as the dispatch boats overhauled him on either side, de Graaf opened fire to port and starboard. Incredibly, thanks to the lightness of his ship and a chance manoeuvre that opened an escape route, de Graaf managed to flee. In December he anchored at the island of Pinos, Cuba, to careen his ship. He could not relax however, for he was not convinced that he had entirely escaped from the trap even now.

In April 1686 a new squadron, this time formed by Grammont, whom de Cussy had appointed Lieutenant of the Coast of Santo Domingo, Brigaut and de Graaf, took to sea. On the last day of the month, Brigaut sighted a ship bearing the colours of the King of Spain near Matanzas. On receiving the news, Grammont set sail for Matanzas, where he arrived three days later, and discovered the remains of a vessel that had been wrecked on the coast during a storm.

Believing that he might find another ship gone adrift, he entered the Bahamas Channel and headed north. Here he was caught in a storm and nothing more was heard of either him or his ship until eighteen months later, when the filibuster, Captain du Marc, returned to Santa Dominica.[36] Du Marc had managed to escape from a Spanish prison and reported to de Cussy that he had heard Grammont and his 180 men had all perished in the storm.

PEACE, THE PRELUDE TO WAR (1685-1688)

That spring, perhaps motivated by the fact that more than 100 of his slaves had been stolen from him by the Spanish and taken to Santo Domingo, de Graaf decided on actions of reprisal.

With an squadron of seven ships and 500 filibusters, he sailed to the Bay of Ascensión in Yucatan. He made landfall and he and his men set off inland. The first city they came to was Tihosuco – it had been abandoned when the watch had warned of the proximity of attackers. They continued their march to Valladolid, where the thirty-six militiamen who had remained to defend the city put up practically no resistance.

In April, news of de Graaf's actions reached the Governor of Yucatan, but before he could respond, de Graaf had re-embarked and was heading for Roatán and, eventually, back to La Tortuga.

Escuadrás Vizcaíno (1687-1692)[37]

On 6 November 1685, Madrid accepted the proposal from a number of Guipûzcoa merchants to arm a corsair squadron of four frigates that would impose order in the Caribbean. Commodore Francisco García Galán, commanding the 34-cannon, 259-ton *Nuestra Señora del Rosario y las Ánimas* and 180 men, was put in charge of a squadron consisting of the *San Nicolás de Bari* (24 cannons, 200 tons and 142 men), the *Nuestra Señora de la Concepción* (140 tons and 66 men), the tender *San Antonio* (60 tons and 36 men) and the galliot *Santiago* (30 tons and 53 men).

The other officers were Francisco de Aguirre as second-in-command, Miguel de Vergara as third, and José de Leoz y Echalar, Martín Pérez de Landeche, Sebastián Pisón, Silvestre Soler and Fermín de Salaverri. The mission was to seek out and crush de Graaf. The squadron was known as the *Escuadrón Vizcaíno* (Biscayan Squadron) or the *Escuadrón Guipuzcoano* (Guipuzcoan Squadron).

Before crossing the Atlantic, the squadron engaged the French near Cape Verde – twelve Vizcaínos were killed, including García Galán. When they reached the Indies, the squadron split up: Salaverri took dispatches to Nueva España, while the rest patrolled the waters of Trinidad, Margarita and La Tortuga. The patrols took three ships, including a Jamaican sloop captained by John Jennings.

Salaverri reached Havana at the beginning of March, and Veracruz in mid April 1687. On his way to Nueva España he had his first encounter with de Graaf, in which he decided not to engage in battle and fled, the Dutchman in hot pursuit. Luck was on Salaverri's side, however, as a passing Cuban coastguard turned the tables on de Graaf. Now the filibusters fled, leaving a straggling canoe to face the coastguards alone. During the fray the brother of corsair Blas de Miguel was killed and the latter swore vengeance on de Graaf.

Salaverri managed to get back to the squadron, restructure his forces and divide them into two patrols. The first, commanded by Leoz on the Rosario, reached Veracruz early in July with his ships so badly damaged that they were practically beyond repair.

Early in 1688 Leoz sailed for Veracruz. En route, he intercepted Roger Whitfield's *Dragon* sailing from Jamaica to New York, and left her in Santiago de

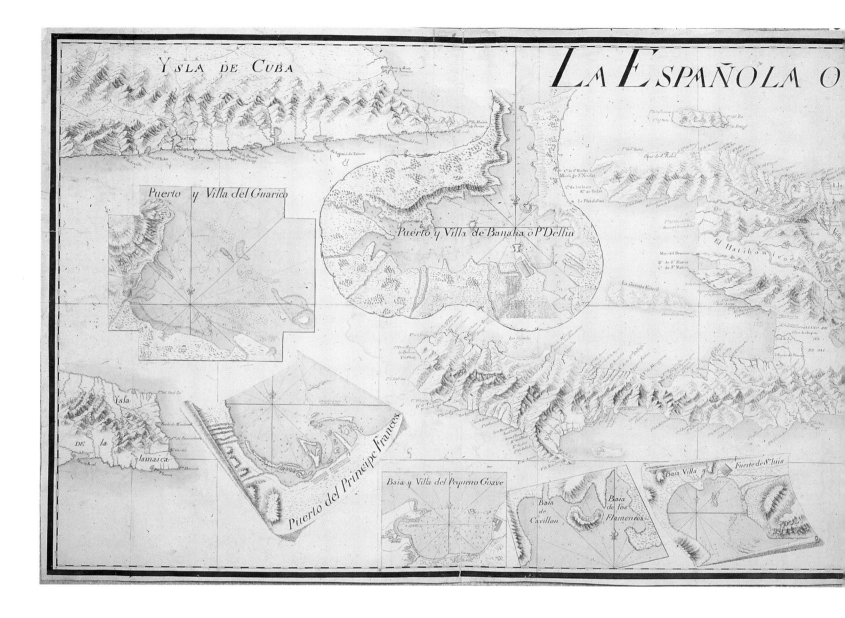

The Peace of Ryswick put an end to many years of conflict.
Spain acknowledged French sovereignty over west Hispaniola and territorial
limits were established very similar to those that today correspond to Haiti
(the French zone) and the Dominican Republic (the Spanish zone).

BLAS MIGUEL SEEKS REVENGE[42]

Blaming de Graaf for the death of his brother, Blas Miguel swore revenge. Accompanied by eight men in a canoe he attempted to surprise the Dutchman in Petit Goave. On the eve of St Lawrence 1687, he took the town without quarter – filibuster style.

But he did not withdraw in time. Blinded by rage and greed, he continued his plundering raids long enough to allow a force of 500 men to be recruited from the surrounding towns and villages. In the ensuing confrontation, his ammunition ran out and he was forced to flee with only twenty-four men.

According to other sources, seventeen of his men were killed and he was taken prisoner with forty-seven others. On the following day he was summarily tried and sentenced, with two of his lieutenants, to be 'torn alive on the rack'. The rest were hanged

Cuba. From here, he proceeded to Santo Domingo, where the contingent was dissolved. Most settled on the island as local coastguards, where they became the scourge of the English.

The damage inflicted on English ships was so serious that, by the end of 1688, the Governor of Jamaica was authorised to use Royal Navy ships to eliminate the Guipuzcoanos and protect English trade from Jamaica. However, when the League of Augsburg was formed, allying the English, Spanish and Dutch against the French, the Royal Navy protection was rendered redundant. The Vizcaínos split up and continued on their adventures separately. In November 1690 their commander, Francisco de Aguirre, was in Havana, and in 1692 the squadron was officially disbanded.

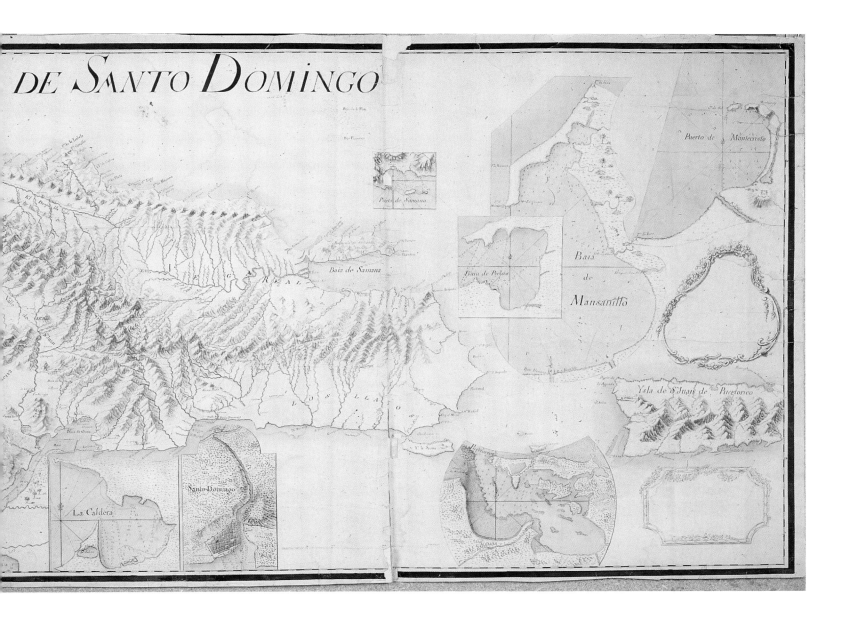

DE SANTO DOMINGO

Isla Vaca, a Strategic Place

In September 1687 the Governor of Santo Domingo, de Cussy, ordered de Graaf to set up a stronghold with 250 men on Isla Vaca (Île-à-Vache), to ensure control of the island. De Cussy wrote to the English Governor of Jamaica, informing him that he was going to take possession of Isla Vaca and that, given the neutrality existing between France and England, he hoped the English would stay away from the area to avoid confrontation.

De Cussy's true objective, however, was to keep the English away from Santa Dominica and to stop the Spanish coastguards, who patrolled those waters, from using the island as a base. De Graaf did indeed build a fortress on the island and assured its control.

FRANCE AGAINST THE LEAGUE OF AUGSBURG (1689-1697)

On 22 May 1688 James II, King of England, issued a proclamation against filibustering and sent a squadron commanded by Robert Holmes, to clean up the waters of the Caribbean.[43] By the end of the year, James had fled to France and William of Orange was proclaimed king.

French protection of the last of the Stuarts triggered an alliance between the remaining European powers, who raised the standard of King William, to defend their respective interests against France. The League of Augsburg allied England, Holland and Spain, among others, who sealed a coalition to evict the French from their American colonies. The policy of repressing filibusters was assumed by all colonial authorities.

The Caribbean was once again the scene of military offensives. France took the initiative and the Governor General of Martinique, the Count of Blenac, attacked St Kitt's. On 27 July 1689 the French mustered before Basse Terre with six warships, fourteen merchant vessels and twenty-three sloops. Some 120 filibusters went ashore and began the siege of Fort Charles, which surrendered two weeks later.

Meanwhile, in December, de Graaf engaged in his Jamaican campaigns. In a short space of time he had captured eight sloops off the north coast through the strategy of devastating, rapid, surprise attacks. The English attempted to counter by preparing a squadron commanded by Captain Edward Spragge on the warship HMS *Drake*, but it failed to be a deterrent to de Graaf.

In early 1690, Ducasse was placed in command of three warships, a sloop and a brigantine to escort 700 reinforcements to the detachment on San Martín, now being besieged by the forces of Sir Timothy Thornhill. The reinforcements arrived in time to save the colony, surprise the English on land and take many prisoners, whom they sent to the island of Nevis.

Between March and May, de Graaf consolidated the blockade of Jamaica: no ship could either reach or leave the island without encountering the squadron of filibusters. One month later, in waters close to the Cayman Islands, the expected encounter took place with HMS *Drake*, escorting a number of merchant ships that had set out to break through the blockade. De Graaf came off badly and retreated to Santa Dominica in mid June.

Here rumours spread of an imminent Anglo-French attack and, although de Cussy considered such an attack unlikely and made no preparations, de Graaf was sent to Isla Vaca.

Believing that the island's forces were sufficient to respond to the hypothetical attack, the French took the offensive and attacked Santiago de los Caballeros.[44] On 6 July 1690 de Cussy, with 900 filibusters and 200 emancipated black slaves, took the city, sacked it and razed it to the ground. Vicious retaliation by forces from Santo Domingo forced them to retreat.

Six months later, in January 1691, the attack at last took place. An English detachment, the Windward Fleet, 200 musketeers, 300 inhabitants of Santiago and a further 100 from Montecristi attacked Guarico. De Cussy made a stand at Sabana Real – the Battle of La Limonade[45] – the final outcome of which was 300 Frenchmen dead, including Franquesnay and de Cussy himself. Port de Paix was burned to the ground, followed by Cabo Francés and Port Prince. When he learned of the attack, Ducasse returned to his countrymen's aid late in January, only to find Cabo Francés devastated and the battlefield strewn with corpses rotting in the sun.

When Ducasse arrived in Martinique, it was to hear that the forces from the Leeward Islands, commanded by Governor Codrington, were besieging Guadeloupe.[46] With two companies of infantry and 600 filibusters, on board the *Jasardeux*, *Mignon*, *Emerillon*, *Cheval Marin* and the 20-cannon merchantmen to bring up the rear, he sailed to the aid of the island. Although at first he attempted to avoid actual combat, he and his men finally disembarked in Grosier on 23 May 1691. The English surrendered two days later, demoralised by the unceasing torrential rains and the numerous deaths by disease.

Ducasse returned to Martinique in triumph but the crews of some of his ships were suffering from yellow fever and these he dispatched to Santa Cruz. On 7 August he sailed to Port de Paix, north of Hispaniola, where 250 of his men died of fever.

Governor Ducasse of Santa Dominica

On 1 October 1691, in recognition of his successes Ducasse was promoted Governor of Santa Dominica. When he took possession of the post, the colony had still not recovered from the Spanish offensive, and Ducasse's first task was to restore morale. In 1692 he reorganised the administration of the colony and moved the seat of government to Cabo Francés, causing a mass exodus from La Tortuga.[47]

In mid February news was received of a new Spanish attack on the colony. Ducasse sent a company of infantry from Petit Goave to Port de Paix as reinforcements for de Graaf and Levasseur and to prevent a second Spanish assault on Santa Dominica. The attack never took place. Gradually the colony recovered and, in January 1693, Ducasse's efforts earned him promotion to Capitaine de Vaisseau.[48]

On his death in 1685 Charles II was succeeded by James II. As a Catholic, the long-term intentions of the new King of England became the object of suspicion among Protestant circles and, after the birth of his son James in June 1688, revolts broke out forcing James II to flee to France six months later. The rise of the House of Orange began a new era of convergent interests between England and Holland against a common enemy, France.

The Offensive against Jamaica

In 1692 Jamaica suffered a devastating earthquake. Port Royal was destroyed and food and other provisions were in desperately short supply. In the summer of 1693 William Beeston[49] was appointed governor and began his term of office with the aim of rebuilding the island. The main obstacle to his endeavour was the shortage of manpower, particularly during wartime.

Early in June 1694 Ducasse proposed that the best way to avoid an Anglo-Spanish whipping was to take the initiative and carry out a major offensive. He chose

Jamaica as his target[50] and sailed from Petit Goave on the 54-cannon *Temeraire*, seconded by Chevalier du Rollon and with the backing of a fleet totalling twenty-two sailing ships and over 3,000 men; they reached the island on the morning of 27 June.

Ducasse split his forces into two divisions. The first anchored fifteen miles east of Port Royal while the second, commanded by Ducasse himself, proceeded to Port Morant, where he disembarked 800 men led by Beauregard. They advanced east, burning and destroying everything in their path.

From Port Morant the English sent warning of the French arrival to the cities in the north but Governor Beeston, fearful of dividing his already scant forces, did not dare deploy his troops.

On 1 July the *Temeraire* and a second French ship weighed anchor and sailed to the Bay of Bluefields. Ducasse had disembarked troops and continued his operations until the end of the month. On 27 July he gathered the main body of his forces in an attempt to take Port Royal. Beeston, who until that moment had made no move, ordered a sortie. But the French managed to get back to their ships under cover of night.

The three largest ships, with the forces of de Graaf, attacked Carlisle, thirty-five miles to the west. They anchored in the afternoon and landed some 1,500 filibusters during the night of 28 July. By the morning, they had managed to isolate the small English garrison. Beauregard commanded the advance guard and de Graaf the main body of the army. Having sacked the city, he sent parties to reconnoitre the surrounding area. Having called his men back, on 3 August Ducasse withdrew and reached Petit Goave the following day. The operation had clearly revealed the vulnerability of the island.

The Anglo-Spanish Counter Attack

One month after the French retreat, Beeston sent a small force to Santa Dominica to bombard the city of L'Esterre, near Leogane, on 11 October 1694.

There they set a course for Petit Goave, only to discover that Beauregard was waiting for them. Burning a number of villages near Isla Vaca they decided to return to Jamaica to await more numerous forces.

In the spring of 1695 an English expedition, consisting of more than twenty ships commanded by Colonel Luke Lillingston and Commodore Robert Wilmot, reached the Antilles. They joined forces with the Spanish troops of Santo Domingo and the Windward Fleet with the intention of striking the definitive blow to the French colonies.[51]

On 15 May they set sail for Guarico, where they put de Graaf's outnumbered defenders to flight. One month later the squadron reached Port de Paix, which they besieged. The French garrison attempted to evacuate the city a few hours before the allied infantry arrived, and then surrendered. The city was razed to the ground and, on 27 July, the allied fleet again set sail. It was then the turn of Port Margot, Planemon and other strongholds – Ducasse meanwhile retreated to Leogane.

At the end of the campaign 600 Frenchmen were dead, 900 were prisoners and the allies had a booty of 1,000 slaves, 150 cannons and over 200,000 pesos. Differences over the sharing-out process led to the disintegration of the alliance and the English and Spanish returned to their respective bases. Ducasse sent de Graaf and La Boulaye to France where, though tried as deserters, they were eventually pardoned.

There were no further campaigns until the following year. The French attempted to send reinforcements for a possible counter-offensive, in the form of a squadron commanded by Bernard-Jean-Louis de Saint-Jean, Baron de Pointis.[52] When he heard the news, Ducasse assembled a major contingent of filibusters, although he did not manage to reach Cabo Francés until the beginning of March 1697.

On 16 March the 84-cannon warship *Esceptre* anchored off Petit Goave. When Ducasse went on board, de Pointis received him in a rage, accusing him of disobeying his orders – the hapless Ducasse had managed to mobilise only 200 filibusters, the rest having set off on their own private ventures.

De Pointis weighed anchor to reassemble the filibusters, but his methods were so brutal that a revolt broke out so savage that it could not be quelled until Ducasse intervened. The filibusters refused to take part in the campaign since they saw no profit in the attack; furthermore, they refused to submit to the authority of de Pointis.

The problem was solved when de Pointis appointed Ducasse commander of all the island forces,[53] while he reserved for himself the command of the contingent from France. Moreover, as an economic incentive, he offered the filibusters an increase in their portion of the booty.

Thus, sufficient forces were mustered to form two divisions. The first composed of troops from the island – 650 buccaneers, 170 soldiers, 110 volunteers and 180 emancipated negroes – commanded by Ducasse on the 40-cannon *Pontchartrain*. In total, 1,110 men sailing on the 18-cannon *Serpente*, the 20-cannon *Gracieuse*, the 18-cannon *Cerf Volant*, the 18-cannon *Saint-Louis*, the 16-cannon *Dorade* and other lesser ships. The second division consisted of the French contingent commanded by de Pointis. Having assembled at Cape Tiburón on 8 April 1697, they set a course south to launch the Cartagena de Indias campaign.

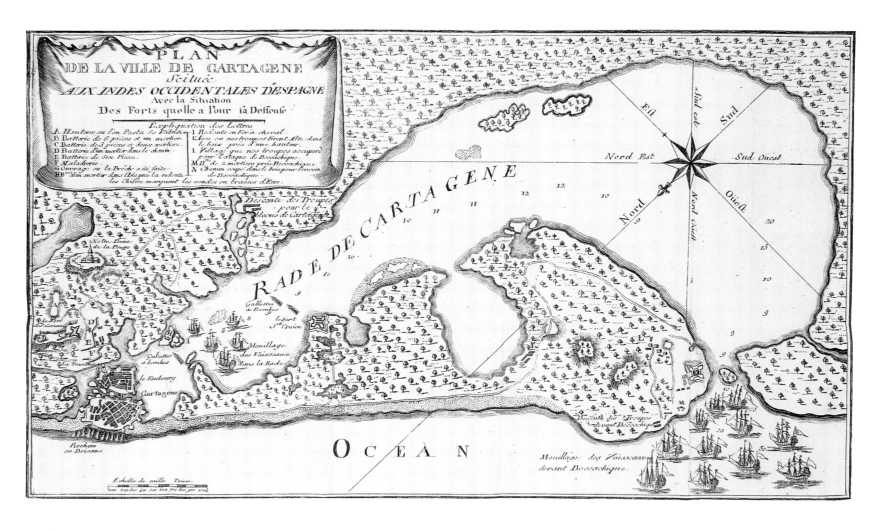

Cartagena de Indias witnessed the last great bucanneer assault. Many were taken prisoner or killed during the assaults, while those who managed to escape later returned and gradually settled down and devoted themselves to other activities in the colony.

The Cartagena de Indias Campaign[54]

On 15 April Ducasse and de Pointis disembarked with 1,200 men, determined to take Boca Chica. While they were preparing their positions, the filibusters captured a coastguard patrol boat carrying reinforcements from Portobelo. As in the good old days, they used the ship to escort a number of vessels to Cartagena. The defenders at the fortress got wind of the ruse, however, and opened fire on the attackers, forcing them to scatter. Outraged by the filibusters' lack of discipline, de Pointis ordered those who returned to be beaten.

During the night, the Spaniards made a sortie, killing seven filibusters and six soldiers and wounding twenty-two others, including Ducasse. Joseph d'Honon de Gallifet, a newcomer to Santo Domingo and, to the majority, an absolute unknown, took over command from Ducasse.

De Pointis ordered the filibusters to assault the hillock of Nuestra Señora de la Popa, while the main body of the forces advanced over the plain. Under orders from Gallifet the filibusters hesitated during their attack and the defenders forced them to retreat.

After this initial failure, the French stormed higher positions, where they placed artillery, consolidating the position on 20 April. Eight days later, the Getsemani quarter of the city was heavily bombarded and two days later Ducasse, now recovered from his wounds, once again took command of the filibusters. On 1 May he met with a Spanish officer outside one of the city gates to negotiate terms of surrender, arguing that the French had opened a breach in the enemy defences. The Spaniards refused and de Pointis ordered the final assault.

After a bloody battle, on 2 May a white flag was hoisted above the walls requesting a ceasefire in which to negotiate the terms of capitulation. Meanwhile, news came that a Spanish column of over 1,000 men was approaching the city. Ducasse was sent with his filibusters and a number of soldiers to intercept, but the column never materialised.

On their return, the filibusters found the gates of the city closed and de Pointis's men imposing the terms of capitulation by force – the Frenchman had prevented Ducasse from entering to avoid the sacking of the city.

The few surviving citizens of Cartagena were urged by de Pointis to hand over all their worldly goods to avoid the wrath of the filibusters. The proceeds from the 'collection' amounted to more than eight million French crowns.

The enraged filibusters demanded their share of the booty, which they reckoned to be a quarter of the total, but de Pointis handed over only 40,000 crowns. Meanwhile, the Frenchman withdrew his troops and loaded the treasure on his ships, leaving Cartagena to the mercy of the filibusters, who sacked the city. Those who resisted were put to the sword while the rest took refuge in the church.

Ducasse broke down the gate with cannon fire and captured all the city's inhabitants. He then tortured the survivors to obtain what booty he could – just a few crowns.

As the fleet left, de Pointis came face-to-face with the Anglo-Dutch fleet, commanded by Vice-Admiral John Neville, which was coming to Cartagena's aid. Most of the French ships either deserted or were captured. As for de Pointis, he managed to slip away at dawn on 10 June, although he was pursued for two days.

Neville continued on to Cartagena, where he found Ducasse's squadron anchored in the bay. He immediately attacked, capturing a number of ships and most of the filibusters. Ducasse managed to break through the blockade and escape to Santa Dominica.

Luck was against the filibusters: those who managed to escape did so with no booty, while those who were captured were forced to work on the reconstruction of the city. On 8 July 1697 Ducasse wrote to Pontchartrain from Leogane, complaining about the way de Pointis had handled the campaign and accusing him of being responsible for the decimation of his filibusters. After much correspondence and a series of lawsuits, Ducasse received a small share of the huge booty wrested from the Spaniards.

On 30 September the Peace of Ryswick recognised France's rights to her American colonies, thereby putting an end to two centuries of conflicts.

The Last Skirmishes

In 1698 two Scottish ships, the *Unicorn* and the *Dolphin*, carrying 1,200 colonists to establish a new trading post on the coast of Darien for the Scottish Gulf of Darien Company,[55] anchored at St Thomas in the Dutch Virgin Islands. The commanders of the ships were unfamiliar with the coast of Tierra Firme and needed a pilot to guide them to their destination. They found their man, Robert Alliston, in a tavern.

Alliston embarked on the venture, taking charge of the vice-admiral's ship, the *Saint Andrew*, and a slow, difficult crossing began. On the night of 26 October one of the passengers saw a light and rocks that seemed to be land. Indeed, he had sighted Nuestra Señora de la Popa, the beach head of Cartagena.

Two weeks later they reached Isla Dorada, in the Gulf of San Blas, to the east of Nombre de Dios, and on 15 November they came to the Gulf of Darien, renamed the Bay of Caledonia. Taking advantage of their good relations with the Indians, they claimed right of purchase and, on the basis of this, legitimate ownership. However, the colony met with a string of serious difficulties: rampant sunstroke, boredom and internal disputes threatened to put paid to an adventure that had only just begun.[56]

At the end of February 1699 Alliston took to sea once more aboard the *Endeavour* with orders to guide Captain John Anderson to Jamaica to obtain provisions. A few days later they returned with victuals and waited for reinforcements supposedly coming from England.

The Windward Fleet,[57] consisting of five large ships and six smaller vessels and commanded by Diaz Pimienta, set sail on 13 February 1700. On 7 March the fleet reached Playón, disembarked 200 men and attacked simultaneously from land and sea. On 11 April a capitulation was signed and the colony was evacuated.

A subsequent colonisation attempt took place with 1,000 men from New England, but this time it was the climate that did the job of evicting them.

The lands of North America also witnessed the establishment of new settlements. One morning in January 1699, at the Spanish colony of Penzacola, five

Life on the upper decks on board ship in the early 18th century is revealed in this illustration: reading and recitation, smoking, the company and entertainments of black slaves and luxurious clothing characterised the lives of upper class passengers, while, in stark contrast, the crews on the lower decks were subjected to severely cramped conditions.

French ships commanded by Iberville requested the help of a coast pilot.[58] On boarding the 58-cannon *François*, the Spanish found to their surprise that Iberville's interpreter was none other than Laurens de Graaf. Such was the meaning of his presence on board, that the visitors were denied permission to enter the harbour, and they were allowed only to send in boats to take on provisions. In a state of maximum alert, the Spanish garrison sent a number of ships in pursuit of the French flotilla, which soon disappeared westward to found the colony of Louisiana, in the present Mississippi city of Biloxi. A census taken in May 1700 registers one 'Le Sieur Graffe' as one of the officers of the colony and servant of His Majesty the King. It is believed that he was one of the original founders of the colony of Mobile, Alabama, although he apparently never made the journey. De Graaf died early in 1704.

The Anglo-Dutch assault on Vigo, 1702.

EPILOGUE

LORDS OF FORTUNE

By the end of the 17th century the national situation in Spain had become critical. The Armada was reduced to a few old, badly equipped ships, the crews were scarce and there were no economic resources to sustain them. The shipyards of Cantabria were all but paralysed by a lack of official orders, delays in payments, accidental fires and enemy attacks. The fleets had been suspended and commercial trade was scanty.

Charles II had married twice but, nevertheless, died childless and the question of who was his rightful successor was the source of all manner of conspiracies and schemings at Court. There were two main candidates for the throne: Philip, Duke of Anjou, son of the Dauphin of France and grandson of Louis XIV; and Charles, Archduke of Austria. In the event it was Philip's claim that was to prove initially stronger.

Charles II died in November 1700. Philip was appointed his successor and arrived in Spain crossing the frontier at Bidasoa on 22 January 1701. One month later, in Madrid, he began to reduce the nation's spending and to introduce administrative reforms that had far-reaching effects among the noble classes.

Philip understood that his most important objective must be to re-establish Spain's maritime communications with America and, in order to protect them, he obtained the support of two escort squadrons sent by Louis XIV in exchange for awarding the *asiento de negros* to the French Company of Guinea.

Between 1700 and 1706 transatlantic Spanish navigation was practically at a standstill,[1] indeed, the only recorded crossings were made by the *azogues* bound for Veracruz in 1701 and 1703. In 1706 the last Ocean Fleet governed by traditional regulations sailed from Nueva España. Fleets also sailed in 1708, 1711, 1712, 1715, 1720 and 1722, and individual azogues did so in 1710, 1719 and 1722.

Concurrently the galleons from Tierra Firme fared no better: a fleet sailed in 1700 and galleons did likewise in 1706 and 1713, but none ever returned. In 1700 the galleons were intercepted by the English while those of 1713 were shipwrecked off the coast of Florida together with the fleet from Nueva España. There was only one further foray, undertaken in 1721 by Baltasar de Guevara. In the composition of the transatlantic fleets, foreign vessels accounted for 31.2 per cent of the tonnage transported between 1700 and 1715 and for 41.1 per cent of the total number of voyages.[2] Furthermore, the cost of French protection was so high that it was estimated the money paid for freight could have bought thirty vessels, including eight 50-cannon ships and two 80-90 cannon ships.[3]

But most damaging to the Spanish Royal Navy was the subordination of her commanders to French officers. On 24 March 1701 Count d'Estrées was appointed Lieutenant General of the seas,[4] and later Ducasse was named Head of the Squadron. The memory of the Count's bombardment of Alicante and the inclusion of Ducasse, whom everyone considered the champion of piracy, led to the resignation of the principal Spanish senior officers such as the Duke of Nájera, Captain General of the Spanish Galleys; the Marquee of Leganés, Captain General of the Ocean; and Juán Tomás Enríquez de Cobrera, Admiral of Castile.

BLACKBEARD, A LEGENDARY PIRATE[5]

One of the most legendary pirates of the early 17th century was Edward Teach, probably born in Bristol although some claim he was born in South Carolina or even Jamaica.

He began his maritime career on the ships of the Royal Navy but, after the end of the Spanish War of Succession, he decided to continue his adventures. His first actions were in 1716 when he assaulted a Spanish merchant vessel transporting flour from Havana, and another loaded with wine from Bermuda; he attacked a third ship en route from Madeira to South Carolina.

His nickname, Blackbeard, was due to his long black beard and a thick mat of hair of the same colour adorned with lit matches that he would set fire to when he entered into combat. Apart from his terrifying aspect he was also famous for being one of the most bloodthirsty of pirates.

One of his most audacious exploits took place in 1717 when he assaulted and seized a 40-cannon French vessel belonging to the French Company of Guinea, renamed *Queen Anne's Revenge*. Blackbeard was the first man ever to jump on board another vessel with a pistol in his hand and a knife between his teeth.

He carried out numerous attacks on vessels of all nationalities and his forces continued to increase until he commanded 400 men on six ships. In North Carolina and Virginia a price was put on his head and £100 were offered for his capture dead or alive.

He died on 22 November 1718 when a vessel named the *Pearl,* belonging to the king and commanded by Lieutenant Maynard, tracked him down. They confronted each other in combat until Maynard was able to slit his throat; his head was taken to Virginia to be displayed for all to see.

Boarding was often the final push that determined the outcome of a sea battle. The blood-thirsty and daring crews of pirate ships were veterans of the European wars and deserters from the royal navies and thought little of confronting merchant ships and, occasionally, the crews of coastguard frigates.

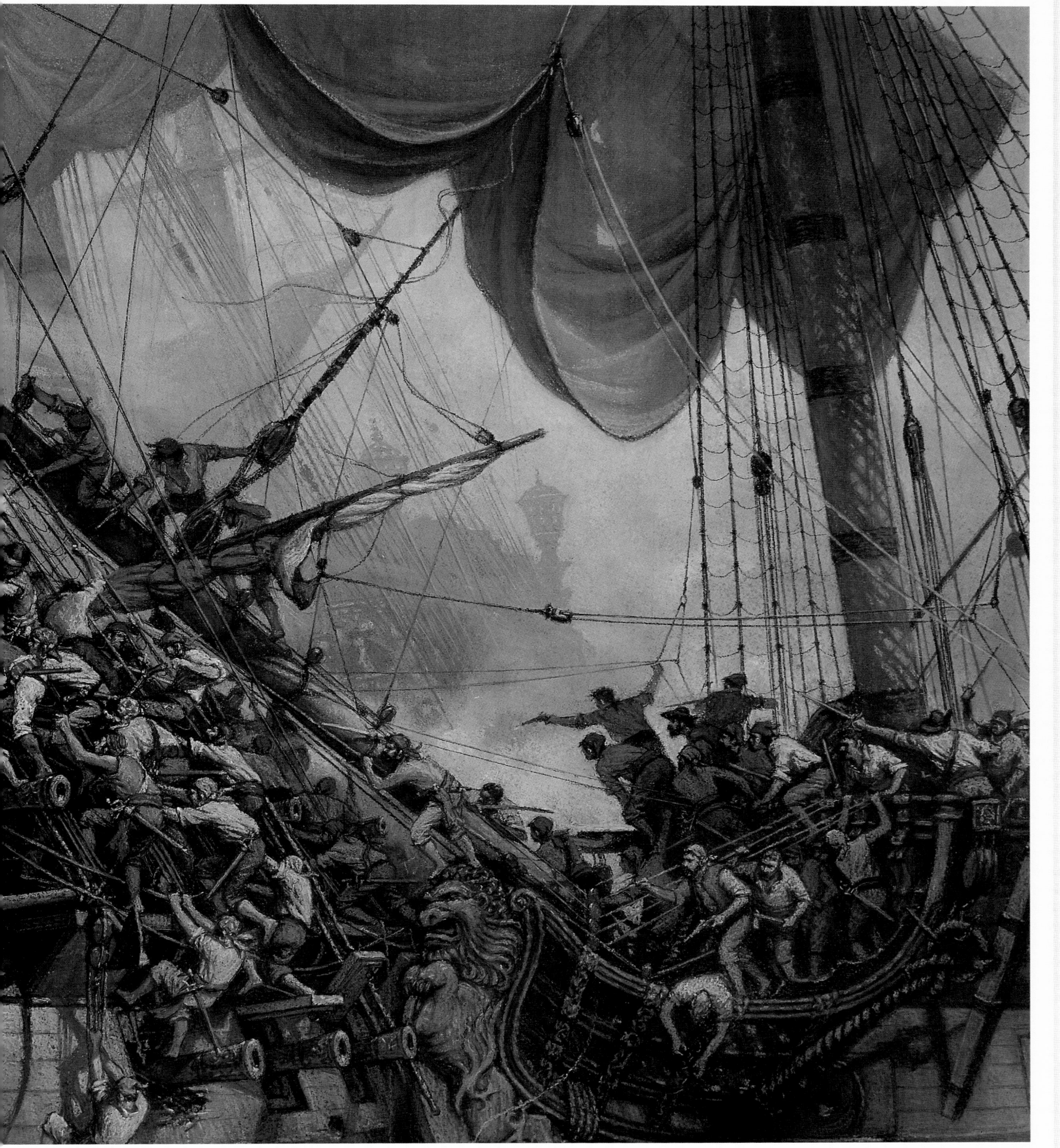

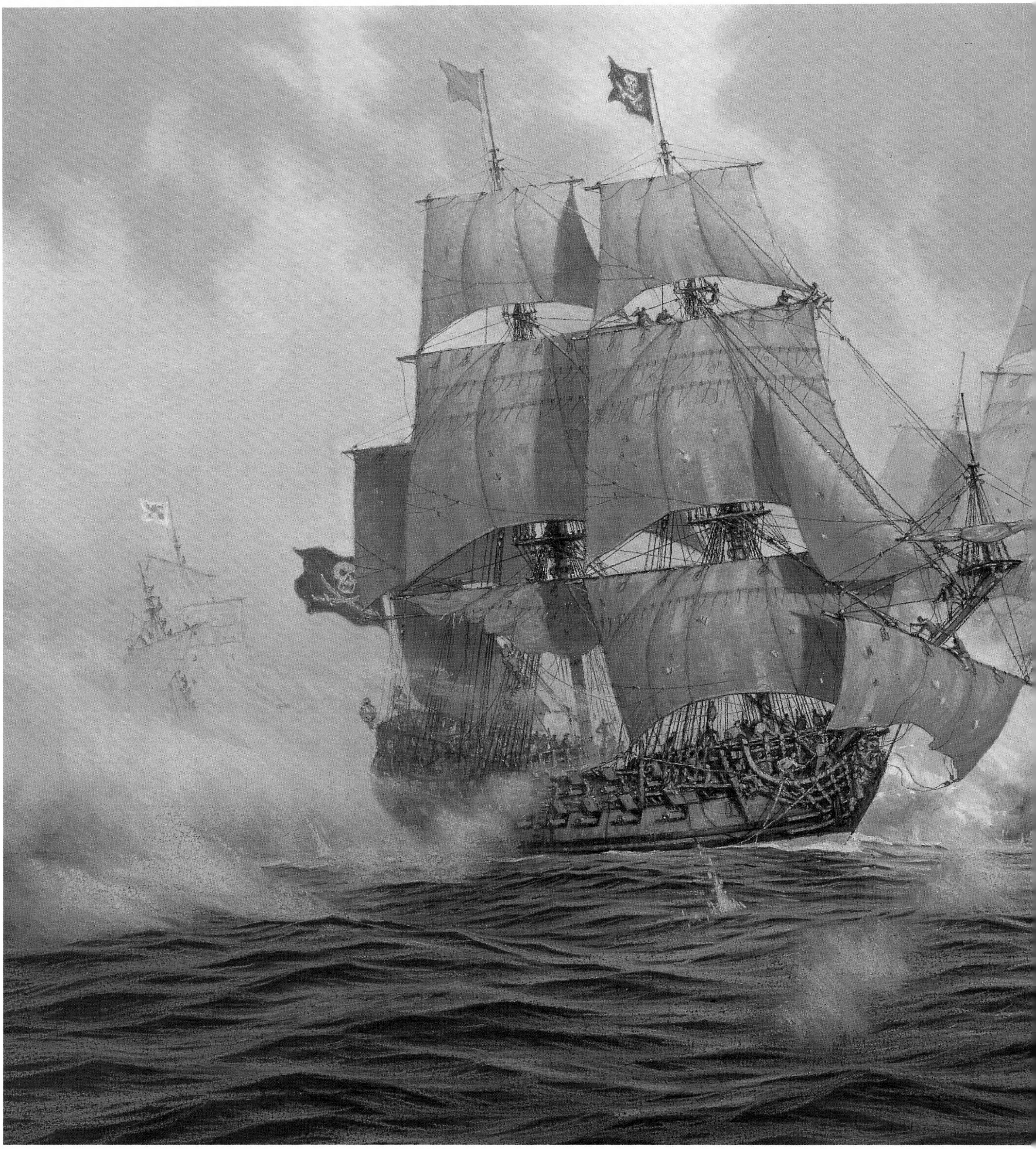

WOMEN PIRATES[6]

A tender reached Jamaica one day in November 1720. The port officers addressed the crew to enquire after their place of provenance and intentions; they were answered that the intention was to buy supplies and that their commander was Jack Rackham. The news spread across the docks: the fearsome pirate known as Calico for his wearing of silk underclothing was in the port.

While Rackham was provisioning his ship a royal vessel commanded by Jonathan Barnet, who had received the order to capture Calico from the Governor of the island, once again asked those on board to identify themselves. When the answer came that it was commanded by Jack Rackham of Cuba, Barnet ordered them to surrender. Far from obeying, Calico hoisted the black flag and ordered his men to fight. The battle was fierce but eventually the tender surrendered and the prisoners were taken to Santiago de la Vega where it was discovered that among them were two women, Anne Bonny and Mary Read.

Anne Bonny was the daughter born to a lawyer from County Cork and one of his servant girls. The lawyer's wife surprised the lovers and the discovery led to a violent separation. Anne was born soon after and her father tried to persuade his wife that this child was nothing to do with him. She would have none of it and reported him to the authorities. He lost his position and eloped with the girl and his daughter, Anne, to Carolina. There he made a fortune as the head of a plantation.

Anne grew up surrounded by sailors and married one John Bonny, who, it is said, had no money and the alliance enraged Anne's father. She abandoned her family and moved to New Providence where she and John managed a tavern for some time. Here Anne met Calico and they became lovers. They decided to flee and, together with a group of men, they seized a brig which was anchored in the port and sailed out to sea, thus beginning their career as pirates.

Mary Read was also the product of an elicit love affair. Her mother had had a short marriage during which she bore a son before her husband, a sailor, went to sea and didn't return. Mary was conceived with another, unknown, man and, after she was born, her mother moved to the country where she lived for four years, during which time Mary's half-brother died.

Back in London the seafaring husband returned and Mary's mother dressed the little girl as a boy to make all believe that this was her son. The story was so convincing that everyone believed it, even Mary's grandmother who assigned them a weekly stipend of £1 for the child's upbringing. Then, when Mary was thirteen years old, her grandmother died and the young girl had to work for her living.

After being in service for some time, she assumed the appearance of a man and enlisted on a war ship from which she deserted; later she enlisted as a soldier in Flanders. There she fell in love with another soldier named Fleming whom she married; they settled down in Breda where they managed a tavern called 'The Three Horseshoes'.

Some time later Fleming died suddenly and Mary closed the inn and enlisted as an infantry soldier in Holland. Finally she enrolled on a vessel that was captured by Calico in the Caribbean and joined his crew.

She had a strong relationship with Anne Bonny – indeed, so loyal was it that Calico suspected they were lovers. All doubts as to this were dissipated, however, when Mary fell in love with a male member of the crew.

After they were captured by Barnet Mary and Anne were sentenced to death in Santiago de la Vega on 28 November 1720. But, while Calico was hanged at Gallows Point, the two women were granted a reprieve. It seems that Anne returned to Carolina to her father's plantation while Mary died of the fever in Santa Catalina in late April the following year.

Jack Rackman was one of the most feared men in Caribbean waters.
Also known as 'Calico' his ship was identified by a black flag with a skull and two crossed sabres; members of his crew included two of the most famous women pirates, Anne Bonny and Mary Read.

The Battle of Vélez Málaga, at which Blas de Lezo lost a leg, was one of the pivotal events of the Spanish War of Succession.

EDICT FOR THE SUPPRESSION OF PIRACY

I, KING GEORGE

We have been informed that several persons, subjects of Great Britain, have, since 24 June of the present year 1715, been committing piracy and robbery at sea, in the West Indies or the proximity of our plantations, causing great damage to British commercial ships and trade in these regions. Although we have designated a regiment we believe necessary to suppress this piracy, to put an end to it more efficiently our Private Council has considered the issue of this royal edict by which we promise and declare that any pirate who gives himself up on 5 September 1718 or earlier to any of our main secretaries of state in Britain or Ireland, or to any governor or sub-governor of any plantation overseas will obtain our gracious pardon of the piracy he may have committed before 5 January. We therefore strictly order our Admirals, Captains and other officers at sea, as well as Governors or Commanders of forts, castles or strongholds of our plantations and the rest of our civil and military officers to arrest those pirates who refuse to hand themselves in as accorded in this edict....

Signed in the Court of Hampton on 5 September 1717 in the fourth year of our reign.

God Save the King

Just as Philip was addressing the needs of his navy, Emperor Leopold was contesting the will of Charles II and claiming the throne for his son. And throughout Europe political relationships were becoming ever more complicated: Louis XIV had acknowledged James Stuart's right as King of England and the Orange clan had begun the preliminaries for war.

Holland, England, Denmark and Germany allied against France in defence of the claims of Charles of Austria and declared war against Philip of the Spanish throne, in May 1702.

A magnificent squadron of fifty ships of the line, transporting 14,000 soldiers set out for Cadiz to fight for the rights of the pretender. Inland, those who had been wronged by Philip's court sided with the archduke while those who had been recently favoured came out in support of the king. During the ensuing years the *azules* (for Charles) and the *blancos* or *blanquillos* (for Philip) confronted one another on the battlefield.[8] Events such as the fall of Gibraltar evidenced the weakness of Spain before her enemies. But none was more damaging to a once-proud nation than the fiasco that befell the fleet of Nueva España.

On 11 June 1702 the fleet set sail from Nueva España, transporting the massive wealth accumulated since the end of Charles II's reign in the holds of nineteen vessels, among them a single war galleon, the flagship, under the command of Manuel de Velasco. The fleet was escorted by twenty-three French vessels commanded by Vice-Admiral Chateau-Renault.

The voyage proceeded without major incident until the fleet reached the Azores. There the officers and men received news of the outbreak of war and the presence of the Anglo-Dutch squadron commanded by Sir Cloudesley Shovell off the Peninsula coast.

Suspecting that Shovell would block Cadiz or await them in the Capes and, despite an invitation from the French to take refuge in Brest, Velasco ordered his ships to make port in the Bay of Vigo. On 22 September the fleet dropped anchor near Redondela, a safe haven with good land defences. Ten days later most of the treasure had been offloaded and was being transported to the Court in 1,500 wagons.

On 21 October Shovell's squadron appeared and two days later the assault began with his soldiers taking the land positions. The gun battle lasted until the 24th, by which time a great number of Hispano-French fighters were either dead or wounded – many because of the last minute order received by both the Spanish and the French to set fire to their own vessels. On the 28th the Anglo-Dutch forces re-embarked and, on the last day of October, set sail for England and Holland, where they arrived to heroes' welcomes and great victory celebrations.

In 1715 Antonio de Ubilla's fleet, which joined up with the galleons in Havana, was also rather unfortunate. On 27 July the ships set sail only to be surprised, three days later, by a sudden hurricane that engulfed them before they could reach the Bahamas Channel. One vessel managed to survive – ten others were lost near Cape Canaveral.

When news of the loss arrived in Havana, Juan Hoyo Solórzano was appointed to dive in search of the sunken goods and, during the following months, four million pesos were ultimately recovered. When just 350,000 pesos had been accumulated and were being guarded by sixty soldiers, 300 men led by Henry Jennings attacked the site with three tenders and two ships. With no difficulty and in the face of only light resistance, they seized the booty and removed it to Jamaica. The Spanish protests were of little effect, merely succeeding in denying Jennings the approval and therefore the support of the English authorities which, according to Daniel Defoe, had led the outlaws to engage in piracy.

At last, the War of Succession came to a close and the signing of the Treaty of Utrecht gave way to a new period during which the relations between European powers were reasonably settled. After the consolidation of the French, English and Dutch colonies and the final rupture of the trade monopoly with America, the presence of pirates in the Caribbean, and their threats to navigation were a common and shared danger for all nations.

England decreed the suppression and persecution of piracy in all her colonies and the corsairs who had hitherto been in the service of the Crown were branded as outlaws. With no sovereign to serve, the lords of fortune set sail to attack any vessel that crossed their path. Some, like William Kidd, would end their days on the gallows; others like Blackbeard would be crushed by the eventual supremacy of the navies of all nationalities sent to annihilate them.

When the Spanish trade monopoly in the Indies was broken the raison d'être of corsairs, buccaneers and filibusters was broken with it and these violent, daring men became pirates, enemies of all commercial shipping and pursued by all. They were finally driven out of the Caribbean by the late 1720s.

PIRATE FLAGS

From the beginning of the 18th century pirates used personal flags to identify themselves when approaching their victims. The idea was to cause terrible fear and thereby secure a rapid surrender without having to fight. The adopted symbols were associated with death – their victims had little time to surrender to the pirate's strength and the red and black colours used to represent blood sent an unequivocal message to the hapless crews of merchant ships

Christopher Condent

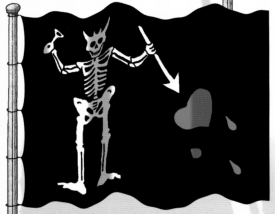

Edward Teach 'Blackbeard'

Jack Rackham 'Calico'

Thomas Tew

Captain Thomas 'The Pirate Lord'
and Captain Edwards

The Jolly Roger or Black Flag –
the banner of the King of Death

The Barbary pirates

Captain Bartholomew Roberts –
'your time is almost up'

Bowsprit pennant of Captain Bartholomew Roberts
ABH: A Barbadian's Head –
*   the head of the Governor of Barbados*
AMH: A Martinican's Head –
*   the head of the Governor of Martinique*

THE PRINCIPAL PLAYERS

AERNOUTS, Hurriaen: Dutch corsair from Curaçao who organised expeditions against the French in North America and the Caribbean. In 1674 he attacked French possessions north of Maine, storming Penobscot, San Jean River, Jemsec and the rest of the province known as New Holland. He took part in several actions with Jan Erasmus Reyning.

ALLISON, Robert: Also known as Alliston. The first reports of his activities in the Caribbean are dated December 1679 when he collaborated with John Coxon in the assault of Portobelo and the expedition to the Pacific. In 1698 he sailed with the Scottish Company of Darien expedition as a pilot.

ANDRIESZOON, Michael: Of Dutch origins but his base was Santa Dominica and he frequently operated in connivance with Laurens de Graaf. His freebooters knew him by the nickname 'Capitaine Michel' or 'L'Andresson' while the English knew him as 'Michel' or 'Mitchel'.

The first record of him is dated 1683, when it seems he took part in the capture of the *situados* of Puerto Rico and Santo Domingo. He took part in the sacking of Veracruz (spring 1683), in the blockade of Cartagena (Christmas 1683), and the assault of the Dutch Indiamen (spring 1684). In August 1684 he was seen on the coast of New England and, at the beginning of the following year, he was seen again in Tierra Firme. In the spring of 1685 his was one of the units that participated in the blockade of Cuba and in July he took part in the assault on Campeche led by de Graaf. After this adventure he retired from the sea and lived his final days peacefully in the French colony of Santa Dominica.

BARRERA Y VILLEGAS, Felipe de la: Spanish officer from Valle de Toranzo near Santillana in Cantabria. He defended Laguna de Términos where he was mayor in 1680 and Campeche in 1683. He died in 1704.

BEESTON, William: Born in Titchfield, Hampshire, in 1636. He emigrated to Jamaica in May 1660 and three years later was elected member of the Council of Jamaica representing Port Royal. He was Judge of the Court of Common Pleas in December 1664. Between 1671 and 1672 he carried out several campaigns as a coastguard. In 1673 he was the Commissioner of the Admiralty in Jamaica and in 1677 he was elected Speaker of the Assembly of Jamaica. His differences with the new governor, the Duke of Carlisle, led to the dissolution of the Assembly and the deportation of Beeston to England by order of the Chief Justice Colonel Long in July 1680. He was later reinstated.

At the end of 1692 he was knighted in Kensington and returned to Jamaica as governor in the summer of 1693. He held the post until 1702 and died soon after.

BINCKES, Jacob: Commander from Friesland who led two expeditions to the West Indies. He was a veteran of the Anglo-Dutch War and had taken part in the two-day battle in Dunkirk in 1666 and Medway in 1667. In 1672 he was appointed commander of the 70-cannon *Woerden* with which he fought in Solevay. In September 1672 five officers including Binckes were unfairly accused of lack of diligence during combat but they were later reinstated.

Ruyter recruited him in Texel for his campaign in the Caribbean in 1673 where he was given command of the frigate *Nordhollandt*. He was promoted to vice-admiral in Amsterdam in March 1676 and was sent to the Caribbean, taking part in the operations in Tobago one year later.

BRASILIANO, Rock: Born in Holland he settled down among the English in Jamaica. According to Exquemeling he was from Groningen, from whence he emigrated to the colony of Bahía in Brazil – hence his nickname. He commanded a small ship and became famous after a highly profitable expedition in Nueva España. He was captured in Campeche and deported to Spain but he returned to Jamaica as a free man. At the beginning of 1668 he joined up with El Olonés when the latter went to Jamaica to sell a ship, and then became a first officer in Lecat's crew. He took part in the attack on Portobelo in 1688, in the campaign of the Gulf of Mexico in 1669 and in the assault on Panama in 1670-71.

CLERC, François Le (Peg Leg): Le Clerc lost his leg fighting against the English in the wars with France. In 1553 Henry II awarded him the first French letter of marque. Together with Jacques Sore and Robert Blondel, he took part in the French campaigns against Spanish interests. On his way back to France in 1559 he attacked Santa Cruz de las Palmas. Henry II ennobled him as reward for his services.

CLIFFORD, George, third Earl of Cumberland (1558-1605): An English nobleman much given to gambling, as a result of which he lost his fortune. He was educated in Cambridge where he stood out as a mathematician. He tried to recover his losses by capturing a Spanish Fleet and, with this purpose, he went to sea in 1589. He managed to arm an expedition with twenty ships accompanied by Sir John

Berkeley. He attacked Lanzarote and Puerto Rico, obtaining substantial booty and leaving the stronghold in Berkeley's hands, although later he abandoned the island due to the casualties among his troops caused by fever. He returned to England at the end of the year without having attained any results of note.

CORSO, Juan: Also known as Corzo or, to the English, Corsario John, he was a famous Spanish corsair of unknown origin who was both feared and hated by his victims. One of Pedro de Castro's subordinates, he was known to have an extremely violent personality. He was active between 1680 and 19 May 1685 when he was caught in a storm in Apalache Bay and was drowned.

COXON, John: Active from 1676, with a French licence he took part in the capture of Santa Marta in June 1677. In 1680 he led an attack on Portobelo and later took part in the Pacific campaign.

Between 1682 and 1683 he was a corsair with a Jamaican letter of marque, which he eventually renounced to continue his adventures as a pirate. He was last heard of in 1688 near the Isla Vaca off the coast of Hispaniola, commanding a barca longa with eighty Englishmen, three French and five Flemish.

CUSSY, Pierre Paul Tarin de: Governor of La Tortuga and Santa Dominica. He rose to interim governor in March 1676 substituting d'Ogeron until the arrival of de Pouançay that same year. Seven years later, on 1 September 1683, he took over from de Pouançay as governor although his official appointment did not take place until the beginning of 1684. He maintained the policy of allowing the filibusters to stay in the colony in order to ensure its prosperity. The main campaigns by Caballero de Grammont, de Graaf and others took place during de Cussy's term of office. After the

attack on Santiago de los Caballeros in 1690 he fought in and was killed at the Battle of Limonade.

DRAKE, Sir Francis (c.1540-1596): Born in Crowndale near Tavistock in about 1540 into a family of farmers, one of twelve children. He was the nephew of William Hawkins, brother of John Hawkins. It seems that he visited Spain as the cabin boy of Jane Dormer, Countess of Feria, and maintained contact with a Jewish convert group who controlled the slave trade associated with the Hawkins family. Sent by John Hawkins, in 1566 he took part in the expedition led by John Lowell. In 1567 he participated in the disastrous journey to Veracruz and fled to England aboard the *Judith*. Between 1570 and 1572 he made several voyages to America and, during the last one, attempted to seize the silver that crossed the Isthmus of Panama.

In 1577 he began his great voyage aboard the *Pelican*, renamed *The Golden Hind*. He assaulted several strongholds and visited California, Las Marianas and several other places until he completed the circumnavigation of the world. He returned to England where he was knighted and celebrated as a national hero.

Between 1585 and 1587 he set out with twenty-one vessels and assaulted the coast of Galicia; then he sailed south where he carried out an unsuccessful attack on Santa Cruz de la Palma. He crossed the ocean until he came in sight of Santo Domingo which he sacked by attacking from land and imposing a tributo de quema. Not content with this, he proceeded to Cartagena, where he also obtained a handsome booty. He returned to England with a huge profit, which nonetheless only just covered his expenses.

Aboard the *Revenge* in 1588 he was part of Admiral Howard's crew who, together with Seymour, fought against the Great Armada sent by Philip II. The devious way in which he captured the Andalucían flagship raised many suspicions. The following year he attempted an act of reprisal against La Coruña attacking the city with eighty ships and 20,000 men. He failed, however, and was removed from command.

His good fortune ended with the expedition he began with John Hawkins in 1595. A sizeable fleet set off for the Caribbean. After the death of Hawkins Drake took command and attempted an assault on San Juan de Puerto Rico, but the encircling manoeuvre which he attempted on land was detected and the assault was repelled.

He continued south where he attacked and torched Río Hacha. He had decided to seize the Mexican silver and for this reason he proceeded to Nombre de Dios, where he met with a well prepared and equipped garrison. He tried to assault Panama but was severely repelled, sustaining 500 casualties. In revenge he destroyed Nombre de Dios. He died of dysentery on 28 January 1596 near Portobelo. His body was placed in a lead coffin and thrown overboard.

DUCASSE, Jean-Baptiste (1646-1715): Born on 2 August 1646 in Saubuse, near Dax. When he carried out his first sea raid he was a ship's boy for the Company of Senegal, boarding in 1677 and sailing several times to Santo Domingo, Florida and Canada.

In March 1686 he joined the French Royal Navy as lieutenant de vaisseau and the following year was promoted to capitaine de frégate. He took part in a campaign against St Kitt's in July 1689 and in early 1690 was put in command of three ships, one tender and one brig to transport 700 men as reinforcements to the isle of San Martín, which was being attacked by the English. After the Spanish attack on the inhabitants of Santa Dominica, Ducasse

sailed to their aid at the end of January 1691, finding what little remained of Cabo Francés.

He participated in the French operations in Guadeloupe in 1691 and in October of that year was appointed Governor of Santa Dominica. In January 1693 Ducasse was promoted to capitaine de vaisseau.

At the beginning of June 1694 he successfully attacked Jamaica and the following year survived the Anglo-Spanish counter-attack, managing to maintain his positions until the arrival of reinforcements from France.

He led the filibusters in the attack against Cartagena de Indias in 1697 but was deceived by de Pointis. In 1700 he resigned from his post as governor and returned to France. One year later, with the Coronation of Philip V of Spain he was sent to the peninsula as Chief of Squadron with the task of defending French interests in Spain and the control of the *asiento de negros*. Philip V promoted him to captain general and with a French squadron he escorted the fleet from Tierra Firme to Cartagena.

At the end of August 1702 he returned to Santa Marta, where he defeated an English squadron of superior strength. On his return he took part in the battle of Vélez Málaga on 24 August 1704, during which he was wounded. After recovering he continued on his escort missions for the Fleets of Nueva España in 1705, 1708 and 1711. As a reward for his services he was appointed lieutenant general of the French Royal Navy in 1707 and received the Golden Fleece from Philip V in April 1712.

In March 1714 Ducasse took command of the forces laying siege to the city of Barcelona, but was forced to retire the following year due to health problems. He died in Bourbon L'Archambauld on 25 June 1715.

ESTRÉES, Jean, Count, later Duke d' (1624-1707): Born on 3 November 1624 in Soleure, now in Switzerland, into an old

family from Picardy. He enlisted in the French army during the Flanders campaigns of 1644-1647. After a brilliant military career he was promoted to lieutenant general in June 1655 and, during the Devolution War of 1667, participated with the French Armada in attacks on Spanish territories in Holland.

He was the Commander of the French squadron at the Battle of Tobago in 1677 and was shipwrecked on the Isle of Aves in May 1678. In 1679 he returned to the Caribbean.

He was appointed Marshal of France in 1681 and led the Mediterranean campaigns, bombarding Tripoli in 1685 and Algiers in 1688. He was made a duke in March 1687 and was Lieutenant General of Brittany in 1701; he died in Paris on 19 May 1707.

EVERTSEN, Cornellis: Dutch filibuster who took part in several campaigns together with Jan Willems. He is mentioned in the operations that took place on the Isle of Pinos in 1685, as well as the campaign against Campeche. Later he participated in the attacks on Jamaica in September 1687 and Honduras in February 1688.

FLORIN, Juan (Juan Florentino, Jean Fleury or Florentine): Possibly the nickname of Giovanni Verrazzano, brother of the famous Florentine cartographer Jerónimo Verrazzano who had settled in France. At the service of François I as a corsair of Jean d'Ango, he established his base between the Azores and the Canaries. He achieved his major success in 1521, when he captured the treasure of Montezuma near the Azores.

After numerous adventures he was captured by Captain Martín Pérez de Irízar in 1527. The mistake of offering a high ransom for his freedom awakened suspicion as to who he was and he was sent to Seville. Once his identity had been confirmed a letter was sent to the king and the prisoner was led to his presence over land. King Charles sent the messenger back with the order to execute Florin the moment their paths crossed. The encounter took place in the port of Pico en route from Toledo to Avila, and he was hanged in the *rollo de justicia* of Colmenar de Arenas, today Monbeltrán.

GRAAF, Laurens Cornelis Boudewijn de, (Lorencillo) (c.1650-1704): It is believed that de Graaf was born in Boost, Holland, around 1650 and was married in the Canary Islands to Petronila de Guzmán. Called Lorencillo by the Spaniards, he was one of the most fearsome freebooters of the 17th century. His wrongdoings began as a member of the artillery on Spanish vessels, in acts of reprisal against the filibusters of Hispaniola, La Tortuga and Jamaica. Captured by these, he decided to join them and became one of their great leaders.

He took part in many operations such as the capture of the *situado* in 1682, the sacking of Veracruz and Cartagena in 1683, the campaigns on Tierra Firme and the sacking of Campeche in 1685. Between 1686 and 1687 he fought against the Spanish forces several times, including the battle of Bajo Alacrán and against the corsairs of Vizcaya.

In 1687 he settled on the Isla Vaca from where he set out on several missions. He was involved in the blockade of Jamaica in 1689 and took an active part in the attacks on Santiago de los Caballeros in 1691 and the sacking of Jamaica in 1694.

The King of Spain offered him an amnesty in exchange for abandoning piracy and joining the Royal Armada. Instead de Graaf accepted to serve Louis XIV, who knighted him and appointed him deputy in the colony of Santa Dominica. During the last days of his life, it appears that he participated in the foundation of the colony of Louisiana. He died in early 1704.

GRAMMONT, François (Agramont): (1650-1686). Born in Paris in about 1650 into a well-to-do family. Legend has it that when he was fourteen he killed a royal officer who was courting his sister, as a result of which he had to go into hiding. He enlisted in the navy under a false name and was rapidly promoted, becoming captain of a frigate at the age of twenty-four. He was short, dark and very active.

He decided to abandon the navy after participating in several campaigns in the Caribbean, which led him to settle on La Tortuga, where he joined the Fraternity and became one of its leaders. He was feared by the Spaniards because of his extreme cruelty to prisoners. He organised assaults on Maracaibo in 1678 and La Guaira in 1680 and took part in the sackings of Veracruz and Campeche in 1683 and 1685, respectively.

It appears that he died when his ship was wrecked in the Straits of Florida in 1686.

GRAND, Pierre le (Peter the Great): A simple man whose career as a buccaneer was also simple, Le Grand was born in Dieppe and appeared in the Caribbean as a pirate. His moment of glory came in 1602: while sailing near Cape Tiburón with twenty-eight companions in a large vessel, they sighted a galleon belonging to the Windward Fleet. They attacked it during the night, captured the ship, set sail for Le Grand's native city and there, later, he sold the vessel. He ended his days as a reputedly honest citizen.

GUZMÁN, Juan, Pérez de (1618-1675): President of the Audiencia of Panama and Knight of the Order of Santiago, de Guzmán was born in Seville and joined the Ocean Armada when he was twenty years old. During his life he sailed in several fleets. He was commander of a company between 1643 and 1647.

In 1651 he returned to the New World and on 19 January 1657 was appointed Governor of Antioquía, in Nueva Granada, although he never occupied the post because he was simultaneously appointed interim Governor of Cartagena. After being promoted to *maestre de campo*, he became Governor of Puerto Rico. On 11 January 1665 he was made president of the Audiencia of Panama and, as such, was active in the recovery of Santa Catalina after Mansfield's occupation.

His good fortune ran out with the arrival of the new Viceroy of Peru, Count Lemos. As a result of disagreements between them, de Guzmán was accused of embezzling a number of bars of silver from the Royal Treasury. Removed from office and arrested in July 1667, he was sent to Peru as a prisoner and his post was taken over by Agustín de Bracamonte. The Council of the Indies exonerated him in January 1668 and ordered him to be reinstated, but the ruling did not reach Peru until a year later.

On 4 February 1669 he sailed from El Callao to Panama aboard the ship *Nuestra Señora de Granada*, arriving in the city two months later to take up his post. In January 1671 he became ill with a disease known as Fuego de San Antonio (a contagious skin disease produced by streptococci, with symptoms that include nausea and high fever).

After Morgan's sacking of Panama, de Guzmán was removed from office on 9 October 1671 with the arrival of the *visitador*, Francisco de Marichalar. Proceedings against de Guzmán lasted from 17 November 1671 to 20 February 1672 and, although he was acquitted, he was by then a shadow of his former self. He returned to Madrid and died in 1675.

HAUSPATER, Johann Adrian (Adrian Juan Pater): One of the great Dutch admirals who took part in the Caribbean campaigns during the first quarter of the 17th century, although he was not so lucky during his period as a corsair. He was taken prisoner in Araya by Luis Fajardo and was sentenced to row in the galleys of Cartagena for three years. He later regained his freedom and went back to piracy.

Sent by the West India Company to establish a colony in Guyana, his attempt failed and he set sail for Panama. He attacked Santa Marta in 1630, taking the city from the fifteen men who were defending it, whom he forced to surrender. He received news that Antonio de Oquendo's huge armada was passing on its way to Brazil and he set off in pursuit and then challenged Oquendo. During the confrontation the Spaniard defeated Hauspater and set fire to his vessel. To avoid burning to death Hauspater jumped into the water and grabbed a rope that was hanging from the ship *Prins Willem*. He finally drowned when his strength gave out on 12 September 1631.

HAWKINS, Sir John (1532-1595): Born in Plymouth into a family of shipbuilders. He became involved in the wine and sugar trade but turned to piracy during the Anglo-French wars.

In 1560 he dropped anchor in the Canaries where he learned of the slave trade from his friend Pedro Ponte, probably via the Spanish ambassador in London, Gomes Suárez de Figueroa, Count of Feria. In 1562 he set out on his first slave-trading expedition – his destination was La Isabela in Hispaniola. His second trip was in 1564, where he traded on the coast of Tierra Firme in the cities of Borburata, Curaçao, Rio Hacha, Santa Marta and Cartagena. Upon his return he shared out large profits and was knighted by Queen Elizabeth.

His third expedition was in 1567. Employing the same methods he made good sales in Margarita and Borburata. In Río Hacha things did not go so well, however, and he 'was forced' to set fire to

the city in order to convince its inhabitants, who had twice refused to do business, that they wished to trade. He was entirely unsuccessful in Cartagena and a storm led him to seek refuge in Veracruz. The Fleet of Nueva España came after him and he confronted it, sustaining numerous casualties, after which he managed to reach Marín, Vigo and finally England.

In 1573 he became navy treasurer and reorganised the Royal Navy to meet the Great Spanish Armada in 1588. In an expedition to the Caribbean in 1595, his luck ran parallel to that of his companion Francis Drake: he died en route to San Juan de Puerto Rico on 22 November due to illness. His body was thrown overboard.

HENDRIJKS, Boudewijn (Balduino Enrico): Considered one of the most important seamen of the Dutch West Indies Company. He was sent to the aid of Bahía but, arriving too late, headed for the Antilles. He attacked San Juan de Puerto Rico, sacking the city and besieging the castle of Morro. Unable to take the castle, he retreated after sustaining a number of casualties. Hendrijks then sailed south, where he assaulted Araya and other minor strongholds. Back in Cuba, he attempted to capture the fleet off the coast of Havana but died of fever in July 1626. His fleet returned to Holland.

HERMITE, Jacob l': A French seaman and Huguenot who took refuge in Holland, where he occupied different posts in the West Indies Company. He directed the Company's first Pacific campaign planning to seize Peruvian silver. He went to sea in 1622 with eleven vessels and 1,600 men heading straight for the Le Maire Straits and the Pacific. He sailed far from the coast to avoid detection and arrived at El Callao on 7 May 1623 – three days after the silver had left for Panama. The city was besieged for 100 days, but to no avail; there were many casualties, including L'Hermite himself. The

fleet returned to Holland after sailing around the world; only two vessels completed the voyage with a small booty.

HEYN, Pieter Pieterszoon (1577-1629): Born in Delfshaven on 15 November 1577. He became a man of the sea when still very young, fighting in the wars against Spain and was taken prisoner in 1597. He was sentenced to the galleys, *ad modum belli*, for four years until he was freed in an exchange of prisoners.

He returned to sea, where he devoted himself to trading and amassing an immense personal fortune. He was appointed director of the Dutch Company of the West Indies, fostering smuggling with the Spanish colonies in America.

In 1622 he was made vice-admiral and took part in the Brazilian campaign, during which he seized twenty-two Portuguese vessels in San Salvador.

After this successful campaign he was given the command of a corsair squadron with which he set out to take a fleet. He achieved this objective in 1628, when he captured the Fleet of Nueva España in the Matanzas Bay.

The booty went to the funds of the West India Company. It was valued at over 11.5 million guilders – 177,000 silver pounds, 66 gold pounds, 1,000 pearls, cochineal, indigo, silks, 37,375 skins, etc. Piet Heyn received only 7,000 guilders from the profits and, dissatisfied with his share, he decided to leave the Company.

His idea was to retire when he returned home but he was promoted to Admiral Lieutenant of Holland in 1629 and was given command of the Dutch naval forces. Sent to destroy the pirates of Dunkirk, he died in combat on 8 June of that year.

HOORN, Nikolaas van (Banoren): Born in Holland, Hoorn was mentioned by Exquemeling, his name also appearing in a number of Spanish documents.

During the Franco-Dutch War (1672-1689) he fought in the North Sea alongside fellow corsairs. He engaged in slave trading in the islands of the French and Spanish colonies, and legend has it that he evaded arrest, probably for illicit trading, ordered by Jean d'Estrées.

At the end of November 1682 he arrived in the Spanish colony of Santo Domingo with 300 slaves. Once there, Governor Francisco de Segura Sandoval confiscated his ship and cargo. Understanding that the actions taken against him were merely in reprisal for the capture of the 'situado' by de Graaf, Hoorn professed his innocence. The governor was of a different opinion and, when he discovered Hoorn's ship to be full of items stolen during his stay in Cadiz, he placed him under arrest aboard his own vessel.

At the beginning of 1683 Hoorn fled to Petit Goave where he was well-received among the freebooters. From then on his career ran parallel to that of de Graaf. He died of gangrene as a consequence of injuries sustained in combat.

HUIDOBRO, Mateo Alonso de: One of the main officers of the Windward Armada, he devoted his life to hunting down well known pirates. He emerged on the scene in 1663, when he contributed 2,000 pesos to the construction of four galleons built in Holland; in return, he was appointed captain of the 572-ton vessel *San Felipe*. The fleet set out in 1667 and arrived in Havana in the autumn of 1668.

In the attack of 1669 he defended Maracaibo against Morgan, but was forced to flee on a barca longa to Mexico with fifty-six men. Initially accused of negligence, he was deported to Spain and tried alongside Alonso de Campos. The Council considered that they had acted boldly and exonerated both men.

He died in 1683 defending the palace of the governor during de Graaf's attack on Veracruz.

IRÍZAR, Martín Pérez de: Born in Rentería, in the province of Guipúzcoa de Irízar was a corsair who served the Emperor with two war galleons of his own. He made important captures, including that of Juan Florin, and was rewarded with a title and coat of arms. He died at the battle of the isle of Alborán, after receiving seven harquebus wounds.

JOL, Cornelis Corneliszoon (Peg Foot): Also known as Cornelius Goll, he was born in Holland at the end of the 16th century. He became a corsair when he was very young and lost his left leg in combat at the age of twenty. His ambition was to capture a fleet and, encouraged by Pieter Heyn's victory, he set off for Cuba in 1629, but had no memorable results. He made two more attempts in 1630 and 1635. In 1633 he joined Diego Lucifer and, with Bellaco y Medio as their admiral, they attacked Campeche and sacked it, later setting fire to the city. Jol attempted to assault Santiago de Cuba in 1638 and two years later, in 1640, he set off in pursuit of Carlos Ibarra's fleet. Having failed to achieve his objective, he withdrew, sustaining great losses in a hurricane that caught him at sea. He died in Holland in 1641.

LECAT, Jelles de (Hels or Ycles): A Frisian at the service of both the Spanish and the English. The first reference to his adventures dates from around 1668 when he was a first officer in Rock Brasiliano's crew.

He took part in the campaign in the Gulf of Mexico and the sacking of Panama together with Henry Morgan. Afterwards, in Jamaica, an attempt was made to capture them but they took refuge in Campeche, where Lecat decided to serve the Spanish

with Reyning. He became a coastguard for some time and nothing more was heard of him after 1673.

LYNCH, Sir Thomas: Governor of Jamaica between 1671 and 1675, and in 1682 and 1684. Born in Cranbrook, Kent, he arrived in the Indies as Officer Junior in the Western Design, 1654, commanded by William Penn. In 1660 he returned to England and, in November of the same year, he requested a passage to Jamaica on one of the king's ships, settling there as a Provost-Marshall. In December 1662, when Windsor arrived in the colony imposing administrative changes, Lynch was appointed Lieutenant Colonel of the Militia. After the establishment of the Council of Jamaica, in April 1663 he was appointed senator and, one year later, president.

Following several disagreements with the governor and other members of the Council, Lynch returned to England. To make the most of his stay in Europe he travelled to Spain and spent the winter in Salamanca learning the language and ways of the people.

His reputation gradually grew and, with the support of the Secretary of State, Lord Arlington, who believed in his talents as a politician, he was considered the person most suitable to put an end to hostilities between the Spanish and the English. In January 1671 he was appointed Governor and Chief of the Naval Forces on Jamaica. He travelled to the Caribbean with a letter for Modyford's arrest – he was accused of '...acting against the King's will and causing havoc and hostilities against the subjects of His Majesty the Catholic King's brother...'.

Lynch remained as head of the island until 1675 when changes in English policy towards Spain led to his being considered pro-Spanish; he was substituted by Vaughan.

In 1682 another change in policy, attempting to satisfy Spanish demands, including putting an end to attacks by Jamaican corsairs, once again saw Lynch as governor of the island. He settled permanently in Jamaica with his family and died there on 24 August 1684.

MANSFIELD, Edward (Mansvelt or Mansafar): Mansfield was born in Holland but became a corsair at the service of the English. He was appointed Admiral of the Fraternity of the Brothers of the Coast and was the mentor of many well known freebooters, including Henry Morgan.

Mansfield was probably involved in the assault of Santiago de Cuba together with Christopher Myngs in 1662. One year later he participated in the sack of Campeche, in the actions on Sancti Espíritus in December 1665, in the campaign against Cartago in April 1666 and in the assault on Santa Catalina.

He died one year later in La Tortuga under strange circumstances, probably by poisoning.

MARTIEN, David: A Dutch vagabond who served under French and English colours. He was a veteran commander of the West Indies when he joined Morris in his adventures in the Gulf of Mexico.

MIGUEL, Blas de: A Cuban corsair, probably a mulatto, who attempted to murder Lorencillo in Petit Goave in revenge for the death of his brother, who was abandoned during the encounter with Miguel de Salaverria. He was taken prisoner and put on trial the following day; Miguel and his two lieutenants were sentenced to be 'broken alive on the wheel', while the rest of the prisoners were hanged.

MODYFORD, Sir Thomas (c. 1620-1679): He was Governor of Barbados between 1660 and 1664 and Governor of Jamaica between 1664 and 1671. Son of the mayor of Exeter, he was born in about 1620. After

the Civil War, during which he fought on the side of the royalists, he attempted to settle in Barbados where he bought a 500-acre plantation and assumed the leadership of the community. He was a member of the Council of Barbados and, with the restoration of the monarchy in 1660, he was appointed governor.

By virtue of his friendship with George Monck and the latter's influence with the king, in February 1664 Modyford was proposed as Windsor's successor in the government of Jamaica, a post he took up in May.

His government stood out for its permissiveness and issue of letters of marque for those who engaged in hostile actions against the Spanish.

In 1671 he was removed from office, arrested and imprisoned in the Tower of London for a little more than a year. After the change of policy in 1675 he was allowed to return to Jamaica, where he died in September 1679.

MOLESWORTHY, Hender: Interim Governor of Jamaica, substituted Lynch in 1684.

MORGAN, Henry (c.1635-1688): Born in Penkarne or Llanrhymny, Wales, in about 1635 into a military family. At the age of nineteen he joined the disastrous expedition of the Western Design as a subordinate member of the crew, and stayed on in Jamaica. During the administrative reshuffle carried out by Windsor, he was appointed Captain of the Regiment in Port Royal. Other sources place him in Barbados where he must have arrived as a *siervo* (lackey), travelling later to Jamaica.

He received a letter of marque and sailed with Commodore Christopher Myngs's squadron in October 1662 for the campaign against Santiago de Cuba. With Morris he took part in the Tabasco campaign in the

spring of 1665 and in Central America during the summer of the same year.

Morgan led the assault on Puerto Príncipe in April 1668 and later the attacks against Portobelo in July 1668, Maracaibo in March 1669, the recovery of Santa Catalina during Christmas 1670 and finally the sacking of Panama in January 1671.

He was arrested and transferred to London in August 1672, although he was never tried. Having been knighted, he returned to Jamaica two years later as Lieutenant Governor to Lord Vaughan, holding the post until removed from office in 1678. He was interim governor for a few months in 1681.

He spent his last years at the head of a plantation and as a member of the upper classes of Jamaican society. He died of dropsy in 1688.

MORRIS, John (1658-72): Born in Jamaica in 1658. It is believed that he took part in an assault on Campeche and Santiago de Cuba together with Myngs and received a letter of marque from Governor Lord Windsor. In June 1664, Morris and a few other captains ignored the order to cease hostilities under the protection of the old letters of marque, and continued the assaults. In 1665 Morris took part in the campaigns against Tabasco and Central America.

Between 1668 and 1671 he was Morgan's lieutenant and joined him in all his actions. When Morgan was taken back to England as a prisoner, the new governor, Sir Thomas Lynch, recommended Morris as 'a good comrade, a good pilot and one who had never been a pirate as far as he knew…'.

MYNGS, Sir Christopher (1625-1666): An officer of the Royal Navy born into a well-to-do family from Norfolk. In May 1653 he boarded the *Elizabeth* during the first Anglo-Dutch war, taking command after the captain was killed during a skirmish with the Dutch when returning from the Mediterranean.

In October 1655 he was promoted to commander of the ship *Marston Moore*, recently returned to Jamaica. Having suffered a great number of hardships in the Indies, the crew mutinied in protest for not having received their pay. In spite of his popularity, Myngs was arrested by the Jamaican command for having supported his men.

He took part in the military actions encouraged from Jamaica and, in 1658, actively participated in its defence. The following year he fostered an act of reprisal against Tierra Firme, attacking Cumaná, Puerto Cabello and Coro. The loss of part of the booty was the cause of Myngs's arrest. He was sent to England but was returned by virtue of his loyal support of King Charles II.

In August 1662 he returned to Jamaica and led the military campaigns organised from there. The most outstanding of these was the destruction of Santiago de Cuba. One year later he took part in the sacking of Campeche.

In late 1664, during the second Anglo-Dutch war, he was promoted to vice-admiral. He served bravely in the battle of Lowestoft in June 1665 and was knighted for his courage and fervour. After the winter patrols he commanded the *Victory* in the Four Days' Fight in June 1666, during which he was wounded several times in the hand and shoulder, never once leaving the bridge. A few days later he succumbed to his wounds at his home in Goodman Fields, Whitechapel.

NAU, Jean David (El Olonés) (1630-1668): Born in Sables d'Olonne in the French region of Poitou in 1630. At the age of twenty he travelled to the Caribbean as an engagé; then he became a buccaneer in Hispaniola and finally a freebooter in the Fraternity of the Brothers of the Coast. He

was especially notorious for the extreme cruelty he showed his prisoners.

He set out for Campeche, where he was shipwrecked and, only after numerous mishaps, managed to reach La Tortuga. In 1668 he captured a frigate near Key Fragoso in Cuba and put its entire crew to the sword. He entered into an association with Miguel el Vasco and other freebooters with whom he attacked Maracaibo and Gibraltar in 1668, seizing substantial booty and severely mistreating their inhabitants. Upon his return he planned to take Nicaragua, but instead he sailed to Honduras, where he stormed Puerto Caballos. After many desertions he was left with only one of his ships, with which he ended up in Darien. The local cannibals avenged all his victims by eating him alive.

OGERON, Bertrand, Sieur de la Bouère d' (1613-1676): The third son of a merchant of the same name, d'Ogeron was born in Rochefort and baptised on March 19 1613. In October 1653, a few months before the death of his father, he became a captain in the Marine Corps.

He arrived in the isle of Martinique in the New World in 1657 and was wounded two years later at the end of the Franco-Spanish war. He took part in a few campaigns on the west coast of Santo Domingo and later lost all his possessions in a shipwreck but managed to return to France in 1660. While preparing his return to the New World in 1662 he joined the French West Indies Company. In 1663 he was one of the thirty men who founded the first colony on the west coast of Hispaniola, Léogane (the French pronunciation of the Spanish name La Yaguana or L'Yaguane).

In the spring of 1664 he was appointed Governor of La Tortuga although he did not occupy the post until 6 June 1665.

In 1668 he travelled to France to attend personal business and, in his absence, de Pouançay acted as his substitute. He

returned to the colony in August 1669 to find resentment rife among the buccaneers due to the severe conditions imposed by the Company. A revolt took place in the spring, forcing d'Ogeron to abandon the island. He was not able to regain control until months later thanks to the aid of vessels and men sent by the Governor of the Windward Isles, Jean Charles Baas-Castelmore, and after offering the filibusters a general amnesty.

He led the disastrous campaign on Puerto Rico in 1673 and returned to Paris in search of a new destiny; but he contracted dysentery and died on January 31 1676 before being received by the king or by Colbert.

PEZ Y MALZARRAGA, Andrés del: An officer of the Ocean Armada and pirate hunter, Pez y Malzarraga was born in Cadiz in 1657, the son of an officer of the Ocean Armada. He enlisted at the age of sixteen and, on 2 July 1672, was part of the Spanish-Dutch squadron that sailed to Palermo during the war with France, where his father and brother were both killed.

In 1681 he was assigned to ships that served as reinforcement to the Windward Armada and, in the summer of 1683, was promoted to captain to command the 8-cannon vessel *Jesús, María y José*, otherwise known as *The Sevillano*.

In 1683 he took part in the defence of Cartagena de Indias and in the battle of El Bajo del Alacrán, where he almost managed to capture de Graaf.

PHIPS, Sir William (1650-1695): Born in 1650 on a plantation near the Kennebeck River in Maine, Phips was the son of an immigrant from Bristol, England. His father died when William was a child and he grew up in poverty.

In 1668 he arrived in Boston and became a carpenter's apprentice. He was a tall, strong man and soon began to travel and trade between the Bahamas and the West Indies. During these voyages he learned of the position of several Spanish vessels in the Caribbean. He married the widow of a rich merchant and she provided him with funds for his expeditions.

He had a great reputation as a treasure hunter, especially known for his find near New Providence of a ship thought to be the *Nuestra Señora de las Maravillas*, sunk in 1656, and for his greatest success, the recovery of the *Nuestra Señora de la Pura y Limpia Concepción*, sunk in 1641.

After several more or less successful expeditions, he travelled to England in 1691. Thanks to his contacts in London and his considerable fortune, he was appointed Governor of Massachusetts and returned to Boston in May 1692.

He died suddenly on 18 February 1695.

PICARD, Pierre le: A French filibuster who carried out campaigns in the Caribbean, the Southern Sea and North America. He was a member of El Olonés's band until they went their separate ways in Panama. In 1668-1669 he led attacks in Veragua. During the Franco-Dutch war it seems he became a corsair at the service of France and after the peace of Nimega he turned renegade. Between 1685 and 1687 he took part in the campaigns of the Southern Seas. He was last heard of on Rhode Island a few years later.

POINTIS, Bernard-Jean-Louis de Saint Jean, Baron de (1645-1707): De Pointis enrolled in the Royal Armada in January 1672, taking part in several combats. In 1677 he was a lieutenant in d'Estrées's second campaign against Tobago. His naval career continued in the Mediterranean and he took part as an artillery lieutenant general in the War of La Liga in 1689. He returned to sea and, in 1696, commanded the naval squadron sent to reinforce the colony of Santa Dominica.

In October 1699 he was promoted to rear admiral and, during the Spanish War of Succession, commanded the *Magnanime* at the Battle of Velez Málaga on 24 August 1704. Seven months later his five-vessel squadron, separated from the rest of the forces during the blockade of Gibraltar, had a disastrous encounter with the squadron of Vice-Admiral Sir John Leake. Three of the ships were captured and the other two, including de Pointis's, were deliberately set on fire.

He died in France on 24 April 1707.

PORTUGUÉS, Bartolomeu: Although born in Portugal, he operated with a letter of marque from the Governor of Jamaica. His first action, in 1662, was to seize a Spanish vessel off the coast of Manzanillo (Cuba) and arm it with four cannons. One year later he captured a merchant ship carrying 100,000 pounds of cocoa and 75,000 escudos in cash. With his new ship he intended to attack Campeche but was captured, tried and sentenced to death. He managed to escape and returned to Campeche, where he seized a ship with which he attempted to return to Jamaica. Shipwrecked in the Jardines de Cuba, he eventually reached his destination after several mishaps.

POUANÇAY, Jacques Nepveu, Sieur de: Fifth French Governor of La Tortuga and Santa Dominica and a prominent instigator of privateering. De Pouançay was the elder of two sons born to Jeanne, older sister of d'Ogeron, and her husband, Thomas Nepveu. He served with his uncle for a few years and substituted him as Governor of La Tortuga during his absence.

He was officially appointed governor on 16 March 1676, substituting de Cussy, who was interim governor at the time. His main objective was to refloat the economy of La Tortuga through piracy and to reinforce the colony of Santo Domingo, where

opportunities were greater – hence his policy of uninterrupted hostilities against his neighbours on Hispaniola, despite the peace treaty between France and Spain.

The intensity of the attacks against Spanish colonies fostered by de Pouançay, fruit of his belief in an imminent Spanish attack, increased after the arrival of Van Hoorn, who joined forces with those of de Graaf, forming a genuine army that perpetrated the boldest attacks of the 17th century.

On 30 September 1683 de Pouançay was replaced by de Cussy as governor of the colony.

REYES, Diego (Diego Grillo or Diego the Mulatto): A mulatto from Havana who operated in La Tortuga and attacked Spanish vessels at the service of the French. He sailed on Jean Lucas's 15-cannon ship and was captured by Mateo Alonso de Huidobro in October 1673. He was eventually hanged in Veracruz.

REYNING, Jan Erasmus (1640-1697): Born in Vlissingen in 1640, Reyning was the son of a sailor from Copenhagen who died in a sea battle during the first Anglo-Dutch war. In 1665-67, during the second Anglo-Dutch War, Reyning was captured and imprisoned in Ireland for eighteen months.

After a brief re-encounter with his wife and children he set sail for Surinam. In 1667 he arrived in the Antilles intending to re-establish the Dutch colony of Cayenne that had been destroyed by the French three years earlier. The French then returned and took him to Martinique as a prisoner, where he served as an oarsman at the service of the retired Governor Robert Le Frichot des Friches, master of Clodore.

Reyning managed to flee to Santo Domingo and became the servant of a buccaneer, who soon set him free. He returned to the Cayman Islands in 1668 and founded his own company of corsairs, with

Jamaican letters of marque, as Captain Casten of Amsterdam.

With this company he reached Port Royal and joined Lecat and Brasiliano. Having been involved in a number of actions in Nueva España, Reyning left Mexico by crossing the Yucatan. He arrived in Caracas where he found a new associate, Francisco Galesio, with whom he captured several English vessels in 1673.

Once the peace treaty was signed between Holland and England in February 1674, Reyning returned to Granada and joined up with Hurriaen Aernouts. Together they attacked Granada, but were captured by the French and taken to a plantation in Martinique. They attempted to flee to Curaçao in a canoe but were caught in a storm that carried them to Maracaibo. Being under suspicion, they were imprisoned for a time by the Spanish. Reyning arrived in Curaçao some time later.

In early 1676 he travelled to Amsterdam to see his family. Here he was appointed commander of an 8-cannon frigate named *The Fortuyn*, part of Admiral Jacob Binckes's expedition, with whom he joined in the battles of Tobago.

Once the war was over, he formed a company for the Spanish Crown to transport slaves from Curaçao to Nueva España. After facing many problems at the hands of corrupt local Spanish authorities, he returned to Holland. The Admiralty named him commander and he then took part in the war of the Great Alliance aboard the 44-cannon *Drakestein* with 170 men. In 1694 he bombarded Brest and was promoted to Extraordinaris-Kapitein for his courage.

Reyning died on 4 February 1697 escorting a convoy to Bilbao. He and his men were caught in a storm while awaiting the high tide. Almost 400 men perished.

RIVERO, Pardal Manoel: A Portuguese corsair, Rivero received his license from Pedro de Ulloa, Governor of Cartagena, on 3 January 1670, taking advantage of the fact that Queen Mariana de Austria had authorised such licenses on 20 April 1669.

After numerous operations, he was shot in the throat and killed by John Morris, Morgan's lieutenant.

RODERIGO, Pieter: Of Flemish origin. In the summer of 1674 Aernouts's campaign conquered the French Acadia, renaming it New Holland. Despite the fact that the English were neutral during the Franco-Dutch war, their ships were attacked by Roderigo and his men, who were finally captured, were accused of piracy and condemned to death, although they were later exonerated. During the Indian conflict known as the War of King Philip, they fought courageously in defence of the English colony.

ROVERBAL, Jean François de la Roque (M. de la Roche or Roberto Baal): A French nobleman who sought to make his fortune through piracy. He took part in the voyages of discovery to Canada. His exploits began in the Caribbean with the capture of Santa Marta. In 1544 he assaulted Cartagena de Indias, where he seized a substantial booty. He then captured a merchant vessel off the coast of Santiago de Cuba and later failed in his attempt to storm Havana.

SEARLE, Robert: Searle was one of the most active Jamaican pirates. He was mentioned for the first time in 1658 when he bought a 60-ton ship armed with eight cannons, which he renamed *The Cagway*. In 1662 he joined forces with Myngs in the assault of Santiago de Cuba.

After peace was signed in 1670 he took part in the reconquest of New Providence, which had been stormed by a Spanish regiment. Taking advantage of his success, he launched an attack against the colony of San Agustín, Florida. He was arrested by Governor Modyford when he returned to Port Royal.

After Rivero Pardal's attack on Jamaica, Searle was a member of Morgan's punitive expedition to Panama.

SHARP, Bartholomew: Born in 1650 in London, Sharp became a corsair during the second Anglo-Dutch war between 1665 and 1667. Together with Dampier he seized Segovia in 1675. His first known action took place in the summer of 1679 when, with a band of French, English and others, he sacked the Bay of Honduras. In an alliance with Allison, Coxon, Cornelius Essex and Tomas Magott, he sacked Portobelo under Coxon's command. Sharp participated in the campaign in the Pacific and returned to England in 1682.

Arrested and charged with piracy, he was tried at the Admiralty and exonerated for lack of evidence in controversial proceedings that raised protests from the Spanish embassy.

He returned to the Caribbean on his own ship and received a letter of marque from Neville, Governor of Jamaica, in January 1684. It is suspected that he took part in the assault on Campeche in July 1685, together with Lorencillo and Gramond. At the end of 1686 and in January 1687, Neville accused him of piracy, but he was once again exonerated due to lack of evidence. In 1688 Sharp was appointed commander of the northern part of the Windward Isles.

In the summer of 1699 he was imprisoned for misconduct by the Danish authorities of Santo Tomás.

STRONG, John: An English corsair and treasure-hunter in the service of William Phips and Sir John Narborough; a very successful diver in search of sunken goods from his vessel *The Concepción*. He attempted similar operations in the Southern Sea and died in La Coruña in 1694.

TESTU, Guillaume le (Giraldo Testu): Le Testu's guarantor was Philippo Strozzi, a relative of Catalina de Medicis. He carried out several violent actions in the Caribbean in the early 1570s. His most outstanding was an alliance with Drake in the Isthmus of Panama. He was shot dead when retreating from a battle.

WINDSOR, Lord Thomas, Seventh Baron of Windsor and First Duke of Plymouth (c.1627-1687): Windsor was the first royalist Governor of Jamaica between 1660 and 1664. An outstanding trait of his policy was that he allowed attacks against Spanish interests even in peacetime.

Born in Kew, Surrey, in about 1627 to a Norman family, he served in the Royalist Cavalry during the civil war and later continued to fight against Cromwell's protectorate. Once the monarchy was restored he was reinstated as seventh Baron of Windsor and Lord Lieutenant of Worcestershire. Thanks to a recommendation from the Committee for Foreign Plantations in the summer of 1661, he was appointed to replace Colonel d'Oyley as Governor of Jamaica.

He took up this post in April 1662 and sent out letters to the Governors of Puerto Rico and Santo Domingo demanding permission to trade. He raised the salaries of the regiment, which he transformed into five militia regiments distributed around the island.

He concluded the works of the port fortress, which he named Fort Charles. He also offered land for settlement to all colonists over the age of twelve, as well as establishing a court and an admiralty.

The greatest change he introduced was after news reached him that the Spanish governors had forbidden trade. His response was a proposal to trade 'by force'.

Windsor recruited freebooters, whom he placed under Myngs's command and sent to assault and destroy Santiago de Cuba in 1662. He returned to England at the end of that year, leaving Sir Charles Lyttelton in his place. The court was upset by this and removed him from office in February 1663. He was replaced by Sir Thomas Modyford.

Windsor was offered no further post until 1676, when he was appointed the Duke of York's Master of the Horse. Five years later he was made Governor of Portsmouth and died in November 1687.

ENDNOTES

PROLOGUE

1. Casado Soto, José Luis: *Los Barcos Españoles y la Gran Armada de 1588*. Madrid: San Martín, 1988.
2. The League of the Cinq Ports was created with the aim of protecting the privileges and commercial interests of the important ports on the southeastern coast of England.
3. The ports of southwestern England saw their privileges in danger and formed a league that opposed the pretensions of the Cinq Ports.
4. The seafaring towns around Bayona formed an association. This relationship between the Cantabrian ports was maintained until the 19th century.
5. Fernández Duro, Cesáreo: *La Marina de Castilla*. Madrid: Reedición Editmex SL, 1995.
6. Fernández Duro: op. cit., pp.67 and 94.
7. August 10 1350: Mensaje del rey de Inglaterra al arzobispo de Canterbury. In Fernández Duro: op. cit., pp.418-419.
8. Ibid., pp.99-108.
9. Ibid., p.105.
10. Gosse, Philip: *The History of Piracy*, London: Longman, Green & Co, 1932.
11. Ibid., pp.117-118.
12. Fernández Duro: op. cit., p.245.
13. Letter of marque to Harry Paye. In Marsden, R.G. (editor): *Documents Relating to Law and Custom of the Sea*. Navy Records Society, 1915, Vol. I, pp.112-114.
14. Fernández Duro: op. cit., pp.167-168.
15. Ibid., p.173.
16. Ibid., p.177.
17. Gosse: op. cit., pp.26-27.
18. Azcárraga y Bustamante, José Luis: *El Corso Marítimo: Concepto, Justificación e Historia*. Madrid: Instituto Francisco de Vitoria, 1950.

CHAPTER 1

1. Lucena Salmoral, Manuel: *Piratas, Bucaneros, Filibusteros y Corsarios en América*. Madrid: Mapfre, 1992, p.52.
2. Real Academia de la Historia (RAH), Colección Muñoz, LXXXV, f.144 v.
3. *Recopilación de las Leyes de los Reinos y de las Yndias*, Vol. V, Book III, Title XIII, Law 4. Madrid: 1681.
4. Lucena: op. cit., p.53.
5. Sáiz Cidoncha, Carlos: *Historia de la Piratería en América Española*. Madrid: San Martín, 1985, p.20.
6. Lucena: op. cit., p.54, quoting Morineau, Jean: *Tels étaient corsaires et flibustiers*. Paris: 1957, p.51.
7. Sáiz Cidoncha: op. cit., p.20.
8. Memoria de las joyas, plumejes y otras cosas enviadas al Emperador desde Nueva España. RAH, Col. Muñoz, LXXVI, f.209.
9. Díaz del Castillo, Bernal: 'Verdadera Historia de los Sucesos de la Conquista de Nueva España, por el Capitán'. In *Historiadores Primitivos de las Indias*, Vol. II, t. XXVI. Biblioteca de Autores Españoles. Madrid: Atlas, 1947, p.205.
10. Díaz del Castillo: op. cit., pp.206-207.
11. Biblioteca Museo Naval (BMN), Ms. 70 and Ms. 72.
12. Díaz del Castillo: op. cit., p.205.
13. Lucena: op. cit., p.55.
14. Díaz del Castillo: op. cit., p.206.
15. Ibid., p.207.
16. Jármy Chapa, M. de: *Un Eslabón Perdido de la Historia. Piratería en el Caribe Siglo XVI y XVII*. Mexico: UNAM, 1983.
17. Sáiz Cidoncha: op. cit., p.22.
18. Archivo General de Indias (AGI), Contaduría General, 1872.
19. Lucena: op. cit., p.57.
20. Picó, F.: *Historia General de Puerto Rico*. Río Piedras: Huracán, p.53.
21. Lucena: op. cit., p.57.
22. Fernández Duro, Cesáreo: *Armada Española, Desde la Unión de los Reinos de Castilla y Aragón*. Madrid: Reedición MNM, 1972. Vol. I, p.207.
23. Sáiz Cidoncha: op. cit., p.23.
24. Carta del Teniente Corregidor de Cádiz al Consejo de Indias. RAH, Col. Muñoz, LXXV, f.54 v.
25. Asalto a la Habana en 1537. De Bry: *América De Bry (1590-1634)*. Madrid: Siruela, 1992, p.23.
26. Sáiz Cidoncha: op. cit., p.28. Also Picó: op. cit., p.54.
27. Pezuela, Jacobo de la: *Historia de la Isla de Cuba*. Madrid: 1968. T. I, pp.182-183.
28. Santa Marta, November 1 1543. RAH, Muñoz, T. LXXXIII, f.105.
29. RAH, Muñoz, T. LXXXIII, f.106.
30. De Bry: *América De Bry (1590-1634)*. Madrid: Siruela, 1992, p.28. Also RAH, Muñoz, LXXXIII, f.231. The pilot he cites was a Sevillian named Juan Álvarez.
31. Sáiz Cidoncha: op. cit., p.25.
32. Carta de los oficiales de la Casa de Contratación, April 1545. RAH, Muñoz, LXXXIV, f.68 v.
33. Sáiz Cidoncha: op. cit., p.25.
34. Lucena: op. cit., p.58.
35. Recopilación…. Vol. IV Book III, Title XIII, Law 5.
36. Lucena: op. cit., p.64.
37. Santo Domingo, May 11 1553. RAH, Muñoz, LXXXVI, f.258 v.
38. Ibid.
39. Ibid., f.251 v.
40. Carta del Gobernador Angulo al Emperador. December 23 1553. Colección de Documentos de Indias, Segunda Serie, Vol. III, p.260.
41. Fernández Duro: op.cit., Vol. I, p.280.
42. *Relación de Diego de Mazariegos sobre la entrada, toma, saqueo que hizo en la Habana el corsario francés Jacques de Soria…el mes de julio de dicho año*. July 10 1555. BMN, Mn. 38, Doc. 17.
43. Mota, F.: *Piratas en el Caribe*. Havana: Casa de las Américas, 1984, p.35.
44. Gall, J. and F.: *El Filibusterismo*. Mexico: F.C.E., 1957.
45. Haring, C.H.: *The Buccaneers in the West Indies in the XVIIIth Century*. London: Methuen, 1910, p.51.
46. Recopilación…. Vol. IV, Book III, Title XIII, Law 8.
47. Documents Relating to…. Vol. I, p.162.
48. Recopilación…, ibid.
49. Sáiz Cidoncha: op. cit., p.31.
50. LHe was called Jean Beautemps.
51. Lucena: op. cit., pp.65-66.
52. Simón, Fray Pedro: *Noticias Historiales de las conquistas de Tierra Firme en las Indias Occidentales*. Nuevo Reino de Granada: 1624. Reprinted in Bogotá in 1892.
53. Relación que se ha tenido en el Consejo de las Indias y noticia de los robos que corsarios franceses han hecho en el Mar de Poniente, en navegación de las Yndias…. BMN, Mn. 38, Doc. 34.
54. Lucena: op. cit., p.67.

CHAPTER 2

1. Cecil told the Spanish ambassador in London that the Privy Council opposed the extension of the ban on trade with the Indies.
2. Documents Relating to… Vol. I, p.172.
3. Georget, Henry and Eduardo Rivero: *Herejes en el Paraíso. Corsarios y navegantes ingleses en las costas de Venezuela durante la segunda mitad del siglo XVI*. Caracas: Arte, 1993, p.41.
4. Georget: op. cit., p.42.
5. Rumeu de Armas, A: *Viajes de Hawkins a América*. Seville: 1947. See also Richard Hakluyt: *Principal Navigations, Voyages, Traffiques and Discoveries of the English Nation*. London: Hakluyt Societ, 1847-1852, Vol. II.
6. Lucena Salmoral, Manuel: *Piratas, Bucaneros, Filibusteros y Corsarios en América*. Madrid: Mapfre, 1992, p.72.
7. Rumeu: op. cit., p.246.
8. One year earlier, in 1563, the Queen had commissioned Thomas Stucley to make a voyage of discovery to Florida on condition that he remain there for two years.
9. Lucena: op. cit., p.72.
10. Georget: op. cit., p.42.
11. Testimony of John Sparke. In Hakluyt, Vol. X, pp.9-63. Cited in the Spanish edition of Georget: op. cit., pp.61-115.
12. Lucena: op. cit., p.74.
13. Lucena: op. cit., p.72.
14. Sáiz Cidoncha, Carlos: *Historia de la Piratería en América Española*. Madrid: San Martín, 1985, p.55.
15. According to others, on the 18th. See Lucena, op. cit., p.75.
16. Some sources state that the attack was planned in connivance with the Treasurer, basing their suppositions on the account by the Comisario of the Audiencia de Santo Domingo, Alonso Pérez Roldán. See Lucena, op. cit., quoting Restrepo Tirado, E.: *Historia de la Provincia de Santa Marta*. Bogotá: Biblioteca de Autores Colombinos, 1953, Vol. I, p.230.
17. Or sold, which seems to be more likely.
18. Sáiz: op. cit., p.56.
19. AGI, Justicia 38.
20. Lucena: op. cit., p.78.
21. Testimonio de Job Hortop, in Hakluyt, Vol. IX, pp.448 and following. See also Georget, op. cit., pp.44 and following.
22. González, Tomás: *Apuntamientos para la Historia del rey Felipe II, por lo tocante a sus relaciones con la reina Isabel de Inglaterra*. Madrid: Memorias de la Real Academia de la Historia, Vol. II, 1832.
23. Letter from Guerau de Spes to the Duke of Alba, London, December 14 1571. AGS, Estado 824, in Colección de Documentos Inéditos para la Historia de España.
24. According to Rumeu, op. cit., pp.249-250, it was on this occasion that the attack was simulated.
25. Sáiz: op. cit., p.59.
26. Juarez Moreno, Juan: *Piratas y Corsarios en Veracruz y Campeche*. Seville: CSIC, 1972, p.19.
27. Relación del suceso de la Armada y Flota de Nueva España en el puerto de San Juan de Ulúa con el corsario Juan de Aquines, en el mes de septiembre de 1568. BMN, Ms. 31, Doc. 83.
28. Before Veracruz was moved to its current site, the port was known as San Juan de Ulúa and the islet opposite was called Isla Gallega. Sáiz, op. cit., p.60.
29. Jiménez Rueda, Julio: *Corsarios Franceses e Ingleses en la Inquisición de Nueva España*. Mexico: Archivo General de la Nación, UNAM, 1945.
30. Recognisance of his ships commissioned to search for contraband and to take pirates. November 15 1571. In Documents Relating to…, p.190.
31. *Recopilación de las Leyes de los Reinos y de las Yndias*, Vol. IV, Book III, Title XIV, Law 5.
32. Ibid.
33. Lucena: op. cit., p.99.
34. Lucena: op. cit., p.100.
35. Its presence was known. AGI, Ind. 427, L. 30, f. 232 r and v.
36. Le Testu was an old acquaintance. On his ship *La Condesa* he had carried out several robberies in 1571. BMN, Ms. 38, Doc. 34. He also committed robbery on Hispaniola. The Spanish ambassador in Paris unsuccessfully claimed back what had been stolen. AGI, Patronato 267, R. 57.
37. In *Sir Francis Drake Revived*, a work by his nephew Francis, son of Thomas Drake, published in 1626, the scene is described in which Drake climbed to the crest of the mountain range that

crosses the isthmus, and, from the top of a tree, the runaway slave chief showed him the Pacific. On his knees, Drake begged God to allow him to 'sail this sea once again on an English ship'.

38. It seems probable that in his fantastic account he confused Veracruz with Venta Cruz or Venta Cruces, which he assaulted and razed to the ground.

39. Letter from Cristóbal Moner, BMN, Ms. 38, Doc. 38.

40. Relación de los daños que los corsarios Yngleses hicieron en la Carrera de las Yndias en S.M. puertos y costas de ellas y sus vasallos…desde el año 1568 hasta 1573. BMN, Ms. 38, Doc. 36.

41. Fernández Duro, Cesáreo: *Armada Española, Desde la Unión de los Reinos de Castilla y Aragón*. Madrid: Reedición MNM, 1972. Vol, I, p.344.

42. Hakluyt, Richard: *El viaje del patrón Andrew Barker, de Bristol, en el año de 1576*. In Georget, op. cit., pp.117-125.

43. Georget: op. cit., p.48.

44. Documents relating to…, pp.234-244.

45. Kamen, Henry: *La Inquisición Española. Una revisión crítica*. Barcelona: Crítica, 1999, p.274.

46. According to Serrano Mangas, the surname Aponte/Ponte was characteristic of the Jewish convert community of Fregenal.

47. Serrano Mangas, Fernando: *La Segura Travesía del Agnus Dei. Ignorancia y Malevolencia en Torno a la Figura de Benito Arias Montano 'El Menor'*. Villanueva de la Serena (Badajoz): Diputación de Badajoz-Editora Regional de Extremadura, 1999.

48. Zamora, Padre Alonso de: *Historia de la Provincia de San Antonio del Nuevo Reino de Granada*. Impreso 1701, Libro IV, Cap. III, p.280.

49. *Relación de lo que declaró un inglés llamado Francisco que se perdió en una pinaza de la armada del capitán Francisco Drac y fue preso en la cienaga de Santa Marta. Monday, 24 March 1586*. BMN, Ms. 38, Doc. 56.

50. *Relación de los daños que se entiende han hecho las Armadas que salieron de Ynglaterra y Tregelingas en la costa de Portugal y Galicia, en todo septiembre de 1585*. BMN, Ms. 38, Doc. 50.

51. Simón, Fray Pedro: *Noticias Historiales de las conquistas de Tierra Firme en las Indias Occidentales*. Nuevo Reino de Granada: 1624. Reprinted in Bogotá in 1892, p.257.

52. Moya Pons, Frank: *Manual de Historia Dominicana*. Santo Domingo: Caribbean Publishers, 1995, p.46.

53. Lucena: op. cit., p.107.

54. Ibid.

55. Lucena: op. cit., p.108.

56. Warning had reached the colony from Cartagena. AGI, Patronato 266, R. 51.

57. Lucena: op. cit., p.109.

58. Fernández Duro: op. cit., p.399.

CHAPTER 3

1. Casado Soto, José Luis: *Los Barcos Españoles y la Gran Armada de 1588*. Madrid: San Martín, 1988. pp.158 and following.

2. Casualty list in Casado, op. cit.

3. Hakluyt, Richard: *Principal Navigations*.

4. González-Arnao Conde-Luque, Mariano: *Derrota y Muerte de Sir Francis Drake*. A Coruña 1589-Portobelo 1596. Xunta de Galicia: 1995.

5. González-Arnao: op. cit., p.53. See also John Norris: *The Expedition of Sir John Norris and Sir Francis Drake to Spain and Portugal, 1589*. London: Ed. R.B. Wernham, Navy Record Society, 1988.

6. González-Arnao: op. cit., p.55.

7. Ibid., p.92.

8. Ibid., p.96.

9. Lucena Salmoral, Manuel: *Piratas, Bucaneros, Filibusteros y Corsarios en América*. Madrid: Mapfre, 1992, p.112.

10. Ibid., p.280.

11. González-Arnao: op. cit., p.128.

12. Ibid., p.129.

13. Ibid., p.130.

14. Ibid., p.149.

15. Cumberland received his commission for this campaign on February 21 1592. Commission to the Earl of Cumberland to Capture Spaniards, with Authority to Divide the Spoil. Documents Relating to…, p.279.

16. González-Arnao: op. cit., p.117.

17. Ibid., p.219.

18. Hakluyt: *Principal Navigations*, Vol. II.

19. Letter from the licenciado Manso de Contreras to the King. Margarita, June 4 1592. AGI Santo Domingo, 184.

20. Appleby Manuscript in Andrews, pp.242-253. Samuel Purchas, Hakluyt Postumus, Vol. XVI, pp.18-22, in Georget and Rivero: op. cit. pp.127-139.

21. Interrogation ordered by Captain Felipe de Linares y Torrellas. La Asunción, May 29 1593. In Vicente Dávila: Encomiendas…, Vol. II, pp.154-158.

22. Testimony of William Parker. In Hakluyt, Vol. X, pp.277-280. Georget, op. cit., pp.245-248.

23. Testimony of William Parker. In Purchas, Vol. XVI, pp.292-297. Georget, op. cit., pp.267-274.

24. Fernández Duro, Cesáreo: *Armada Española, Desde la Unión de los Reinos de Castilla y Aragón*. Madrid: Reedición MNM, 1972. Vol. III, pp.117-133.

25. Rumeu de Armas, A: *Viajes de Hawkins a América*. Seville: 1947. See also Richard Hakluyt: *Principal Navigations*.

26. Sir Francis Drake and Sir John Hawkins to Queen Elizabeth. Plymouth, August 13 1595 (E.c.) PRO. SP. 12/253 n∫ 79l.

27. Maynarde, Thomas: *Sir Francis Drake and his Voyage 1595*. Additional Ms., 5209.

28. Fernández Duro: Armada…, Vol. II, pp.96-100.

29. Commission to Sir John Hawkins and Sir Francis Drake against the Spaniards. Westminster, January 21 1595 (O.S.).

30. Lucena: op. cit., p.114. The author mentions 2,500 men, which would seem to be an underestimation.

31. González-Arnao: op. cit., pp.140-141.

32. Lloyd: op. cit., pp 183-186

33. Simón, Fray Pedro: *Noticias Historiales de las conquistas de Tierra Firme en las Indias Occidentales*. Nuevo Reino de Granada: 1624. Reprinted in Bogotá in 1892. Vol. VII, p.300.

34. Testimony of Sir Anthony Sherley. Hakluyt, Vol. X, pp.266-276.

35. *Relación de lo sucedido a la Armada Ynglesa en el puerto de Nombre de Dios a 8 de henero de 1596*. BMN, Mn. 38, Doc. 65.

36. Simón: op. cit., Vol. VIII, p.30.

37. *Toma de Saint Vincent y Puertobello por el cap*. William Parker…. Georget, op. cit., p.272.

38. Lucena: op. cit., pp.117-118.

39. Testimony of Sir Robert Dudley. In Hakluyt, Vol. X, pp.203-212. Georget, op. cit., pp.141-152.

40. Georget: op. cit., p.50.

41. Testimony of Sir Robert Dudley. In Hakluyt, Vol. X, pp.203-212. Georget, op. cit., pp.141-152.

42. Testimony of Robert Davie. In Hakluyt, Vol. X, pp.213-226. Georget, op. cit., pp.153-167.

43. Testimony of Lawrence Keymis. In Hakluyt, Vol. X, pp.441-501. Georget, op. cit., pp.168-229.

44. Testimony of Thomas Masham. In Hakluyt, Vol. XI, pp.1-15. Georget, op. cit., pp.251-265.

CHAPTER 4

1. Deive, Carlos Esteban: *Tangomangos. Contrabando y Piratería en Santo Domingo (1522-1606)*. Santo Domingo: Fundación Cultural Dominicana, Inc., 1996, p.175.

2. Lucena Salmoral, Manuel: *Piratas, Bucaneros, Filibusteros y Corsarios en América*. Madrid: Mapfre, 1992, p.127.

3. Deive: op. cit., p.174.

4. Ibid., p.175.

5. Moya Pons, Frank: *Manual de Historia Dominicana*. Santo Domingo: Caribbean Publishers, 1995, p.51.

6. BMN, Mn. 38, Doc. 22.

7. Deive: op. cit., pp.82 and 112.

8. Ibid., pp.99-100.

9. Memorials of López de Castro. In Rodríguez Demorizi, Emilio: *Relaciones Históricas de Santo Domingo*. Ciudad Trujillo: Archivo General de la Nación, Vol. II, 1945, pp.161-188.

10. Deive: op. cit., pp.82, 83 and 88.

11. Peña Batllé, Manuel Arturo: *La Isla de la Tortuga*. Madrid: Cultura Hispánica, 1951. Reprinted: Santo Domingo: Editora de Santo Domingo, S.A., 1974, p.76.

12. Serrano Mangas, Fernando: *La Segura Travesía del Agnus Dei. Ignorancia y Malevolencia en Torno a la Figura de Benito Arias Montano 'El Menor'*. Villanueva de la Serena (Badajoz): Diputación de Badajoz-Editora Regional de Extremadura, 1999, pp.58-77.

13. Sáiz Cidoncha, Carlos: *Historia de la Piratería en América Española*. Madrid: San Martín, 1985, p.119. Deive identifies him as Pablos Barlandingen. Deive, op. cit., p.203.

14. Moya: op. cit., p.64.

15. Deive: op. cit., p.237.

16. Ibid., p.68.

17. Ibid., pp.67 and following.

18. BMN, Ms. 38, Doc. 22.

19. Grocio, Hugo: *De la Libertad de los Mares*. Madrid: Centro de Estudios Constitucionales, 1956.

20. Sáiz: op. cit., p.125.

21. Ibid., p.124.

22. Lucena: op. cit., p.120.

23. Deive: op. cit., p.178.

24. Ibid., p.229.

25. Ibid., pp.230-231.

26. De Bry: *América De Bry (1590-1634)*. Madrid: Siruela, 1992, p.476.

27. Ibid., p.472.

28. Lucena: op. cit., p.120.

29. Copia del CHAPTER de carta del Conde de Gondomar a S.M. acerca de haberse deshecho la compañía que se firmó en Inglaterra para ir al río de las Amazonas. BMN, Mn. 38, Doc. 78.

30. Ibid., p.120.

31. Ibid., p.120.

CHAPTER 5

1. Lucena Salmoral, Manuel: *Piratas, Bucaneros, Filibusteros y Corsarios en América*. Madrid: Mapfre, 1992, p.129.

2. Ibid., p.131.

3. Ibid., p.132.

4. Ibid., p.133.

5. Ibid., p.134. Quoting Bradley, P.T.: *Relación del viaje y sucesos de la Armada Olandessa*.

6. Ibid., p.125.

7. Serrano Mangas, Fernando: *La Segura Travesía del Agnus Dei. Ignorancia y Malevolencia en Torno a la Figura de Benito Arias Montano 'El Menor'*. Villanueva de la Serena (Badajoz): Diputación de Badajoz-Editora Regional de Extremadura, 1999, pp.250-251.

8. Lucena: op. cit., p.144.

9. Serrano Mangas: op. cit., p.259.

10. Lucena: op. cit., p.145.

11. Biblioteca Nacional (BN), Ms. 18719, 45.

12. Ibid., p.146.

13. Picó, F.: *Historia General de Puerto Rico*. Río Piedras: Huracán, p.90.

14. Sáiz Cidoncha, Carlos: *Historia de la Piratería en América Española*. Madrid: San Martín, 1985, p.150.

15. Ibid., p.151.

16. Lucena: op. cit., p.138.

17. Ibid.

18. The order was issued on December 31 1557, at the height of the war with France, in response to the activities of French corsairs.

19. Serrano Mangas: op. cit., p.269.

20. Lucena: op. cit., p.141.

21. Lucena: op. cit., p.142.

22. Serrano Mangas: op. cit., p.254.

23. Ibid., p.255.

24. Lucena: op. cit., p.147.

25. AGI, Indiferente, 1873.

26. Rahn Phillips, Carla: *Seis galeones para el Rey de España*. Madrid: Alianza Editorial, 1991, pp.21-24. Also Fernández Duro, Cesáreo: Disquisiciones Nauticas. Vol. II, pp.285-286.

27. AGI, Escribanía de Cámara, 968. Also BMN, Navarrete, XXIV.

28. Haring, C.H.: *The Buccaneers in the West Indies in the XVIIIth Century*. London: Methuen, 1910, p.303.

29. Peña Batllé, Manuel Arturo: *La Isla de la Tortuga*. Madrid: Cultura Hispánica, 1951. Reprinted: Santo Domingo: Editora de Santo Domingo, S.A., 1974, p.35.
30. Ibid., p.136. Quoting Durtertre.
31. Ibid., p.137.
32. Lucena: op. cit., p.
33. Peña Batllé: op. cit., p.118.
34. Ibid., p.119.
35. Ibid.
36. Documents Relating to…, pp.470 and following.
37. Peña Batllé: op. cit., p.137.
38. Ibid., p.137.
39. Moya Pons, Frank: *Manual de Historia Dominicana*. Santo Domingo: Caribbean Publishers, 1995, p.78.
40. Peña Batllé: op. cit., p.140.
41. Ibid., p.141.
42. Ibid., p.154.
43. Exquemeling, Alexander Oliver: *Piratas en la América y luz a la defensa de las costas de las Indias Occidentales*. Madrid: 1681 and 1793. Seville: Ed. Facsimilar, Hispano Americana de Publicaciones, 1987.
44. Ibid., p.145.
45. Ibid., p.146.
46. *Relación sucinta de la restauración de la Isla de Tortuga que la defendían las Armas de Francia y la gobernaba M. Timaleon de Fontenay, caballero de la religión de San Juan*. AGI, Patronato 276, R.6. Also *Memorias de lo obrado en la facción de las yslas de la Tortuga y la Española, contra los Franceses e Yngleses, 1654*. BMN, Ms. 1841.
47. Peña Batllé: op. cit., pp.145-146.
48. Ibid., p.148.
49. Ibid., p.149.
50. Ibid., p.154.

CHAPTER 6

1. Moya Pons, Frank: *Manual de Historia Dominicana*. Santo Domingo: Caribbean Publishers, 1995, p.46, p.84.
2. With this objective in mind, they kept the Fleet in view of the defenders as a permanent threat of possible disembarkation.
3. Moya Pons: op. cit., p.85.
4. *Relación de la feliz vitoria que han tenido las Armas de Su Majestad (Dios le guarde) en la ciudad de Santo Domingo, isla Española, contra la Armada Inglesa de Guillermo Pen…*. BMN, Mn. 38, Doc. 83.
5. Moya Pons: op. cit., p.85.
6. *Relación de lo sucedido de la Armada Inglesa de Guillermo Pen en la Isla de Xamaica y las perdidas de gente y Baxeles que ha tenido…*. BMN, Mn. 38, Doc. 85.
7. Guizot: *Histoire de la République d'Angleterre*. Vol. II, pp.194-197. In *Relación del viaje y sucesos que tuvo desde que salió de la ciudad de Lima, hasta que llegó a estos Reinos de España, el Dr. D. Diego Portichuelo de Rivadeneira…*. Undated reprint: Documentos relacionados.
8. Lucena Salmoral, Manuel: *Piratas, Bucaneros, Filibusteros y Corsarios en América*. Madrid: Mapfre, 1992, p.176.
9. Ibid.

10. Marley, David F.: *Pirates and Privateers of the Americas*. Santa Barbara (California): ABC-CLIO, 1994, p.278.
11. Ibid.
12. Ibid., p.279.
13. Lucena: op. cit., p.176.
14. Marley: op. cit., p.429.
15. Lucena: op. cit., p.177.
16. Marley: op. cit., p.429.
17. Ibid.
18. Lucena: op. cit., p.177.
19. Fernández Duro, Cesáreo: *Armada Española, Desde la Unión de los Reinos de Castilla y Aragón*. Madrid: Reedición MNM, 1972. Vol.v, p.43.
20. Lucena: op. cit., p.179.
21. Jarmy Chapa, M. de: *Un Eslabón Perdido de la Historia. Piratería en el Caribe Siglo XVI y XVII*, p.193. Also Lucena, ibid., p.178.
22. Juárez Moreno, J.: *Piratas y corsarios en Veracruz y Campeche*. Seville: CSIC, 1972, pp.21 and following.
23. Lucena: op. cit., p.177.
24. Peña Batllé, Manuel Arturo: *La Isla de la Tortuga*. Madrid: Cultura Hispánica, 1951. Reprinted: Santo Domingo: Editora de Santo Domingo, S.A., 1974, pp.185 and following.
25. Ibid.
26. Ibid., p.227.
27. Ibid., p.230.
28. Ibid., p.232.
29. Ibid., p.231. Quote: extract from the *Recopilación Diplomática*, Vol. XIII, Colección Trujillo, de Américo Lugo.
30. Ibid., p.236.
31. Ibid., p.125.
32. Exquemeling, Alexander Oliver: *Piratas en la América y luz a la defensa de las costas de las Indias Occidentales*. Madrid: 1681 and 1793. Seville: Ed. Facsimilar, Hispano Americana de Publicaciones, 1987.
33. Lucena: op. cit., p.174. Quoting Gall: op. cit., pp.109-110.
34. Moya Pons: op. cit., p.89.
35. Ibid.
36. Ibid., p.90.
37. Peña Batllé: op. cit., p.241.
38. Lucena: op. cit., p.186.
39. Exquemeling: op. cit., p.67.
40. Lucena: op. cit., p.187.
41. Exquemeling: op. cit., pp.76 and following.
42. Exquemeling: op. cit., p.98.
43. Marley: op. cit., p.255.
44. Lucena: op. cit., p.179.
45. Ibid., p.179. He quotes Haring: *The Buccaneers in the West Indies in the XVII Century*. London: 1910, p.129.
46. Marley: op. cit., pp.259-260.
47. The aspects related to slave traffic are taken from Vega Franco, Marisa: *El tráfico de esclavos con América (Asientos de Grillo y Lomelín)*. Seville: Estudios Hispanoamericanos-CSIC, 1984.
48. Lucena: op. cit., p.180.
49. Marley: op. cit., pp.255-258.
50. Ibid., p.246.
51. Alvarado García, E.: *Historia de Centroamérica*. Tegucigalpa: undated, p.126.
52. Lucena: op. cit., p.186.
53. Ibid., p.190.
54. Marley: op. cit., pp.264 and following.
55. Ibid., p.320.
56. Lucena: op. cit., p.255.

57. Exquemeling: op. cit., pp.135 and following.
58. Lucena: op. cit., p.194.
59. Fernández Duro: *Armada Española…*.Vol. v, p.173.
60. *Absolución de Mateo Alonso Huidobro y Alonso Campos*. In Fernández Duro, ibid., p.174.
61. Lucena: op. cit., p.255.
62. Marley: op. cit., p.348.
63. Ibid.
64. Ibid., pp.272-273.
65. Ibid., p.219.
66. Ibid., p.229.
67. Lucena: op. cit., p.196.
68. Marley: op. cit., p.349.
69. Lucena: op. cit., pp.197-200. Also Exquemeling, op. cit., pp.192 and following.
70. Marley: op. cit., pp.307-309.
71. Ibid., p.220.
72. Ibid., p.269.

CHAPTER 7

1. Lucena Salmoral, Manuel: *Piratas, Bucaneros, Filibusteros y Corsarios en América*. Madrid: Mapfre, 1992, p.205.
2. Marley, David F.: *Pirates and Privateers of the Americas*. Santa Barbara (California): ABC-CLIO, 1994, p.296, quoting Exquemeling, op. cit.
3. López Cantos, A.: *Historia de Puerto Rico (1650-1700)*. Seville: CSIC, 1975, p.290.
4. Royal Decree in Fernández Duro, Cesáreo: *Armada Española, Desde la Unión de los Reinos de Castilla y Aragón*. Madrid: Reedición MNM, 1972. Vol.v, p.169.
5. Marley: op. cit., p.297.
6. Lucena: op. cit., p.206.
7. Marley: op. cit., p.4.
8. Ibid., pp.51-52.
9. Fernández Duro, Cesáreo: *Armada Española, Desde la Unión de los Reinos de Castilla y Aragón*. Madrid: Reedición MNM, 1972. Vol.v, pp.183 and following.
10. Peña Batllé, Manuel Arturo: *La Isla de la Tortuga*. Madrid: Cultura Hispánica, 1951. Reprinted: Santo Domingo: Editora de Santo Domingo, S.A., 1974, pp.251-252.
11. Lucena: op. cit., p.209.
12. Marley: op. cit., p.421.
13. Ibid., p.87.
14. Ibid., p.88.
15. Ibid.
16. Lucena: op. cit., p.209.
17. Marley: op. cit., p.164.
18. Ibid.
19. AGI, Panamá, pp.95-96.
20. Serrano Mangas, Fernando: 'El proceso del pirata Bartholomew Sharp, 1682'. In *Temas Americanistas*, Vol. IV, 1984, pp.14-18.
21. Lucena: op. cit., p.209.
22. Marley: op. cit., p.139.
23. Lucena: op. cit., p.210.
24. Ibid.
25. Marley: op. cit., p.105.
26. *Pesquisa contra Francisco de Segura. Presidente de la Audiencia de Santo Domingo, por haber dejado salir de aquel puerto a Nicolas Van Horen. zaalandés, siendo pirata y habiendo saqueado Veracruz*. AGI, Escribanía de Cámara, 25a, 25b and 25c.

27. *Averiguación sobre los culpables en la entrada y saqueo de Veracruz por el pirata Lorenzo*. AGI, Escribanía de Cámara, 297a.
28. Marley: op. cit., p.12.
29. Lucena: op. cit., p.205.
30. Marley: op. cit., p.13.
31. Ibid., p.108.
32. Ibid.
33. Gaztañeta e Yturribalzaga, Antonio de: *Arte de Fabricar Reales*. Barcelona: Ed. Facsimilar, Lunwerg, 1992.
34. Marley: op. cit., pp.315-320.
35. Ibid., p.285.
36. Ibid., p.112.
37. Ibid., p.380.
38. Juárez Moreno, J.: *Piratas y corsarios en Veracruz y Campeche*. Seville: CSIC, 1972, pp.360 and following.
39. Lucena: op. cit., p.223.
40. Ibid., p.224.
41. Fernández Duro: *Armada Española…*. Vol. v, pp.278 and following.
42. Ibid.
43. Juárez Moreno: op. cit., p.411.
44. Moya Pons, Frank: *Manual de Historia Dominicana*. Santo Domingo: Caribbean Publishers, 1995, p.94.
45. Ibid., p.95.
46. Marley: op. cit., p.125.
47. Peña Batllé: op. cit., p.257.
48. Moya Pons: op. cit., pp.94-95.
49. Marley: op. cit., pp.44-45.
50. Lucena: op. cit., pp.225-226.
51. Ibid., p.226.
52. Ibid., p.227.
53. Marley: op. cit., pp.126-127.
54. The Cartagena campaigns are magnificently described in De la Matta Rodríguez, Enrique: *El asalto de Pointis a Cartagena de Indias*. Seville: CSIC, 1979.
55. Fernández Duro: *Armada Español…*. Vol. v, p.307.
56. Marley: op. cit., pp.7-8.
57. Ibid.
58. Marley: op. cit., p.117.

EPILOGUE

1. As regards the changes that took place in the period between 1700 and 1715, see Pérez-Mallaína, Pablo Emilio: *Política Naval Española en el Atlántico (1700-1715)*. Seville: Escuela de Estudios Hispanoamericanos, CSIC, 1982.
2. Ibid., p.27 (table).
3. Ibid., p.138.
4. The rise to the throne of Philip V brought with it the appointment of numerous superior naval officers and the restructuring of the Spanish Armada according to the model conceived by Colbert.
5. Captain Charles Johnson: *Robberies and Murders of the Most Notorious Pirates*. London: Conway Maritime Press, p.67.
6. Ibid., pp.103-129.
7. Ibid., pp.189-207.
8. The traditional kingdoms of the Peninsula also aligned themselves during the war of the factions. Castile mostly supported Philip, while Aragon was largely in favour of Charles.

GENERAL BIBLIOGRAPHY

ALVARADO GARCÍA, E: *Historia de Centroamérica. Tegucigalpa*: undated.

ALSEDO Y HERRERA, Dionisio de: *Piraterías y agresiones de los ingleses y otros pueblos de Europa a la América Española desde el siglo XVI al XVIII.* Madrid: 1883.

AZCÁRRAGA Y BUSTAMANTE, José Luis: *El corso marítimo: concepto, justificación e historia.* Madrid: Instituto Francisco de Vitoria, 1950.

BARRIONUEVO, Jerónimo de: *Avisos de D. Jerónimo de Barrionuevo* (1654-1658). In Colección de Escritores Castellanos, Madrid: 1893.

CASADO SOTO, José Luis: *Los barcos españoles y la Gran Armada de 1588.* Madrid: San Martín, 1988.

Colección de documentos inéditos de Ultramar. Madrid: 1885-1900, 13 vols.

Colección de documentos relativos al descubrimiento, conquista y colonización de las posesiones españolas en América y Oceanía. Madrid: 1864-83, 42 vols.

CHAUNU, Huguette and Pierre: *Seville et l'Atlantique (1504-1650).* Paris: 1955-56.

Compagnie qui fit le voyage, Un de ceux de la,: Un flibustier français dans la mer des Antilles en 1618-1620 manuscrit inedit du debut du XVIIe siecle Editions J.-p.Moreau, 1987.

DE BRY: *América de Bry (1590-1634).* Madrid: Siruela, 1992.

DEIVE, Carlos Esteban: *Tangomangos. Contrabando y piratería en Santo Domingo (1522-1606).* Santo Domingo: Fundación Cultural Dominicana, Inc., 1996.

DE LA MATTA RODRÍGUEZ, Enrique: *El asalto de Pointis a Cartagena de Indias.* Seville: CSIC, 1979.

DESJEAN, Jean Bern, Baron de Pointis: *Relation de l'expedition de Cartagena faite par les françoi en 1697.* Amsterdam: 1698. Reprinted in Spanish by: Arrázola, Roberto: 'Genuina y detallada relación de la toma de Cartagena'. In *Historial de Cartagena.* Buenos Aires: 1943.

DÍAZ DEL CASTILLO, Bernal: 'Verdadera historia de los sucesos de la conquista de Nueva España, por el capitán…'. In *Historiadores Primitivos de las Indias.* Vol. II, T. XXVI. Madrid: Biblioteca de Autores Españoles, Atlas, 1947.

DURTERTRE, Jean Baptiste: *Histoire générale des Antilles habitués par les françois.* Paris: 1667-1671.

EXQUEMELING, Alexander Oliver: *Piratas de la América y luz a la defensa de las costas de las Indias Occidentales.* Madrid: 1681 and 1793. Seville: Ed. Facsimilar, Hispano Americana de Publicaciones, 1987.

FERNÁNDEZ DURO, Cesáreo: *Armada Española, desde la unión de los reinos de Castilla y Aragón.* Madrid: Reprinted MNM, 1972. Vols. I to V.

– *La Marina de Castilla.* Madrid: Reedición Editmex S.L., 1995.

– *Disquisiciones Nauticas.* Vol. II. Facsimile, MNM, Madrid: 1995.

GALL, J and F.: *El Filibusterismo.* Mexico: F.C.E., 1957.

GARCÍA ARIAS, L.: *Historia del principio de la Libertad de los Mares.* Santiago: 1946.

GAZTAÑETA E YTURRIBALZAGA, Antonio de: *Arte de Fabricar Reales.* Barcelona: Ed. Facsimilar, Lunwerg, 1992.

GEORGET, Henry; Eduardo Rivero: *Herejes en el Paraiso. Corsarios y navegantes ingleses en las costas de Venezuela durante la segunda mitad del siglo XVI.* Caracas: Arte, 1993.

GONZÁLEZ, Tomás: *Apuntamientos para la Historia del rey Felipe II, por lo tocante a sus relaciones con la reina Isabel de Inglaterra.* Madrid: Memorias de la Real Academia de la Historia, Vol. VII, 1832.

GONZÁLEZ-ARNAO CONDE-LUQUE, Mariano: *Derrota y Muerte de Sir Francis Drake.* A Coruña 1589 - Portobelo 1596. Xunta de Galicia, 1995.

GOSSE, Philip: *The History of Piracy.* London: Longman, Green & Co, 1932.

GROCIO, Hugo: *De la libertad de los mares.* Madrid: Centro de Estudios Constitucionales, 1956.

HARING, C.H.: The Buccaneers in the West Indies in the XVIIIth Century. London: Methuen, 1910.

– *Comercio y navegación entre España y las Indias.* Mexico: FCE, 1979.

HAKLUYT, Richard: Principales viajes, expediciones, tráfico comercial y descubrimientos de la nación inglesa. Edited, translated and with an introduction by José M™ Pérez Bustamante. Madrid: Atlas, 1988-1992, Vol. II.

JÁRMY CHAPA, M. de: Un eslabón perdido de la Historia. Piratería en el Caribe siglos XVI y XVII. Mexico: UNAM, 1983.

JIMÉNEZ RUEDA, Julio: *Corsarios Franceses e Ingleses en la Inquisición de Nueva España.* Mexico: Archivo General de la Nación, UNAM, 1945.

JUÁREZ MORENO, Juan: *Piratas y Corsarios en Veracruz y Campeche.* Seville: CSIC, 1972.

KAMEN, Henry: *La Inquisición Española. Una revisión crítica.* Barcelona: Crítica, 1999.

LABAT, P. Jean Robert: *Voyage et nouveaux voyages aux isles de l'Amerique*, Paris: 1722.

LAVEDAN, Antonio: *Tratado de los usos, abusos, propiedades y virtudes del Tabaco, Café, Té y Chocolate.* Madrid: 1796.

LÓPEZ CANTOS, A.: *Historia de Puerto Rico (1650-1700).* Seville: CSIC, 1975.

LUCENA SALMORAL, Manuel: *Piratas, bucaneros, filibusteros y corsarios en América.* Madrid: MAPFRE, 1992.

MARDSEN, R.G. (Editor): *Documents relating to Law and Custom of the Sea.* Navy Records Society, 1915.

MARLEY, David F: *Pirates and Privateers of the Americas.* Santa Barbara (California): ABC-CLIO, 1994.

MORENO, J.J.: *Asaltos Piratas a Veracruz y Campeche durante el siglo XVII.* Seville: 1972.

MORINEAU, Jean: *Tels étaient corsaries el flibustiers.* Paris: 1957.

MOTA, Francisco M.: *Piratas en el Caribe.* Havana: Casa de las Américas, 1984.

– *Piratas y corsarios en las costas de Cuba.* Havana: Gente Nueva, 1997.

MOYA PONS, Frank: *Manual de Historia Dominicana.* Santo Domingo: Caribbean Publishers, 1995.

NORRIS, John: *The Expedition of Sir John Norris and Sir Francis Drake to Spain and Portugal, 1589.* London: Ed. R.B. Wernham, Navy Record Society, 1988.

Ordenanzas del Buen Gobierno de la Armada del Mar Océano de 24 de Henero de 1633. Madrid: CSIC Histórico de la Marina, 1974.

OTERO LANA, Enrique: *Los Corsarios Españoles durante la decadencia de los Austrias.* Madrid: Ed. Naval, 1992.

PEÑA BATLLÉ, Manuel Arturo: *La Isla de la Tortuga.* Madrid: Cultura Hispánica, 1951. Reprinted Santo Domingo: Editora de Santo Domingo, S.A., 1974.

PÉREZ MARTÍNEZ, Héctor: *Piraterías en Campeche.* Campeche: Universidad Autónoma del Sudeste, 1984.

PÉREZ-MALLAINA, Pablo Emilio: *Política Naval Española en el Atlántico (1700-1715).* Seville: Escuela de Estudios Hispanoamericanos, CSIC, 1982.

Person of quality, A: A full account of the proceedings in relation to captain Kidd. London: 1701.

PEZUELA, Jacobo de la: *Historia de la Isla de Cuba.* Madrid: 1968.

PICÓ, F.: *Historia General de Puerto Rico.* Río Piedras: Huracán.

PORTICHUELO DE RIVADENEIRA, Diego: *Relación del viaje y sucesos que tuvo desde que salió de la ciudad de Lima, hasta que llegó a estos Reinos de España, el Dr. D. Diego Portichuelo de Rivadeneira….* Undated reprint: Documentos relacionados.

RAHN PHILLIPS, Carla: *Seis galeones para el Rey de España.* Madrid: Alianza Editorial, 1991.

Recopilación de las Leyes de los Reinos y de las Yndias. Madrid: 1681.

RESTREPO TIRADO, E: *Historia de la Provincia de Santa Marta.* Bogotá: Biblioteca de Autores Colombinos, 1953, Vol. I.

RODRÍGUEZ DEMORIZI, Emilio: *Relaciones históricas de Santo Domingo.* Ciudad Trujillo: Archivo General de la Nación, 1945.

RUMEU DE ARMAS, A: *Viajes de Hawkins a América.* Seville: 1947.

SÁIZ CIDONCHA, Carlos: *Historia de la Piratería en América Española.* Madrid: San Martín, 1985.

SIMÓN, Fray Pedro: *Noticias Historiales de las conquistas de Tierra Firme en las Indias Occidentales.* Nuevo Reino de Granada: 1624. Reprinted Bogotá: 1892.

SERRANO MANGAS, Fernando: 'El proceso del pirata Bartolomew Sharp, 1682'. In *Temas Americanistas.* Vol. IV, 1984.

– *La Segura Travesía del Agnus Dei. Ingorancia y Malevolencia en Torno a la Figura de Benito Arias Montano 'El Menor'.* Villanueva de la Serena (Badajoz): Diputación de Badajoz-Editora Regional de Extremadura, 1999.

VEGA FRANCO, Marisa: *El tráfico de esclavos con América (Asientos de Grillo y Lomelín).* Seville: Estudios Hipanomericanos-CSIC, 1984.

ZAMORA, P. Alonso de: *Historia de la Provincia de San Antonio del Nuevo Reino de Granada.* Impreso 1701.

ARCHIVES CONSULTED

Archivo General de Indias, Seville (AGI)
Archivo General de Simancas, Simancas (Valladolid) (AGS)
Archivo Histórico Nacional, Madrid (AHN)
Biblioteca del Museo Naval, Madrid (BMN)
Biblioteca Nacional, Madrid (BN)

INDEX OF NAMES

INDEX OF PLACE NAMES

INDEX OF SHIPS

PHOTOGRAPHIC CREDITS

PROLOGUE

p.10: Museo de la Catedral de Palma de Mallorca (Oronoz).
pp.12-13: Museo Nacional d'Art de Catalunya (MNAC).
p.14: Museo de la catedral de Palma de Mallorca (Oronoz).
p.15: Theatrum Orbis Terrarum, de Abraham Ortelius, Antwerp (Mithra-Index).
p.17: Retablo de la virgen de los navegantes. Iglesia de San Pedro, Zumaia. Archivo Fotográfico del Untzi Museoa-Museo Nard de San Sebastián.
p.18: Museo de la Catedral de Palma de Mallorca (Oronoz).
p.19: Barco argelino partiendo de un puerto bárbaro. Andries van Eertvelt. National Maritime Museum Picture Library, Greenwich.
p.21: Roca en una playa. Jacob de Gruyter. National Maritime Museum Picture Library, Greenwich.

CHAPTER I

p.22: Archivo Lunwerg.
p.24-25: Archivo General de Indias, Seville.
p.26.1: Archivo General de Indias, Seville.
pp.26-27: Archivo General de Indias, Seville.
p.28: Moctezuma's plume. Museum, Vienna.
p.29: Archivo Lunwerg.
p.30: Archivo General de Indias, Seville.
p.31: Museo Naval, Madrid.
p.33: Archivo General de Indias, Seville.
pp.34-35: Cartography. Archivo Lunwerg.
p.36.1: Original illustration by Javier Escudero. Archivo Lunwerg.
p.36.2: Small crossbow, 18th-Century; I. 289. Museo Naval, Madrid.
p.36.3: Sand clock, 16th-Century; I. 1304. Museo Naval, Madrid.
p.37.1: Portuguese nautical astrolabe. Recovered from the pilot's cabin of the wrecked Nuestra Señora de Atocha. Christie's, New York.
p.37.2: Nautical astrolabe from 1571. Modern replica. I. 1853. Museo Naval, Madrid.
p.37.3: Antonio Gaztañeta's log, Norte de la navegación, Seville, 1692.
p.38-39: Museo Naval, Madrid.
p.40: Diccionario de las artes de la pesca. Sánez Reguard. Museo Naval, Madrid.
p.41: Original illustration by Javier Escudero. Archivo Lunwerg.
p.42: Archivo General de Indias, Seville.
p.43: De Bry's América. Engraving. Biblioteca del Museo Naval, Madrid.
p.44: National Maritime Museum Picture Library, Greenwich.
p.45: Archivo General de Indias, Seville.

CHAPTER II

p.46: (Index).
p.48: National Maritime Museum Picture Library, Greenwich.
p.49: De Bry's América. Engraving. Biblioteca del Museo Naval, Madrid.
p.50: Archivo Lunwerg.

p.51: De Bry's América. Engraving. Biblioteca del Museo Naval, Madrid.
p.53: Biblioteca del Museo Naval, Madrid.
p.54: Biblioteca del Museo Naval, Madrid.
p.55: Biblioteca del Museo Naval, Madrid.
pp.56-57: Museo Naval, Madrid.
pp.58-59: Archivo Lunwerg.
p.61: Archivo Lunwerg.
p.63: De Bry's América. Engraving. Biblioteca del Museo Naval, Madrid.
p.65: The British Museum, department of drawings and engravings. London.
p.67: Archivo General de Indias, Seville.
p.68: Archivo General de Indias, Seville.
p.69: National Maritime Museum Picture Library, Greenwich.
pp.70-71: Archivo General de Indias, Seville.
pp.72-73: Cartography. Archivo Lunwerg.
p.75: British Library, London. Bridgeman-Index.
p.76: Archivo General de Indias, Seville.
p.77: Prisma.
pp.78-79: Archivo Lunwerg.

CHAPTER III

p.80: By kind permission of The British Library, London.
p.82: Public Record Office. Image Library, MPF. 318, London.
p.84: Torre de Belem, Lisbon. Archivo Lunwerg.
p.85: Archivo General de Indias, Seville.
p.87: De Bry's América. Engraving. National Portrait Gallery, London (Oronoz).
p.88: Archivo General de Simancas, Valladolid.
p.89: Archivo Lunwerg.
p.91: Archivo General de Indias, Seville.
p.93: By kind permission of The British Library, London.
p.95: Biblioteca del Museo Naval, Madrid.
p.96: Servicio Histórico Militar, Madrid.
p.97: Archivo General de Indias, Seville.
pp.98-99: Duque del Infantado's weapons collection. Museo Naval, Madrid.
p.100: Bay and city of Portobello, Panama, 1688. Archivo General de Indias, Seville. Oronoz.
p.101: Plymouth City Museums and Art Gallery Collection.
p.102: Private collection (Bridgeman-Index).
p.103: Medallion of Nicholas Hilliard (1547-1619). Christie's Images, London (Bridgeman-Index).
p.105: Portrait of Philip II. Antonio Moro. Real Monasterio de San Lorenzo de El Escorial, Madrid.
p.106: Oil painting attributed to Johann Andreas Thiele (active 1670-1680). Roudnice Lobkowicz Collection. Nelahozeves Castle, Czech Republic. Bridgeman-Index.

CHAPTER IV

p.108: The Somerset House Conference, 1604. Juan Pantoja de la Cruz (1551-1608). National Maritime Museum Picture Library, Greenwich.
p.110: View of London early in the 18th century. Engraving (Aisa).
p.111: Biblioteca Nacional Madrid.
pp.112-113: City and port of Seville. Sánchez Coello. Museo de América, Madrid (Oronoz).
p.114: Letter from Hispaniola by Andrés de Morales. Archivo Lunwerg.
p.115: National Maritime Museum Picture Library, Greenwich.
p.116: Seascape. Adam Willaerts. Museo del Prado, Madrid.
p.117: Archivo General de Indias, Seville.
pp.118-119: Original illustration by Javier Escudero. Archivo Lunwerg. Dice and kitchen utensils retrieved from the wrecked galleons Conde de Tolosa and Guadalupe. Playing cards and dominoes from the Museo Naval, Madrid.
p.120: View of the city of Amsterdam. 16th-17th Century. Etching signed by Jollain (Aisa).
p.121: Plan of the port of Acapulco. Archivo General de Indias, Seville (Oronoz).
p.123: Museo Naval, Madrid.
p.125: Museo Naval, Madrid.

CHAPTER V

p.126: Museo del Prado, Madrid.
p.129: Archivo General de Indias, Seville.
p.130-131: Archivo Lunwerg.
p.132: Archivo General de Indias, Seville.
p.133: Museo del Prado, Madrid.
p.134.1: Archivo Lunwerg.
p.134.2: Museo Naval, Madrid.
p.135: National Maritime Museum Picture Library, Greenwich.
p.136: Biblioteca Nacional, Madrid (Oronoz).
p.137: National Maritime Museum Picture Library, Greenwich.
p.139: Archivo General de Indias, Seville.
p.141: Archivo Lunwerg.
p.142: Biblioteca del Museo Naval, Madrid.
p.143: Duque del Infantado weapons collection. Museo Naval, Madrid.
p.144: Museo del Prado, Madrid.
p.145: Museo del Prado, Madrid.
p.147: Biblioteca del Museo Naval, Madrid.
p.149: Archivo General de Indias, Seville.

CHAPTER VI

p.150: National Maritime Museum Picture Library, Greenwich.
p.153: The Baby King (fragment). Jacob Jordaens. Kunsthistoriches Museum, Vienna. Archivo Fotográfico Fournier Artes Gráficas, S.A.
p.154-155: Graphic rendering, Archivo Lunwerg.
p.156: Historical Portraits Society, London.

p.159: La Kermesse (fragment). Peter Paul Rubens, c. 1635-1638. Museé du Louvre, Paris. Archivo Fotográfico Fournier Artes Gráficas, S.A.
p.161: Biblioteca del Museo Naval, Madrid.
p.163: Archivo General de Indias, Seville.
p.164.1: Private collection.
p.164.2: Archivo General de Indias, Seville.
p.164.3-165.1: Biblioteca del Museo Naval, Madrid.
p.164.4: Private collection.
p.169: Portrait of Sir Cloudisley Shovell. Michael Dahl. National Maritime Museum Picture Library, Greenwich.
p.170: Biblioteca del Museo Naval, Madrid.
p.172: Biblioteca del Museo Naval, Madrid.
p.173: Biblioteca del Museo Naval, Madrid.
p.175: Archivo General de Indias, Seville.

CHAPTER VII

p.176: Archivo General de Indias, Seville (Oronoz).
p.179: National Maritime Museum Picture Library, Greenwich.
p.180: (Prisma).
pp.184-185: National Maritime Museum Picture Library, Greenwich.
p.186: Biblioteca del Museo Naval, Madrid.
p.187: Archivo General de Indias, Seville (Oronoz).
p.190.1: Simulation of the wrecking of the galleon Conde de Tolosa.
p.190.2: Photo: Jonathan Blair.
p.191: All items retrieved from the wreckage of the galleons Nuestra Señora de Guadalupe, Nuestra Señora de la Pura y Limpia Concepción and Conde de Tolosa. Most now deposited at the Museo de las Atarazanas, Santo Domingo (Dominican Republic).
pp.194-195: Plan of Hispaniola at the beginning of the 18th century. 20-B-2. Museo Naval, Madrid.
p.197: National Maritime Museum Picture Library, Greenwich.
p.199: Biblioteca del Museo Naval, Madrid.
p.201: National Maritime Museum Picture Library, Greenwich.

EPILOGUE

p.202: Archivo General de Indias, Seville.
p.205: Archivo General de Indias, Seville.
pp.206-207: Blackbeard taking the French vessel El Guineano, 1717. John Michael Groves. Private collection.
pp.208-209: The capture of The Sheba Queen. John Michael Groves. Private collection.

PHOTOGRAPHERS

Matías Briansó
Joaquin Cortés
Jonathan Blair
Pedro Borrell
Manel Pérez
Adalberto Ríos

ACKNOWLEDGEMENTS

I would like to thank the following for all their assistance
during the research and writing of this book:

Alejandro Selmi, Carlos León, Genoveva Enríquez, Gerardo Vivas,
Guillermo Santoni, Ignacio del Hierro, Javier Escudero, Jean-Yves Blot,
José Chez Checo, Lourdes Odriozola, Manu Izaguirre, Miguel Quadra-Salcedo,
Miguel Rosa, Patricia Meehan, Pedro Borrell and Victoria Stappel.

All the staff at the Museo Naval de Madrid,
especially Rear Admiral José Ignacio González Aller and Dolores Higueras.

All the staff at the Archivo General de Indias, Archivo General de Simancas,
Archivo Histórico Nacional and the Biblioteca Nacional.

The editors at Lunwerg, especially Carmen García, Andrés Gamboa
and Miguel Ángel Palleiro.

Special thanks to Fernando Serrano Mangas and Jorge Pla
for many hours of effort and collaboration, without which
the work would never have been completed.

And fondest regards to Virginia, Ôñigo and María,
who sacrificed so much of their precious time.

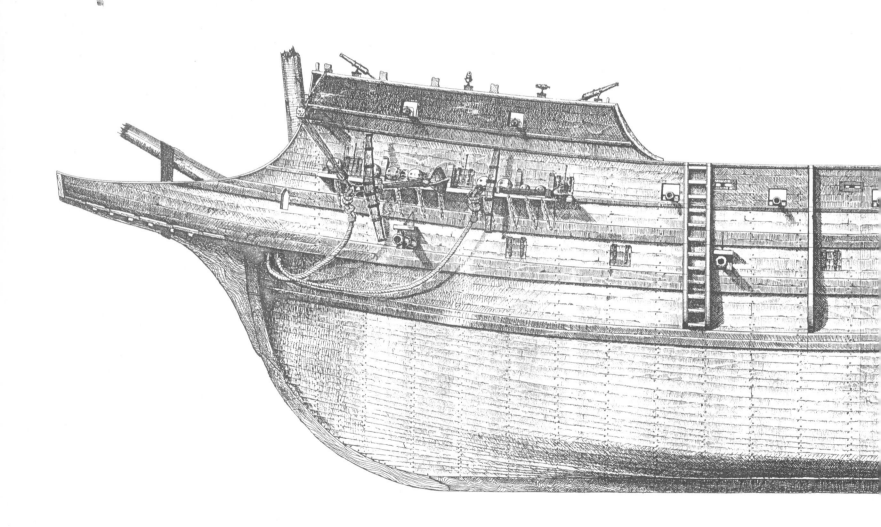

SPANISH GALLEON,
17th CENTURY